World Economic Situation and Prospects

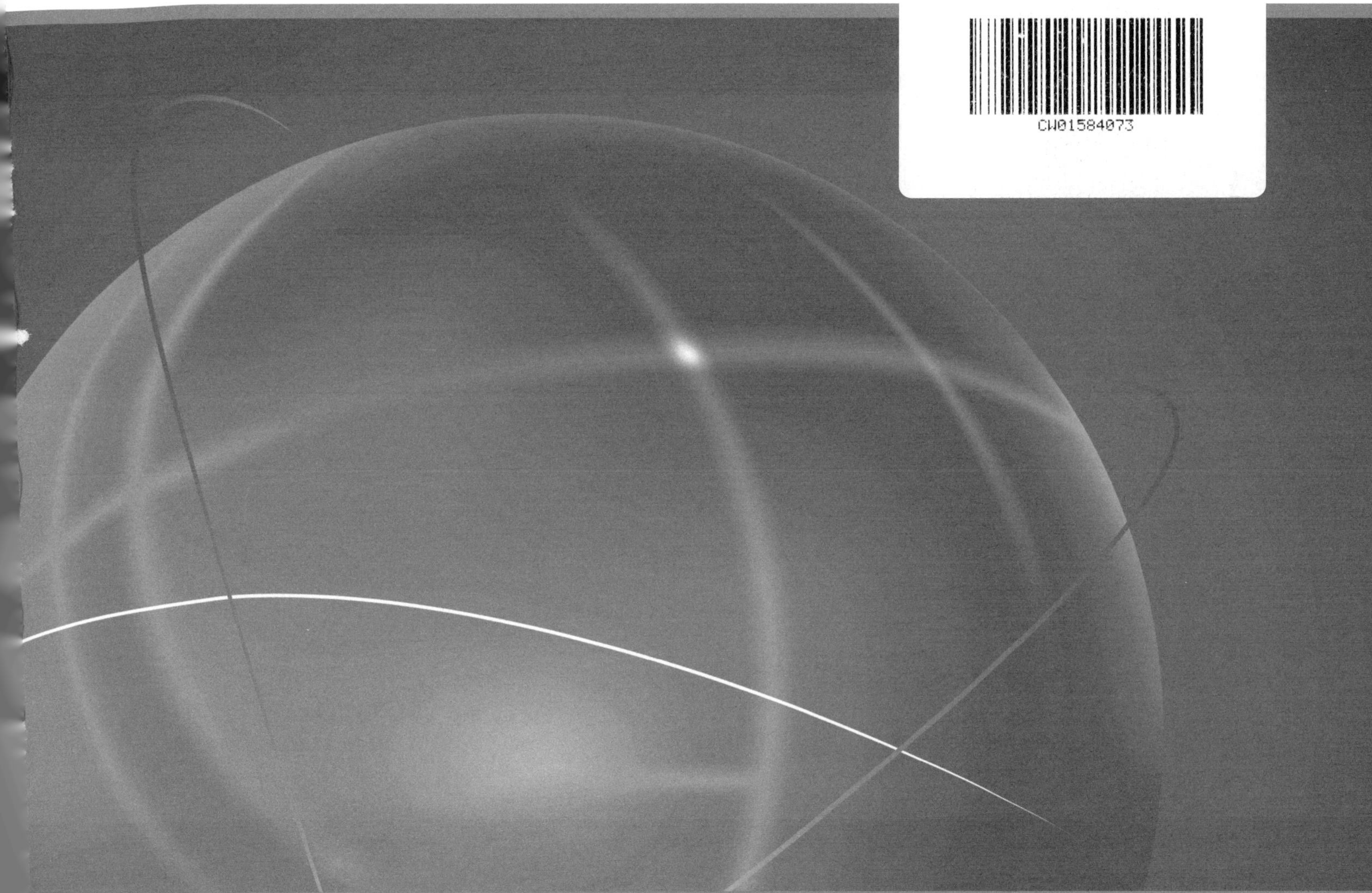

United Nations
New York, 2022

The *World Economic Situation and Prospects 2022* is a report produced by the United Nations Department of Economic and Social Affairs (UN DESA), in partnership with the United Nations Conference on Trade and Development (UNCTAD) and the five United Nations regional commissions: Economic Commission for Africa (UNECA), Economic Commission for Europe (UNECE), Economic Commission for Latin America and the Caribbean (UNECLAC), Economic and Social Commission for Asia and the Pacific (UNESCAP) and Economic and Social Commission for Western Asia (UNESCWA). The United Nations World Tourism Organization (UNWTO) also contributed to the report.

For further information, visit https://www.un.org/en/desa or contact:

UN DESA

Liu Zhenmin, Under-Secretary-General

Department of Economic and Social Affairs
Room S-2922
United Nations
New York, NY 10017
USA

☎ +1-212-9635958
✉ undesa@un.org

UNCTAD

Rebeca Grynspan, Secretary-General

United Nations Conference on Trade and Development
Room E-9042
Palais de Nations, 8–14
1211 Geneva 10
Switzerland

☎ +41-22-9175806
✉ sgo@unctad.org

UNECA

Vera Songwe, Executive Secretary

United Nations Economic Commission for Africa
Menelik II Avenue
P.O. Box 3001
Addis Ababa
Ethiopia

☎ +251-11-5511231
✉ ecainfo@uneca.org

UNECE

Olga Algayerova, Executive Secretary

United Nations Economic Commission for Europe
Palais des Nations
CH-1211 Geneva 10
Switzerland

☎ +41-22-9174444
✉ unece_info@un.org

UNECLAC

Alicia Bárcena, Executive Secretary

Economic Commission for Latin America and the Caribbean
Av. Dag Hammarskjöld 3477
Vitacura
Santiago, Chile
Chile

☎ +56-2-22102000
✉ secepal@cepal.org

UNESCAP

Armida Salsiah Alisjahbana, Executive Secretary

Economic and Social Commission for Asia and the Pacific
United Nations Building
Rajadamnern Nok Avenue
Bangkok 10200
Thailand

☎ +66-2-2881234
✉ escap-scas@un.org

UNESCWA

Rola Dashti, Executive Secretary

Economic and Social Commission for Western Asia
P.O. Box 11-8575
Riad el-Solh Square, Beirut
Lebanon

☎ +961-1-981301
@ https://www.unescwa.org/contact

ISBN: 978-92-1-109183-0
eISBN: 978-92-1-001183-9
Print ISSN: 1995-2074
Online ISSN: 2411-8370
United Nations publication
Sales No. E.22.II.C.1

Foreword

The world is now two years into the COVID-19 pandemic, and the end is nowhere in sight.

The human, economic and social toll of the pandemic has been devastating. Rising poverty, job losses, shredded safety nets, health-care systems pushed to the brink, and the impacts of a changing climate are placing the Sustainable Development Goals further out of reach.

Inequalities are intensifying, setting the stage for an uncertain, uneven and unfair recovery.

In some countries, ambitious vaccination roll-outs and bold economic support and stimulus packages are paving the way towards recovery.

But progress is not being shared equally.

More than a quarter of developing countries have yet to achieve their pre-pandemic levels of output, hampered by severely inadequate access to vaccines and limited financial resources. Job creation has been insufficient to make up for earlier losses, with employment deficits disproportionally affecting women and youth.

Against this backdrop, the risk of new COVID-19 variants emerging and spreading threatens to derail any recovery prospects.

At the same time, rapidly rising inflation in many parts of the world will result in higher interest rates, limiting borrowing and constraining fiscal space at exactly the time countries should be investing in jobs, education, health care, and the green economy.

For developing countries already drowning in debt, this is a recipe for defaults and prolonged economic distress.

In this fragile and uneven period of global recovery, the *World Economic Situation and Prospects 2022* calls for better targeted and coordinated policy and financial measures at the national and international levels.

As detailed in this report, national fiscal and monetary authorities need to carefully sequence, calibrate and coordinate their policies to avoid sudden disruptions. Internationally, the world needs to come together to reform the global financial system. This requires the full mobilization of governments, international financial institutions, credit-rating agencies and others.

We must act across a wide range of challenges – from addressing illicit financial flows, to injecting more fairness into the global tax system, and encouraging more private investment into developing countries.

We must also overhaul the international debt architecture, so developing countries can access the financing and debt relief they need to spur recovery in the short term and invest in resilient and sustainable development over the longer term.

This must include investments in education systems, universal health coverage and social protection, jobs in the green, digital and care economies, and access to COVID-19 vaccines for all, so we can put the pandemic behind us.

The time is now to close the inequality gaps within and among countries.

If we work in solidarity – as one human family – we can make 2022 a true year of recovery for people and economies alike.

The United Nations system stands ready to work with every country to make our way through this global crisis, and build the resilient, inclusive, equal and sustainable world economy that every person needs and deserves.

António Guterres
United Nations Secretary-General

Explanatory notes

The following symbols have been used in the tables throughout the report:

...	**Three dots** indicate that data are not available or are not separately reported.
–	**A dash** indicates that the amount is nil or negligible.
-	**A hyphen** indicates that the item is not applicable.
-	**A minus sign** indicates deficit or decrease, except as indicated.
.	**A full stop** is used to indicate decimals.
/	**A slash** between years indicates a crop year or financial year, for example, 2021/22.
–	**Use of a hyphen between years**, for example, 2021–2022, signifies the full period involved, including the beginning and end years.

Reference to "dollars" ($) indicates United States dollars, unless otherwise stated.
Reference to "billions" indicates one thousand million.
Reference to "tons" indicates metric tons, unless otherwise stated.
Annual rates of growth or change, unless otherwise stated, refer to annual compound rates.
Details and percentages in tables do not necessarily add to totals, because of rounding.

For **country classifications**, see Statistical annex.

Data presented in this publication incorporate information available as at **30 November 2021**.

Starting in 2010, data for the Ukraine excludes the temporarily occupied territory of the Autonomous Republic of Crimea and Sevastopol.

The following abbreviations have been used:

APP	Asset purchase programme
ASEAN	Association of Southeast Asian Nations
CAPE	Cyclically Adjusted Price Earnings
CIS	Commonwealth of Independent States
ECB	European Central Bank
EMU	European Economic and Monetary Union
G20	Group of 20
G7	Group of 7
GCC	Gulf Cooperation Council
GDP	gross domestic product
ICT	information and communications technology
ILO	International Labour Organization
IMF	International Monetary Fund
OECD	Organisation for Economic Co-operation and Development
OPEC	Organization of the Petroleum Exporting Countries
PEPP	Pandemic Emergency Purchase Programme
PPP	purchasing power parity
S&P	Standard and Poor's
UN DESA	United Nations Department of Economic and Social Affairs
UNCTAD	United Nations Conference on Trade and Development
WESP	World Economic Situation and Prospects
WHO	World Health Organization

Acknowledgements

The World Economic Situation and Prospects 2022 is a report produced by the United Nations Department of Economic and Social Affairs (**UN DESA**), in partnership with the United Nations Conference on Trade and Development (**UNCTAD**) and Economic Commission for Africa (**UNECA**), Economic Commission for Europe (**UNECE**), Economic Commission for Latin America and the Caribbean (**UNECLAC**), Economic and Social Commission for Asia and the Pacific (**UNESCAP**) and Economic and Social Commission for Western Asia (**UNESCWA**). The United Nations World Tourism Organization (**UNWTO**) also contributed to the report. The forecasts presented in the report draw on the World Economic Forecasting Model (WEFM) of UN DESA as well as inputs from the United Nations regional commissions.

Under the general guidance of Liu Zhenmin, Under-Secretary-General for Economic and Social Affairs; Elliott Harris, United Nations Chief Economist, Assistant-Secretary-General for Economic Development; and Shantanu Mukherjee, Director of the Economic Analysis and Policy Division (EAPD); Hamid Rashid, Chief of the Global Economic Monitoring Branch (GEMB) of EAPD led and coordinated the writing of the report with a core team of authors from **GEMB**, comprising, Helena Afonso, Grigor Agabekian, Ian Cox, Andrea Grozdanic, Ingo Pitterle, Julian Rodrick Slotman, Sebastian Vergara, Yasuhisa Yamamoto and Zhenqian Huang. The core team benefited from the research and analytical support from Ali Bargu, Lennart Claas Niermann and Lea Steininger.

The contributions of Cornelia Kaldewei, Leah C. Kennedy, Poh Lynn Ng and Gabe Scelta from **UN DESA**; Rachid Amui, Bruno Antunes, Regina Asariotis, Rashmi Banga, Chantal Line Carpentier, Stefan Csordas, Cambiz Daneshvar, Marco Fugazza, Taisuke Ito, Richard Kozul-Wright, Nicolas Maystre, Alessandro Nicita, Janvier Nkurunziza, Ralf Peters, Mesut Saygili, Miho Shirotori, Vincent Valentine, Dong Wu from **UNCTAD**; Bartholomew Armah, Joseph Atta-Mensah, Jean Paul Boketsu Bofili, Hopestone Kayiska Chavula, Adrian Gauci, Chaoyi Hu, Bosede Olanike from **ECA**; José Palacín Lucio from **ECE**; Claudio Aravena, Sonia Gontero, Ramon Pineda, Daniel Titelman, Cecilia Vera from **ECLAC**; Shuvojit Banerjee, Zheng Jian, Michal Podolski, Kiatkanid Pongpanich, Sweta Saxena, Vatcharin Sirimaneetham from **ESCAP**; Mohamed Bchir, Jan Gaska, Mohamed El Moctar Mohamed El Hacene, Ahmed Moummi, Souraya Zein from **ESCWA**; Sandra Carvão, Michel Julian and Javier Ruescas from **UNWTO**; Joaquin Salido Marcos and Susanna Wolf from **UN-OHRLLS** are duly acknowledged.

The report was edited by Gretchen Luchsinger, with graphic design by Mackenzie Crone and cover design by Parvati Mcpheeters.

Sustainable Development Goals

Goal 1. End poverty in all its forms everywhere

Goal 2. End hunger, achieve food security and improved nutrition and promote sustainable agriculture

Goal 3. Ensure healthy lives and promote well-being for all at all ages

Goal 4. Ensure inclusive and equitable quality education and promote lifelong learning opportunities for all

Goal 5. Achieve gender equality and empower all women and girls

Goal 6. Ensure availability and sustainable management of water and sanitation for all

Goal 7. Ensure access to affordable, reliable, sustainable and modern energy for all

Goal 8. Promote sustained, inclusive and sustainable economic growth, full and productive employment and decent work for all

Goal 9. Build resilient infrastructure, promote inclusive and sustainable industrialization and foster innovation

Goal 10. Reduce inequality within and among countries

Goal 11. Make cities and human settlements inclusive, safe, resilient and sustainable

Goal 12. Ensure sustainable consumption and production patterns

Goal 13. Take urgent action to combat climate change and its impacts

Goal 14. Conserve and sustainably use the oceans, seas and marine resources for sustainable development

Goal 15. Protect, restore and promote sustainable use of terrestrial ecosystems, sustainably manage forests, combat desertification, and halt and reverse land degradation and halt biodiversity loss

Goal 16. Promote peaceful and inclusive societies for sustainable development, provide access to justice for all and build effective, accountable and inclusive institutions at all levels

Goal 17. Strengthen the means of implementation and revitalize the Global Partnership for Sustainable Development

Executive summary

Global growth prospects

After a strong recovery in 2021, global growth momentum is losing steam

Global economic recovery hinges on a delicate balance amid new waves of COVID-19 infections, persistent labour market challenges, lingering supply-chain constraints and rising inflationary pressures. After a global contraction of 3.4 per cent in 2020 and following an expansion of 5.5 per cent in 2021, the highest rate of growth in more than four decades, the world economy is projected to grow by 4 per cent in 2022 and 3.5 per cent in 2023. World gross product in 2021 was 1.9 per cent higher than in 2019 but still 3.3 per cent below the level of output projected prior to the pandemic. These aggregate growth figures, however, mask marked divergences in the pace of recovery across countries and regions.

Global recovery in output in 2021 was largely driven by robust consumer spending and some uptake in investment. Trade in goods bounced back, surpassing the pre-pandemic level. But growth momentum slowed considerably by the end of 2021 including in big economies like China, the European Union and the United States of America, as the effects of fiscal and monetary stimuli dissipated and major supply-chain disruptions emerged. Growth impetus generally has been weaker in most developing countries and economies in transition. While higher commodity prices have helped commodity-exporting countries at large, rising food and energy prices have triggered rapid inflation, particularly in the Commonwealth of Independent States (CIS) and Latin America and the Caribbean. Recovery has been especially slow in tourism-dependent economies, notably in the small island developing States.

Output losses relative to pre-pandemic projections will remain substantial in most developing countries

According to current forecasts, half of the world's economies will exceed pre-pandemic levels of output by at least 7 per cent in 2023. In East Asia and South Asia, average gross domestic product (GDP) in 2023 is projected to be 18.4 per cent above its 2019 level, compared to only 3.4 per cent in Latin America and the Caribbean. This does not necessarily mean that countries will fully regain their output relative to trend output growth before the pandemic. Despite a robust recovery, East Asia and South Asia's GDP in 2023 is projected to remain 1.7 per cent below the levels forecast prior to the pandemic. Africa and Latin America and the Caribbean are projected to see gaps of 5.5 and 4.2 per cent, respectively, compared to pre-pandemic projections. These persistent output gaps will exacerbate poverty and inequality and undermine sustainable development.

The global outlook faces major uncertainties and risks

Near-term global growth prospects face major risks with the pandemic far from over. With new waves of infections spreading quickly, the human and economic tolls are expected to increase. The growth outlook presented in this report therefore remains susceptible to an upsurge in cases and potential restrictions on economic activities. Limited access to vaccines poses a particular challenge to most developing countries and transition economies as a resurgence of the virus will likely affect them more than the developed countries, which have achieved relatively high vaccination coverage. By December 2021, the number of vaccine doses per 100 people in the least developed countries stood at just 23.9 against 147.4 in the developed countries. Limited supplies of vaccines from manufacturers and domestic fiscal constraints continue to limit access for many developing countries.

Rising inflationary pressures in major developed economies and a number of large developing countries present additional risks to recovery. Global headline inflation rose to an estimated 5.2 per cent in 2021, more than 2 percentage points above its trend rate in the past 10 years. The inflationary pressure was particularly pronounced in the United States, the euro area and Latin America and the Caribbean. A faster-than-expected tightening of global monetary conditions represents another major challenge. Any unexpected shifts in the monetary policy stances of the Federal Reserve in the United States could abruptly change investor expectations and trigger large adjustments in portfolio allocations, while significantly altering capital flows to developing countries.

International trade and investment registered mixed performance

International trade performance was mixed in 2021. Merchandise trade bounced back, with global trade in goods surpassing the pre-pandemic level. Trade in services has remained subdued, however, as many cross-border services, particularly international travel and tourism, have yet to recover. Our baseline scenario projects that global trade in goods and services will grow by 5.7 per cent in 2022 after an expansion of 11 per cent in 2021. Although trade in services is yet to recover, it is expected to gradually improve as external demand patterns normalize. The trade outlook remains susceptible to potential restrictions in economic activities, however, with the new Omicron variant of COVID-19 posing considerable risks and policy uncertainties.

In many parts of the world, investment has rebounded from the pandemic-induced slump, supported by an easing of COVID-19 restrictions, large fiscal stimulus packages and ultraloose monetary policies. After contracting by 2.7 per cent in 2020, global investment expanded an estimated 7.5 per cent in 2021, driven by strong albeit moderating growth in China and the United States. Beyond the headline figures, however, the global investment picture is more troubling. In many countries, the rebound is the result of favourable base effects and an exceptionally supportive fiscal and monetary policy environment. As financial conditions tighten and fiscal support is withdrawn, investment growth will likely return to the slow pace that prevailed before the pandemic. Medium-term investment prospects are particularly challenging for developing and transition economies that heavily depend on fossil fuels.

Labour market recovery is lagging

Employment levels are projected to remain well below pre-pandemic levels during 2022–2023 and possibly beyond. The pace of job creation has been largely inadequate to offset earlier employment losses although the picture varies across regions. While labour markets in developed countries are gradually improving as recovery gathers pace, employment growth in developing countries remains weak amid lower vaccination progress and limited stimulus spending. This divergence is projected to continue in the near-term. In developed economies, full employment recovery is projected in 2023 or in some cases in 2024. The developing economies, especially those in Africa, Latin America and the Caribbean, and Western Asia, are expected to see much slower recovery of jobs.

Global poverty is projected to remain at record highs

Adverse impacts of the pandemic on growth and employment have significantly undermined progress on global poverty reduction, dashing hopes of achieving the Sustainable Development Goal of ending extreme poverty. The number of people living in extreme poverty globally is projected to decrease slightly to 876 million in 2022 but is expected to remain well above pre-pandemic levels. Fast-developing economies in East Asia and South Asia and developed economies are expected to experience some poverty reduction. In contrast, poverty is forecast to further increase in the world's most vulnerable economies. Insufficient fiscal space and the slow recovery of employment in general will undermine poverty reduction in many developing countries in the near term. This is particularly the case in Africa, where the absolute number of people in poverty is anticipated to rise through 2023.

Higher inequality may emerge as a longer-term legacy of the COVID-19 crisis

Higher levels of inequality within and between countries are emerging as a longer-term consequence of the pandemic. For the vast majority of developing countries, a full recovery of GDP per capita will remain elusive. The gap between what they will achieve and what they would have achieved without the pandemic will persist well into 2023. In contrast, GDP per capita in the developed economies is expected to almost fully recover by 2023 relative to pre-pandemic projections.

Uneven recovery of employment and income across different population groups is increasing inequalities within countries. In particular, the crisis has exacerbated the gender divide, especially in developing countries, where women experienced a sharper decline in employment and labour force participation than men. Many women face serious barriers to re-entering the labour force, especially women with young children. Support for unpaid domestic work, including childcare, will remain crucial to reversing the gender divide in the recovery of jobs. More broadly, an inclusive and sustainable recovery will require putting gender considerations at the heart of social protection and labour market policies.

Fiscal asymmetries are shaping recovery and development prospects

Governments around the world will need to continue accommodative fiscal stances and avoid the temptations of premature fiscal consolidation. This will help ensure a robust, inclusive and sustainable recovery. Yet differences in fiscal space and structural constraints across countries will continue to limit the ability to support pandemic-related expenditures, including vaccination, as well as to provide relief to the most vulnerable and support the restoration of employment.

Fiscal and debt situations are extremely challenging for low-income developing countries. With very limited fiscal space to confront the pandemic and support recovery, they are taking resources to respond to the crisis from other critical areas, including public investment and education. Unsustainable external debt burdens, additional borrowing during the pandemic and increasing debt-servicing costs have put a rising number of countries on the verge of a debt crisis. They are in urgent need of further and coordinated international support for debt relief.

Reinvigorating multilateralism is essential to confront the health and climate crises

Reinvigorating multilateralism will remain critical to contain the pandemic and accelerate a robust and inclusive global recovery. Manifestly unequal access to vaccines and inadequate commitments to addressing debt challenges, however, illustrate that multilateralism still needs to rise to the challenge of steering a recovery that is broad-based and inclusive. Stronger and more ambitious international cooperation is an imperative to beat the pandemic, put the world back on track towards sustainable development and pursue bold climate action.

The pandemic triggered an unprecedented monetary policy response

Since the onset of COVID-19, countries around the world have rolled out extraordinary measures to mitigate adverse economic and financial impacts. The monetary response has broadly followed the playbook of the 2008–2009 global financial crisis but with unprecedented speed, scale and scope. Central banks aggressively cut short-term interest rates to increase liquidity, reduce borrowing costs and support economic activities. But coming on the heels of a decade of monetary accommodation, policy rates in developed economies quickly approached their effective lower bound. Developed country central banks thus relied heavily on unconventional monetary policy tools, particularly large-scale asset purchase programmes (APPs), to stabilize financial markets and stimulate recovery.

Asset purchase programmes have become a primary stimulus tool in developed countries

For many developed country central banks, APPs, often referred to as quantitative easing, have become the primary tool for monetary stimulus during the COVID-19 crisis. Since March 2020, the central banks of Japan, the United Kingdom, the United States and the euro area have added roughly $10.2 trillion in security assets to their balance sheets, with total assets soaring to over $25.9 trillion by the end of September 2021. Balance sheets have also risen sharply as a share of GDP. In the second quarter of 2021, total financial assets on central bank balance sheets ranged from 35 per cent of GDP in the United States to 130 per cent in Japan.

In implementing APPs, central banks purchased long-maturity securities such as government bonds or mortgage-backed securities from financial institutions. This provided liquidity to restore market confidence and financial stability, lower long-term borrowing costs, boost credit flows and reduce the cost of servicing existing debt. APPs are expected to stimulate aggregate demand, employment and economic growth while helping central banks achieve their inflation targets.

Many developing country central banks implemented asset purchase programmes for the first time

The pandemic saw a turning point for monetary policy in many developing countries, where central banks introduced APPs for the first time as they confronted large capital outflows, growing risks of financial instability and rising government financing costs. During 2020, 27 central banks – 10 in Africa, 9 in Asia and 8 in Latin America and the Caribbean – embarked on APPs. While these programmes have been broadly modelled after those in developed economies, they mainly aimed to boost market confidence and reduce market dysfunctionality and have been much smaller in scale and shorter in duration. By the second quarter of 2021, the Reserve Bank of India was the only major developing country central bank continuing significant asset purchases.

The programmes have been effective in addressing financial distress and kickstarting recovery...

Empirical evidence suggests that the APPs have been generally effective in addressing financial distress and supporting the recovery of economic activities in the early stages of the current crisis. During both the global financial crisis and the COVID-19 pandemic, the programmes helped to stabilize financial markets by providing liquidity, easing financial conditions and reducing uncertainty. They also lowered long-term borrowing costs, supporting a rebound in investment and consumption of durable goods and allowing countries to emerge quickly from recession.

...but the longer-term growth impacts of asset purchase programmes are less clear

There is growing evidence that when normal market functioning is restored and the economy is recovering, new purchases do not provide significant additional stimulus. The slow economic recovery from the global financial crisis suggests that the effectiveness of central bank asset purchases may not extend beyond the early recovery phase. Although monetary policies in developed countries were exceptionally accommodative in the 2010s, investment failed to pick up significantly. Abundant liquidity and ultralow borrowing costs often did not stimulate bank lending to the real economy. In some cases, ultralow interest rates and underpriced risks encouraged the emergence of "zombie firms" with low productivity. In several countries, especially the United States, firms have been using cheap and abundant liquidity for stock buy-backs rather than new investments. In the second quarter of 2021, buy-backs among companies listed on the Standard and Poor's (S&P) 500 index totalled $199 billion, close to an all-time high. Large-scale buy-backs have negatively affected investment and capital accumulation and reduced firms' abilities to cope with an economic downturn, especially if buy-backs are increasingly funded with new debt.

Prolonged ultraloose monetary policies have created macroeconomic vulnerabilities

A prolonged period of ultraloose monetary policies, with central banks pumping massive amounts of liquidity into financial markets to keep long-term interest rates low, has created significant macroeconomic and financial vulnerabilities. Large-scale APPs in developed countries have encouraged speculative behaviour among investors, with the search for higher yields triggering a borrowing binge in some developing economies. Public and publicly guaranteed debt in low- and lower-middle-income countries owed to private creditors rose by 264 per cent during 2010–2019, compared with a 7 per cent decline from 1998–2007. Excessive external borrowing, especially from private creditors, has exacerbated debt sustainability concerns for many developing countries.

Asset price bubbles pose a threat to financial stability

The additional liquidity from large-scale APPs has fuelled asset price inflation in virtually every asset class, including bond, equity and real estate markets. Stock prices have recorded especially large gains in the United States, where current valuations are approaching levels only seen prior to the bursting of the dot-com bubble in 2001. This has spurred fears of ever-expanding asset price bubbles as the disconnect between financial markets and economic fundamentals continues to widen. If monetary conditions were to shift abruptly, with major central banks quickly tapering asset purchases and raising policy rates, asset price bubbles would likely burst. Sharp market corrections could trigger a rising number of bankruptcies and inflict substantial economic damage on a fragile recovery, with adverse global spillover effects. Financial stability concerns are compounded by the higher-risk exposure of investors, as APPs have pushed market participants towards higher-yielding assets.

Higher asset prices have disproportionately benefited the wealthy

Evidence from developed countries suggests that APPs have had adverse distributional effects, disproportionately benefiting rich households and widening wealth inequalities. Capital gains from rising stock, bond or housing prices account for a significant share of total income for top earners, especially the top 1 per cent, but are negligible for groups in the bottom of the income distribution. In addition, wealthy households invest a much larger share of their portfolios in financial assets, especially equities, which have registered the strongest price gains since the onset of the current crisis. According to preliminary estimates, the top 1 per cent of income earners in the United States registered net wealth gains of about $3.5 million per person between the first quarter of 2020 and the second quarter of 2021. The bottom 20 per cent recorded an increase of only about $5,300 per person. The APPs also likely increased gender inequalities since women tend to have less wealth and income than men and are less likely to invest in risky assets. These findings underscore the need for central banks to pay attention to the distributional consequences of APPs.

Central banks face difficult trade-offs in unwinding policy support

While concerns about higher inflation after the global financial crisis proved unfounded, developed country central banks are now facing rising inflationary pressures. Rapid consumer price inflation from the strong recovery in demand and supply-side disruptions is pressuring monetary authorities to scale back, if not unwind, their APPs. This time, the tapering of asset purchases is happening at a much faster pace than after the global financial crisis. Unwinding and eventually exiting APPs will not be easy. Central banks, especially the Federal Reserve and the European Central Bank (ECB), face the challenge of scaling back bond purchase programmes without creating financial market turmoil and destabilizing global financial flows. The risk of policy mistakes, either by withdrawing stimulus too fast or by delaying the tightening for too long, is substantial. Beyond this immediate challenge, the more fundamental question is if – and if so, how quickly – central banks will reverse asset purchases and reduce the size of their balance sheets.

Rapidly rising interest rates could add considerable pressure to public finances

Debt service costs in several developed countries have become more sensitive to short-term interest rates in part due to APPs. If interest rates were to rise more sharply and rapidly than expected, public finances could come under pressure, especially in countries with high debt burdens. In the United States, for example, interest expenses accounted for about 10 per cent of total government revenues in 2020. This ratio is forecast to increase to about 14 per cent by 2030 in the baseline scenario but may soar to 22 per cent in 2030 under a higher interest rate scenario, which could lead to difficult choices on the expenditure side. The fiscal implications of a sudden unwinding of APPs could be equally consequential for developing countries, especially those with open capital accounts and high levels of external public debt. Higher interest rates following the end of APPs could trigger large capital outflows and further aggravate debt sustainability for many developing countries with significant levels of hard currency-denominated external debt. The "taper tantrum" of May 2013 serves as a reminder of these risks.

The crisis presents an opportunity for central banks to support climate action

To mitigate the adverse effects of APPs and facilitate the unwinding process, a set of complementary policies should be put in place. Macroprudential policies can play an important role in strengthening the resilience of the financial system. They can slow asset price growth and restrain excessive risk-taking, especially in sectors that pose greater risks to the financial system. Fiscal and taxation policy reforms can minimize the adverse side effects of APPs. More progressive income taxation, including through levies on capital gains and taxes on corporate stock buy-backs, can help to discourage speculative behaviour, reduce inequalities and improve macroeconomic outcomes. Finally, APPs offer central banks an opportunity to finance climate action, mitigate climate risks and help transition to a low-carbon economy. When unwinding their asset purchases, central banks may choose to hold on to assets of sectors and firms with lower carbon footprints. At the same time, central banks can develop new principles and guidelines to prioritize low-carbon assets for future APPs.

Regional outlook

The robust economic expansion of the United States has slowed amid mounting inflationary pressures

In the United States, robust growth in 2021, estimated at 5.5 per cent, is forecast to decelerate to 3.5 per cent in 2022. Recovery has largely depended on domestic demand; external demand has been weak. Rapid growth in domestic demand has faced increasing supply-side constraints due to global supply-chain disruptions and logistics backlogs, particularly the shortage of industrial inputs, including semiconductors. Resulting inflationary pressures are projected to persist well into 2022 given persistent labour shortages, which may worsen if a new wave of infection takes hold. The consumption-driven recovery will lose momentum once the effects of fiscal stimulus on household spending dissipate. Uncertainties over the COVID-19 pandemic, mounting inflationary pressures and associated monetary policy decisions impact economic prospects.

The economy of the European Union confronts strong headwinds and surging inflation

The economy of the European Union returned to growth in 2021 along with the gradual easing of containment measures, continuation of accommodative macroeconomic policies and a sharp rebound in leading export destinations, particularly China and the United States. Following a 6 per cent contraction in 2020, the region's GDP grew by an estimated 4.7 per cent in 2021. The region faced serious headwinds in the second half of the year, however, fanned by supply-chain disruptions and shortages of workers. The automotive industry, crucially important for many European Union countries, had to scale back production due to semiconductor shortages. In late 2021, another wave of the pandemic prompted the reintroduction of containment measures that are disrupting many service sector activities. Inflation in the second half of the year surged to levels not seen for years; however, the ECB, while scaling back its APP, is likely to maintain its low borrowing costs at least until early 2023. Growth is expected to moderate to 3.9 per cent in 2022 due to the lower base effect and tapering of ECB asset purchases but a massive recovery plan financed by joint debt issuance will likely improve medium-term growth prospects.

China's economy faces near-term challenges, while pursuing high-quality growth

China's economy expanded an estimated 7.8 per cent in 2021, with growth projected to moderate to 5.2 per cent in 2022. Rapid recovery in the first half of 2021, driven by strong exports due to the reopening of developed countries and robust investment, has lost momentum. The reintroduction of restrictive measures under the "zero-COVID-19" policy has taken a toll on services and consumption while policy-induced property market cooling and temporary power rationing to phase out fossil fuels have weighed on investment. At the same time, the default of a large real estate firm has shaken financial markets and confidence in the sector. The Government still has multiple policy tools to stimulate economic activity, however, as low inflation offers room for monetary easing. A swift recovery from the pandemic has boosted government revenues for more targeted fiscal spending. Going forward, China's transition towards development driven by consumption and higher-end manufacturing will lead to more sustainable but slower growth, with significant international spillover effects.

Lifted restrictions and higher commodity prices underpin recovery in the Commonwealth of Independent States and Georgia; economic activity rebounds in South-Eastern Europe

Economic growth resumed in the CIS area in 2021 as mobility and activity restrictions were eased or removed, domestic demand strengthened and the external environment became more favourable, including through sharp increases in commodity prices. The aggregate GDP of the CIS and Georgia, after shrinking by 2.6 per cent in 2020, expanded by an estimated 4.3 per cent in 2021. Growth is projected to moderate to 3.2 per cent in 2022. In small energy-importing countries, recovery in remittance flows and tourism revenues supported economic activities. Labour market conditions improved significantly. Most of the CIS area experienced a strong upsurge in inflation in 2021, however, spurred by supply disruptions, higher food and energy prices, stronger demand and in some cases currency depreciations. Monetary authorities in almost all countries reacted to the inflationary spike with policy tightening. Governments have taken various measures to limit price increases and mitigate impacts on their populations. The area's economic outlook has multiple downside risks, such as increased volatility in commodity prices, slow progress in vaccination against COVID-19, mounting geopolitical tensions and rising risks in the banking sector. The broad recovery in the European Union along with increasing tourism demand accelerated recovery of the South-Eastern European economies in 2021. But the pace will likely weaken in 2022 as governments scale back fiscal support amid debt sustainability concerns.

New COVID-19 waves and an uncertain policy environment cloud Africa's recovery prospects

In Africa, aggregate GDP is projected to expand by 4.0 per cent in 2022, slightly up from an estimated 3.8 per cent in 2021. While improving vaccination rates and terms of trade will support more robust economic growth, the continent will remain far below its pre-pandemic output trends. Moreover, a nascent recovery will remain fragile and subject to risks from recurrent waves of COVID-19 infection as most of the region's population remains unvaccinated. Political instability and conflict in many subregions will further aggravate existing problems and undermine economic potential. The poverty rate is projected to remain elevated, with an increase in the absolute number of people in extreme poverty. For commodity exporters, higher commodity prices have provided much needed fiscal space.

In contrast, tourism-dependent African countries face a much longer path to recovery. Countries across the region are struggling with elevated debt burdens and rising interest payments. These will limit fiscal space to support economic recovery and implement the 2030 Agenda for Sustainable Development, underscoring the critical role of multilateral support, including to expedite vaccine distribution and facilitate debt relief.

After solid economic recovery, downside risks are rising for East Asia

East Asian economies have rebounded from the worst of the pandemic with GDP growth estimated at 6.7 per cent in 2021 after slowing to 1 per cent in 2020. Recovery is, however, still in the early stages, and the resurgence of COVID-19 cases has disrupted prospects otherwise supported by strong policy stimulus and external demand. More people in extreme poverty, a slow labour market recovery and rising climate risks will continue to inhibit progress on the 2030 Agenda for Sustainable Development. Looking ahead, the region's economic growth is forecast to moderate to 4.9 per cent in 2022 as base effects disappear. Weaker export demand, prolonged supply-side challenges, rising concerns around financial instability and the possibility of a sharper-than-expected slowdown in China's economy, all amid a lingering pandemic with new variants, pose downside risks. Containing the pandemic will remain a policy priority in the near term; macroeconomic policies should remain accommodative and targeted to ensure an inclusive and sustainable recovery.

South Asia's recovery gathers momentum but more constrained policy space and downside risks lie ahead

The recovery continues to gain momentum in South Asia amid contained COVID-19 infections and higher mobility, robust remittance inflows and broadly supportive macroeconomic policy stances. After an estimated expansion of 7.4 per cent in 2021, regional GDP is projected to grow at a more moderate pace of 5.9 per cent in 2022. The recovery, however, is still fragile, uneven and subject to pandemic-related uncertainties and downside risks. Labour market recovery is lagging, indicating severe socioeconomic challenges for large segments of the population. Stalling and reversing the recent rise in poverty and inequality largely depends on achieving robust, sustained and inclusive growth. A lasting recovery moving forward may prove challenging, however, as fiscal and monetary policy space become more constrained and global financial conditions tighten. Policymakers will need to maintain critical support for recovery and job creation such as by prioritizing public infrastructure and green investments that crowd-in private finance.

Uneven recovery among Western Asian economies points to further polarization

In Western Asia, the region's GDP grew by an estimated 4.7 per cent in 2021 after contracting by 3.4 per cent in 2020. Economic recovery has been led mainly by growth in domestic demand. With the relaxation of pandemic control measures and progress on vaccination, economic activities showed rapid recovery in most economies in the region in the second half of 2021. In parallel with robust domestic demand, the unemployment rate declined towards pre-pandemic levels in Israel, Saudi Arabia and Turkey. Employment recovery has been slower in other countries and the employment situation remains dire in Iraq, Lebanon, the State of Palestine, the Syrian Arab Republic and Yemen. A strong recovery is forecast to continue, mainly in oil-exporting countries given the expected increase in crude oil production. Regional GDP growth is projected to accelerate to 4.8 per cent in 2022. Recovery remains fragile, however, in non-oil exporting middle- and low-income countries.

Latin America and the Caribbean's recovery is losing traction amid fading external tailwinds and tighter macroeconomic policies

Latin America and the Caribbean's economy rebounded from the COVID-19 crisis amid favourable external conditions, successful vaccine roll-outs and strong domestic policy support. After contracting by a record 7.4 per cent in 2020, the region's GDP grew by an estimated 6.5 per cent in 2021. But the pandemic threatens to leave lasting scars on the region's economies, including higher unemployment and poverty, greater inequality and larger debt burdens. Regional GDP growth is projected to slow sharply to 2.2 per cent in 2022 as tailwinds from higher commodity prices and buoyant demand from China and the United States are expected to fade. At the same time, tighter monetary and fiscal policies will weigh on domestic demand, with central banks raising policy rates to combat soaring inflation and governments increasingly shifting from fiscal stimulus to the consolidation of public finances. The regional outlook remains subject to significant downside risks, including the spread of new COVID-19 variants, a sharp tightening of global financial conditions, and mounting social and political instability.

In summary, the world has emerged from the depths of a paralysing economic crisis. The recovery in economic output and the labour market remains uneven across countries due to large differences in vaccine access and policy space. At the same time, the crisis has undermined and reversed some hard-won achievements in realizing the 2030 Agenda for Sustainable Development. The past two years have seen sharply rising numbers of people in extreme poverty, widening gender gaps in labour markets, and escalating income and wealth inequality, within and between countries. Going forward, the fragile recovery faces strong headwinds amid the spread of the new variants of COVID-19, persistent labour market challenges, lingering supply-chain constraints and rising inflationary pressures. Policymakers confront difficult policy trade-offs, as countries aim to move from a rebound in output to a robust, inclusive and sustainable recovery. This will require better targeted and coordinated monetary, fiscal, and labour market policies, supported by new technologies. The international community needs to strengthen and reinvigorate multilateralism to ensure equal and universal access to vaccines, address debt challenges, and accelerate the transition towards low-carbon economies.

Table of contents

Chapter III

Page

Boxes

Boxes: figures

Figures

Tables

Page

Statistical annex

Country classifications

Annex tables

CHAPTER I

Global economic outlook

Global growth prospects

The growth outlook in a pandemic world

Global growth is gradually converging to its long-term trend

Global economic recovery from the COVID-19 pandemic hinges on a delicate balance amid new waves of infection, labour market challenges, lingering supply-side constraints and rising inflationary pressures weighing heavily on near-term growth prospects. The global economy grew by 5.5 per cent in 2021 – the highest growth rate since 1976 – after contracting by 3.4 per cent in 2020. World gross product in 2021 was 1.9 per cent higher than in 2019 but still 3.3 per cent below the level projected before COVID-19. The recovery of output in 2021 largely represented the resumption of household spending and investment, which had come to a screeching halt in 2020 amid lockdown measures worldwide. The world economy is projected to grow by 4 per cent in 2022 and 3.5 per cent in 2023, converging towards its long-term trend of around 3 per cent per year between 2010 and 2019. But these aggregate figures mask strong divergence in growth prospects as a significant number of developing countries are struggling to recover from the pandemic.

Easing supply-side disruptions and containing inflation are crucial to support global growth

The projected growth rates for 2022 mark a small upward revision from the forecasts in the *World Economic Situation and Prospects 2021*, even as significant downside risks emerged during the fourth quarter of 2021 (table I.1). The growth momentum of the first three quarters of 2021 – especially in the United States, the European Union and China – slowed as the stimulating effects of fiscal and monetary measures began to dissipate and supply-side challenges emerged at the end of the year. The easing of supply-side constraints and the taming of inflationary pressures will remain critical to keep the global economy on the projected near-term growth trajectory. Growth prospects, however, face significant risks and uncertainties, including new mutations of COVID-19, such as the Omicron variant that began spreading in late November 2021. Growth forecasts presented in this report remain susceptible to potential lockdowns and other restrictive measures worldwide. In addition, as major central banks start to withdraw their extraordinary policy support, global financial conditions may tighten considerably, weighing on global recovery.

Output losses relative to pre-pandemic projections will remain substantial in developing countries

According to current forecasts, the gross domestic product (GDP) of 16 hard-hit developing countries – including many small island developing States – will be more than 5 per cent smaller in 2022 than in 2019.[1] Well over a fifth of developing countries, 28 in total, will have to wait until 2022 to see GDP return to pre-crisis levels. Twenty or nearly a fifth of developing countries will still be below their 2019

1 The GDPs of the Bolivarian Republic of Venezuela and Lebanon will be more than 30 per cent smaller than before the pandemic. These sharp contractions are due to domestic economic fragilities compounded by the impact of the pandemic.

output levels by the end of 2023. On the other hand, by 2023, more than half of the world's economies will exceed their 2019 output levels by at least 7 per cent. In East and South Asia, average GDP in 2023 is projected to be 18.4 per cent above its 2019 level, compared to only 3.4 per cent in Latin America and the Caribbean (figure I.1). But this does not mean that countries will regain lost output. In fact, despite the robust recovery, East and South Asia's GDP in 2023 is projected to be 1.7 per cent below the level forecast prior to the pandemic. Africa and Latin America and the Caribbean are expected to see losses of 5.5 and 4.2 per cent, respectively, compared to pre-pandemic projections.

Figure I.1

Change from 2019 average gross domestic product

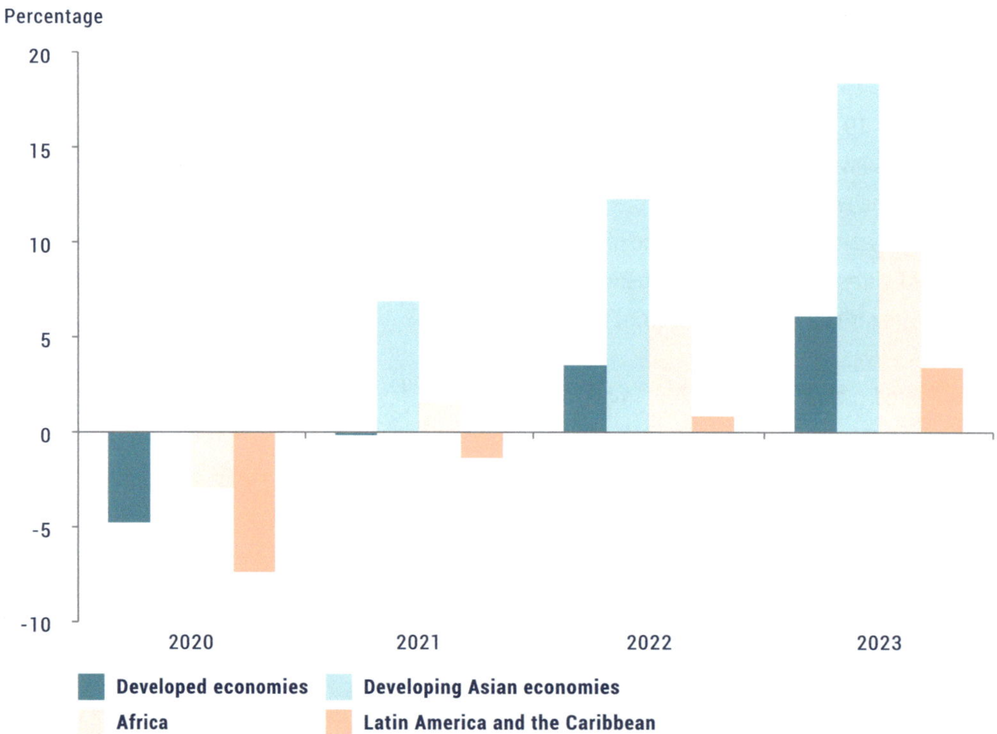

Source: UN DESA estimates and forecasts.
Notes: Africa excludes Libya; Latin America and the Caribbean excludes the Bolivarian Republic of Venezuela.

Inequality between countries is widening

The recovery of GDP per capita across developed and developing countries is uneven

A full economic recovery measured in terms of GDP per capita will remain elusive for developing countries in the near term. In 2022, the per capita output of developing countries and economies in transition is projected to be more than 2 per cent below the level expected prior to the pandemic. The GDP per capita gap between what they will achieve and what they could have achieved without the pandemic will persist well into 2023 (figure I.2). On the other hand, the GDP per capita of the developed economies is projected to almost fully recover by 2023 relative to pre-pandemic projections. The uneven pace of recovery between developed and developing countries will widen income inequality across countries and make it all but impossible to reduce global inequality by 2030, as targeted in the global Sustainable Development Goals.

Figure I.2
GDP per capita losses by development status

Percentage change between current and pre-pandemic forecasts

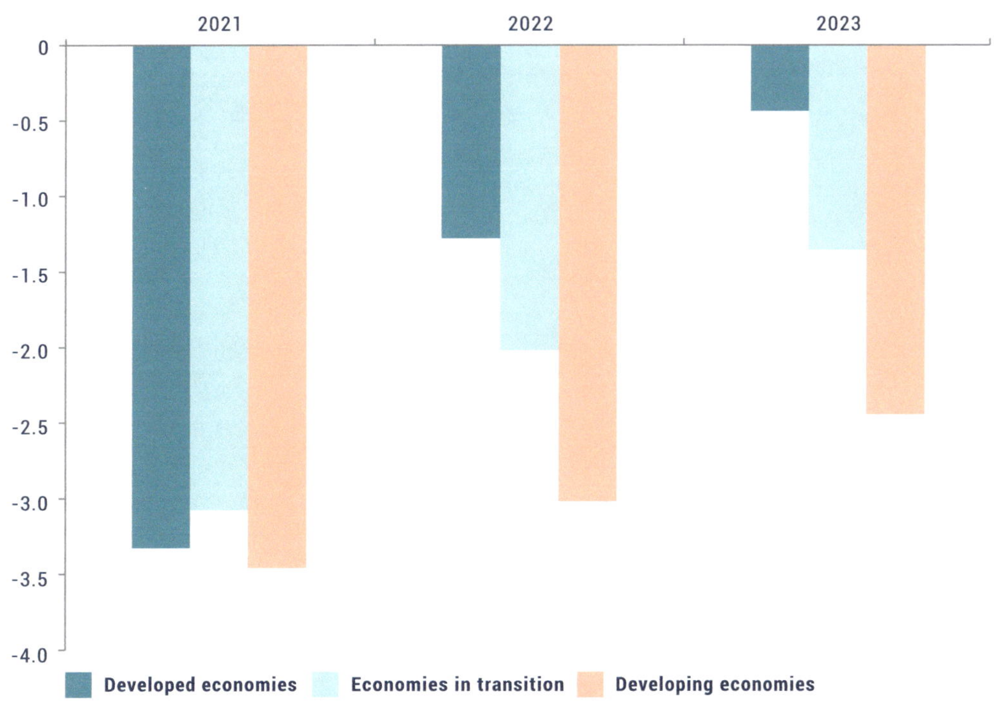

Source: UN DESA estimates and forecasts.

Table I.1

Growth of world output and gross domestic product, 2020-2023

					Change from *WESP 2021*	
Annual percentage change	**2020**	**2021[a]**	**2022[b]**	**2023[b]**	**2021**	**2022**
World	-3.4	5.5	4.0	3.5	0.8	0.6
Developed economies	-4.8	4.8	3.7	2.5	0.8	1.1
United States of America	-3.4	5.5	3.5	2.4	2.1	0.8
Japan	-4.6	2.2	3.3	2.7	-0.8	1.5
European Union	-6.0	4.7	3.9	2.6	-0.1	1.2
Euro area	-6.5	4.7	4.0	2.5	-0.3	1.4
United Kingdom of Great Britian and Northern Ireland	-9.8	6.2	4.5	2.0	-0.6	2.5
Other developed countries	-3.3	4.0	3.7	2.7	-1.0	1.5
Economies in transition	-2.6	4.4	3.2	2.9	1.0	0.2
South-Eastern Europe	-3.1	6.2	4.0	3.6	2.2	0.9
Commonwealth of Independent States and Georgia	-2.6	4.3	3.2	2.8	0.9	0.2
Russian Federation	-3.0	4.2	2.7	2.3	1.2	0.3
Developing economies	-1.6	6.4	4.5	4.7	0.8	0.0
Africa[c]	-2.2	3.8	4.0	3.6	0.3	0.4
Northern Africa[c]	-2.4	4.8	4.8	2.8	-0.1	0.7
East Africa	1.3	4.0	4.8	5.7	1.0	0.7
Central Africa	-2.4	2.0	3.3	3.5	-0.9	-0.3
West Africa	-0.8	3.2	3.7	4.0	0.7	0.1
Southern Africa	-6.2	2.9	2.6	2.9	0.1	0.0
East and South Asia	0.0	6.8	5.0	5.4	0.4	-0.2
East Asia	1.0	6.7	4.9	5.4	0.3	-0.3
China	2.3	7.8	5.2	5.5	0.7	-0.6
South Asia[d]	-4.7	7.4	5.9	5.6	0.5	0.6
India[d]	-7.1	9.0	6.7	6.1	1.7	0.8
Western Asia	-3.4	4.7	4.8	3.5	0.8	1.4
Latin America and the Caribbean	-7.4	6.5	2.2	2.5	2.7	-0.3
South America	-7.0	6.7	1.6	2.4	2.9	-1.1
Brazil	-4.1	4.7	0.5	1.9	1.5	-1.7
Mexico and Central America	-8.2	6.1	3.4	2.7	2.3	1.0
Caribbean	-7.2	3.2	11.5	3.7	-0.6	8.7
Least developed countries	0.8	1.4	4.0	5.7	-3.5	-0.6
Memorandum items						
World trade[e]	-8.3	11.0	5.7	4.0	4.0	1.9
World output growth with PPP weights[f]	-3.3	5.6	4.2	3.8	0.7	0.4

Source: UN DESA.
Notes: (a) estimated, (b) forecast, (c) excludes Libya, (d) growth rates are on a calendar year basis (for fiscal year growth figures, please refer to the statistical annex), (e) includes goods and services, and (f) based on a 2015 benchmark.

The pandemic is far from over

Despite the roll-out of vaccines from early 2021, the COVID-19 pandemic is far from over. From 1 April through 1 December 2021, an average of 9,432 people died every day around the world, significantly higher than the 6,061 deaths per day recorded during the same period in 2020.[2] By early December 2021, COVID-19-related deaths since the start of the pandemic had reached 5.2 million. Yet the total number of deaths directly and indirectly attributable to the pandemic is much higher. Excess deaths have been highest in some economies in transition and a number of Eastern European and Latin American countries.[3]

The emergence of a more transmissible and deadly COVID-19 variant poses a major risk...

Over 2021, the epicentre of the pandemic shifted multiple times. For much of the year, developing and transition countries saw a growing share of infections and deaths as they lagged in vaccination. But in the fourth quarter of 2021, as colder temperatures in the Northern Hemisphere led to more indoor social activities, Europe and the United States began to experience new outbreaks, with severe cases mostly affecting the unvaccinated. Countries in Europe with relatively lower vaccination rates have experienced stronger increases in cases. Moreover, the emergence in late November 2021 of the Omicron variant, which is likely to be more transmissible than earlier variants and with a better ability to evade vaccines, sounded new alarm bells across the world. Governments from major developed countries, including in Europe, Japan and the United States, responded by introducing travel restrictions from Southern Africa[4] where Omicron was first detected. A number of developing countries also swiftly imposed entry restrictions on travellers from Southern Africa.

...with potentially significant impacts on economic activity

New COVID-19 variants and the reintroduction of quarantine and mobility restrictions could significantly restrain economic activities. Although the actual impact is impossible to assess in advance, new variants could severely impair market confidence and derail economic recoveries. The willingness to work in person could decline again, posing downside risks to an already slow recovery of labour markets and intensifying supply-chain disruptions. The long-awaited recovery of service industries, from hospitality to international travel and conferences, could also be further postponed. Efforts to push ahead with reopening and attract tourists in tourism-dependent countries, particularly the small island developing States, could be easily reversed.

2 According to the COVID-19 Data Repository at John Hopkins University (last accessed 21 December 2021).
3 See The Economist's COVID-19 tracker (accessed on 14 December 2021).
4 The list of countries included Angola, Botswana, Eswatini, Lesotho, Malawi, Mozambique, Namibia, South Africa and Zimbabwe.

Vaccine inequities remain a formidable challenge

Access to COVID-19 vaccines remains a challenge in many developing countries and transition economies, driven in many cases by fiscal constraints. By the end of 2021, the number of doses per 100 people in the least developed countries stood at just 23.9, against 147.4 in the developed countries (figure I.3). In most developing countries, acute vaccine shortages – as opposed to vaccine hesitancy – continue to prevent higher vaccination coverage, leaving these countries highly vulnerable to renewed waves of infection. Unsurprisingly, the concentration of deaths due to COVID-19 shifted from developed to developing countries through much of 2021 (figure I.4), yet a few major developed countries, such as the United States, still experienced among the highest numbers of deaths per 100,000 people.

Figure I.3

Number of doses per 100 people

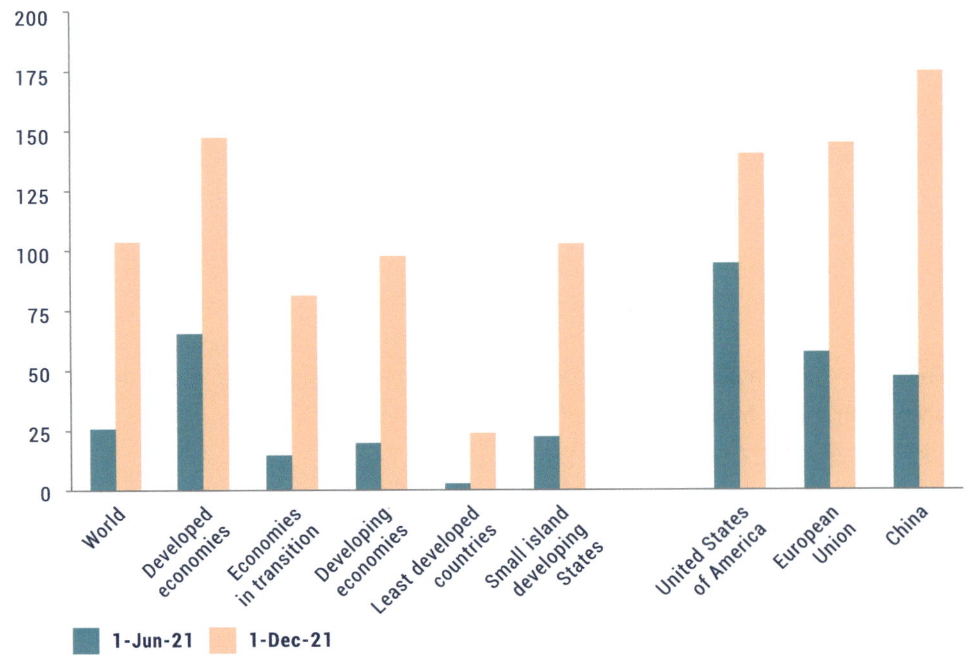

Source: UN DESA, based on data from Our World in Data (accessed on 20 December 2021).

Figure I.4
Share of monthly COVID-19 related deaths by development status

Source: UN DESA, based on data from Johns Hopkins University.

Uneven progress in vaccination imposes large economic costs globally

Progress in vaccination was critical to resume economic activities and recover output in 2021. Countries with high vaccination rates managed to ease restrictions, allowing demand to surge and economic growth to come back more quickly. Low vaccination rates and recurring waves of infection in many developing countries, on the other hand, demanded continued restrictions. If they had achieved levels of vaccination similar to those in high-income countries, low-income countries could have raised output in 2021 by $38 billion or 8 per cent of their collective GDP (UNDP, 2021).[5] Vaccination is clearly a necessary condition for reopening economies but not a sufficient condition for accelerating growth and recovery. Many other factors, including public and private investments to improve labour markets and create jobs, will also determine the size and pace of recovery.

Export controls and prioritization of bilateral agreements continue to affect access to vaccines in developing countries

This report's baseline scenario assumes sufficient progress in vaccination to allow the lifting of restrictions on economic activities and obviate the need for new restrictions during the forecast horizon. It remains particularly crucial to scale up vaccination in developing countries to restore confidence and boost aggregate demand. This will, however, remain contingent on accelerating vaccine deliveries. COVAX, the global vaccine distribution initiative, announced in September 2021 that it aims to ship 2 billion doses by the end of the first quarter of 2022. Achieving this target would yield a fully vaccinated

5 Further, the global GDP loss from not vaccinating people in all countries, relative to a counterfactual of global vaccinations, is higher than the cost of manufacturing and distributing vaccines worldwide (Cakmakli and others, 2021).

coverage rate of about 35 per cent. As of early December 2021, however, only about 610 million doses had been shipped. The COVAX target faces significant uncertainty amid the export controls of major suppliers, the prioritization of bilateral agreements over COVAX and regulatory approval processes (COVAX, 2021).

The Group of 20 (G20) summit in Rome in October 2021 affirmed the clear imperative of vaccinating at least 40 per cent of the population in all countries by the end of 2021 and 70 per cent by mid-2022, in line with WHO's global vaccination strategy. The G20 will need to take urgent measures to boost the supply of vaccines in developing countries and mitigate relevant supply and financing constraints.

Rising inflation is emerging as a new risk

Global inflation increased significantly in 2021...

Global inflation largely remained restrained, often below central bank targets, in the past decade, despite massive increases in global liquidity after the 2008–2009 global financial crisis. Global headline inflation surged to an estimated 5.2 per cent in 2021, however, more than 2 percentage points above its trend rate in the past 10 years. The rise was particularly pronounced in the United States and the euro area, and in Latin America and the Caribbean. Medium-term market-implied inflation expectations over a five-year period in the United States and the euro area increased slightly throughout 2021 but remained moderate, below 2.5 and 1.8 per cent, respectively (IMF, 2021d). This would suggest that inflation expectations remain well anchored and should allow inflation to return to its pre-pandemic rates if labour shortages and supply-side bottlenecks dissipate and global food and energy prices stabilize in 2022.

...amid supply-side disruptions, the release of pent-up demand and high commodity prices

The rise in inflation in 2021 was largely due to a unique combination of idiosyncratic supply-side bottlenecks, a stronger-than-anticipated rebound of demand and high commodity prices. Commodity prices surged, with steep increases in metals, coal, crude oil and natural gas. Crude oil prices rose by 70 per cent to $70 per barrel on average. The drivers of escalating energy prices included high electricity demand caused by hot weather in some countries, low renewable energy production due to unfavourable weather conditions and high energy demand overall (World Bank, 2021a). Food prices shot up by 22 per cent in 2021, reaching their highest level in a decade, spurred by sharp increases in vegetable oil, cereal and dairy prices (FAO, 2021). High food prices hurt the consumption of the poor, whose situation is already very strained. Underlying drivers encompassed reduced harvests due to adverse weather, labour shortages and high consumption demand. Major supply bottlenecks and port congestion raised shipping costs and led to higher import prices.

In 2022, some upward pressure on prices is expected to ease as central banks tighten monetary policy. The timing and sequencing of central bank responses to inflationary pressures will remain critical, however. If monetary policy stances are tightened too quickly, they will inevitably derail recovery. On the other hand, if monetary tightening and normalization are delayed for too long, inflation expectations may become entrenched and self-fulfilling. Major central banks will need to coordinate and clearly communicate their responses to inflationary pressures to ensure financial market stability and support recovery.

Under the baseline scenario, the global headline inflation rate is forecast to fall to 3.8 per cent in 2022 and 3.1 per cent in 2023, returning to its pre-pandemic trend. These forecasts are contingent on the dissipation of the supply-chain disruptions plaguing the global economy by the second half of 2022. Renewed restrictions due to new COVID-19 variants could translate into higher inflationary pressures, however. In addition, climate change has increased the frequency and severity of extreme weather events, which may also adversely affect supply chains and cause upward pressures on prices.

Inflationary pressures are projected to gradually ease throughout 2022

Employment, poverty and inequality

Labour markets are lagging

Global employment has yet to fully recover from the unprecedented shock of the COVID-19 pandemic, despite the gradual lifting of lockdown restrictions, immense efforts to protect employment and support businesses, and the rebound in global output. While aggregate output in 2021 returned to pre-pandemic levels in most major economies, the recovery of employment lagged and even stalled in many parts of the world. According to the International Labour Organization (ILO), by the third quarter of 2021, total working hours remained 4.7 per cent below pre-pandemic levels, equivalent to the loss of 137 million full-time jobs (ILO, 2021d). The sluggish speed of job creation cannot compensate for earlier employment losses particularly in sectors hit hardest by the pandemic. New waves of infection, for example in Europe and the Commonwealth of Independent States (CIS), are forcing the reintroduction of partial lockdowns and slowing job recovery, especially in the services sector.

Global output recovered but employment remains well below pre-pandemic levels

The crisis has had a devastating impact on employment in tourism, hospitality, travel and retail trade. It has disproportionately affected vulnerable groups, including youth, women and migrant workers, as well as workers with lower educational attainment and skills. Exacerbation of the gender divide is evident, especially in developing countries, with women seeing greater declines in employment and labour force participation than men (IMF, 2021d). Currently, many women confront serious barriers to re-entering the labour force, especially women with young children (Fabrizio and others, 2021). Supporting unpaid domestic work, including childcare, as well as reopening schools will be crucial in reversing gendered labour outcomes going forward.

In countries able to implement large-scale fiscal stimulus measures, mechanisms to protect businesses and jobs helped mitigate fallout from the crisis on employment (figure I.5). The ILO finds that, on average, a 1 per cent increase in annual GDP in the fiscal policy response is associated with a 0.3 percentage point increase in working hours (ILO, 2021d). The Organisation for Economic Co-operation and Development (OECD) estimates that without government-funded job retention schemes, the fall in the number of employees would have been 50 per cent larger, resulting in a decline in employment of more than 6 per cent (OECD, 2021a). Specific stimulus programmes, such as the Paycheck Protection

Income support and job retention schemes prevented larger downturns in labour markets

Program in the United States and the Australian JobKeeper Payment programme, have had significant positive impacts in preventing larger job losses.[6]

Institutional settings have determined different strategies to mediate impacts on employment. In the United States, substantial income support accompanied a rise in unemployment, while in European countries, furlough and short-time work schemes allowed a reduction in working hours. In the long-term, countries that experienced higher unemployment will be more likely to suffer from a long-lasting decline in labour force participation but may eventually see a more efficient redeployment of labour (Bartholomew and Diggle, 2021).

Figure I.5

Fiscal stimulus and changes in working hours, 2020

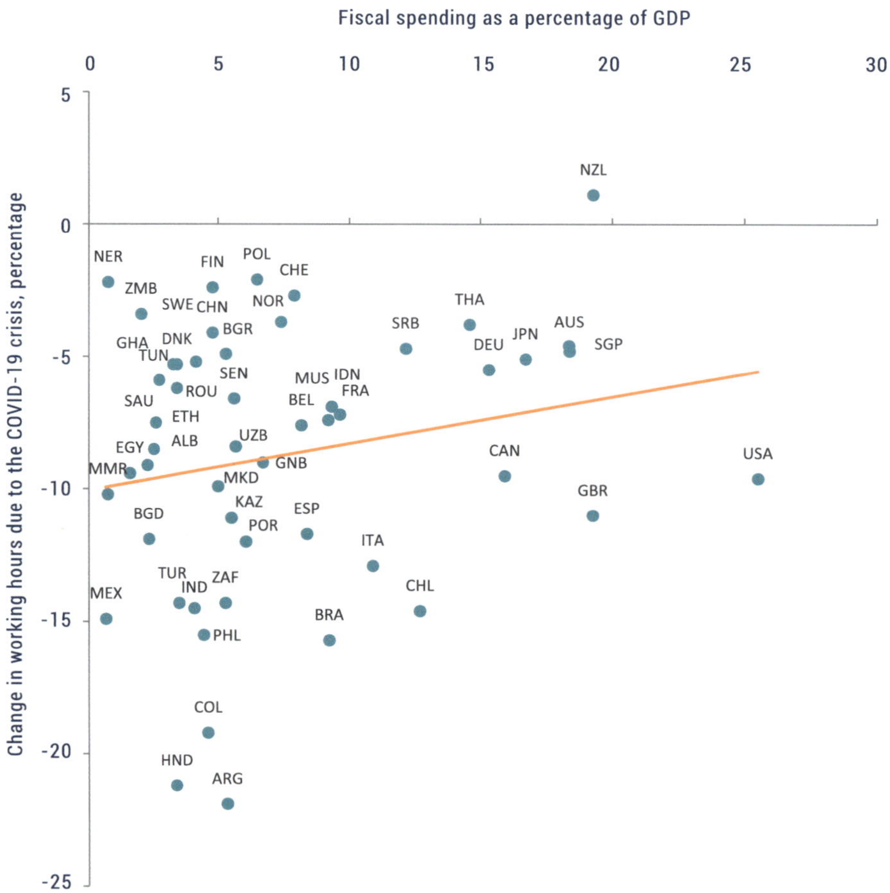

Source: UN DESA, based on data from the ILO and the IMF World Economic Outlook database, October 2021.
Note: Changes in working hours are based on ILO modelled estimates.

6 The Paycheck Protection Program increased employment by 2 million jobs (about a 3 per cent increase) between April and June 2020 (Autor and others, 2020). The JobKeeper programme reduced total employment losses by at least 700,000 positions between April and July 2020 (Bishop and Day, 2020). Andrews and others (2021) point to the importance of measures being temporary, targeted and adaptive as economic conditions change. They highlight that it is not only size but also policy design that matters.

A notable divergence has emerged between developed and developing economies in part due to uneven progress in vaccination and the size of fiscal stimulus packages. In 2021, employment largely recovered in developed countries. While the rise in working hours in the euro area and Japan reflected workers taking on more hours at the same firms where they were previously employed, in the United States it was associated with lower unemployment rates (Shin, 2021). By contrast, employment growth in developing countries stalled; some countries continued to experience employment losses.[7] Jobs in the informal sector in developing countries were hit hard as job retention programmes only protected the formal sector. This divergence in employment outcomes between developed and developing countries is projected to widen in the near term given the faster growth of the working-age population in developing countries and more limited fiscal space to support recovery.

Fear and discouragement are keeping many workers from rejoining the labour force

Although headline unemployment rates moderated in 2021 and further reductions are expected in 2022, especially in developed economies, the figures are less representative of actual labour market conditions as millions of prospective workers remain outside the labour force. In 2020, 81 million workers globally became inactive compared with 33 million who moved to formal unemployment (ILO, 2021c). Currently, many workers are reluctant to return to work because of health concerns. Employment numbers also do not reflect large variations in incomes, skill mismatches, and job quality and satisfaction levels. In developing economies, a precise assessment of unemployment is further complicated by rising informality. In addition, the slow job recovery is weighing on the quality of human capital as workers lose skills or skills become obsolete, which may contribute to increases in structural and long-term unemployment and lead to a higher youth employment gap.

Enormous labour shortages affect labour markets in both the United States and Europe

Among developed economies, the United States has been steadily adding jobs since early 2021, including in the most affected sectors, such as travel, leisure and hospitality. The unemployment rate declined from 8.1 per cent in 2020 to 5.6 per cent in 2021 and is projected to subside further in 2022. Yet the labour market remains more than 6 million jobs short relative to pre-pandemic levels (Furman, 2021). Further, the labour force participation rate remains well below pre-crisis levels at about 61.6 per cent. It is especially low for individuals aged 55 or older and those without a college education. Paradoxically, the United States is facing an acute shortage of workers, with job openings increasing significantly and hires largely stable since the end of 2020 (figure I.6). As the recovery gathers momentum, shortages may gradually subside, but the reluctance to return to work, especially among low-pay workers who left employment in massive numbers in 2021, could delay the process. In the medium term, implementation of a massive infrastructure plan may lead to higher demand for workers and further improvement in labour markets.

In Europe, labour market conditions in 2021 varied significantly (figure I.7). Unemployment rates fell to low single-digit levels, around or below 3 per cent, in the Czech Republic, Germany and Poland, while unemployment rates remained elevated in Greece, Italy and Spain. Despite supply-side disruptions and the resurgence of COVID-19 cases in some countries by the end of 2021, labour demand is expected to

7 Between the fourth quarter of 2020 and the third quarter of 2021, the deficit in working hours in high-income countries decreased from 5.4 per cent to 3.6 per cent over pre-pandemic levels. In the same period, the gap in working hours in low-income countries expanded from 3.7 per cent to 5.7 per cent (ILO, 2021d).

strengthen in the near term as service sectors gradually return to full activity. Manufacturing output has recovered, and firms are attempting to expand output to deal with massive backlogs of earlier orders. This is subject to the evolution of new virus variants and mobility restrictions, however. European countries are also facing massive labour shortages that are causing significant logistical bottlenecks. At the same time, many workers remain furloughed, which complicates an accurate assessment of labour utilization rates. As furlough schemes are phased out, workers may not necessarily be employed in their previous jobs and may be unwilling to seek employment in sectors with worker shortages.

Figure I.6

Growth in job openings and hires in the United States

Source: UN DESA, based on data from the United States Bureau of Labour Statistics.

Note: The job openings rate is computed by dividing the number of job openings by the sum of employment and job openings; the hires rate is computed by dividing the number of hires by employment.

Figure I.7

Labour market slack in selected European Union countries, second quarter of 2021

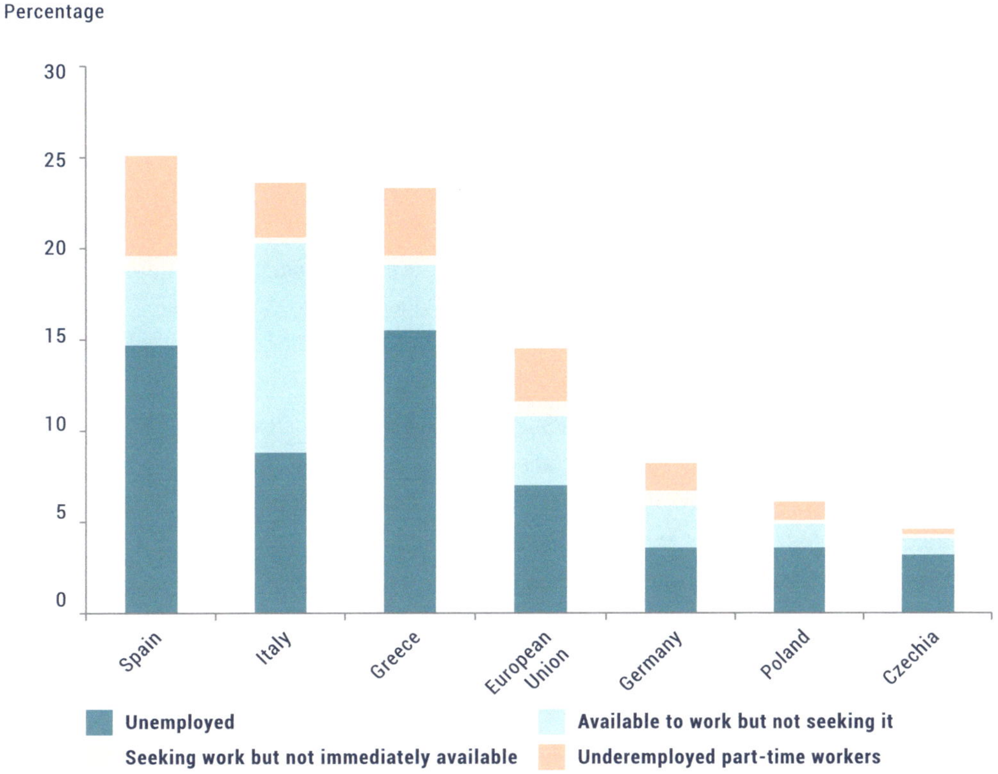

Source: UN DESA, based on data from Eurostat.

Unattractive job offerings and labour market uncertainties help explain labour shortages

Although unemployment rates remain above pre-pandemic levels, certain sectors are experiencing massive labour shortages, especially in Australia, Canada, European countries and the United States (United Nations, 2021b). Two factors help to explain this situation. First, despite the gradual recovery of labour markets, many available jobs appear to be low quality and/or poorly paid and thus are unattractive. In OECD countries, the persistent increase in "domestic outsourcing", which means contracting out work to another company in the same country, is one reason explaining the increase in low-pay jobs with mediocre working conditions (OECD, 2021a).

Second, the pandemic triggered a large-scale labour reallocation shock, especially in developed economies, altering both labour demand and supply. Demand for certain professions, such as in information technology, data analysis, project management and numerous other occupations, has strengthened during the pandemic. Demand for construction and travel-related workers, street vendors and medium-skilled clerks crumbled. Changes in the pattern of labour demand were accompanied by shifts in the labour supply. Many workers abandoned their jobs over safety considerations or because of pay dissatisfaction. Some opted for retirement earlier than planned or began looking for better and more stable positions.

Many developing countries face the prospect of long-lasting slack in labour markets

Among developing regions, unemployment remains precariously high in Latin America and the Caribbean, often at double digits. In 2021, most job recovery took place in the large informal sector, which suffered the bulk of job losses. To address growing working poverty, including food insecurity, governments extended social protection programmes to informal workers, such as in Argentina, Brazil, Peru and the Plurinational State of Bolivia. While growth has recovered, registered unemployment rates may continue to increase as some workers who dropped out of the labour force early in the pandemic gradually start to look for jobs (ECLAC, 2021a). In most of sub-Saharan Africa, fiscal space remains severely constrained to supporting job growth. In the third quarter of 2021, unemployment in South Africa reached 34.9 per cent, the highest rate in the world. In comparison, employment in the Russian Federation has almost returned to its pre-pandemic level, with the unemployment rate below 5 per cent since early 2021. Unemployment in China has fallen since early 2020 and was back to the pre-pandemic level by mid-2021.

The recovery of labour markets in developing countries is not expected before 2023

Labour market conditions in developed economies are expected to improve but a full employment recovery is projected only in 2023. For low-income countries, this may be as far out as 2024. In Africa, Latin America and the Caribbean, and Western Asia in particular, lasting slack in labour markets calls for continued fiscal support and active labour market policies. The outlook is marred, however, by uncertainties associated with the pandemic and the effectiveness of policies to revitalize job creation. Many longer-term impacts of the pandemic on employment, such as the accelerated pace of automation, the reconfiguration of supply chains and offshoring, and teleworking, are not yet fully understood.

Poverty to remain at a decade high amid rising inequalities

The COVID-19 pandemic has significantly increased poverty and inequality globally, causing a substantial reversal in progress towards sustainable development. According to estimates by the United Nations Department of Economic and Social Affairs, progress in reducing extreme poverty has been set back by several years in most countries. Botswana, Kenya, Morocco and Samoa are among the countries that have lost up to a decade's worth of poverty eradication efforts. Developed countries, in contrast, were mostly able to support household incomes and even reduce the number of people in poverty through strong transfer and social protection programmes. Even wider gaps in prosperity levels among world regions may be one of the lasting legacies of the crisis.

The number of extremely poor people may remain at record highs in the coming years

An unprecedented 85 million more people entered extreme poverty in 2020 globally.[8] The number is projected to remain well above pre-pandemic levels for the next several years, likely at record highs for the last decade (figure I.8). Only slight declines are expected in 2022, to about 876 million people. Fast-developing economies in East and South Asia as well as developed economies will likely see a reduction in poverty in the near term. But it is anticipated to increase further in the world's most vulnerable economies. In Africa, home to almost 70 per cent of the world's extremely poor people, the

8 This figure is comparable to the latest World Bank estimates, which showed that the number of people in extreme poverty increased by 77 million from 2019-2020 and by 97 million relative to pre-pandemic projections (Gerszon Maler and others, 2021).

absolute number of people in poverty is projected to rise through 2023 (figure I.9). This will take place amid rapidly growing populations, weak income growth and limited fiscal space. In sub-Saharan Africa, high rates of multidimensional poverty are expected to amplify pandemic-related shocks in education and employment (UNDP and OPHI, 2021).

Poverty projections are subject to major uncertainties, though. The economic outlook could easily worsen with a more transmissible and deadly COVID-19 variant or new waves of infection, especially in countries with low vaccination rates. In addition, the capacity to reduce poverty will be largely constrained by insufficient fiscal space across the developing world, the slow recovery of employment in some countries and tightening global monetary conditions. Extreme weather, conflicts and political fragility could also further affect poverty prospects.

Figure I.8
Global number of people living in extreme poverty

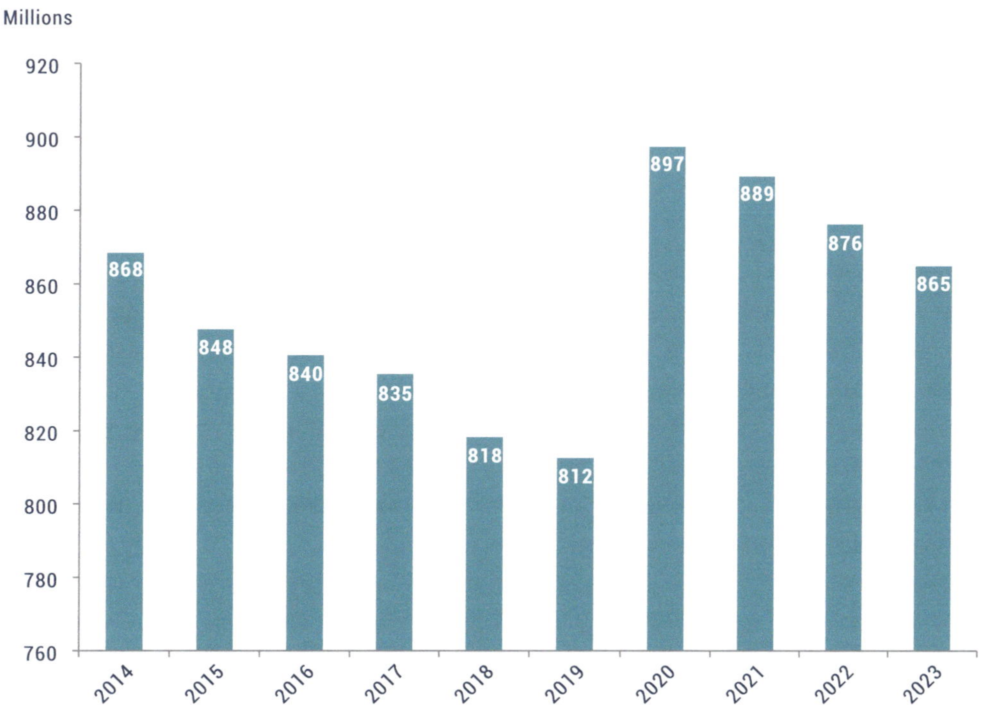

Source: UN DESA.
Note: Estimates were derived using the latest growth forecasts from the World Economic Forecasting Model. Extreme poverty refers to $1.90 per day (in 2011 PPP).

Figure I.9
Change in the number of people living in extreme poverty in developing countries

Source: UN DESA.
Note: Estimates derived using the latest growth forecasts from the World Economic Forecasting Model. Extreme poverty refers to $1.90 per day (in 2011 PPP). Numbers above the bar represent the number of people living in extreme poverty in 2020.

Conditions for faster poverty reduction have worsened

Projections suggest that poverty reduction rates have returned to the pre-pandemic pace of 2-4 per cent per year. This is too slow to eradicate extreme poverty by the global goal of 2030, however, barring major changes in global economic conditions, such as another commodity supercycle boosting growth in commodity-dependent developing economies. Most developing countries experienced structural investment challenges in the previous decade, leading to relatively low growth and insufficient reduction in poverty rates, as in Africa and Latin America and the Caribbean. If anything, conditions for significant poverty reduction have deteriorated, including through greater informality, higher public debt and persistent slack in labour markets.

People on lower incomes globally face a larger hit from the pandemic

The COVID-19 pandemic is increasing inequalities between and within countries, amid disparities in unemployment rates and shares of labour income in developed and developing economies. In the first two quarters of 2021, global labour income fell by 5.3 per cent. About 108 million workers are now extremely and moderately poor, a vast majority of them in developing countries (ILO, 2021e). Further, the pandemic has taken a harsher toll on those at the bottom of the income distribution. While average incomes of people in the bottom 40 per cent of the global income distribution were estimated to be 6.7 per cent lower in 2021 compared to 2019, those of people in the top 40 per cent were down only 2.8 per cent (Sanchez-Paramo and others, 2021). Divergent employment prospects between developed and developing countries will likely prevent major reductions in inequality across countries in the near term.

The pandemic is exacerbating pre-pandemic divergences in job conditions

Asymmetric impacts on employment and income between population groups are increasing inequality within countries.[9] The divide between high-skilled and low-skilled occupations continues to grow. This is due not only to different levels of pay and benefits and varying degrees of employment vulnerability but also crucially to the ability to work remotely.[10] Many low-skilled workers face more hazardous working conditions in front-line sectors, such as retail, catering, health care and personal care services, which are associated with high risks of COVID-19 exposure. The pandemic has accelerated the ongoing disappearance of medium-skilled jobs, further contributing to the increasing polarization of incomes. In 2020, global employment decreased the most for medium-skilled workers (-4.7 per cent), followed by low-skilled workers (-3.3 per cent) and high-skilled workers (-1.3 per cent), compared to 2019 (ILO, 2021d).

An increase in learning poverty in developing countries will have long-term repercussions

The pandemic has worsened prospects for a dramatic loss in human capital and the most dire education crisis in a century for developing countries. This is due to prolonged school closures, lasting up to 250 days, or in some cases, with schools yet to reopen. Poor learning outcomes have resulted despite government efforts to deliver remote learning. The share of 10-year-olds in developing economies who cannot read a basic text has reached an estimated 70 per cent, an increase of 17 percentage points from 2019 (World Bank, 2021d). Without robust, large-scale plans to recover these losses, the effects of delayed education will likely be felt for decades, widening inequality between and within countries, especially for girls.

Other pre-pandemic transformations in work, such as rising precarity, pose significant challenges. The pandemic sped up expansion of the gig economy, where workers are often classified as self-employed rather than employees. While expanding livelihood opportunities, this trend will preclude more workers from collective bargaining, including for basic benefits such as paid sick leave and access to unemployment insurance. Amid shrinking fiscal space and the phasing out of social protection measures, the withdrawal of fiscal support could further increase inequality within countries by adversely affecting the most vulnerable workers.

---

9 The trajectories of stock markets in developed economies also point to rising inequalities within countries. Since the start of the pandemic, stock prices have surged to unprecedentedly high levels, leading to large increases in wealth for the richest segments of the population.

10 The digital divide aggravates inequalities. Even for those professions where telecommuting is feasible, insufficient access to the Internet and inadequate digital infrastructure remain impediments to remote work in many countries, especially in rural areas. While over 95 per cent of the population in Denmark, Norway and the Republic of Korea used the Internet in 2020, the figure was only 35 per cent in Sri Lanka and 11 per cent in Chad.

International trade, investment and financial markets

Demand recovery has buoyed international trade and commodity prices

A divergent recovery in trade flows

Recovery of goods trade beat expectation but services trade has remained subdued

International trade performance was mixed in 2021. Merchandise trade was stronger than expected, with global trade in goods surpassing pre-pandemic levels (figure I.10a). Strong demand for pandemic-related goods such as medical supplies and goods related to lifestyle changes such as electronic devices buoyed merchandise trade in the first half of the year. In the second half, however, supply-chain challenges amid labour shortages in Europe and the United States and new waves of COVID-19 slowed growth. Trade in services remains subdued as the COVID-19 pandemic lingers; many countries have yet to fully reopen their borders.

The pandemic weighs on the outlook for international trade...

World trade is expected to continue improving, fuelled by stronger demand as more countries reopen and restart productive activities. The baseline scenario projects that global trade in goods and services will grow by 5.7 per cent in 2022 after an expansion of 11.0 per cent in 2021. Risks to forecasts are still on the downside, however. The pandemic remains the largest risk, particularly if more transmissible and deadly variants take hold and disrupt economic activities. Trade tensions, including unresolved ones between China and the United States, and between the European Union and the United Kingdom,[11] could weigh on trade flows. Although trade in services could strengthen due to the normalization of patterns of demand, with the relative increase in demand for durable goods expected to shift back, services could stabilize along a lower trajectory if the impact of the pandemic turns out to be long-lasting (UNCTAD, 2021d; WTO, 2021).

11 Trade tensions between the European Union and the United Kingdom intensified during 2021, particularly over the Northern Ireland Protocol to the Brexit Withdrawal Agreement, which prevents checks along the border between Northern Ireland (in the United Kingdom) and the Republic of Ireland (in the European Union). This could impose border checks within the United Kingdom when goods flow to Northern Ireland from other parts of the country.

Figure I.10

World merchandise trade, by volume, January 2018 to September 2021

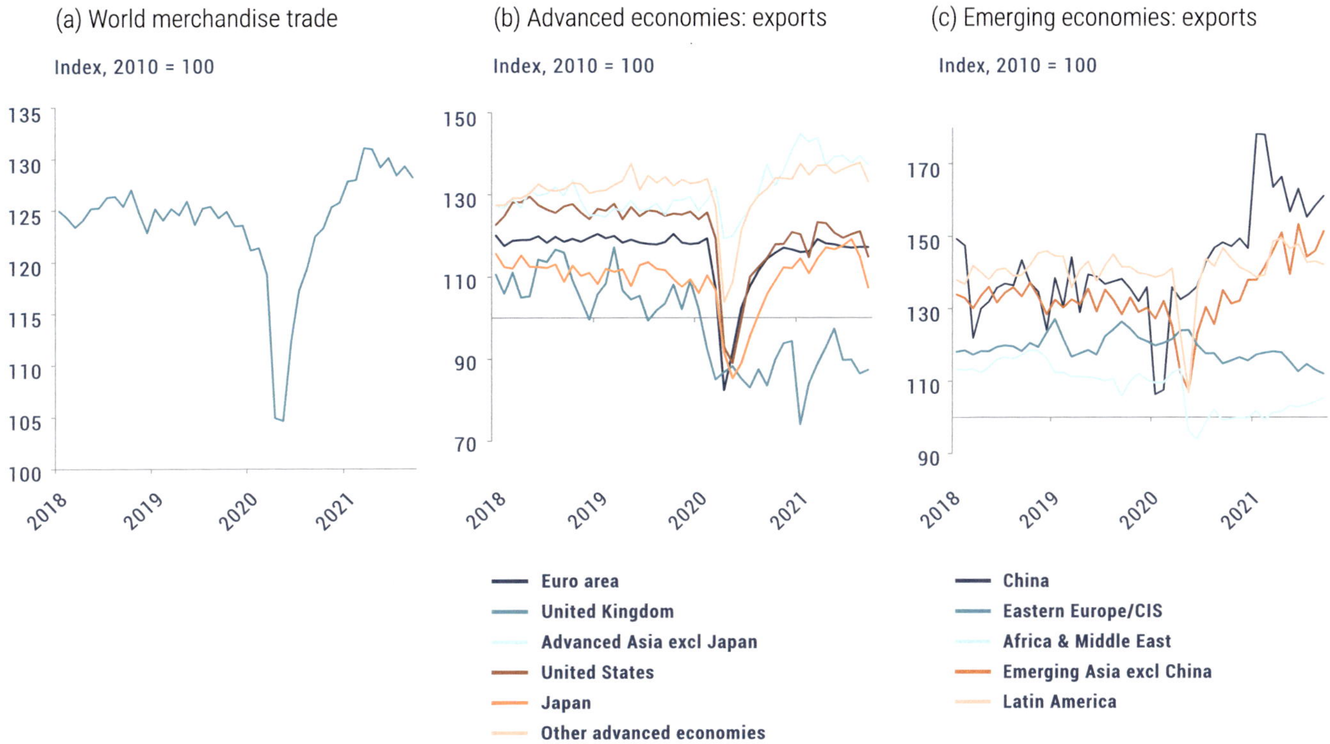

Source: CPB Netherlands Bureau for Economic Policy Analysis, World Trade Monitor database (accessed on 3 December 2021).
Note: Regional groupings are not strictly comparable to those in the World Economic Situation and Prospects 2022 but illustrate regional tendencies.

...along with unresolved supply-side constraints

Ongoing supply shortages and network disruptions will continue to be a drag on global merchandise trade in the near term. Although they are expected to recede over time, their duration and severity are uncertain. Supply-chain constraints are likely to persist in 2022 for several reasons. First, businesses usually do not hold excessive inventory to avoid additional storage costs, which means that producers and retailers may not effectively respond to consumer demand swings due to renewed waves of COVID-19 infection. Second, industry consolidation and dependence on key manufacturers contribute to supply-chain chokepoints. For instance, in 2021, strong demand for semiconductor-related goods and disruptions in the output of some major producers increased delivery times[12] and constrained output in related industries, particularly car production.

12 The average delivery time of semiconductors increased from 12 weeks in early 2020 to more than 20 weeks in July 2021 (King, 2021).

Third, possible renewed virus waves as well as extreme weather events could keep costs of shipping high and disrupt operations at a few critical international container ports,[13] impeding the growth of merchandise trade. During the pandemic, misallocation of containers led to a significant rise in shipping costs, which increased sevenfold from an average of $1,446 per container at the end of 2019 to above $10,000 in September and November 2021.[14] The recovery in energy prices also contributed to higher rates. New virus variants could prolong bottlenecks in international shipping, resulting in delays and further cost hikes. Furthermore, labour shortages, ageing infrastructure, a lack of warehouse abilities at ports as well as shortages of truck drivers in key destination countries have increased port congestion, which is still not fully resolved.

The rebound in exports has been particularly strong in China and other Asian economies

While global merchandise trade has recovered to the pre-pandemic level, there is clear regional divergence (figure I.10). Rebounds in goods exports are more evident in China and other developing Asian countries. Given China's strict virus containment measures and policy stimulus, its factories continued to operate at full capacity in the first half of 2021 and managed to increase exports to meet recovering demand in developed countries. Strong demand from developed countries as well as China buoyed trade performance in several other Asian and Latin American economies. In contrast, merchandise trade in the United Kingdom, Africa and the Middle East has remained subdued. For the United Kingdom, the weakness reflects trade disputes with the European Union. For Africa and the Middle East, the agreement by the Organization of Petroleum Exporting Countries Plus (OPEC+) to reduce oil production has largely suppressed exports. Contingent on the evolution of COVID-19, such geographical variations are expected to recede over time as more countries reopen and resume local productive activities.

Although trade in services has seen weaker performance than trade in goods, it is expected to gradually improve as external demand patterns normalize. Services trade registered positive growth in the second quarter of 2021 across regions but from a low base (figure I.11). During 2021, the global Services Purchasing Manager's Index expanded, recently edging up for both developed and developing countries after a slowdown due to the Delta wave of COVID-19.

13 Disruptions to maritime transport and port operations have also triggered a humanitarian crew-change crisis. Hundreds of thousands of seafarers have been unable to leave ships, remaining stranded at sea far beyond the expiration dates of their contracts (UNCTAD, 2021b).

14 Freightos Data (accessed on 6 November 2021).

Figure I.11.
Growth in services exports

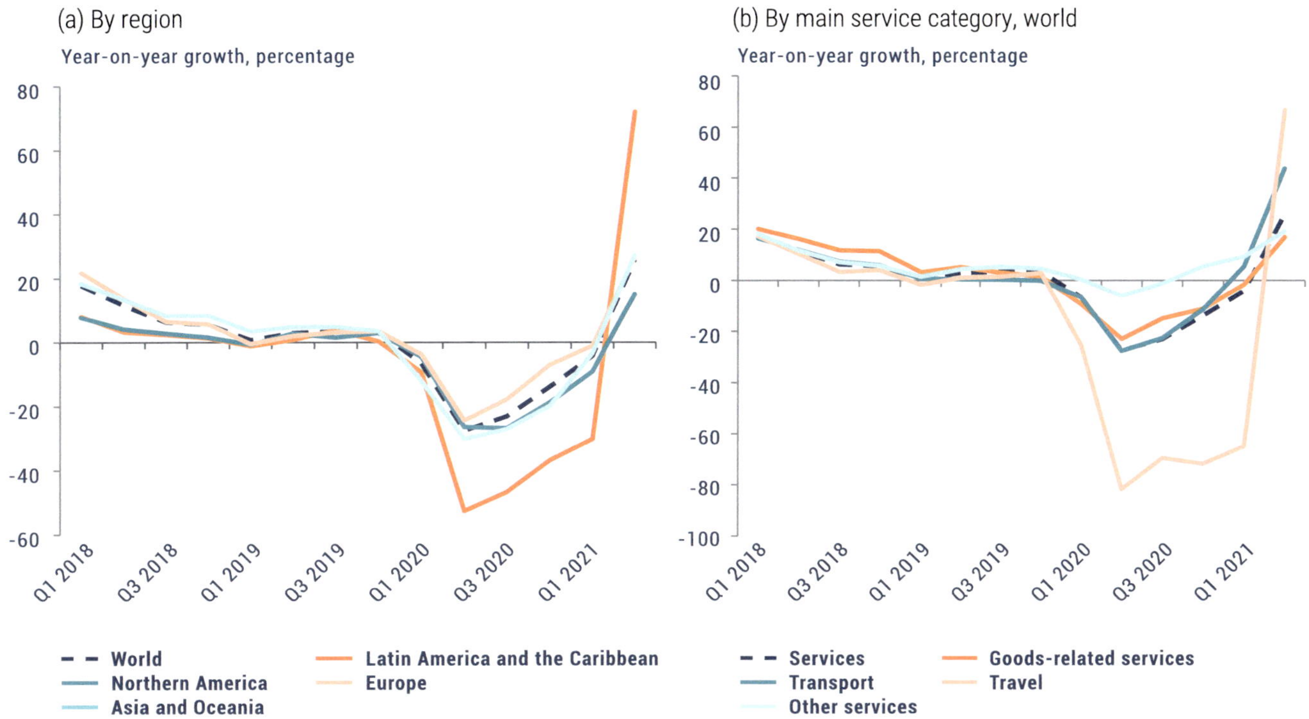

Source: UNCTADStat (accessed on 6 November 2021).
Note: On panel (a), there are no data for Africa.

International tourism is still well below the pre-pandemic level

International tourism experienced a modest improvement in the third quarter of 2021, underpinned by reopening mostly in Europe and the Americas. This was due to progress in vaccination and the resulting relaxation of travel restrictions. From January to September 2021, however, international tourist arrivals were 20 per cent below levels in 2020 and 76 per cent below levels in 2019 (UNWTO, 2021a). Despite an important rebound projected in 2022, driven by unleashed demand, international tourism is unlikely to return to the pre-pandemic level in the near term. As figure I.12 shows, international tourist arrivals plunged by 73 per cent in 2020, dropping to levels of several decades ago. Further restrictive measures and limits on non-essential travel due to new variants could cause a significant setback to the recovery of tourism-dependent economies, in particular the small island developing States.[15]

15 Tourism revenues in the small island developing States declined by $43 billion in 2020, a 70 per cent drop in nominal terms. This represents 43 per cent of the total decline in the exports of goods and services in these countries.

Figure I.12
International tourist arrivals and tourism receipts

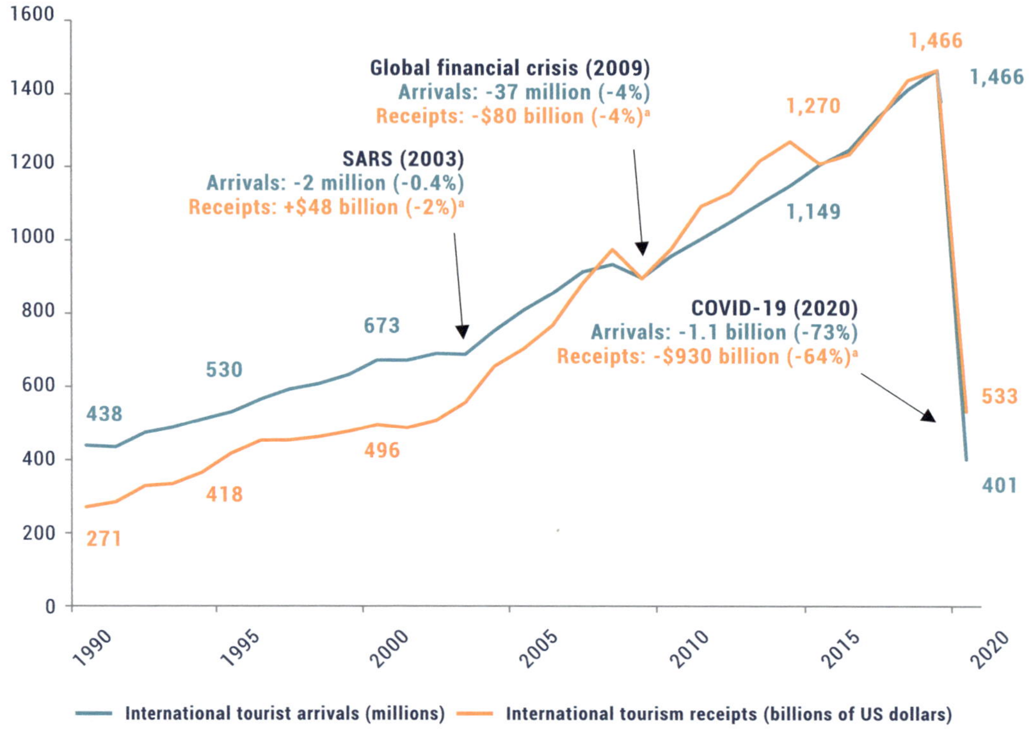

Source: UNWTO.
Note: (a) Real percentage change (local currencies, constant prices).

Targeted trade policies can mitigate pandemic impacts

While the global trade outlook is subject to downside risks, appropriate and targeted policy measures could help mitigate these. There is a clear need for multilateral efforts to address on-going trade tensions and ensure "vaccines for all". Negotiations under the 12th World Trade Organization Ministerial Conference[16] are expected to put forward a strong global response to the pandemic and provide a foundation for more rapid and equitable vaccine production and distribution.

In addition, there is an acute need for tourism-dependent countries to find alternative revenue sources. Some are developing domestic and rural tourism,[17] which could simultaneously help local economies in rural and depressed areas to boost job creation and protect natural resources and cultural heritage, while empowering women, youth and indigenous peoples. For small island developing States, expanding information and communications technology (ICT) and digitally enabled services could open economic opportunities (box I.1). Amid ongoing trade tensions and supply-chain disruptions, many countries

16 The 12th World Trade Organization Ministerial Conference, scheduled to take place from 30 November to 3 December 2021, was postponed due to the emergence of the Omicron variant. Negotiations on the response to the pandemic are still going on with a call for agreement by the end of February 2022.

17 Domestic tourism proved its resilience in 2021. While international air traffic was down by 82 per cent from January to October 2021, compared to 2019 levels, domestic traffic tapered off by 31 per cent, according to the International Air Transport Association.

have also started to shift production closer to consumers. The European Union and the United States have announced ambitious plans to boost domestic production of semiconductors.

Box I.1

The COVID-19 crisis: an opportunity for information and communications technology and digitally enabled services in small island developing States

The COVID-19 pandemic triggered the largest drop in economic output since the Great Depression. Yet ICT and digitally enabled services have exhibited strong resilience since they allow individuals and businesses to operate remotely (figure I.1.a). Developing ICT and digitally enabled services has emerged as an important opportunity for small island developing States to move towards a post-pandemic recovery. This could potentially help them improve virtual connectivity to markets and enhance tourism-related services, which could at least partially offset massive losses from reduced exports of travel services. Economic losses in tourism due to the pandemic led Jamaica's economy to contract by 11 per cent in 2020. Fiji's GDP declined by 19 per cent in 2020, with unemployment rising to 35 per cent and government revenue shrinking by 40-50 per cent.

A number of small island developing States have developed ICT and digitally enabled services, both before and during the pandemic. In 2019, exports of ICT services reached 30.7 per cent of Guinea-Bissau's services exports. During the pandemic, Samoa developed a payment system called MauaPay to connect domestic and international banking systems and facilitate international trade in goods and services. In Vanuatu, drones were used to deliver childhood vaccinations to remote areas (ITU, 2019). Several Caribbean countries built a partnership with a hospital in Canada to provide digital health services to help children suffering from cancer.

Small island developing States still face multiple challenges, however, in leveraging ICT services as an engine for growth and development. Small domestic markets and a limited number of suppliers compound a lack of awareness and inability to fully use available tools such as online maps and streaming services. The latter is partly due to the absence of relevant local online content in local languages. Taking advantage of the recent paradigm shift to move personal data storage to the cloud is complicated by requirements for more data usage and the fact that small island developing States have higher connection costs than most countries.

Improving digital infrastructure, such as through submarine cables connecting to the Internet via optical fibre, has brought cheaper and faster access compared to the more costly and slower alternatives of satellite transmission and microwave radio. Many small island developing States lag behind, however. Plans to develop submarine cable access have not progressed in Kiribati, Nauru, Timor-Leste and Tuvalu, for instance (Johnson, 2021). Since costs could be substantial, countries may need to seek financing from various sources such as private companies and multilateral development banks.

Figure I.1.a
Evolution of global exports

Index, 2011 = 100

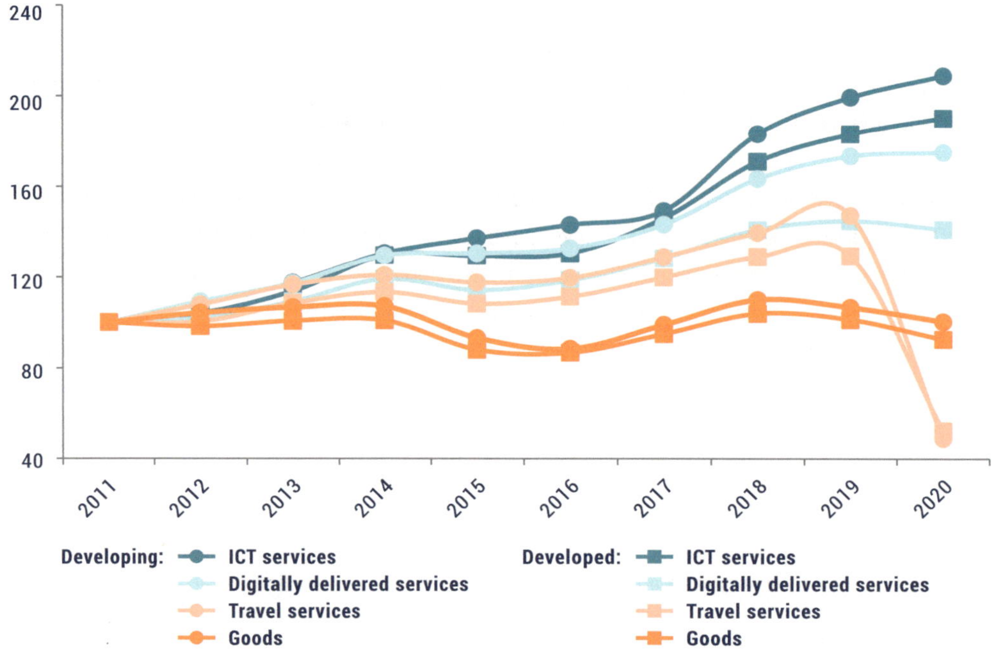

Source: Elaboration based on UNCTADstat (accessed in October 2021).

Small island developing States could also develop tourism-related digital services, such as to enhance travel intermediaries. Some studies show that a substantial amount of money spent by tourists is not retained by local businesses or workers but ends up leaving countries via foreign-owned tour operators, airlines, hotels, and imported drinks and food. Such "tourism leakage" is estimated to amount to about 80 per cent of all money spent by tourists in the Caribbean (WTTC, 2017). Countries could establish and manage online travel platforms that usually take a commission of 15–18 per cent of the price of a hotel room or 3–4 per cent of airfares (The Economist, 2017).

While the pandemic has hit small island developing States disproportionately, ICT and digitally enabled services could help them overcome geographical remoteness. Reliable, fast and affordable connectivity through enhanced digital infrastructure, platforms and services has significant potential. It can help SIDS recover, diversify their economies and make progress towards sustainable development.

Authors: Dong Wu, Vincent Valentine and Bruno Antunes, United Nations Conference on Trade and Development

Commodity prices rise amid strong demand and supply-side disruptions

Commodity prices have increased across the board...

Prices of almost all commodity products trended upward in 2021.[18] Demand for commodities accelerated in tandem with sizeable policy stimulus and vaccine-led reopening plans. The supply side was slower to catch up due to the resurgence of COVID-19, extreme weather events and logistical problems. Overall, the commodity price index of the United Nations Conference on Trade and Development increased by 30 per cent in the first nine months of 2021 (figure I.13a). Rising prices coupled with supply-side disruptions increased inflationary pressures in different parts of the world throughout 2021.

...but are expected to weaken

Looking forward, a modest and gradual decrease in commodity prices is expected. While the factors that drove up prices will gradually dissipate in 2022, there is rising downward pressure on prices. OPEC+ members could loosen supply restraints on oil production while monetary tightening in the United States and a potential slowdown in China's growth could also ease global demand. In the coming years, a global green energy transition could bring mixed impacts on commodity prices as demand will decline for fossil fuels but accelerate for key minerals for electric vehicles and green infrastructure, such as copper and lithium (UNCTAD, 2021d).

Fuel price hikes have taken the lead across all commodity groups (figure I.13b). The OPEC+ agreement on unprecedented crude oil production cuts in early 2020 brought the price above the pre-pandemic level. In October 2021, the West Texas Intermediate spot price of crude oil crossed $80 per barrel, a seven-year high. Higher oil prices have increased inflationary pressures in oil-importing countries such as Brazil, India and Singapore, which could trigger additional monetary policy tightening and cause a setback to recovery. While OPEC+ is phasing out production cuts to meet recovering demand, major oil producers remain reluctant to unleash spare production capacity due to COVID-19 related uncertainties.

Prices of minerals, ores and metals have also bounced back to pre-pandemic levels. After prices reached an all-time peak in July 2021[19] due to recovering demand, however, mining disruptions in Australia, Chile and Peru as well higher shipping costs and disruptions in logistics sent prices down. In 2022, prices are expected to moderate further as global demand shifts from goods to services.

18 All commodity prices increased in 2021 except for precious metals. Prices of precious metals moderated in 2021 after reaching an all-time high in August 2020. This was driven by changing demand for gold, perceived as a safe haven in times of crisis and uncertainty.

19 The UNCTAD minerals, ores and non-precious metals price index began in January 1995. The reading in July 2021 was the highest since that point.

Figure I.13
Major commodity prices, January 2018 to September 2021

(a) UNCTAD commodity price index, all groups

Index, 2019 = 100

(b) UNCTAD commodity price subindices

Index, 2019 = 100

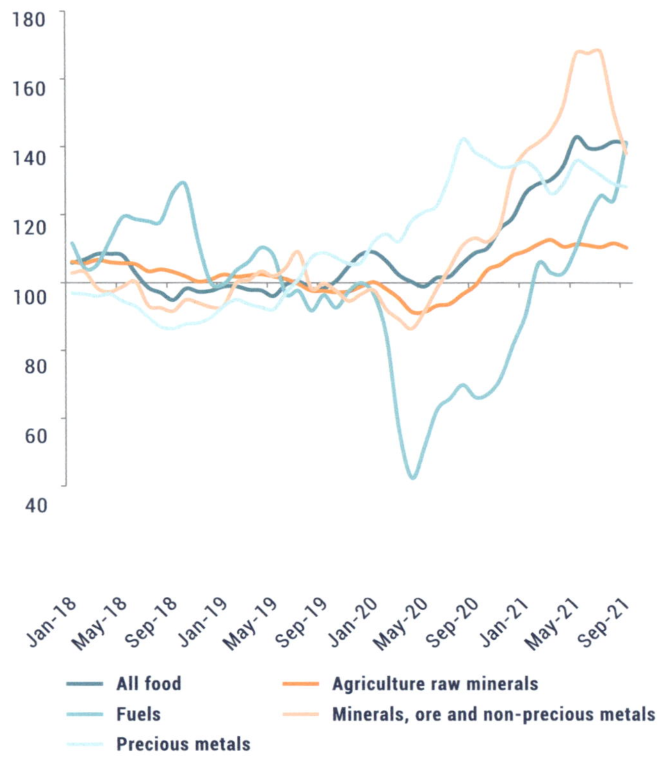

Source: UNCTAD.

Surging food prices threaten food security in low-income countries

Food prices rose in 2021 given lower elasticity of demand along with unfavourable weather conditions for key agricultural commodities such as soybeans, sugar and cereals.[20] Disruptions in supply chains and logistics networks increased transport costs. Higher fuel prices also boosted the costs of agricultural inputs and drove up the prices of grains and oilseeds. While food prices appeared to stabilize in the third quarter of 2021, they had increased nearly 20 per cent since the end of 2020. Low-income countries have been particularly vulnerable as surging food prices feed inflation and threaten food security. The Food and Agriculture Organization and World Food Programme (2021) warn that continued high food prices could undercut food access in many countries, including Afghanistan, the Bolivarian Republic of Venezuela, Haiti, Liberia, Nigeria and Sierra Leone.

20 Adverse weather conditions linked to La Niña severely affected grain production in South America and the United States towards the end of 2020 and into 2021.

Global investment rebounds but structural challenges lie ahead

Macroeconomic stimuli have contributed to strong investment growth

In many parts of the world, investment has rebounded from the pandemic-induced slump, supported by an easing of COVID-19 restrictions, large fiscal stimulus packages and ultraloose monetary policies. After contracting by 2.7 per cent in 2020, global investment expanded an estimated 7.5 per cent in 2021.

The recovery has been driven by strong albeit moderating growth in China and the United States, which together accounted for almost 50 per cent of gross fixed capital formation in 2021. In the United States, gross fixed investment rose by 9 per cent in the first three quarters of 2021. Amid strong monetary and fiscal policy support and buoyant consumer demand, investment in machinery and equipment and intellectual property products soared (figure I.14). Investment growth is projected to moderate in 2022 as sentiment indicators have softened in recent months and the Federal Reserve is shifting to a less accommodative policy stance. The recently passed Infrastructure Investment and Jobs Act, however, will provide a boost to public investment over the coming years. The $1.2 trillion package includes about $550 billion in new spending, which will be spread over five years.[21]

In China, strong export performance and government stimulus buoyed investment in manufacturing and real estate in the first half of 2021. Yet investment growth slowed in the second half of the year as the Government restarted restrictions in line with its "zero-COVID-19" policy and implemented measures to curb the property market. Investment nevertheless is expected to remain an engine of economic growth in the coming years. While the construction boom is likely to end, targeted fiscal policies, including tax incentives and subsidies, will support investment in innovation and technological upgrading as well as in green industries.

21 Since annual fixed investment is about $4 trillion, additional spending of $110 billion would provide a stimulus of about 2.5 per cent.

Figure I.14

Annual investment growth in selected developed economies, by asset type

Source: UN DESA, based on data from CEIC and EuroStat.
Note: Figures are in constant prices. Data for the United Kingdom, euro area and Japan are total investment; data for the United States are private investment.

Strong investment growth may not last as the policy landscape changes

Beyond the headline figures, the global investment picture is more troubling. In many countries, the 2021 rebound did not signal sustained improvement in investment conditions but primarily resulted from favourable base effects and exceptionally supportive fiscal and monetary policies. As financial conditions tighten and fiscal support is withdrawn, investment growth will likely return to the slow pace that prevailed before the pandemic (figure I.15). In some cases, investment performance may worsen as the crisis has reinforced structural obstacles to investment such as the lack of skilled workers.

A low-carbon transition weighs on the investment prospects of fossil fuel-dependent countries

Medium-term investment prospects are particularly challenging for developing and transition economies that heavily depend on fossil fuels. In fact, despite the sharp rise in oil and gas prices over the past year, investment in many large fossil fuel producers has been slow to recover. As the world transitions towards net-zero carbon emissions, these countries face massive economic and financial losses. Comprehensive plans are therefore needed to ensure that investment promotes economic diversification towards new low-carbon technology sectors. In addition, the issue of stranded assets needs to be addressed.[22] A recent study estimates that fossil fuel assets worth $11 trillion to $14 trillion could become worthless by 2036 (Mercure and others, 2021).

Figure I.15

Annual investment growth in selected developing and transition economies

Percentage

Source: UN DESA, based on data from national authorities.
Note: e = estimates.

Global financial conditions remain highly accommodative

Loose global financial conditions have supported economic recovery...

Exceptionally accommodative global financial conditions largely supported the recovery of output while maintaining short-term financial stability and keeping financial market volatility relatively contained throughout 2021. Financing conditions for businesses remained largely favourable and corporate balance sheets generally strengthened (Standard and Poor's, 2021). Corporate bond issuance was strong as firms took advantage of the favourable funding environment. Bond spreads for investment grade and high-yield issuers in developed countries narrowed further in 2021 and remain close to all-

22 Stranded assets comprise investments, infrastructure, equipment, contracts and know-how that suffer from unforeseen or premature write-downs or devaluation due to the energy transition. See *World Economic Situation and Prospects 2020* for a discussion on coping with stranded fossil fuel assets (United Nations, 2020).

time lows. At the same time, unprecedented policy support that included massive injections of liquidity provided by the major central banks in developed countries has resulted in excessive risk-taking and a further build-up of financial vulnerabilities.

With inflationary pressures rising quickly, a growing number of central banks in both developed and developing countries have started tightening their monetary policy stances or signalled their intention to do so. With shifts in monetary policy, global financial conditions are expected to tighten substantially in 2022. The move away from ultraloose financial conditions poses significant risks for the full recovery of the world economy, amid record levels of private and public debt and elevated asset prices. Developing countries with elevated external debt, insufficient international reserves and large current account deficits and external financing needs are particularly vulnerable to a sharper-than-expected tightening of financial conditions.

...but may not sufficiently benefit low-income countries

Net capital flows to emerging markets and developing countries remained moderate throughout 2021, although large emerging economies recorded sizeable inflows of portfolio capital, especially in the first half of the year (figure I.16). Foreign direct investment inflows rebounded more quickly than expected, driven by cross-border infrastructure investment, especially in the power sector (UNCTAD, 2021a). This allowed most central banks to build up foreign exchange reserves. But trends in different asset categories diverged (IMF, 2021d). While hard currency debt issuance and equity flows recovered, cumulative local currency debt flows since January 2020 (excluding China) are still negative. Many low-income countries have not benefited from benign global financing conditions. According to UNCTAD (2021a) estimates, foreign direct investment flows to low-income countries further declined in the first half of 2021.

Figure I.16
Portfolio flows to emerging market economies

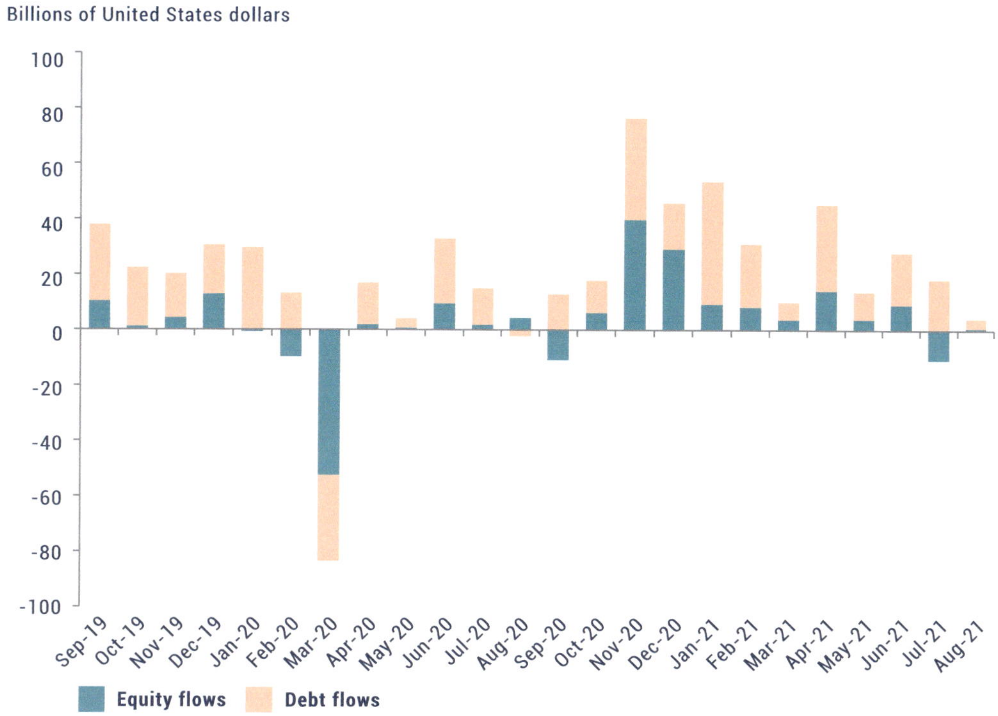

Source: Institute of International Finance.

Tighter financial conditions may trigger market corrections and undermine debt sustainability

The prospect of the gradual withdrawal of monetary support has pushed up longer-term government bond yields in developed economies from a very low base (figure I.17). Yield spreads among major economies are projected to further widen as monetary policy paths diverge. In fact, while the emergence of the Omicron variant of COVID-19 has added a fresh bout of uncertainty, the Federal Reserve and the Bank of England are expected to tighten monetary policy relatively sooner and more aggressively than the European Central Bank and the Bank of Japan. Rising expectations of a faster-than-expected adjustment by the Federal Reserve have also pushed up the value of the dollar. The dollar index, which measures the value of the dollar against the currencies of six developed countries, increased by 7 per cent between January and November 2021, which shows persistently strong global demand for dollar-denominated assets. The dollar may appreciate even further if monetary conditions in the United States tighten, which will make the servicing of dollar-denominated external debt costlier for many developing countries and present significant challenges to debt sustainability.

Figure I.17

Ten-year government bond yields in selected developed economies

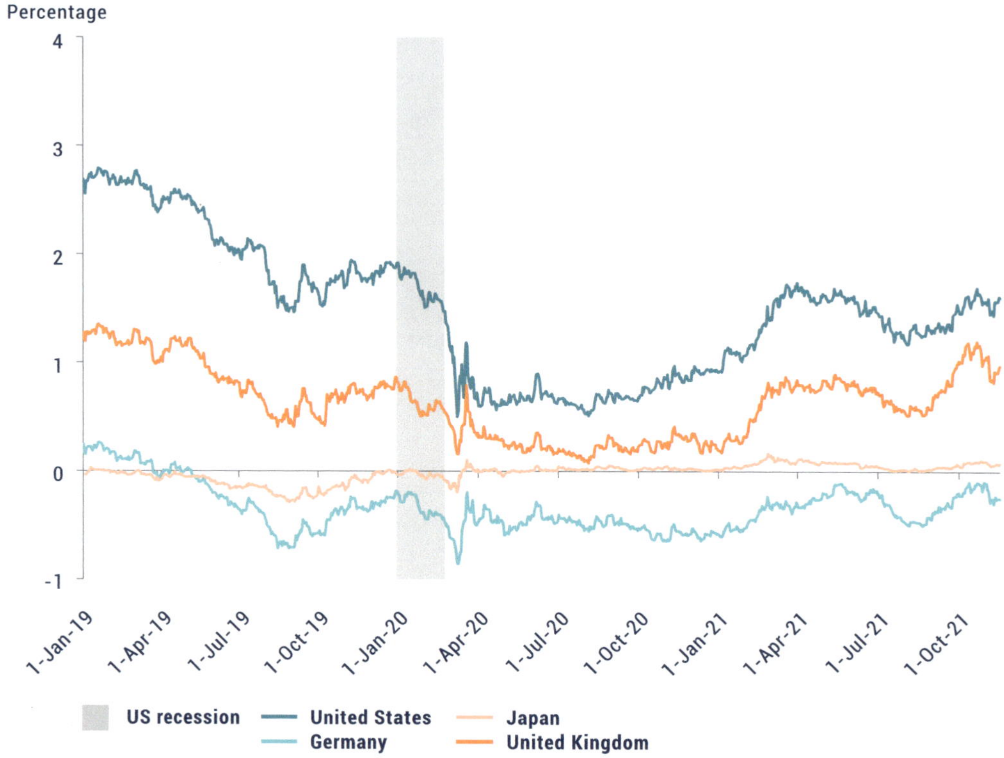

Sources: Federal Reserve, European Central Bank and investing.com.

The combination of low interest rates in developed countries, abundant global liquidity and prospects of economic recovery has resulted in lower volatility across asset classes. This has boosted risk appetite among investors, leading to a broad increase in the prices of risky assets. As a result, equity markets recorded significant gains in 2021. In the United States, for example, the major stock indices reached record highs. While this was also supported by strong earnings and rising profit margins, stock prices in the United States and several other countries appear to be significantly overvalued relative to long-term trends and fundamentals, exacerbating fears of market corrections in response to tighter financial conditions. An abrupt tightening of financial conditions could create large negative spillover effects for developing countries, including capital outflows and depreciation of domestic currencies, as experienced during the 2013 "taper tantrum".

A changing policy landscape

Fiscal asymmetries are shaping recovery and development prospects

Proactive fiscal policies are essential to mitigate the pandemic

The pandemic underscored the critical importance of fiscal policy for fighting a catastrophic crisis and supporting recovery. Proactive fiscal policies or the lack thereof are playing decisive roles in how countries are managing the pandemic, mitigating its impacts and supporting recovery. Yet enormous fiscal asymmetries and financing gaps across countries are leading to profound differences in vaccination progress, financial support to firms and households, and economic recovery prospects. While developed countries have deployed large fiscal packages, developing countries, especially low-income countries, struggle with enormous fiscal challenges. Many are at risk of a sovereign debt crisis. This fiscal and financing divide is contributing to sharply divergent prospects for recovery and, at the same time, preventing effective containment of the pandemic and endangering economic recovery globally.[23]

Fiscal stimulus packages are supporting recovery in developed countries

In developed countries, massive fiscal stimulus packages have played a crucial role in containing the crisis and supporting ongoing recovery (Gourinchas and others, 2021). Loose monetary policy and expanded central bank balance sheets have allowed governments to borrow at low costs while reducing debt-servicing costs and rollover risks. As the pandemic becomes more contained, priorities are shifting towards strengthening social protection and supporting long-term investments and productive capacities, such as in green energy and digital technologies, and enhanced research and development. Examples include the Next Generation EU recovery plan in the European Union and the Infrastructure Investment and Jobs Act in the United States.

Premature fiscal consolidation would be very costly for recovery...

Policymakers need to resist the temptation of a premature fiscal consolidation as previous crises have proven such a step to be self-defeating. In developed countries, for example, fiscal consolidation after the global financial crisis had strong adverse effects on growth, resulting in even higher debt-to-GDP ratios (Fatas and Summers, 2018). Fiscal measures should continue to focus on essential pandemic-related expenditures, provide relief to the most vulnerable and support employment growth, with strategies broadly aligned towards supporting sustainable development. The composition of fiscal outlays should take a strategic approach, such as by boosting public investments in physical and digital infrastructure that can crowd-in private investments, and through targeted fiscal incentives to promote decarbonization, renewable energy and innovation. Investments in human capital, education and public health care should remain priorities.

Pressures for fiscal consolidation will intensify, especially in developing countries. Faster-than-expected monetary tightening in the United States would have severe implications for fiscal positions, especially as the recent rise in public debt has increased the vulnerability of fiscal policy to higher

23 History generally shows that government capacity to issue debt is crucial in tackling emergencies, including wars, economic and financial crises, and pandemics (Eichengreen and others, 2021).

debt-servicing and rollover costs. Countries will need to assess their fiscal rules and establish credible debt sustainability frameworks. In the medium-term, addressing debt sustainability will require a combination of fiscal restraint when appropriate, robust growth and moderate inflation, according to country-specific circumstances. Countries with unsustainable external debt need fast and coordinated international support for debt relief.

Figure I.18

General government gross debt

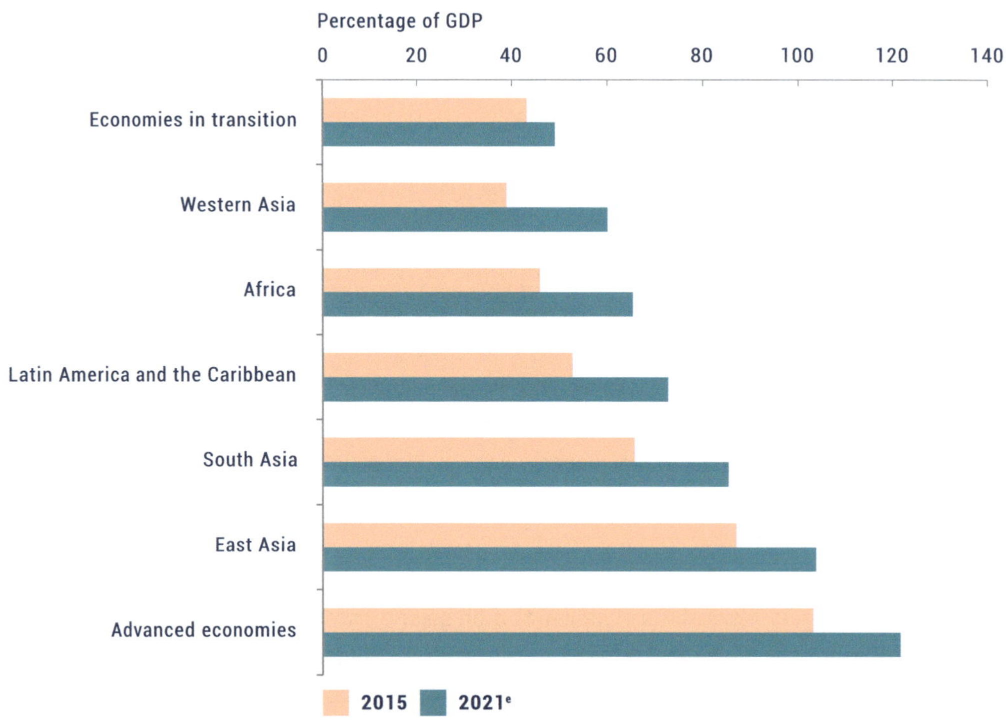

Source: IMF World Economic Outlook Database.
Note: e = estimates.

...but limited fiscal space constitutes a major constraint in developing countries

Many developing countries lack the fiscal space to effectively address the shock of the pandemic much less invest in sustainable development. Countries in Africa and Latin America entered the crisis with weak fiscal positions, which constrained their ability to pursue stimulus measures, roll out vaccination and expand social protection. Amid higher public debt, lower fiscal revenues and tightening global conditions, developing countries now face rising pressures for consolidation (figure I.18) even as escalating debt-servicing costs are already diverting resources from public investments and the COVID-19 response. In addition, most developing countries lack fiscal capacities for dealing with mounting climate risks. Enlarging fiscal space, in the short term, will require further international support, including increased liquidity, debt relief and concessional financing.[24] In the medium term, though, greater fiscal space depends on strengthening tax revenues through progressive taxation and establishing a multilateral mechanism for debt restructuring.

Low-income developing countries are in a very fragile fiscal and debt position

The fiscal and debt situation is extremely difficult in low-income developing countries. Nearly half are in debt distress or at risk of it (IMF, 2021a). Elevated external debt burdens (figure I.19), additional borrowing during the pandemic and increasing debt-servicing costs have pushed a rising number of these countries to the brink of a debt crisis. For more than half the countries in sub-Saharan Africa, debt-servicing costs account for a quarter of government revenue. Worrisomely, many low-income countries have cut public investment and capital spending and have implemented major reallocations of resources from key development areas, including Cameroon, Liberia and Mauritania in Africa, Myanmar and Nepal in Asia, and some small island developing States such as Tonga and Samoa (IMF, 2021a). About two-thirds of low- and lower-middle income countries have cut education budgets since the onset of the pandemic (World Bank and UNESCO, 2021). Some estimates also suggest that the pandemic has impacted social spending on child protection, nutrition, and water and sanitation (UNICEF, 2021).

Figure I.19

External debt stock as a share of gross national income

Percentage

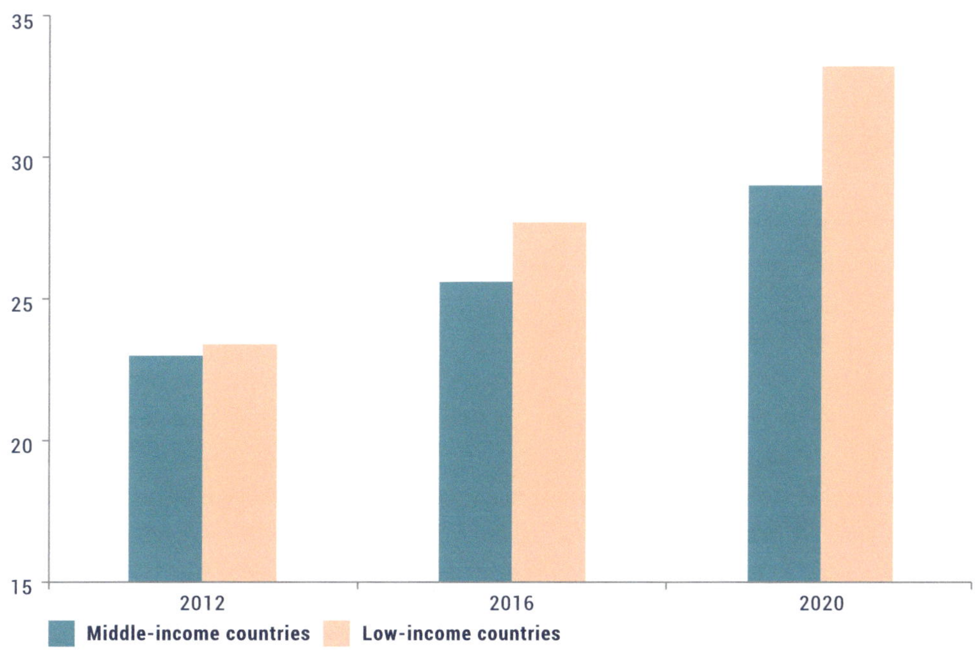

Source: World Bank International Debt Statistics, October 2021.

24 Countries could also explore new avenues, like intragovernmental borrowing. Intragovernmental debt, or the difference between gross debt and net debt, is still very low in developing countries. Intragovernmental borrowing from government-owned pension funds and insurance funds can help to ease some financing constraints. This is a short-term solution that creates a critical long-term liability, however. Countries with weak revenues that consider using this option for financing investments that do not stimulate productivity and growth should proceed with caution.

Support from the international community to low-income countries has been insufficient

The international community's policy responses to the plight of low-income countries have been significant but not sufficient. The G20 Debt Service Suspension Initiative, which paused debt servicing to bilateral and multilateral creditors until December 2021, did not write off or reduce debt burdens and provided limited debt relief to low-income countries. Of 73 eligible countries, only 50 requested suspended debt servicing in 2020 and 2021. Many refrained from this option because they feared credit downgrades.[25] The initiative delivered an estimated $12.7 billion in debt relief (G20, 2021) or about 23 per cent of debt repayments (IMF and World Bank, 2021). Moving forward, the Common Framework for Debt Treatment beyond the DSSI is an agreement between G20 and Paris Club countries to coordinate and cooperate on debt treatment for low-income developing countries. While this is a step in the right direction, including through its consideration of debt cancellations, it only applies to low-income developing countries.

The new allocation of Special Drawing Rights increases liquidity but does not solve financing challenges in developing countries

In August 2021, the International Monetary Fund (IMF) increased the allocation of Special Drawing Rights, distributing an extra $650 billion among member States proportionate to their existing quotas. The least developed countries received 2.4 per cent of the new allocation, which is about 1.3 per cent of their GDP. While this is an important measure to enhance liquidity and ease financing constraints (box I.2), it is not expected to solve the financing challenges in developing countries. Even if the Special Drawing Rights are redistributed through IMF trust funds, a country can only access these additional resources through an IMF-supported programme that presupposes a balance of payments need. It is unclear whether additional Special Drawing Rights on the balance sheets of central banks can prevent exchange rate depreciation and minimize exchange rate risks if foreign reserves dwindle.

Box I.2

Strengthening the impact of Special Drawing Rights

Special Drawing Rights are an international reserve asset that the IMF can issue to supplement existing reserves required for addressing a long-term global crisis. Special Drawing Rights represent unconditional liquidity and are not considered a loan from the IMF. Once they are allocated, IMF member countries can hold them as part of their foreign exchange reserves or exchange them with other countries (or prescribed holders) for freely usable currencies. Contrary to wide belief, the IMF Articles of Agreement do not require Special Drawing Rights to be administered by countries' central banks. Fiscal agencies can decide on their use in accordance with national legal frameworks. Allocations are cost free, but use incurs an interest cost (currently 0.05 per cent) paid to the IMF on the difference between a country's cumulative allocations and its holdings. Countries with holdings that exceed their allocations receive interest payments on the difference from the IMF.

In August 2021, the IMF issued a historic new allocation of Special Drawing Rights, equivalent to $650 billion. Several countries with strong external positions have expressed interest in a voluntary

25 Strikingly, 35 of the 37 beneficiaries of the Heavily Indebted Poor Countries Initiative are now on the list of the Debt Service Suspension Initiative. These countries received bilateral debt relief during the first decade of the twenty-first century only to return to the same debt crisis situation a decade later, illustrating the systemic nature of debt problems in the developing world.

channelling of these to countries most in need while preserving their reserve asset characteristics. In their June 2021 Carbis Bay Communiqué, Group of 7 (G7) countries called for a total global reallocation of $100 billion. Three mechanisms are currently under discussion to address both immediate liquidity needs and longer-term financing requirements for sustainable development.

A first option is the donation or on-lending of Special Drawing Rights through the IMF Poverty Reduction and Growth Trust, which facilitates concessional lending for low-income and other vulnerable countries through IMF programmes. It allows lending countries to earn the interest rate on the Special Drawing Rights, thus offsetting the cost of a deficit in their accounts. A reserve account covers the credit risk associated with on-lending. Lenders can also seek early repayment if needed, allowing on-lent Special Drawing Rights to retain their reserve asset characteristics. Some countries have already channelled their existing allocations this way, which tripled the concessional lending capacity of the IMF in 2020 (Georgieva, 2021).

As a second option, the IMF is developing a new Resilience and Sustainability Trust to channel Special Drawing Rights towards affordable long-term financing for low-income countries, small island developing States and vulnerable middle-income countries, with a focus on tackling the climate crisis. This is in line with calls from the United Nations Secretary-General to establish a new trust fund at the IMF to address the needs of such countries (United Nations, 2021a). The design of such a trust could include safeguards to cover interest payments and credit risk, similar to those of the Poverty Reduction and Growth Trust, and preserve the reserve asset characteristics of Special Drawing Rights.[a] The facility should be finalized quickly and ensure broad accessibility to low- and middle-income countries.

A third option is to channel Special Drawing Rights through new or existing trust funds at multilateral development banks and/or regional development banks, which are already prescribed holders of Special Drawing Rights. Such funds have or could develop financial mechanisms to allow the Special Drawing Rights to retain their reserve asset characteristics, based on the model of the Poverty Reduction and Growth Trust. These funds could leverage new resources for sustainable development, including near-term needs such as vaccine purchases and longer-term sustainable development priorities. Some of this new financing could be channelled through national development banks to leverage their local knowledge and expertise.

While these options can provide much needed additional financing, they should do so at a zero or minimal interest rate to minimize additional debt burdens for developing countries. Further, they should not be subject to onerous conditions, including for fiscal consolidation, which would hamper a sustainable recovery and risk further long-term economic damage. Given the enormous financial needs in confronting the pandemic and supporting recovery, countries in a position to channel their excess Special Drawing Rights should act quickly. Crucially, this should not crowd out official resources for development cooperation, such as official development assistance.

a In their October 2021 Communiqué, the G20 finance ministers and central bank governors endorsed the establishment of such a mechanism and called on the IMF and World Bank to collaborate closely to develop and implement financing under the new trust.

Author: Cornelia Kaldewei, Financing for Sustainable Development Office, United Nations Department of Economic and Social Affairs

Gearing up labour market policies and social protection

Policies supporting employment

Countries have implemented a variety of policies to minimize pandemic fallout on employment. Labour market policies, focusing on formal workers, were adopted or expanded. They comprised wage subsidies, reforms to labour regulations, shorter working-time arrangements and job retention schemes, along with active labour market policies to provide skills training and job placement support. Social safety nets expanded at a historic speed to assist vulnerable groups in the informal sector who are not covered by contributory social programmes. These introduced new temporary benefits, expanded the coverage and generosity of existing benefits, and changed eligibility criteria.[26] Demand-side measures aimed at increasing liquidity for firms and providing tax relief and credit facilities, often through deferrals of taxes on income and profits or postponement of the payment of value added taxes.

Supporting job creation is critical to avoid long-lasting scars from the pandemic

While there is still uncertainty around the magnitude, scope and durability of changes in labour markets, the pandemic will likely have long-lasting effects on employment. Making recovery inclusive hinges on speeding up job creation and the placement and reallocation of workers. Policymakers should not underestimate the role of fiscal and labour market policies in this. Continued fiscal support is required to sustain social safety nets for those who remain in need. Measures to ensure workplace safety must accompany steps to ramp up employment programmes, create incentives for hiring and enact active labour market policies.

Job retention schemes have prevented a further rise in unemployment in developed countries, especially in Europe. Developing countries have focused on policy measures like shorter working-time arrangements and changes in labour regulations. In Latin America, Colombia, Costa Rica and Peru reduced working hours or wages and instituted advance annual leave or even temporary work suspensions (Blofield and others, 2020). Argentina, Brazil and Chile provided wage subsidies to employers and workers to retain jobs and provide income stability. Low-income developing countries were proactive in implementing regulatory changes and shorter working hours while wage subsidies were less common due to budgetary and financing constraints.

Public employment services should target women, youth, migrants and low-skilled workers

As vaccinations progress and mobility increases, countries need to expand active labour market policies. These could include support to small and medium enterprises, targeted sectoral policies, active promotion of employment, assistance in job searches, and skills training through investment in public employment services, with a focus on youth, women, migrants, and low-skilled and self-employed workers. Active labour market policies can advance the reallocation of workers into sectors with growing job opportunities, improve the acquisition of new skills and generate better matches between jobs and jobseekers. These policies can also help the labour market reintegration of groups

26 About 186 countries have implemented 734 conditional or unconditional cash transfer programmes, the most utilized social protection response during the pandemic and particularly important for low-income countries (Gentilini and others, 2020).

that suffered disproportionate displacement. Previous evidence confirms the potential of these policies in labour market recovery.[27]

Gender policy measures are essential for an inclusive recovery of employment

Governments need to take proactive measures to incorporate gender dimensions across social protection and labour market policies. Initiatives might include reforms to unemployment benefits, better targeted and designed training programmes, specific hiring incentives and increased availability of childcare. Canada, Switzerland and Mexico have undertaken institutional coordination and information sharing to advance gender-inclusive policies that improve women's employment and income prospects, reduce the unequal distribution of unpaid care responsibilities and address gender-based violence. Support to specific sectors where women are overrepresented should also be considered, for example, hospitality, essential services and social care.[28]

To make employment programmes more effective, public employment services should use skills demand and supply surveys to understand and cater to labour market needs. Services and firms need to work together to assess needs for skills and design training programmes accordingly for those who are un- and underemployed. Enhancing efforts to assess changing demands and provide targeted reskilling programmes can help avoid skills mismatches that may occur due to structural changes, like digitalization and automation, or those caused by the pandemic. Many countries are currently working on redesigning public employment services. In Europe, Austria has established comprehensive, long-term measures aimed at workers who lost jobs during the pandemic. France and the United Kingdom plan to expand services focusing on young people by increasing front-line staff in public employment services.

Social protection to build resilience

Expanding public revenue in the medium term is critical to strengthening social protection

Social protection systems are essential to resilience as amply demonstrated during the pandemic. Yet the extent to which new social assistance policies will persist in developing countries is largely uncertain. Governments will need to expand public revenues and mobilize financial resources in the medium term to strengthen social protection systems. The pandemic has led to some important policy innovations, for example, in the delivery of social assistance in urban areas and through accelerated crisis preparedness. These offer insights that could be applied to more comprehensive and integrated social protection systems moving forward. Adaptive social protection offers an integrated approach that combines traditional social protection with disaster risk management and climate change adaptation. It can help to build resilience in vulnerable households before, during and after shocks such as droughts, floods or pandemics. This constitutes a shift towards a more long-term approach centred on investing in the capacity of households to deal with and adapt to sudden crises.

27 In OECD countries, active labour market policies have shown particularly positive effects in the long run, especially training programmes (Kluve, 2016).

28 Previous analysis of the effectiveness of active labour market policies in Latin America shows that programmes focusing on women had better outcomes than those focusing on men (Ibarraran and Rosas, 2009; Kluve, 2016).

New technologies can help better identify social programme beneficiaries

Determining social programme beneficiaries requires up-to-date information on incomes and living situations. Since the onset of the pandemic, many countries have used innovative data-driven methods to find new ways to identify beneficiaries. For instance, Pakistan combined information on several factors to qualify nearly 100 million people for the Ehssas emergency cash programme, including assessments of household property, vehicles and telephone bills. Nigeria used a mixed approach blending census data and satellite imagery, processed with machine learning algorithms, to calculate the size and location of dwellings as part of determining poverty levels. These technology-enabled interventions expanded the reach of cash transfers compared to pre-pandemic levels (Gentilini and others, 2020).[29] Such innovations could create dynamic social registries that are updated throughout the year and can help quickly identify households in need in times of crisis.

Monetary policy: overcoming the addiction to easy money

Central banks deployed a wide range of monetary measures to support the recovery...

Global monetary policy responses to the COVID-19 crisis were extraordinary around the world. Central banks cut short-term interest rates, lowered reserve bank requirements, established new lending facilities, used forward guidance and changed their monetary policy frameworks. Major central banks such as the Federal Reserve, the European Central Bank and the Bank of Japan and some central banks in developing countries engaged in asset purchase programmes (see chapter 2). The Federal Reserve also temporarily expanded the number of countries that were offered swap lines from 5 to 14, including 4 developing countries. Such measures helped stabilize financial markets, reduce uncertainty and support the recovery.

...but as inflation gathers pace, monetary conditions are expected to tighten quickly

As economic activity gathers pace and inflationary pressures gain momentum in the United States and many developing countries, exceptionally accommodative monetary policy stances are gradually shifting. A few major central banks have announced plans for or started gradual normalization. The Federal Reserve, for example, initiated the tapering of its asset purchase programme by the end of November 2021 while the Bank of Canada scaled back its programme even earlier.[30] Changes in monetary conditions have been rapidly gaining steam in developing and transition economies especially since the second half of 2021 (figure I.20). Central banks have increased interest rates in a growing number of countries, including Brazil, Chile, Hungary, Mexico, the Russian Federation and South Africa.[31] In 2021, a few central banks, for example in Brazil and the Russian Federation, took drastic measures, increasing interest rates by 725 and 325 basis points, respectively.

29 Other approaches, such as the use of electricity consumption data in Guatemala or a voter database paired with satellite image data and phone records in Togo, also showed encouraging early results.

30 The European Central Bank and the Bank of Japan have not yet signalled changes in their policy stances as of December 2021.

31 One of the few exceptions is Turkey, where the central bank cut interest rates by 2 percentage points in October 2021, prompting a significant depreciation of the domestic currency.

Figure I.20

Central bank interest rate decisions, 2020 and 2021

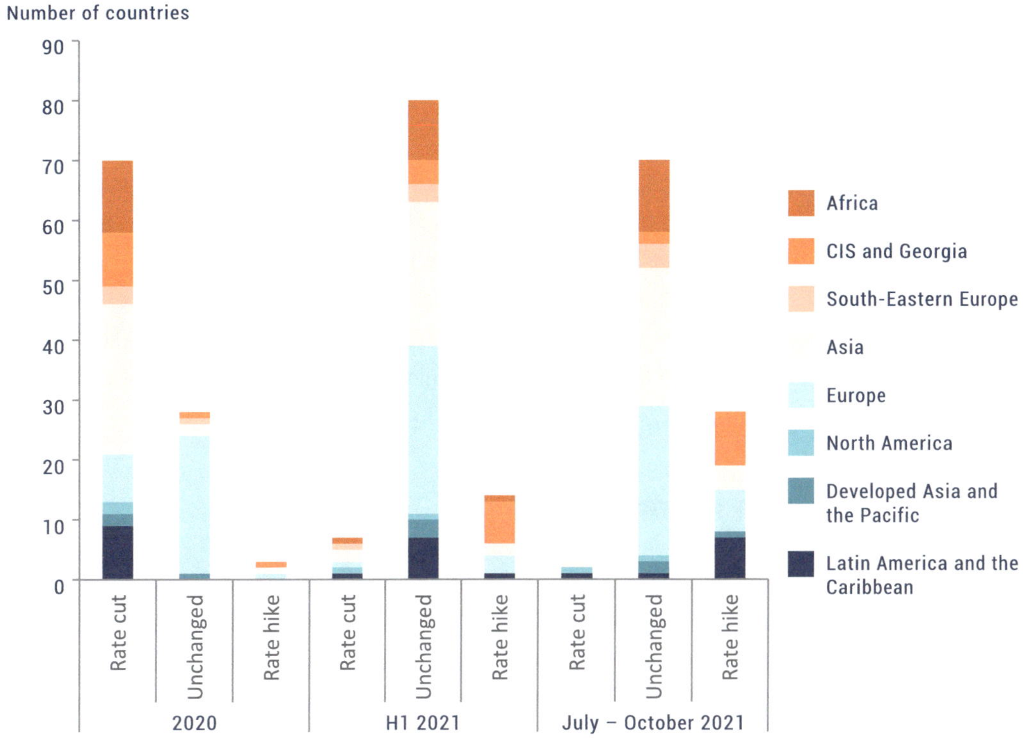

Source: UN DESA, based on data from CEIC (accessed on 23 November 2021).
Notes: 101 central banks are covered based on available data. H1 = first half of 2021.

Amid rising inflation and persistent slack in labour markets, monetary policymakers face major challenges ahead

The shift in monetary policy support is a major challenge for the world economy amid a still raging pandemic, elevated levels of sovereign and private sector debt and record-high stock market valuations in developed countries. The challenge that monetary policymakers face is exacerbated by the difficulty in assessing trade-offs between growth, employment and inflation, given the significant and simultaneous impacts of the crisis on labour markets, global supply chains and potential output.[32] In addition, the trajectory of inflation is surrounded by major uncertainties associated with the pandemic, the rapid spending of accumulated savings and changes in consumption patterns. Supply-chain problems seem to be intensifying inflationary pressures as supply has not kept up with the release of pent-up demand in many sectors.

In particular, the Federal Reserve faces the challenge of scaling down its asset purchase programme. It must ensure appropriate timing and pacing to maintain global financial stability and prevent premature fiscal consolidation. The recent rise in inflation has raised serious concerns in the United States that this could become a longer-term phenomenon. If that proves to be the case, faster-than-expected

32 The uneven impact of the COVID-19 pandemic across sectors and the massive reallocation of resources further complicates assessment of overheating points. Guerrieri and others (2021) discuss how a desire to facilitate the reallocation process can lead to favouring a more expansionary monetary policy because higher inflation can facilitate the adjustment of relative wages and provide the right price signals to encourage mobility.

monetary tightening, with the Federal Reserve raising interest rates several times throughout 2022, could derail recovery at a time when the economy is still operating with 6 million fewer people in the labour market. It could also trigger global financial turmoil, including large corrections in asset prices. For many developing countries, a sudden rise in interest rates could trigger capital outflows and worsen their growth outlook and debt situation, especially those with elevated foreign-denominated external debt.

Developing countries should prepare for monetary tightening in the United States

In developing countries, monetary policy normalization needs to proceed with caution. Where economic activity is on a relatively robust trajectory and vaccination rates are elevated, central banks may act to tame rising inflationary pressures. Yet overly aggressive tightening could undermine the recovery of employment. Developing countries should also prepare for a faster-than-expected monetary adjustment in the United States, for example, by limiting maturity mismatches in their balance sheets. Foreign exchange interventions and temporary capital controls can help strengthen the capacity of monetary policy to respond to country-specific inflation and growth dynamics.

Multilateralism in a world of crises

Reinvigorating multilateralism remains essential to confronting the health and climate crises

The pandemic has been a stark reminder that the world must remain united and respond collectively to global crises. The need for a well-functioning multilateral system is more evident than ever. Yet vast disparities in vaccine roll-outs between developed and developing countries, limited progress in tackling mounting climate risks and inadequate commitments to addressing debt challenges show that multilateralism falls short of effective responses to global challenges. Ongoing crises are exacerbating development asymmetries and increasing inequalities, worsening the health and climate emergencies, and making progress towards the 2030 Agenda for Sustainable Development more difficult if not impossible. Reinvigorating multilateralism will determine whether the world can get back on a track towards sustainable development. The draft Doha Programme of Action for the least developed countries addresses these issues and requires comprehensive action by all stakeholders to ensure that these most vulnerable countries are not left behind.[33]

Addressing intellectual property issues would strengthen the global vaccine supply

Developing countries, especially low-income countries, continue to face enormous hurdles in securing access to vaccines. Realizing an agreed target to vaccinate 70 per cent of the global population by mid-2022 (WHO, 2021) requires accelerated vaccine redistribution. Countries with high volumes of vaccines must provide doses to low- and lower-middle-income countries through swaps delivery schedules with COVAX and the African Vaccine Acquisition Trust, fulfil donation pledges and release manufacturers from previous contracts so they can channel doses to countries with low vaccination rates. Other crucial elements are the elimination of trade restrictions on exports of medical equipment, raw materials and vaccines, and the expansion and diversification of the global vaccine supply

33 On 21 December 2021, the Preparatory Committee approved the draft Doha Programme of Action for the least developed countries and decided to recommend it to the Fifth United Nations Conference on the least developed countries for adoption.

chain.[34] The multilateral system needs to address intellectual property and technology transfer issues as a priority. Absent a clear path to approve and scale up the production of new vaccines, enacting intellectual property waivers remains the best option to improve supplies.

The world is falling short on climate action despite commitments to reduce carbon emissions

Climate change poses an urgent global challenge requiring highly ambitious actions on mitigation and adaptation. In August 2021, the Intergovernmental Panel on Climate Change issued its Sixth Assessment Report (IPCC, 2021a). It provides stark warnings of increasingly extreme heatwaves, droughts and flooding, among many other forms of climate fallout.[35] In November 2021, the 26th Conference of the Parties to the United Nations Framework Convention on Climate Change concluded with significant new commitments to climate action intended to move towards net-zero emissions in the next few decades. Led by the European Union and the United States, over 100 countries pledged to reduce methane emissions by 30 per cent by 2030. Backed by $19.2 billion in public and private funding, 100 countries agreed to end and reverse deforestation by 2030. India set a goal of reaching net-zero emissions by 2070 and ensuring renewable energy makes up 50 per cent of its energy mix by 2030. China promised to reduce its methane emissions this decade. In total, net-zero commitments now cover 80 per cent of total emissions, but even so, pledges fell short of keeping warming below 1.5 degrees Celsius, considered the threshold for avoiding the worst consequences of climate change. Global temperatures are estimated to rise from 1.8–2.7 degrees Celsius by the end of the century, depending on the implementation of announced targets (Climate Action Tracker, 2021). In terms of net-zero goals, only Chile, Costa Rica, the European Union and the United Kingdom have adequately designed targets.[36]

Climate impacts on infrastructure could be enormous for small island developing States

To avoid the worst damages from global warming, the world needs to halve global carbon emissions by 2030 and reach net-zero emissions by 2050, yet it is uncertain that countries will do what is necessary before the climate crisis becomes unmanageable. There are significant risks that climate change could push 132 million more people into poverty in the next decade and displace more than 216 million individuals by mid-century (World Bank, 2021b). Climate impacts on essential infrastructure could be enormous, especially for the most vulnerable countries, including the small island developing States.[37] Accelerated capacity building and adaptation of infrastructure will be critical.[38] Progress will largely

34 The 12th World Trade Organization Ministerial Conference offers an opportunity for member States to achieve more rapid vaccine production and more equitable distribution.

35 The report projects that, depending on the scenario, a mean global temperature increase of 1.5 degrees Celsius relative to pre-industrial times will likely be reached by 2040. If emissions are not slashed in the next few years, this temperature rise may be realized even earlier.

36 Of major importance is the EU Climate Law, which entered into force in July 2021. It sets a binding objective of climate neutrality in the European Union by 2050 and a binding target of reducing net domestic greenhouse gas emissions by at least 55 per cent compared to 1990 levels by 2030. The law also envisages strong action on climate change adaptation and resilience-building as well as related stocktaking, assessment and review, starting in 2023.

37 In many small island developing States, critical infrastructure assets are at high and growing risk of climate change impacts such as coastal flooding from as early as the 2030s (Monioudi and others, 2018; IPCC, 2018).

38 Recent research emphasises the role of resilient infrastructure as "a lifeline for sustainable development", with large net benefits of investing in more resilient infrastructure in low- and middle-income countries (Hallegatte and others, 2019).

depend on better access to affordable financing, which should favour more grants over loans to avoid increasing already onerous debt burdens.

Debt relief measures for low-income countries remain insufficient to confront the pandemic and support the recovery

For many developing countries with unsustainable debt levels, a comprehensive approach to debt relief is needed. This includes plans for timely and orderly debt restructuring. The "doing too little, too late" approach has proven harmful in previous crisis, delaying recoveries, fuelling unsustainable social tensions and raising the cost of debt restructurings. Since debt relief efforts have been insufficient, many countries are facing unbearable trade-offs between servicing debt, containing the crisis and promoting recovery.

The Common Framework for Debt Treatments beyond the DSSI agreed by G20 and Paris Club countries could kickstart a more permanent and comprehensive debt restructuring mechanism. But some aspects need further consideration. Only low-income countries are eligible to participate, even though many middle-income countries also need urgent debt relief. In addition, there is no clear mechanism to ensure the participation of private creditors, who account for a large share of creditors in many countries (figure I.21). Many countries also hesitate to join the Common Framework due to the fear of triggering technical defaults or sovereign rating downgrades, which would in turn raise borrowing costs and limit access to financial markets.[39] Finally, the Common Framework lacks commitments by creditors and debtor countries to align newly found fiscal space with agreed climate and development goals.[40]

A new accord to reform the international tax system aims at reducing tax avoidance by large multinational firms...

In 2021, 136 countries reached a landmark accord to reform the international tax system, a major policy development geared towards reducing tax avoidance.[41] The agreement aims to redistribute a share of the profits of the 100 largest multinationals to increase tax revenues in countries where firms earn their profits. It applies to multinationals with global sales above 20 billion euros and profitability above 10 per cent. The new rules stipulate that 25 per cent of residual profits (profit beyond 10 per cent of revenue) will be allocated to market jurisdictions. The OECD has estimated that up to $125 billion in profits could be reallocated to more than 130 countries a year by 2023 (OECD, 2021b). The agreement also commits to introducing a global minimum corporate tax rate of 15 per cent for firms with revenues above 750 million euros to minimize their use of tax havens and low-tax jurisdictions. As such, it helps to reduce race-to-the-bottom tax strategies.[42] The agreement is expected to increase global tax revenue by $150 billion annually.

---

39 As of November 2021, only three countries (Chad, Ethiopia and Zambia) had requested to participate in the Common Framework.

40 This is an important issue as climate vulnerable countries pay higher costs to service their debt and climate risks increase sovereign risks (Volz and others, 2020).

41 Estimates suggest that governments forego about $240 billion annually through multinational practices such as base erosion and profit shifting (OECD, 2021c).

42 Between 1985 and 2018, the global average corporate tax rate fell from 49 per cent to 24 per cent; estimates suggest that about 36 per cent of multinational profits are shifted to tax heavens (Torslov, Wier and Zucman, 2021).

Figure I.21

Public and publicly guaranteed external debt, by creditor

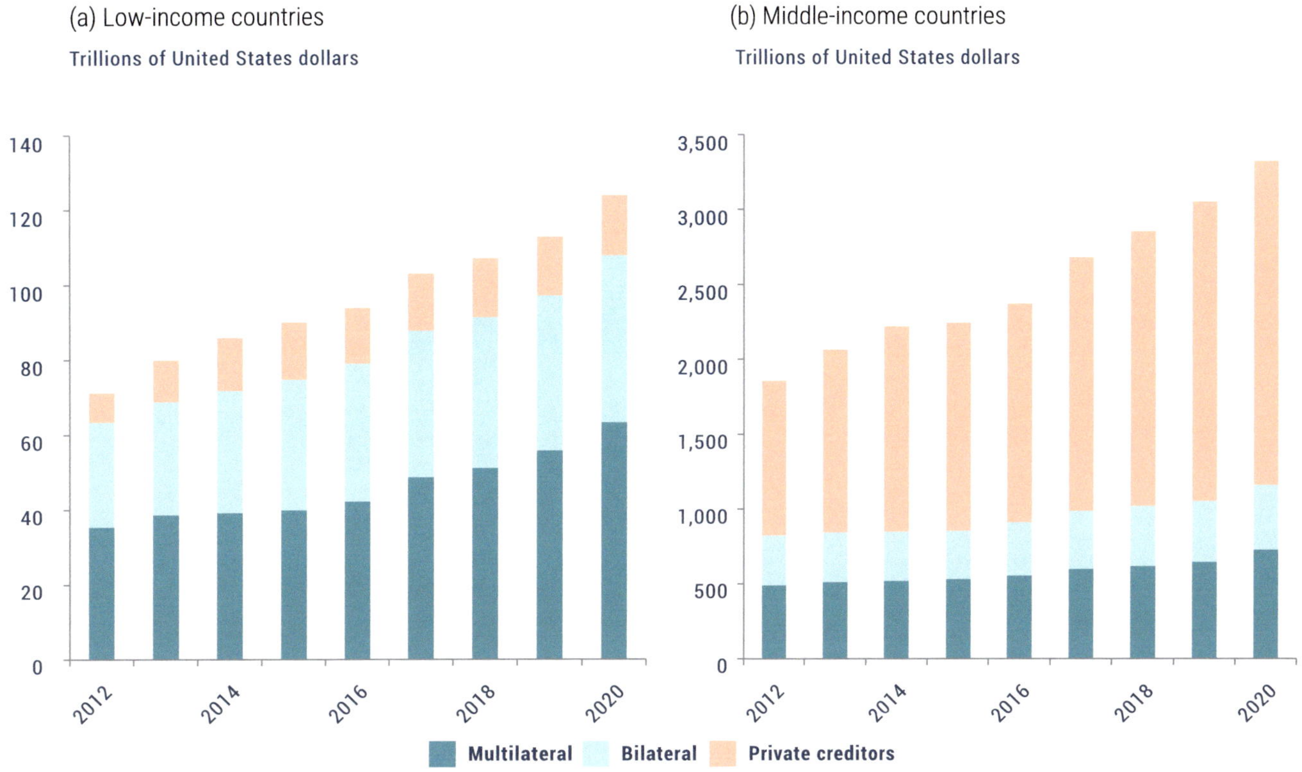

Source: World Bank, International Debt Statistics, October 2021.

...but most beneficiaries will likely be a few large developed countries

While this agreement represents a commitment to reforming the status quo in global taxation, it still has major shortfalls that need to be fixed so that benefits reach developing countries and not just a few large developed economies. A 15 per cent global minimum corporate tax sets the bar too low, for instance, and potentially makes this a global standard. This would particularly affect developing countries that rely relatively more on corporate taxes as a source of government revenue.[43] Further, the main beneficiaries will likely be a small number of developed countries with existing multinational headquarters, undermining the principle of fairness assumed to underlie the accord (ICRICT, 2021). Developing countries in fact stand to lose out due to its allocation principles and absence of dispute resolution mechanisms. In response, the Group of 77, representing 134 developing countries, has reiterated its long-standing call to establish a global tax body within the United Nations. It could spearhead further reforms to tax regulations globally through transforming the United Nations Committee of Experts on International Cooperation in Tax Matters into an intergovernmental forum (Ocampo, 2021).

43 A report by the Tax Justice Network (2021) highlights that developed countries lose more in absolute terms due to corporate tax abuse by multinationals but that the relative hardship caused by these practices is much higher in poorer countries. Losses due to corporate tax abuse in low- and lower-middle-income countries account for 48 per cent of their public health budgets, while in high- and upper-middle-income countries they account for 10 per cent.

CHAPTER II

The monetary policy response to COVID-19: direct impacts and spillovers

The COVID-19 pandemic triggered the worst global economic downturn in almost a century. Since the onset, countries around the world have rolled out extraordinary macroeconomic measures to save people's livelihoods, limit economic damage and kickstart recovery. With less room to reduce interest rates than during the 2008-2009 global financial crisis, central banks, especially in developed countries, relied more heavily on unconventional monetary policy tools. The most notable involved large-scale asset purchases to spur liquidity, prevent financial meltdown and stimulate economic activities.

These policies were effective in stabilizing financial markets and boosting aggregate demand during the early stages of recovery. But initial positive effects have lost strength over time. The continuation of ultraloose monetary policies, with central banks pumping massive amounts of liquidity to keep long-term interest rates low, could worsen the mispricing of risks and further inflate equity prices in major financial markets, while exacerbating wealth inequality.

This chapter reviews the global monetary response to COVID-19, focusing on large-scale asset purchase programmes (APPs) deployed by central banks in developed and developing countries. It discusses how these policies have supported economic recovery and assesses negative side effects and risks. It presents the challenges major central banks face in tapering asset purchases and managing risks of financial market instability that could arise from a disorderly adjustment of asset prices.

The global monetary response to COVID-19

The pandemic triggered an unprecedented monetary response

The monetary response to the pandemic has broadly followed the global financial crisis playbook but with unprecedented speed, scale and scope.[1] The initial COVID-19 shock presented two immediate challenges for central banks. First, the nature of the shock was highly unusual, with strongly correlated supply- and demand-side shocks amid unprecedented economic uncertainty. Second, after a decade of ultraloose monetary policies, central banks, especially in developed countries, had limited room for pursuing conventional monetary policies.

These twin challenges prompted central banks to deploy a wide range of monetary policy tools that included unconventional measures such as forward guidance, APPs and expanded lending operations (Cantú and others, 2021). In addition to expanding existing facilities and reactivating measures adopted during the global financial crisis, central banks established many new programmes. The monetary

1 English, Forbes and Ubide (2021) provide a comprehensive review of the monetary response to the COVID-19 pandemic.

response strongly complemented fiscal policies, often blurring traditional distinctions between the two (Bartsch and others, 2020).[2]

Amid continued uncertainty about the near-term economic outlook, central banks in developed countries have generally chosen to keep their monetary policy stances exceptionally accommodative well into 2021 to boost aggregate demand, reduce unemployment and close output gaps. A combination of supply-chain bottlenecks, energy price increases and the release of pent-up demand, however, has pushed inflationary pressures in many parts of the world, presenting an additional challenge. While economic recovery remains highly uncertain, a growing number of central banks, especially in developing and transition economies, have started to tighten monetary policy stances, pre-empting the prospect of higher inflation beyond the near term. At the same time, a few major developed country central banks have announced plans for gradual policy normalization. In the United States of America, the Federal Reserve started tapering its monthly asset purchases in late November 2021.

Interest rate measures and reserve policies

Aggressive cuts in interest rates and reserve requirements boosted liquidity

When COVID-19 hit in early 2020, central banks quickly and aggressively cut short-term interest rates to increase liquidity, reduce borrowing costs and support economic activity. Policy rates in developed countries were already at low levels, however – often close to or at the effective lower bound (figure II.1).[3] This was due to a long-term decline in the natural rate of interest (i.e., the real interest rate consistent with full employment and stable inflation) and prolonged monetary accommodation. In February 2020, the GDP-weighted average policy rate in developed countries was 0.9 per cent, far below the 3.5 per cent in August 2008 before the global financial crisis.[4] In as many as 23 developed countries (Denmark, Japan, Sweden, Switzerland and 19 euro area countries), policy rates were at or below zero when the pandemic began. Likewise, rates in developing countries were generally lower than at the onset of the global financial crisis although monetary conditions varied widely within this group. Among a sample of 36 developing countries, the average policy rate in February 2020 was 3.2 per cent compared to 7 per cent in August 2008. As a result, the magnitude of rate cuts in response to COVID-19 was considerably smaller than it was during the global financial crisis.

Several central banks provided additional liquidity to financial institutions by reducing the bank reserve requirement ratio (such as Brazil, China, Malaysia, the Philippines and the United States), lowering the remuneration rates on reserves (China, New Zealand and Turkey) or enhancing flexibility for instruments that count as reserves (Malaysia and the Philippines).

2 English, Forbes and Uribe (2021), for example, note that some central bank lending programmes amounted to quasi-fiscal operations.

3 The effective lower bound is the limit on how low policy rates can go. Below the lower bound, it becomes profitable for financial institutions to exchange central bank reserves for cash.

4 At the time of the Lehman Brothers collapse in September 2008, the average rate was still 3.1 per cent.

Figure II.1
Central bank policy rates in developed and developing countries

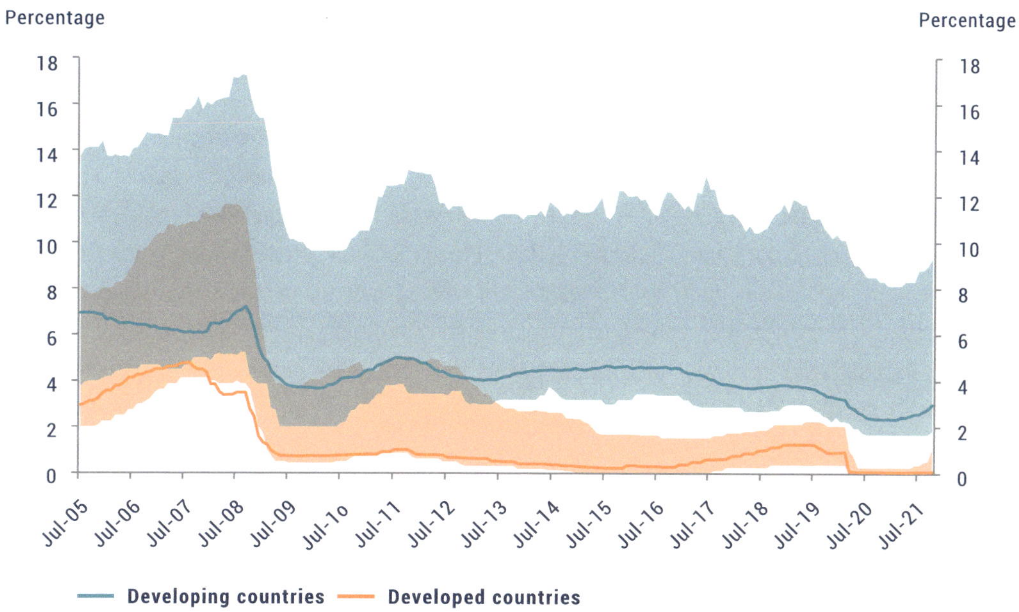

Sources: UN DESA, based on data from the Bank for International Settlements, CEIC and World Bank Open Data (accessed on 17 November 2021).
Note: The lines display the GDP-weighted average policy rates for a set of 36 developing countries and a set of 14 developed economies plus the euro area. The shaded areas indicate the range between the twenty-fifth and seventy-fifth percentile of the respective policy rates.

Expanded lending and foreign exchange operations

Central banks supported credit availability for the private sector

Most central banks in developed and developing countries expanded emergency lending operations at the outset of the pandemic. They adjusted existing facilities, for example, by increasing their size (such as China, Colombia and the Republic of Korea), broadening eligible collateral (Canada, Chile, Japan and Singapore) and changing the maturity of instruments (Canada, India and the United States). They also established entirely new programmes.[5] In addition to providing short-term liquidity to banks and other financial institutions, central banks deployed measures to support the flow of credit to households and non-financial corporations. "Funding for lending" programmes, which provide banks with access to low-cost funding to lend to businesses and consumers, have become an important policy instrument (Casanova and others, 2021). In 2020, several central banks introduced such programmes, including the European Central Bank (ECB) through the third phase of the Targeted Long-Term Refinancing Operations Programme, the Bank of England, the Reserve Bank of Australia, the Saudi Arabian Monetary Authority and the Swiss National Bank. These programmes differed from standard lending facilities in that banks could only access the funds if they increased lending to the private sector – either generally or to certain segments such as small and medium-sized enterprises or industries hit hard by the pandemic. In a similar vein, many developing country central banks, especially in Latin

5 For instance, in March 2020, the Central Bank of Argentina approved a new scheme of credit lines for micro-, small and medium-sized enterprises. The Bank of Canada launched the Standing Term Liquidity Facility to provide temporary liquidity support for eligible financial institutions.

America and East Asia, introduced or expanded measures to channel credit to small and medium-sized enterprises. One example is Chile's Fondo de Garantía para Pequeños Empresarios (Small Business' Guarantee Fund), which expanded significantly in size and scope.

Extended and new currency swap lines helped stabilize exchange rates

During the early stages of the pandemic, capital outflows from developing countries threatened exchange rate stability, while soaring demand for dollar-denominated assets strained offshore dollar funding markets. In response, the Federal Reserve reduced the costs and extended the maturity of its standing dollar liquidity swap lines with the Bank of Canada, the Bank of England, the Bank of Japan, the ECB and the Swiss National Bank. With nine other central banks, it also reopened temporary swap lines activated during the global financial crisis (Australia, Brazil, Denmark, Mexico, New Zealand, Norway, the Republic of Korea, Singapore and Sweden). Developing country central banks used different forms of foreign exchange interventions to improve liquidity and mitigate exchange rate volatility. For instance, they signed or renewed currency swap lines with each other (such as Argentina and China, China and Thailand, China and Turkey, Indonesia and the Republic of Korea, and India and Sri Lanka), lowered foreign exchange reserve requirements for banks (China, Indonesia, Peru and Turkey) and conducted foreign exchange repurchase operations (Brazil) and exchange-rate hedging (Colombia).[6]

Forward guidance and asset purchase programmes

APPs have become a primary stimulus tool in developed countries

As policy rates in many countries reached or came close to their effective lower bound,[7] central banks began to rely more heavily on unconventional monetary policy tools, including forward guidance and large-scale APPs.[8]

Forward guidance, used by major developed country central banks, signals that interest rates will remain low for a prolonged period. The Federal Reserve, for example, committed to keeping the federal funds rate at a target range between 0–0.25 per cent "until labor market conditions have reached [...] maximum employment and inflation [...] is on track to moderately exceed 2 percent for some time" (Federal Reserve, 2021). Other central banks have provided a combination of state- and time-contingent forward guidance.

Given limited conventional monetary policy space, large-scale APPs have become the primary stimulus tool for many developed country central banks during the COVID-19 crisis. The programmes have taken a variety of forms depending on the country context and institutional framework. Developed country central banks adjusted and massively expanded existing programmes introduced during the global financial crisis while also launching new ones. In developing countries, 27 central banks adopted APPs

6 A few countries, such as Argentina, China, India and Peru, also adjusted capital flow management measures, aiming to incentivize inflows and mitigate outflows (OECD, 2020).

7 In the second quarter of 2020, policy rates approached or hit their effective lower bound in almost all developed countries and several developing countries, including Chile, Israel, Peru, the Republic of Korea and Thailand.

8 Negative interest rates were not widely used in response to the pandemic. Denmark, Japan and Switzerland have remained the only economies with policy rates in negative territory.

as a new policy tool. The rest of this chapter will focus on the role of APPs in the crisis response, the macroeconomic and distributional implications, and challenges in exiting the policy.

Central banks' large-scale asset purchase programmes

Central bank purchasing of longer-term financial assets, also known as quantitative easing, is still a relatively new monetary tool, first introduced by the Bank of Japan in 2001.[9] The Federal Reserve, the ECB and the Bank of England adopted quantitative easing in response to the global financial crisis in 2008-2009 after lowering short-term interest rates to close to zero. As economic growth remained subdued and inflation below target during much of the decade after the crisis, all four central banks continued to use the asset purchase mechanism albeit with some pauses.[10]

Mechanism and transmission channels

APPs are expected to support market functioning and boost economic activity

The ultimate objective of large-scale asset purchases by central banks is to boost economic activity and bring inflation back to target. In theory, APPs are expected to work as follows (for a more detailed look at several potential transmission channels, see box II.1). Central banks purchase long-maturity securities, such as government bonds or mortgage-backed securities, from banks and other financial institutions (for example, pension funds) in exchange for short-term liquidity in the form of cash-equivalent bank reserves. Central banks buy these long-term securities to complement demand from financial intermediaries, including during high economic uncertainty when the latter consider these securities too risky. Demand for mortgage-backed securities fell sharply during the global financial crisis, for instance, as market participants lost confidence in their financial value. Many considered them toxic assets even though they were collateralized debt obligations of issuers. The Federal Reserve's purchase of these securities pushed up their prices, reduced their yields and restored market confidence, a sine qua non for proper functioning of the financial market.

Asset purchases by central banks also inject additional liquidity, which, at least in theory, should encourage banks to lend more. At the same time, the decline in government bond yields reduces longer-term borrowing and debt-servicing costs in the private sector, for example, for mortgages, auto loans and consumer debt. This is expected to boost consumption and investment, stimulating economic growth and job creation as well as enabling the central bank to achieve its inflation target. APPs thus have multiple objectives: to restore market confidence and financial stability, lower long-term borrowing costs, boost credit flows and reduce the cost of servicing existing debt. All of these are expected to stimulate aggregate demand, employment and economic growth. How APPs work

9 The rest of the chapter mainly refers to the policy as APPs.

10 The Federal Reserve paused its asset purchases between October 2014 and March 2020; the ECB between January and November 2019.

in practice, however, varies significantly across countries and over time (see the discussion on APP achievements and side effects).

Box II.1

Transmission channels of asset purchase programmes

Since the global financial crisis, quantitative easing has received a great deal of attention in theoretical and empirical research. Yet its effects are still not fully understood and remain debatable if not controversial. While traditional benchmark models of monetary policy predicted that quantitative easing would be largely ineffective (see, for example, Eggertsson and Woodford, 2003; Woodford, 2012), new research has identified a variety of potential transmission channels to the real economy.[a] A core argument for APPs is that central bank purchases of government bonds (or other financial assets) reduce long-term interest rates and boost asset prices through a portfolio rebalancing effect, a liquidity effect and a signalling effect.

The portfolio rebalancing effect is predicated on the assumption that investors have varying preferences for specific maturities. In this environment, a central bank's bond purchases change the relative supply of different assets, affecting their relative prices. In response, investors rebalance their holdings, bidding up the values of remaining government bonds and their close substitutes. As a result, long-term yields fall and the yield curve flattens. The portfolio rebalancing effect is associated with a decline in the term premium.[b]

The liquidity effect is especially relevant during the immediate crisis phase, when central banks step in and, via APPs, provide a liquidity backstop to the financial market (Ferdinandusse and others, 2020). During financial turmoil, market participants lose confidence in the value of assets or, relatedly, in the solvency of their trading counterparts. This situation can quickly lead to liquidity spirals, fire sales and negative feedback loops as money markets "dry up" and uncertainty rises. When central banks enter with large APPs, they step in as deep-pocketed market makers of last resort. They provide a floor for asset prices, restoring confidence and liquidity in the market. This liquidity effect can help central banks address specific bottlenecks in financial market segments where liquidity is needed and confidence is low.

Finally, the signalling effect is related to forward guidance strategies used by central banks to influence expectations about future short-term interest rates. Market participants may interpret large-scale asset purchases as an additional commitment by the central bank to keep short-term policy rates at (or close to) the effective lower bound for an extended period. As expectations for future short-term interest rates shift downwards, long-term interest rates also fall. The signalling channel is largely muted in the early stages of recovery when inflation is well below target. The effect becomes more

a For an overview and discussion of various transmission channels, see, for example, Gern and others (2015), Bundesbank (2016) and Bernanke (2020).

b The term premium is the amount by which the yield on a long-term bond is greater than the yield on shorter-term bonds.

relevant as recovery progresses, inflation picks up and uncertainty about the future path of interest rates increases.

The reduction in long-term interest rates – through portfolio rebalancing, signalling, and, to a limited extent, additional liquidity – is expected to improve overall financing conditions in the economy and boost aggregate demand in several ways. For one, higher or restored asset prices are expected to give rise to a wealth effect, boosting spending by businesses and households. At the same time, lower yields should exert downward pressure on the domestic currency, potentially stimulating net exports, producing an exchange rate effect. In addition, lower long-term interest rates are likely to reduce borrowing costs for governments, providing extra room for fiscal expansions, resulting in a fiscal effect. Finally, quantitative easing may stimulate the real economy through a bank lending effect. As banks receive cheap liquidity in the form of central bank reserves, they have more room to increase lending to the private sector.

Author: Ingo Pitterle, United Nations Department of Economic and Social Affairs

Asset purchase programmes in developed economies: the trillion-dollar bazooka

Developed country central banks massively expanded their balance sheets

The magnitude of APPs to respond to COVID-19 is reflected in the massive expansion of the balance sheets of major central banks. Since March 2020, the central banks of Japan, the United Kingdom, the United States and the euro area have added roughly $10.2 trillion in security assets to their balance sheets, with total assets soaring to over $25.9 trillion by the end of September 2021 (figure II.2a).[11] Balance sheets have also ballooned as a share of GDP. In the second quarter of 2021, total financial assets on central bank balance sheets ranged from 35 per cent of GDP in the United States to 130 per cent of GDP in Japan (figure II.2b).

The Federal Reserve responded to distressed financial markets in the early stages of the crisis by expanding its balance sheet by about $3 trillion between March and June 2020. Since then, it has been buying $120 billion of Treasury securities and mortgage-backed securities each month. As a result, the Federal Reserve's total assets have more than doubled since the pandemic started, rising from $4.2 trillion to about $8.6 trillion.[12] In contrast to earlier quantitative easing programmes that focused on longer-term securities, the Federal Reserve has recently purchased Treasury securities across a broader range of maturities. In the second quarter of 2021, it held 24.8 per cent of total debt of the Government of the United States. In November 2021, the Federal Reserve began to taper its purchases of securities. After reducing the volume of net asset purchases by $15 billion in November and December, the Federal Reserve decided to speed up the tapering process to counter persistently

11 Total assets of the four major developed country central banks slightly exceeded the combined assets under management of the top four global asset managers.

12 This amount includes $2.6 trillion in mortgage-backed securities implicitly guaranteed by the United States Government and $5.5 trillion in United States Treasury securities.

high inflation. From January 2022 on, net asset purchases are expected to decrease by $30 billion per month and end in March 2022.

The ECB implemented its 1.85 trillion-euro Pandemic Emergency Purchase Programme (PEPP) in March 2020 to counter COVID-19-induced risks for the euro area.[13] The programme complements existing APPs, which have a monthly target pace of 20 billion euros. Expected to end in March 2022, PEPP includes purchases of private and public sector securities, including corporate bond securities, asset-backed securities, covered bonds, central government bonds, and regional and local government bonds. The ECB's total assets have increased from about 4.7 trillion euros in March 2020 to 8.4 trillion euros in October 2021.

The Bank of Japan supported the flow of credit to the private sector by raising the upper limit on the amount of outstanding corporate bonds and commercial paper (long and short maturities) to 20 trillion yen. The additional purchases have been extended until at least the end of March 2022 (Bank of Japan, 2021). The bank committed to further supporting public finances by announcing potentially unlimited purchases of government bonds after already holding 43 per cent of outstanding government debt at the end of 2019 (Benigno and Pesenti, 2021). The Bank of Japan is the only major central bank to continuously engage in purchases of exchange-traded funds (ETFs) and Japan real estate investment trusts (J-REITs).

The Bank of England has expanded its quantitative easing programme by about £450 billion since the pandemic began. In total, it has purchased £895 billion worth of bonds since November 2009, almost exclusively United Kingdom government bonds. Unlike other major developed country central banks, the Bank of England already has an exit strategy from the extraordinary policies put in place during the crisis. It plans to raise the key policy rate from 0.1 per cent to 0.5 per cent before reducing its balance sheet by not reinvesting the proceeds.

13 The ECB announced the programme with an initial 750 billion euros, a sum that increased by 600 billion euros in June 2020 and by 500 billion euros in December 2020.

Figure II.2

Balance sheets of major developed country central banks

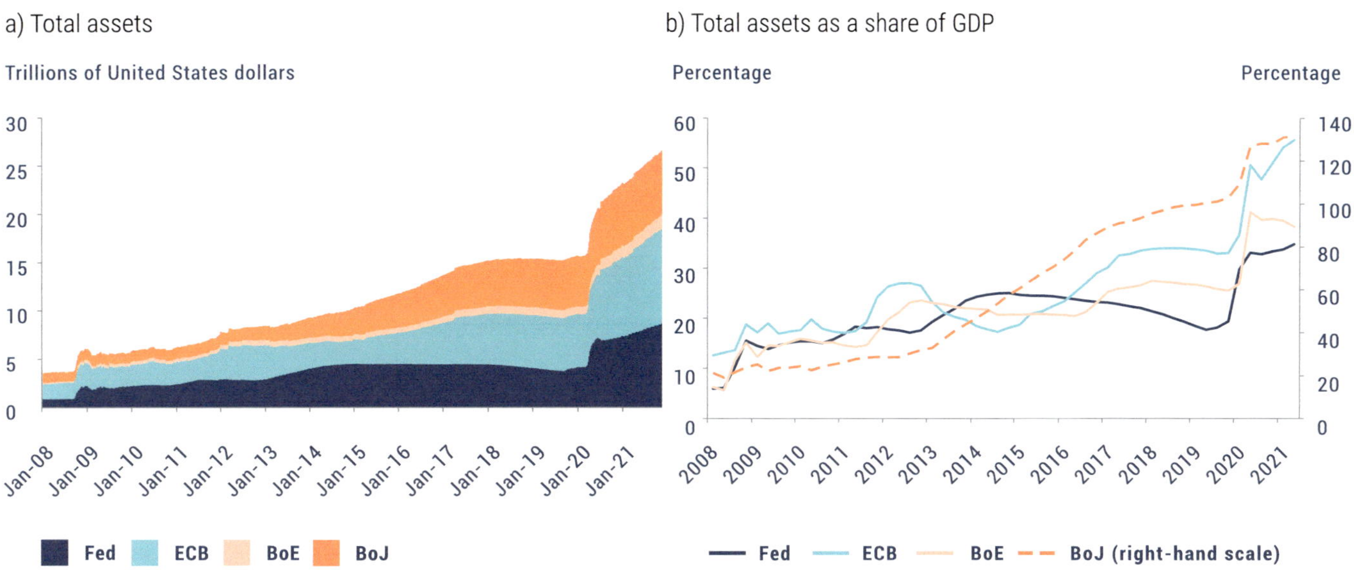

Sources: UN DESA, based on data from the Federal Reserve (Fed), the European Central Bank (ECB), the Bank of England (BoE), and the Bank of Japan (BoJ) (all accessed on 17 November 2021) and CEIC (accessed on 2 November 2021).
Note: For panel a, euro, yen and sterling values were converted into United States dollars by using constant exchange rates from August 2021. In panel b, the figure shows the total assets at the end of the quarter as a share of quarterly GDP (seasonally adjusted, annualized, current prices).

Asset purchase programmes in developing countries: a paradigm shift in monetary policy?

Many developing country central banks implemented APPs for the first time

The pandemic has marked a turning point for monetary policy in developing countries. Many central banks introduced APPs for the first time as they experienced rapidly deteriorating financial conditions, large capital outflows and rising government financing costs. Over the course of 2020, 27 central banks – 10 in Africa, 9 in Asia and 8 in Latin America and the Caribbean – announced or implemented APPs.

While these programmes have been broadly modelled after those in developed economies, there are important differences in scope and purpose. Unlike central banks in developed countries, those in most developing countries still had room to cut policy rates when launching APPs. The measures were mainly introduced in response to market turmoil in the early stages of the pandemic, when investor panic, rising risk premiums and substantial capital outflows triggered a free fall in bond prices and a consequent sharp increase in yields as well as currency depreciation. These APPs mainly aimed to boost market confidence and reduce market dysfunctionality. Several central banks explicitly mentioned the need to reduce the costs of COVID-19 (such as Angola, Bolivia, Cabo Verde and Rwanda). Others used APPs to support fiscal needs (Ghana, Indonesia and Mauritius) (Fratto and others, 2021).

Developing countries' APPs have been smaller and shorter in duration

Overall, developing countries' APPs have been much smaller in scale and shorter in duration than those in developed countries.[14] The size of most APPs in developing countries ranged from just above $300 million to around $30 billion, accounting for 0.3 per cent to 6 per cent of GDP.[15] A few developing country central banks conducted one-off purchases at various times between March and May 2020. By the second quarter of 2021, the Reserve Bank of India was the only major developing country central bank continuing with significant asset purchases (BIS, 2021a). While most developing country central banks have focused on purchasing public securities denominated in local currencies, several have also purchased private securities, bank bonds or even equities. The majority have conducted asset purchases in secondary markets but a few also resorted to purchasing bonds directly from governments, reflecting their intention to support fiscal needs (Fratto and others, 2021).

Have asset purchase programmes met their objectives?

Stabilizing markets during financial turmoil

APPs have been effective in addressing financial distress...

Central banks' large-scale APPs have become an important monetary policy tool to address financial distress in a crisis. During both the global financial crisis and the COVID-19 pandemic, the programmes helped to stabilize markets by providing liquidity, easing financial conditions and reducing uncertainty. Through the large-scale purchase of securities, central banks quickly injected sufficient liquidity in distressed markets, reducing risk premiums and facilitating arbitrage across asset classes. A fast and ambitious response helped avoid fire sales and destabilizing price spirals that could spur the collapse of financial systems (Schnabel, 2021).

The response to the global financial crisis demonstrated that asset purchases are particularly effective in filling liquidity gaps and stabilizing markets under certain conditions. First, when the balance sheets of market participants are weak, resulting in liquidity disruptions and widening bid-ask spreads, central bank purchases have a larger effect on prices. Second, APPs need to be very large and announced quickly. When markets are crumbling and uncertainty is soaring, central banks have no time to be modest and slow.[16] Third, assets should be bought flexibly, allowing for targeted interventions as conditions in various market segments change over time. In the emergency phase, central banks should purchase securities from the most distressed segments of financial markets.

14 A lack of deep and liquid capital markets in developing countries means that APPs are not always a viable policy option.

15 By comparison, net purchases in the Federal Reserve's latest quantitative easing programme amounted to about 20 per cent of GDP in the United States during March 2020 and October 2021.

16 For instance, the significant size of the Federal Reserve's initial programme in 2008-2009, where total asset purchases accounted for about 10 per cent of annual GDP, and the quick absorption of provided liquidity staunched increasing panic on financial markets.

...due to central banks' swift and bold actions

During the COVID-19 pandemic, developed country central banks generally followed these principles, drawing on lessons from the global financial crisis. In March 2020, financial markets across the world were in turmoil as key funding markets experienced severe dislocations. The market for United States Treasury securities, considered one of the world's safest assets, saw a sharp sell-off as panicked investors rushed to exchange them for cash (Schrimpf and others, 2020). In the European Union, liquidity dried up even in traditionally deep markets such as the German Bund market. Corporate bond spreads soared and stock prices plummeted.

In the face of acute financial stress, the major developed country central banks acted swiftly and boldly, announcing large programmes and buying more and different ranges of assets than during earlier APPs. The Federal Reserve made its purchases of Treasury and mortgage-backed securities open-ended. It also shed its unwillingness to purchase corporate bonds and joined the ECB, the Bank of England and the Bank of Japan in buying investment grade and later even lower-grade corporate bonds (Cantú and others, 2021). In Europe, the newly announced PEPP allowed flexible purchases based on markets and jurisdictions, which helped to break the cycle of worsening financial conditions and reduce market panic. Following the announcement of the PEPP and the European Union recovery fund, sovereign yield spreads in the euro area declined notably (figure II.3). At the same time, money market rates realigned with the ECB policy rate. The purchases quickly restored market functioning, safeguarding the transmission of monetary policy (Schnabel, 2021) (see box II.2).

Figure II.3

Euro area GDP-weighted sovereign yields and ICE swap rates

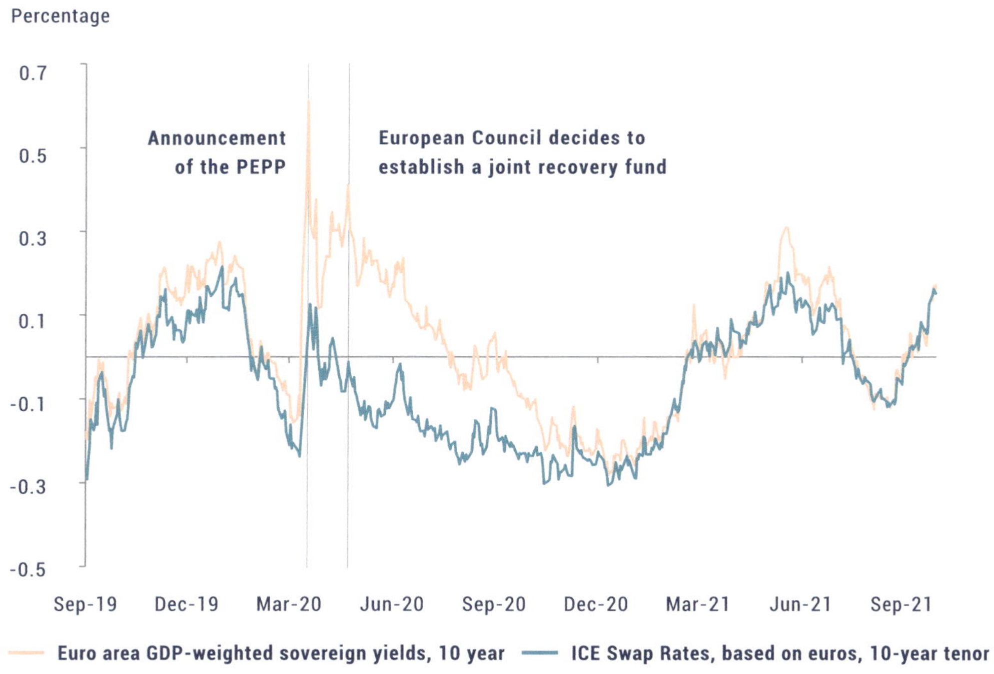

Sources: UN DESA, based on data from the ECB and Federal Reserve Bank of St. Louis (accessed on 11 November 2021).

Note: The ICE Swap Rate is the principal global benchmark for swap rates and spreads for interest rate swaps; it is a proxy for a risk-free rate. The PEPP is the ECB's Pandemic Emergency Purchase Programme.

APPs in developing countries reduced bond yields without weakening currencies

New APPs by developing countries also promoted financial stability during the emergency phase of COVID-19 (Fratto and others, 2021; Sever and others, 2020). It is difficult to disentangle the effects of APPs from those of other monetary policy interventions and from spillovers from accommodative macroeconomic policies in developed countries. Preliminary evidence, however, shows that APPs in developing countries have had some positive impacts as they reduced bond yields and boosted equity prices during periods of market illiquidity. The IMF (2020) estimates that the size of the impact of domestic APP announcements on local currency sovereign bond yields ranged from 20 to 60 basis points. In addition, decisive actions by developed and emerging market authorities may have supported investor confidence, helping to reverse panic selling and capital outflows. At the same time, APPs did not lead to a significant depreciation of currencies in developing countries.[17]

Benefits of APPs during the crisis phase should not mask potential risks

These positive experiences may motivate more central banks in developing countries to consider APPs as an additional monetary policy tool, especially if conventional policy space becomes limited. The recent successful experience with the programmes, however, may overstate their future effectiveness. This is because they were implemented simultaneously with uniquely accommodative macroeconomic easing in developed countries. Further, the financial markets did not anticipate these bold and timely measures. The element of surprise potentially maximized the impact of APPs, preventing asset fire sales and restoring market confidence. APPs in fact may only be suitable for developing countries under certain preconditions, such as stable economic fundamentals, credible monetary policy frameworks and good governance. Without these in place, APPs can carry substantial risks, contributing to higher inflation, increasing depreciation pressures and raising risk premiums while potentially undermining central bank credibility (Hofman and Kamber, 2020).

Box II.2

Backstopping sovereign bond markets via quantitative easing – the special case of the euro area

In the European Economic and Monetary Union (EMU), monetary policy is conducted centrally for all member States by the ECB, even though national governments continue to retain and exercise fiscal sovereignty and issue debt denominated in their common currency, the euro. This institutional set-up suggests an implicit responsibility for the ECB to guarantee the sovereign debt of individual member countries, which makes it difficult to pursue and achieve the primary goal of price stability in the euro area.

When financial turmoil due to the COVID-19 pandemic hit the EMU in March 2020, the resulting downturn affected member States asymmetrically. The effects were especially pronounced in some Southern European countries: Interest rate spreads between German and Italian sovereign bonds, for instance, doubled from 140 basis points to 280 basis points in less than a month. This difference in sovereign financing costs was in part due to varying perceptions of fiscal space in these two countries

17 This is likely due to the moderate size of the programmes and the fact that purchases were sterilized in many cases, with central banks intervening to offset the effect on exchange rates.

(Schnabel, 2021) and their potentially different ability to service existing debt during an economic crisis.

While the ECB initially refused to address rising sovereign yield spreads, worsening financial conditions prompted a public commitment from the ECB President to directly target sovereign spreads with backstop support for all European sovereign bonds. Preliminary evidence suggests that this announcement contributed to shrinking sovereign bond spreads and rebounding stock prices even more than the ECB's actual purchases of sovereign bonds during the immediate crisis phase (Corradin and others, 2021; Delatte and Guillaume, 2020). Similarly, during the European sovereign debt crisis of 2010-2013, when government bond yields spiked, the announcement of theoretically unlimited purchase programmes lowered the spreads of the sovereign bonds of distressed countries without programmes ever being activated (Acharya and others, 2019).

Compared to the large spreads during the European sovereign debt crisis, such as between German and Greek bunds, the divergence in March-April 2020 was relatively contained. Spreads followed a steady downward trend after the initial jump (Ortmans and Tripier, 2021). The difference between the two episodes may be explained by the prompt monetary and fiscal policy response to COVID-19 as well as significant EMU reform since the last crisis (Baldwin and others, 2015). Nonetheless, the sharp spike in sovereign yield spreads in early 2020 showed that not all member States have public debt with a safe asset status at all times. Without the ECB's public and explicit commitment, borrowing costs would remain higher for some countries, rendering them more vulnerable to external shocks and affecting financial stability in the entire EMU. As a sustainable solution, debt mutualization via European Commission bond issuance has been proposed (Brunnermeier and others, 2016) although several member States remain strongly opposed to it. In July 2021, member States agreed to pool debt obligations of up to 750 billion euros to finance a newly created recovery fund.

Author: Lea Steininger, Vienna University of Economics and Business

Fostering economic recovery

APPs have lowered long-term borrowing costs...

Once the initial objective of stabilizing financial markets is achieved, APPs are expected to foster economic recovery in the short run. Empirical evidence from the global financial crisis suggests that APPs have generally been effective in reducing long-term borrowing costs, which can be a necessary but not sufficient condition for economic recovery. Several studies of the euro area, the United Kingdom and the United States indicate that announcements of large-scale APPs were associated with significant reductions in the yields of government bonds and other assets (Gagnon, 2016; Krishnamurthy and Vissing-Jorgensen, 2011; Andrade and others, 2016; Christensen and Rudebusch, 2012). This translated to lower borrowing costs for the private sector.[18]

Several factors determine the effectiveness of asset purchases in reducing bond yields. First, the impact is stronger when there are no entrenched deflationary pressures. If the yield curve is already

18 Gilchrist and others (2015), for example, find that the efficacy of unconventional policy in lowering real borrowing costs has been comparable to that of conventional policy.

relatively flat, asset purchases can barely reduce yields further. Second, a credible commitment by the central bank to provide sustained monetary accommodation leads to a stronger effect on bond yields.[19] When markets tend to believe that a central bank will not unwind asset purchases on a whim, lower bond yields can translate to lower borrowing costs for the economy as a whole especially during the early phase of recovery. And third, targeting a variety of long-maturity assets can lead to a more broad-based decline in borrowing costs. For example, the expansion of the ECB's APP in 2015 at a time of relative financial calm lowered long-term euro area sovereign bond yields by about 30-50 basis points within a day after the announcement. It also reduced the spreads of non-targeted corporate bonds by about 20 basis points compared to risk-free rates.

...helping to kickstart economic recovery

Record-low long-term borrowing costs have supported economic recovery at least in the initial stage. For instance, the economy of the United States was out of recession by the end of 2009, after the first round of quantitative easing was introduced in November 2008. Research estimates that the programme boosted economic output in the United States by 1-3 per cent (Kim, Laubach and Wei, 2020). Preliminary evidence suggests that pandemic-related APPs have also helped kickstart economic recovery, allowing the major developed countries to emerge quickly from recession. A study by Feldkircher and others (2021) finds that in the United States, APP-related monetary expansion stimulated economic activity during the early stages of the crisis mainly through a rise in stock market returns and an easing of financial conditions. Investment growth responded positively right after stimulus measures were introduced. Gross fixed capital formation in the euro area, the United Kingdom and the United States expanded strongly in the third quarter of 2020 after contracting in the previous two to three quarters. At the same time, consumption of durable goods recovered quickly in the second half of 2020, especially in the United States.

Providing longer-term support to economic growth

APPs become less effective after the early recovery phase

While there is broad-based consensus that APPs are an effective policy tool during periods of financial distress and can also help to initiate economic recovery, the benefits of sustained use are less clear. When normal market functioning is restored and the economy is recovering, the macroeconomic effects, including through liquidity provision and portfolio rebalancing, will likely become less important. Once long-term yields are at very low levels, new purchases do not provide significant additional stimulus (see, for example, Gern and others, 2015; United Kingdom, House of Lords, 2021). In addition, transmission channels to the real economy can be hampered by several structural factors, such as the underpricing or mispricing of risks, adverse incentives for banks to lend to the real sector and asymmetric wealth effects from rising asset prices sustained by APPs.

19 For example, the unconventional monetary policy measures adopted by the Bank of Japan between 2010 and 2012 had only a limited impact. Stronger effects were associated with measures adopted in 2013 when the Government provided political backing for the Bank of Japan to pursue an aggressive monetary stimulus (Dell' Ariccia and others, 2018).

The slow economic recovery from the global financial crisis in terms of both output and employment suggests that the effectiveness of central bank asset purchases may dissipate quickly beyond the crisis and early recovery phase. It may also point to the limitations of sustained monetary expansion without supportive fiscal policies. Although monetary policies remained exceptionally accommodative after the global financial crisis, investment failed to pick up significantly. In the euro area and United Kingdom, for example, investment in equipment and machinery grew much more slowly from 2010 to 2019 than from 1998 to 2007 (figure II.4).

Figure II.4

Annual growth in non-residential fixed investment in equipment and machinery

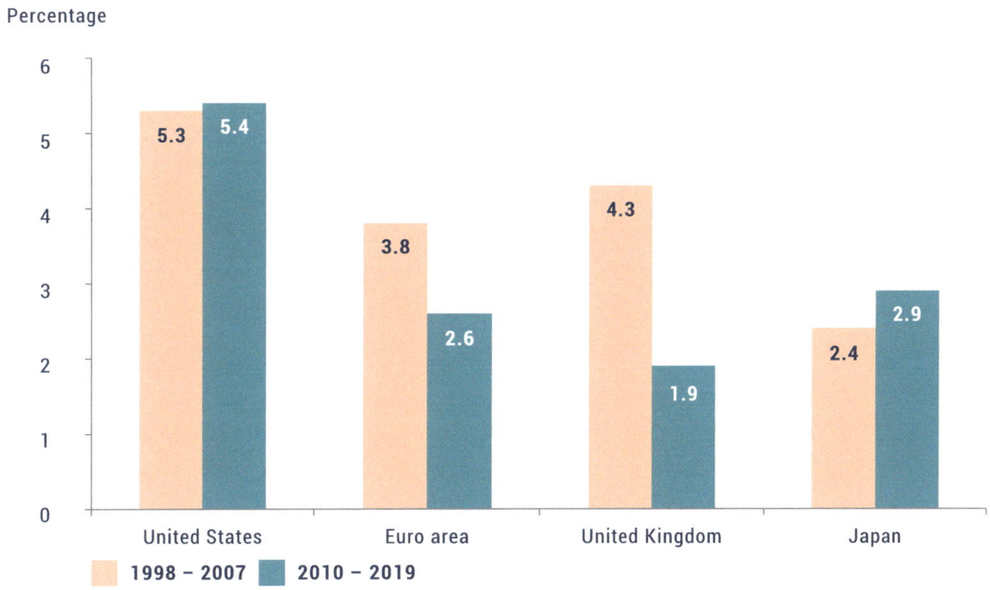

Sources: UN DESA, based on data from CEIC, Eurostat and Federal Reserve Economic Data (FRED).
Note: Growth rates are calculated by taking geometric means of investment (in constant prices) during the reference periods. Data on the United States include only private investment.

Cheap liquidity has often not stimulated bank lending to the real economy...

A persistently weak bank lending channel partly explains why large-scale asset purchases did not necessarily boost private investment in major developed economies. Evidence on asset purchases after the global financial crisis indicates that commercial banks responded in part by shifting their portfolios into assets with low-risk weights rather than lending to the real economy. They did this to minimize the requirements of regulatory capital. Fatouh and others (2019), for example, find that banks in the United Kingdom that received reserve injections through the Bank of England's APP in 2009-2012 engaged in carry trade strategies towards bonds from other European Union sovereigns, such as Greece, Italy, Ireland, Portugal and Spain.[20] In the euro area, Horst and Neyer (2019) find that

20 For the United States, Rodnyansky and Darmouni (2015) did not find any impact on bank lending when asset purchases targeted treasuries in the second phase of quantitative easing after the global financial crisis. When mortgage-backed securities were targeted, as in the first and third phases of quantitative easing, there was a positive effect on lending.

increasing excess reserves can have no or even a contractionary impact on the supply of bank credits because banks may face rising marginal costs from holding deposits due to regulatory issues.

Preliminary evidence from the United States during the COVID-19 crisis also suggests APPs play a limited role in enhanced bank lending. Bank lending in 2020 was hampered by financial constraints at the firm level rather than the bank-level constraints observed in 2008. Many banks in the United States entered the pandemic in strong financial positions, well capitalized and with ample liquidity. Since APPs can mainly relax financial constraints at the bank level rather than at the firm level, the programmes have likely been less effective (Sims and Wu, 2020). Similarly, since bank reserves were much larger in 2020 than in 2008, the direct effect of a further increase in reserves on the liquidity premium is smaller, reducing the overall effectiveness of APPs (Occhino, 2020).

...while encouraging the creation of "zombie firms" with low productivity

Abundant liquidity, ultralow interest rates and reduced financial pressure have also led to a rise in so-called "zombie companies", defined as firms that are unable to cover debt-servicing costs from current revenue over an extended period. Banerjee and Hofmann (2018) find that such companies deleveraged at a slower pace after the global financial crisis. On the one hand, weak banks allowed them to roll over loans rather than writing them off. On the other hand, low interest rates raised incentives for assuming excessive risks or taking bank loans for low-productivity investments that would have been deemed infeasible with higher interest rates. The greater share of zombie companies is likely to have weighed on aggregate productivity not only because these firms are less productive than others but also because they may crowd out investment and employment in healthy firms (Caballero and others, 2008; Adalet McGowan and others, 2017).

Firms use additional liquidity for stock buy-backs rather than productive activities

An additional factor holding back investment is a massive increase in stock buy-backs. While in many countries, including China, Japan, France and the United Kingdom, the volume of stock repurchases has risen considerably since the global financial crisis, the trend has been most pronounced in the United States (Aramonte, 2020). Amid persistently low interest rates and large tax cuts in 2017, share buy-backs reached a record level prior to the COVID-19 crisis (figure II.5). After a pause in the early stages of the pandemic, firms resumed these. In the second quarter of 2021, buy-backs among companies listed on the Standard and Poor's (S&P) 500 index totalled $199 billion, equivalent to about 3.5 per cent of the GDP of the United States. This marked an increase of 124.3 per cent from the second quarter of 2020 and was only 11 per cent below the all-time high of $223 billion in the fourth quarter of 2018. Buy-backs have increasingly been debt financed, contributing to a faster rise in corporate leverage and increasing financial fragility. In 2019, about a quarter of firms bought back stocks by issuing new debt, compared to only 4 per cent of companies in 2007. While pushing up stock prices, large-scale buy-backs may negatively affect capital accumulation and reduce firms' abilities to cope with an economic downturn, especially if they are funded with new debt. Moreover, increases in stock prices often just benefit senior corporate executives and major shareholders while depressing investments in productive capital.

Figure II.5
Stock buy-backs in the United States and the financing tools of firms that bought back stock

a) Stock buy-backs, market value

Billions of United States dollars

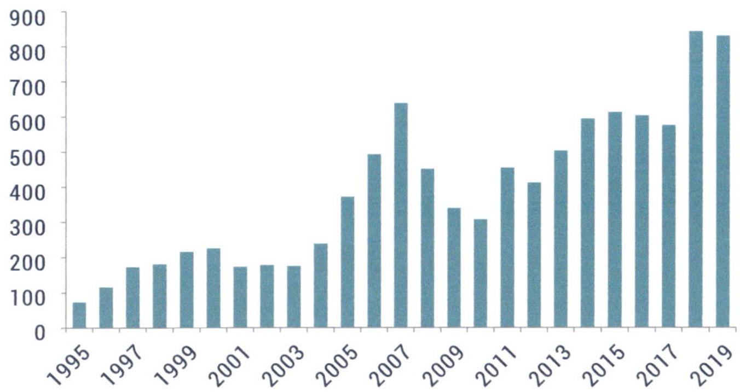

b) Financing tools of firms that bought back stock

Percentage

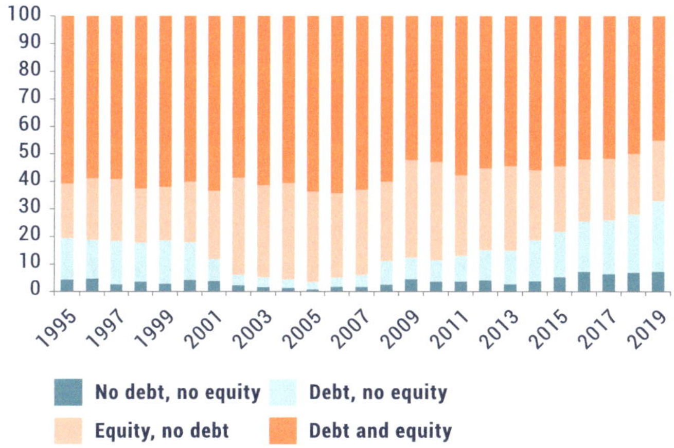

Source: Aramonte, 2020.

Prolonged implementation of APPs could be self-defeating

Prolonged implementation of APPs will likely reduce their effectiveness. First, the signalling effect gradually weakens as recovery progresses and market participants adjust their expectations. Evidence suggests that late-stage programmes shift expectations less than earlier programmes (Yu, 2016). Second, low long-term yields could convey a negative signal about economic prospects, undermining consumer and investor confidence. Third, wealth effects may not boost private consumption significantly since wealthy households with very low marginal propensity to consume primarily benefit from rapidly rising asset prices. As a result, rising wealth is unlikely to translate into significantly stronger aggregate demand. Separately, persistent low rates due to APPs may impair bank profitability and negatively affect credit supply as net interest margins become compressed (Hesse and others, 2018).

Side effects and risks of large-scale asset purchase programmes

APPs adversely affect wealth distribution and may increase macrofinancial risks

Large-scale APPs have played an important role in stabilizing financial markets and reviving economies following the COVID-19 shock. A prolonged period of ultraloose monetary policies has also created macroeconomic and financial vulnerabilities, however. If not managed well these could undermine global recovery. By continuously providing an immense volume of liquidity through asset purchases, central banks risk feeding inflationary pressures while further encouraging search-for-yield and speculative behaviour among investors. This is due to the underpricing of risk, which aggravates the misallocation of capital and increases financial stability risks. At the same time, concerns have been growing over the distributional effects of APPs as rising asset prices disproportionately benefit wealthy households.

Macroeconomic effects

Inflationary concerns

When major developed country central banks began large-scale asset purchases after the global financial crisis, there was widespread concern that the expansion of balance sheets and resulting increase in the monetary base would trigger higher inflation and potentially de-anchor inflation expectations.[21] Figure II.6 illustrates how the monetary bases in Japan, the United Kingdom, the United States and the euro area have increased since 2008 (including a jump since March 2020). Massive expansion of the monetary base, however, has not led to higher inflation in these economies. On the contrary, headline inflation has generally remained low, frequently falling short of central banks' 2 per cent target rate. In the decade after the crisis, consumer price inflation averaged 2.3 per cent in the United Kingdom, 1.6 per cent in the United States, 1.3 per cent in the euro area and 0.3 per cent in Japan.[22]

Concerns about higher inflation after the global financial crisis proved unfounded...

An evaluation of APPs launched in response to the global financial crisis suggests that the impact on inflation has been very limited past the medium term. For instance, based on options data for the United States, Reis (2016) shows that while early rounds of quantitative easing had a sizeable effect on expected inflation, further rounds had little or no effect. Similarly, euro area evidence indicates that APPs put upward pressure on inflation only during the first two years (Gambetti and Musso, 2017; Clemens and others, 2017) and that APP announcements raised inflation expectations only modestly by 20 to 30 basis points (Rieth and Gehrt, 2016).

21 When purchasing long-term securities from financial institutions, central banks create new bank reserves, thus expanding the monetary base (i.e., the sum of currency in circulation and bank reserves).

22 Core inflation, excluding volatile food and energy prices, was even lower.

Figure II.6

Base money in selected major developed economies

Index, January 2008 = 100

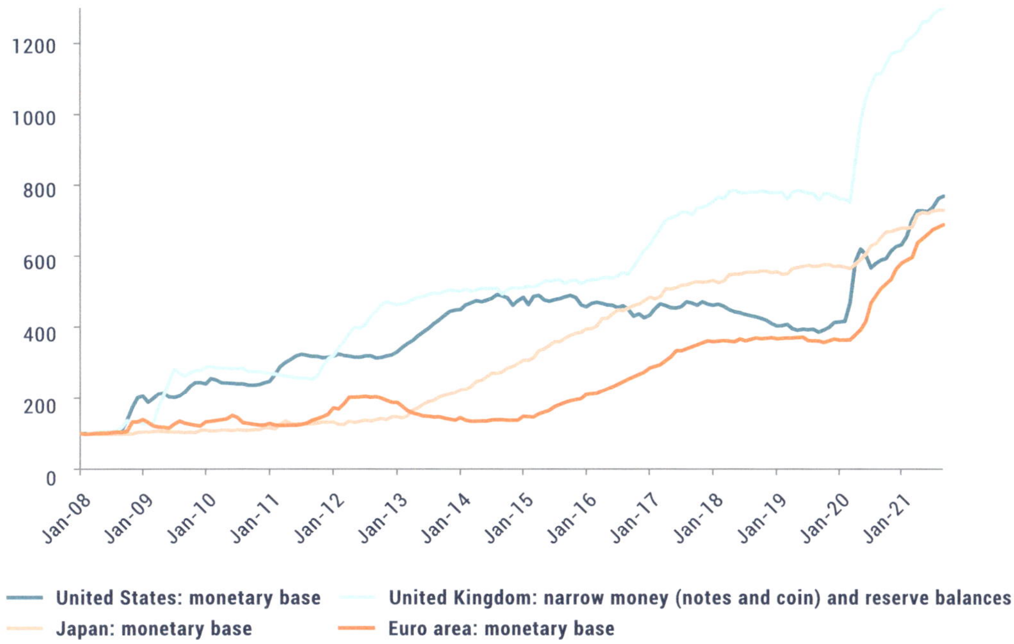

Sources: UN DESA, based on data from the Federal Reserve Bank of St. Louis, Bank of England, Bank of Japan and ECB (accessed on 30 October 2021).

Why has the rapid expansion of the monetary base not led to significantly higher inflation? The main reason is that after the initial crisis phase, most of the additional liquidity created by central banks did not reach the real economy. In fact, the global financial crisis weakened financial intermediation with consequences felt beyond the immediate crisis phase. Rather than increasing credit flows to households and firms, banks and other financial institutions used additional liquidity to shore up their balance sheets (figure II.7a). For their part, financially stressed households and firms were often reluctant to borrow or invest. In the United States, for instance, growth of total bank credit in the 10 years after the crisis was weaker than during the decade before the crisis (figure II.7b). Similar trends were observed in the United Kingdom and the euro area.[23]

...but monetary conditions today are very different

Monetary conditions today, however, differ considerably from those after the global financial crisis. Inflation risks are now emerging as a concern in many developed economies. Unlike during the global financial crisis, economies have faced both demand-side and supply-side shocks during the pandemic. While the demand-side shocks dissipated by the third quarter of 2020, the supply-side shocks persist in the major developed economies. The rapid increases in headline inflation over the past year are primarily due to quickly recovering demand amid strongly supportive fiscal policies and across-the-board supply-side disruptions, including massive dislocation in labour markets. Consumer demand in

23 From a monetary perspective, the rapid increase in the monetary base was offset by declines in the money multiplier and the money velocity.

the United States and the euro area recovered much faster than supply. Unfortunately, central banks do not have specific tools at their disposal to address supply-side bottlenecks such as labour gaps, shortages of products such as semiconductors, or other supply-chain disruptions impeding the flow of goods and services and increasing inflationary pressure.

Notwithstanding prevailing supply-side constraints, APPs may indirectly exacerbate supply-side pressures and contribute to inflationary pressures if bank lending channels remain weak in the near term and firms face constraints in increasing investments and boosting productive capacity, as discussed above. To ease supply-side bottlenecks and inflationary pressures, it will remain critical for central banks in the developed economies to ensure that banks extend credit to the real sectors of the economy and do not just finance stock buy-backs or financial speculation.

Figure II.7

Reserves of depository institutions and growth of total loans in the United States

a) Reserves of depository institutions

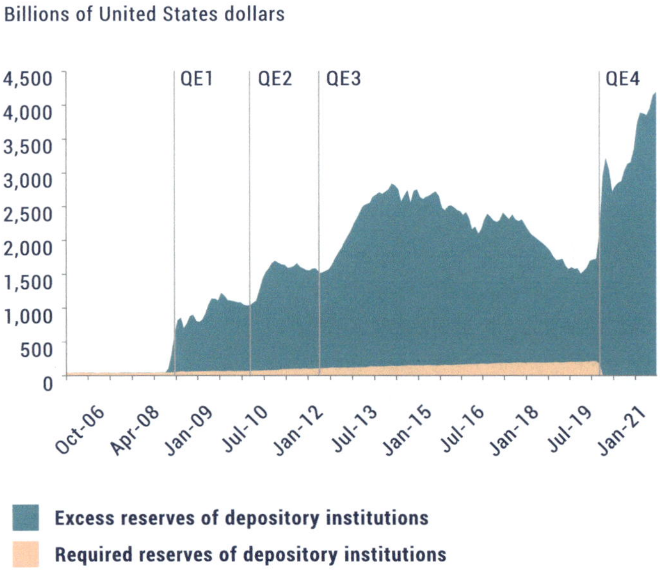

Source: UN DESA, based on data from the Federal Reserve Bank of St. Louis (accessed on 30 October 2021).
Note: QE1 to QE4 are the Federal Reserve's quantitative easing programmes.

b) Growth of total loans

Source: UN DESA, based on data from CEIC (accessed on 30 October 2021).

Asset prices and financial instability

APPs have fuelled asset price inflation

While asset prices are affected by many factors other than monetary policy, the additional liquidity from large-scale APPs has fuelled asset price inflation in virtually every asset class. The most immediate impact has been on bond prices. Over 2020, the average price of the S&P Global Developed Sovereign Bond Index increased by 12 per cent compared to about 2 per cent per year from 2015 to 2019.[24] Prices of corporate bonds have also experienced sharp increases. After a dip in March 2020, the returns rebounded quickly, growing by 12 per cent in the United States and 5 per cent in the euro area (figure II.8b).[25]

Equity prices have soared during the pandemic...

As investors rebalance their portfolios and search for higher risk-adjusted returns, prices of other asset classes have increased as well. Stocks have recorded especially large gains in the United States. In the 10 years after the first round of quantitative easing implemented by the Federal Reserve in response to the global financial crisis, the S&P 500 and the NASDAQ Composite Index rose by over 200 per cent and nearly 380 per cent, respectively. By comparison, both indices had not recorded gains in the 10 years before that point despite some fluctuations (figure II.8a). Since the Federal Reserve announced its latest APP in March 2020 to combat the COVID-19 crisis, the S&P 500 has surged by 75 per cent while the NASDAQ Composite Index has doubled (figure II.8b). Equity prices have also moved higher elsewhere albeit less strongly than in the United States. In the European Union, for example, the Dow Jones Euro Stoxx Index recovered quickly from the pandemic, rising by almost 70 per cent during March 2020 and November 2021 (figures II.8a and II.8b).[26]

...along with prices of real estate, bonds and other assets

Ultraloose monetary policies have driven down mortgage rates and pushed up real estate prices since the global financial crisis and particularly since the onset of the pandemic. Globally, residential property prices adjusted for inflation were 6 per cent higher in the first quarter of 2021 than in 2019. Again, price increases have been particularly strong in the United States, where the Case-Shiller Home Price Index rose by a staggering 23 per cent between March 2020 and July 2021 (figure II.8b). Historically low interest rates have also boosted the prices of other financial products, such as high-yield bonds, and prompted increased speculative activities in meme stocks and cryptocurrencies. The price of the S&P 500 High-Yield Corporate Bond Index increased by 38 per cent from March 2020 to October 2021; the price of Bitcoin, the dominant cryptocurrency, soared by nearly 80 per cent during the same period.

24 Based on the S&P Global Developed Sovereign Bond Index (accessed on 29 October 2021).
25 As of September 2021.
26 Unlike the major United States stock market indices, the Dow Jones Euro Stoxx remains lower than it was before the global financial crisis and the dot-com bubble.

Figure II.8

Asset valuation changes and asset composition in the United States and Europe

(a) Asset valuation changes since October 1998

UNITED STATES

Index, October 1998 = 100

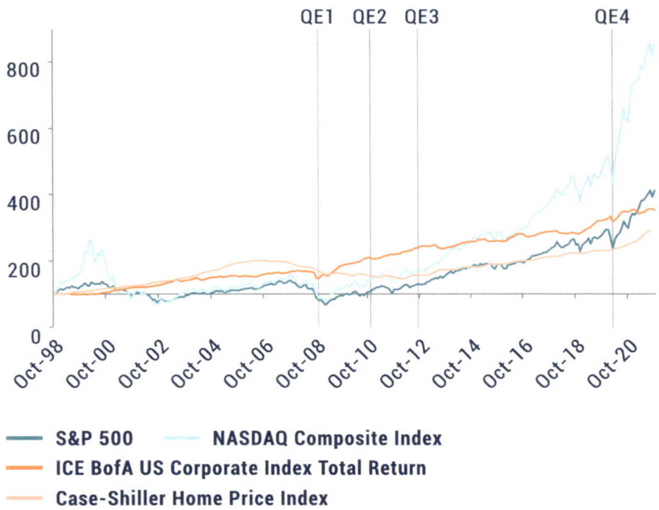

EUROPE

Index, October 1998 = 100

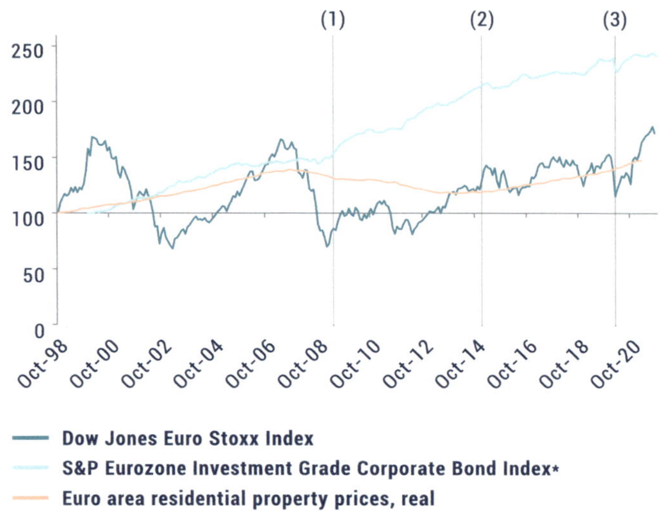

(b) Asset valuation changes during the COVID-19 pandemic

UNITED STATES

Index, 1 March 2020 = 100

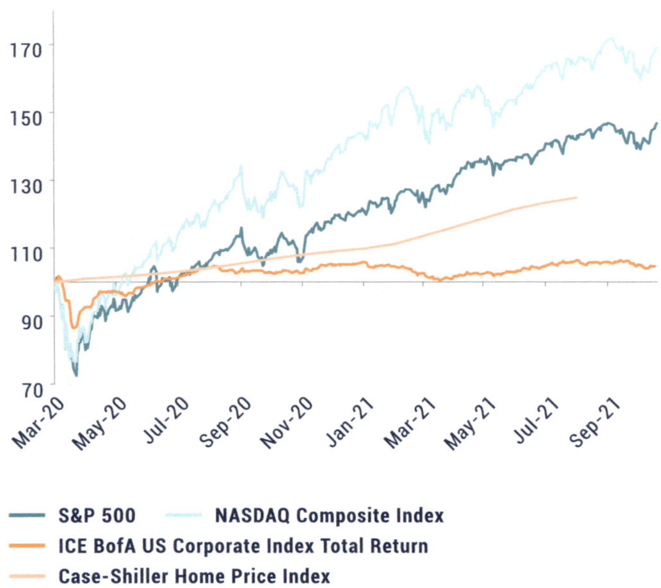

EUROPE

Index, 1 March 2020 = 100

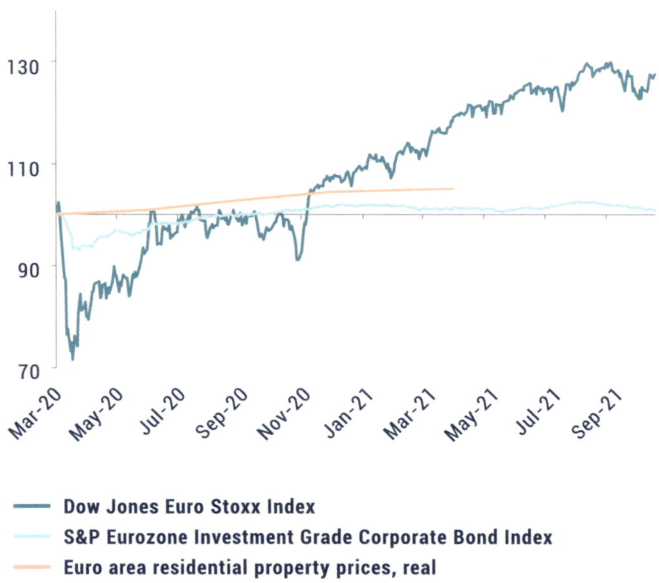

Sources: Bank for International Settlements (accessed on 19 October 2021), Federal Reserve Bank of St. Louis (accessed on 11 November 2021), Investing.com (accessed on 20 October 2021) and S&P Global (accessed on 29 October 2021).

Notes: S&P = Standard and Poor's. BofA = Bank of America. Panel a, right figure: (1) The ECB engaged in the large-scale purchase of covered bonds in May 2009; (2) the ECB announced an expanded APP in January 2015; (3) the ECB announced its PEPP in March 2020. *The S&P Eurozone Investment Grade Corporate Bond Index starts from December 1999 and is thus indexed by using December 1999 = 100. QE1 to QE4 are the Federal Reserve's quantitative easing programmes.

Asset bubbles may burst due to abrupt monetary policy shifts

The valuations of different financial assets, especially equities, appear increasingly detached from underlying fundamentals. In the United States, for instance, the cyclically adjusted price earnings (CAPE) ratio, which measures the relative price of equities by comparing their current price to the average 10-year earnings, has risen by over 50 per cent since April 2020, more than after any other recession in the past 120 years.[27] As a result, equity markets in the United States have rarely seemed more overvalued than they are now, with CAPE ratios approaching levels only seen prior to the bursting of the dot-com bubble in 2001.[28]

This has spurred fears of ever-expanding asset price bubbles as the disconnect between financial markets and economic fundamentals continues to widen. Table II.1 shows that while investment in developed economies bounced back after the collapse in the second quarter of 2020, the upward momentum slowed significantly in the first half of 2021. Despite some recovery in investment during the second half of 2020, global economic conditions are currently characterized by persistent supply-side bottlenecks that have been feeding inflationary pressures. It is likely that supply-side bottlenecks will persist, in the United States and other economies, at least until the first quarter of 2022. If monetary conditions shift abruptly, with the Federal Reserve quickly tapering asset purchases and raising policy rates, asset price bubbles may burst. Sharp market corrections could trigger a rising number of bankruptcies and cause substantial macroeconomic damages, with adverse global spillover effects.

Table II.1

Changes in quarterly gross fixed capital formation

Percentage

	2019 Q3	2019 Q4	2020 Q1	2020 Q2	2020 Q3	2020 Q4	2021 Q1	2021 Q2
Euro Area	0.4	-0.5	-4.3	-12.3	14.8	2	0.8	0.7
United Kingdom	1.3	-1.6	-1.2	-20.7	19	4.4	-1.8	-0.5
United States	0.7	0	-0.1	-7.2	5.2	3.7	2.3	0.5
Japan	0.9	-3.1	0.2	-3.2	-2	2.9	-0.9	1.4

Sources: CEIC and OECD (accessed on 29 October 2021).

Note: Data are quarter-on-quarter growth rates of gross fixed capital formation (constant prices, seasonally adjusted). Euro area data exclude Cyprus, Ireland and Malta.

Financial stability concerns are compounded by the higher risk exposure of investors as APPs have pushed market participants towards higher-yielding assets. As a result, portfolios have become more sensitive to interest rate changes and market volatility. Excessive risk-taking may accelerate any negative shock, leading to broader financial instability. Since leverage on corporate balance sheets was

27 Data on the CAPE ratio for the United States are provided by Robert Shiller.
28 Stock market valuations in other large economies are generally not as high as in the United States but in some cases still appear stretched in view of subdued economic prospects.

already at an all-time high before the pandemic, the latest round of APPs may have further aggravated financial stability risks.[29]

APPs affect the composition of global liquidity and climate risks

In addition to inflating asset prices, APPs can undermine financial stability in other ways (Caldentey, 2017). While base money expansions did not translate into more money circulating in the economy at large, asset purchases have had an indirect impact on the composition of global liquidity. Through the portfolio balancing effect, they have altered the relative profitability of investing in various asset classes, strengthening the international bond market. Rapidly growing bond markets have facilitated additional debt issuances and the build-up of the asset management industry, which in 2020 controlled about $103 trillion of assets globally, up by 11 per cent from 2019 (Heredia and others, 2021). The high level of concentration, interconnectedness and procyclicality of the asset management industry poses substantial risks to financial stability (Caldentey, 2017). Moreover, central banks' purchase operations and portfolio holdings have climate implications that may trigger physical and financial risks given market failure and externalities (box II.3).

Box II.3

Greening asset purchase programmes to mitigate climate risks

Asset purchases by central banks are not necessarily market neutral. When central banks purchase bonds, they tend to give greater weight to sectors with a higher share of carbon emissions. This is because highly carbon-intensive firms are overrepresented in the bond market as they can easily use their large holdings of fixed assets as collateral for issuing bonds (Papoutsi and others, 2021) (figure II.3.a). For instance, the ECB has exhibited a tendency to purchase bonds in carbon-intensive sectors like utilities and transportation (Barker, 2015; Matikainen and others, 2017). As of July 2020, carbon-intensive sectors comprised 62.7 per cent of the value of outstanding corporate bonds held by the ECB (Dafermos and others, 2020a). Likewise, 57 per cent of the value of all bonds in the Bank of England's Corporate Bond Purchase Scheme was from carbon-intensive sectors as of June 2020 (Dafermos and others, 2020b).

29 The adverse effect of asset purchases on bank profitability has also been seen as a potential financial stability risk but so far these concerns appear largely unfounded.

Figure II.3.a

Sector shares of the market portfolio, ECB holdings and emissions

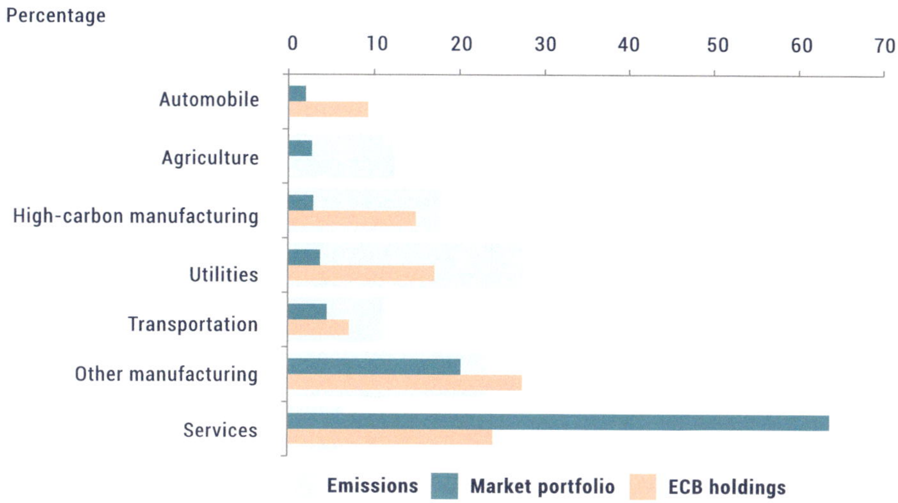

Source: Papoutsi, Piazzesi and Schneider, 2021.

The carbon bias of APPs has had undesirable side effects. When central banks purchase bonds irrespective of their ecological footprint, they provide an implicit subsidy to fossil fuels and other high-emissions industries, encouraging investment in these sectors. Climate change, in turn, poses different risks to the stability of the financial system, including physical, liability and transition risks.

Tackling climate change requires a "whole-of-government" approach. While central banks may not be at the very centre of climate policies, as public institutions, they play an important role in promoting the transition to a low-carbon economy. Monetary policies should do more to address climate-related risks and provide necessary incentives to green the financial system. Central banks have taken some action by forming the Network for Greening the Financial System, with a membership of 100 central banks and financial regulators as of November 2021. Its primary objectives include integrating sustainability into central bank portfolio management.

Central banks ought to acquire low-carbon assets, such as green bonds, sustainability bonds, or assets that meet minimum environmental, social, and governance (ESG) standards. The ECB, for example, has made green bonds and sustainability-linked bonds eligible for central bank operations (ECB, 2021). Sweden's Riksbank announced that it would "only offer to purchase bonds issued by companies deemed to comply with international sustainability standards and norms" from January 2021 onwards (Riksbank, 2020). Similarly, in November 2021, the Bank of England published details of how it will green its Corporate Bond Purchase Scheme (Bank of England, 2021). Such policy moves will promote the growth of green financial markets and reduce the cost of capital for investments in clean energy relative to carbon-based energy. Moving beyond climate considerations, central banks can also play a more active role in fostering sustainable investments more broadly.

Distributional effects: making the rich richer?

Higher asset prices have disproportionately benefited the rich...

After early studies largely focused on the macroeconomic and financial effects of APPs, interest in their distributional impact has grown in recent years (for example, Bernoth and others, 2016; Metzger and Young, 2020; Bonifacio and others, 2021; BIS, 2021b). As discussed, central bank asset purchases affect financial markets and the real economy, and, consequently, distributional outcomes, in various ways. In principle, faster economic growth and improved job markets, which are key longer-term objectives of APPs, should benefit low-income groups. Experiences in the past decade, however, have raised doubts about the long-run positive effects of the programmes on output and employment. While they have boosted prices across a broad range of asset classes, these have disproportionately benefited wealthy households as they not only hold more assets but also larger shares of risky assets than other groups. While the distributional impact of APPs is not uniform across countries and time periods, the programmes have likely increased wealth inequalities, especially in developed countries.

...as income and wealth composition differ across groups

APPs affect different groups unevenly due to large variations in sources of income. Capital gains account for a significant share of total income for top earners, especially the top 1 per cent, but are negligible for other groups (figure II.9a). Low-income earners, in turn, rely heavily on transfers and welfare programmes. The sharp increase in asset prices has thus primarily lifted the incomes of the wealthy.[30]

Another factor in the impact of APPs on wealth distribution is that different groups own varying asset types. Wealthy households hold a large share of their wealth in financial assets, especially stocks (figure II.9b), which at least in the United States have recorded stronger price gains than other asset classes in the past two decades.[31] In addition to directly owning shares of publicly listed companies, many wealthy households invest in private equity and venture capital firms, which have also experienced sharp increases in value. By contrast, less wealthy individuals hold most of their assets in real estate, where prices have grown at a slower pace.

Rapid but uneven increases in asset prices, coupled with differences in the composition of asset holdings across wealth groups, imply that wealthy households have reaped most of the direct gains from APPs. In the United States, the wealthiest 10 per cent of households held nearly half of all assets in stocks in 2016, while the corresponding figure for the bottom 20 per cent was only 2 per cent (figure II.9b). Assuming this asset composition still holds, the top 10 per cent in the United States may have recorded wealth gains of about 44 per cent since March 2020, compared to only 15 per cent for the bottom 20 per cent as of October 2021. In the European Union, likewise, the top 10 per cent has held a

30 By contrast, transfer or welfare programmes usually vary little with economic activity (Amaral, 2017).

31 In fact, ownership of stocks is heavily concentrated among the wealthiest households. In the United States, over 90 per cent of those in the top 10 per cent of the wealth distribution owned stocks in 2019 compared with 21 per cent of those in the bottom 25 per cent (Smart, 2021).

Figure II.9

Income and asset composition in the United States and Europe

(a) Income composition

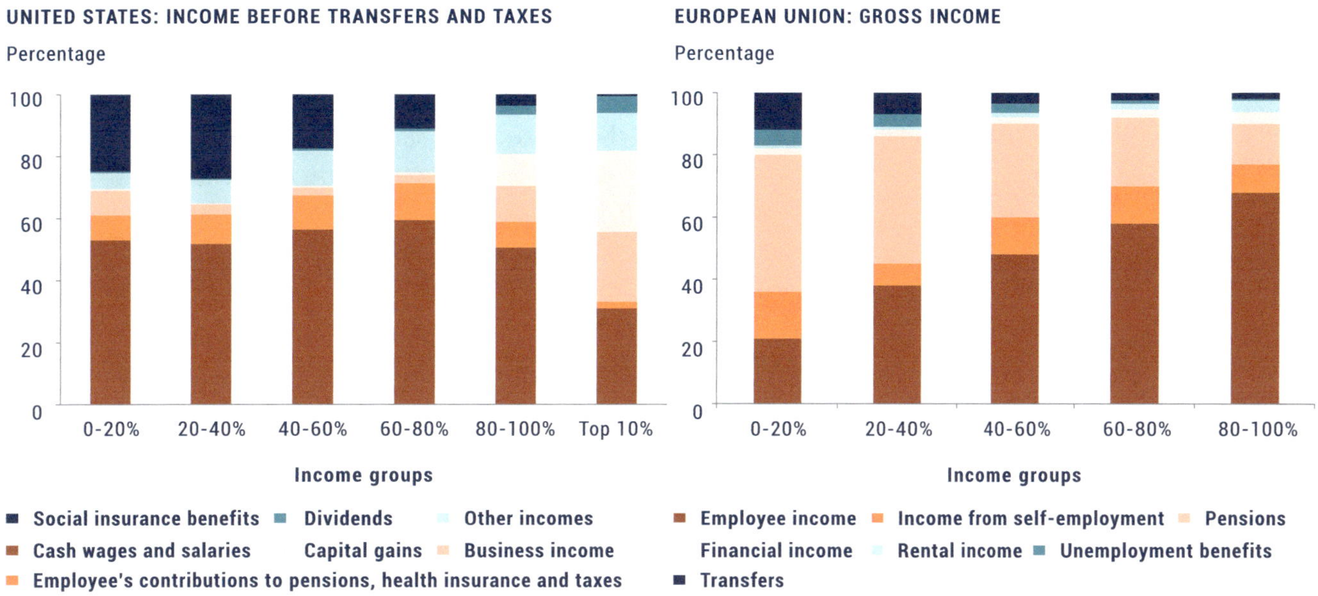

(b) Asset composition

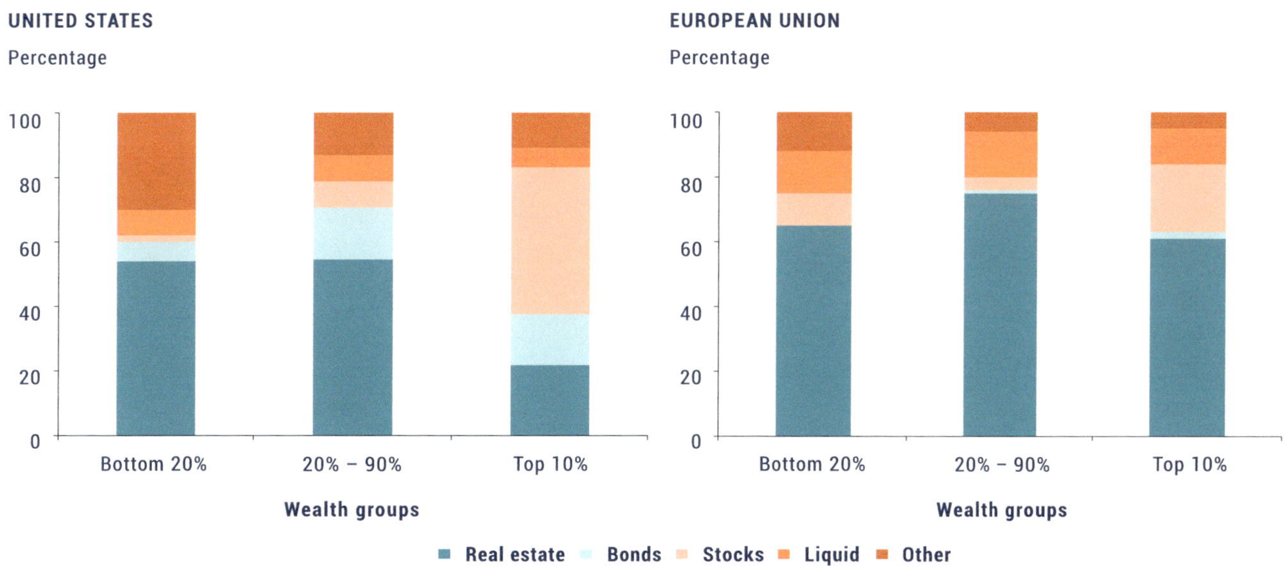

Sources: Panel a, left: United States, Congressional Budget Office, Distribution of Household Income 2017 (accessed on 25 October 2021). Panel a, right: Lenza and Slacalek, 2018. Panel b: Bonifacio and others, 2021.

larger share of wealth in stocks than other groups and is estimated to have recorded stronger wealth gains since the beginning of the pandemic.[32]

The top 1 per cent have experienced the largest wealth gains

The asymmetric effect of APPs is more striking when considering absolute wealth gains. Between the first quarter of 2020 and the second quarter of 2021, the top 1 per cent of income earners in the United States registered net wealth gains of about $3.5 million per person, while the bottom 20 per cent recorded only an increase of about $5,300 per person.[33] Longer-term wealth trends provide further evidence of the negative distributional effects associated with APPs. In the 10 years before the global financial crisis, the wealth of the top 20 per cent and the bottom 20 per cent of income earners in the United States grew at a similar pace (figure II.10). After three rounds of quantitative easing, wealth trends diverged sharply among income groups, widening further after a fourth round in 2020.[34]

Figure II.10
Growth of wealth across income groups in the United States

Index, Q1 1998 = 100

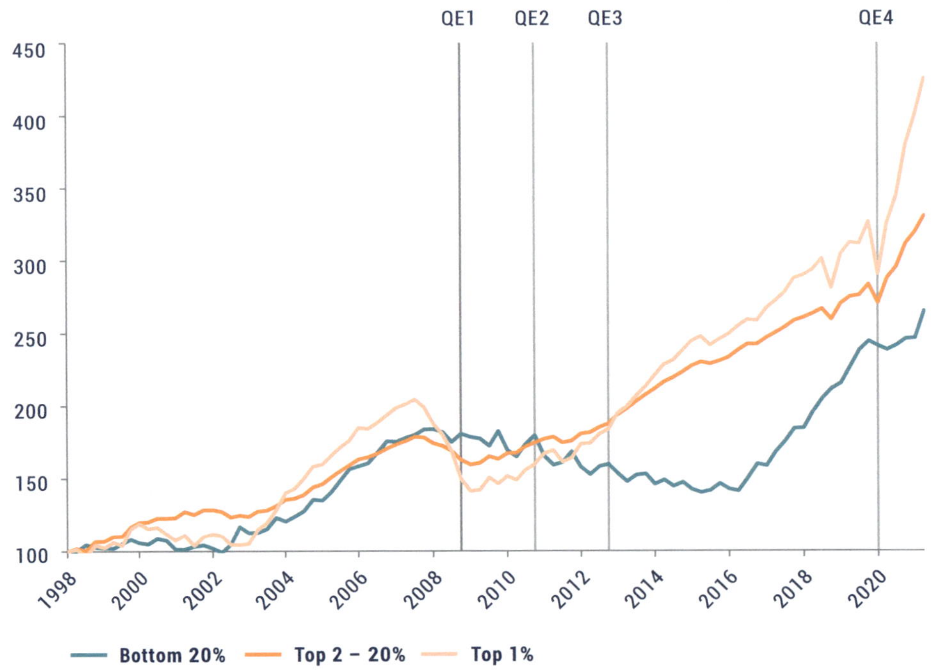

Sources: UN DESA, based on the Federal Reserve Distributional Financial Accounts (accessed on 21 October 2021).
Note: QE1 to QE4 are the Federal Reserve's quantitative easing programmes.

32 The smaller gap in wealth gains in the European Union compared to the United States is consistent with Domanski, Scatigna and Zabai (2016), who argue that increases in house prices tend to decrease inequality if home ownership prevails, while increases in other asset prices tend to increase inequality.

33 Calculated based on data from the Federal Reserve's Distributional Financial Accounts (accessed on 4 October 2021).

34 Other factors, such as the slow and uneven labour market recovery from the global financial crisis, contributed to diverging wealth trends.

APPs have widened inequalities in several developed economies

Developed countries other than the United States that have implemented APPs have experienced similar trends in income and wealth inequalities. For instance, Bernoth and others (2016) indicate that ECB asset purchases have likely increased wealth inequality in the euro area due to increases in stock prices. In the United Kingdom, research finds that positive effects from APPs are higher at the top of wealth and income distribution and lower at the bottom. The richest 10 per cent of households gained, on average, £350,000 during the first round of quantitative easing in 2009, more than 100 times the gains seen by the poorest 10 per cent (United Kingdom, House of Lords, 2021). The Bank of Japan's QE and QQE (quantitative and qualitative easing) programmes increased income and wealth inequality through a rise in the price of financial assets that benefited primarily richer income groups and widened income gaps among different income groups (Yoshino, Taghizadeh-Hesary and Shimizu, 2018). In a recent speech, the Governor of the Bank of Canada admitted that quantitative easing can widen wealth inequality as the programmes boost the value of assets that are not evenly distributed across society (Macklem, 2021).

APPs may contribute to gender and intergenerational inequalities

Since APP effects are primarily transmitted via higher asset prices, the programmes also have an implicit gender bias, favouring men over women. On average, women have lower incomes and less wealth. They tend to be more risk averse, with ownership rates of risky financial assets lower for women than men. APPs are thus likely to benefit men more strongly than women (Metzger and Young, 2020). When APPs are sustained over a long period, they can also increase intergenerational inequality. In the United States, for example, older persons tend to be more active in investing in equity markets. In 2019, 43 per cent of stocks in value terms were owned by investors aged 65 and above (Smart, 2021). Older persons may thus benefit disproportionally from asset price increases.[35]

Besides boosting asset prices, APPs also have distributional implications by affecting inflation, employment and wages. In most cases, however, the adverse distributional effects from higher asset prices likely outweigh the positive effects associated with modest employment and wage gains.[36]

35 APPs impact pension funds as well but the actual impacts remain inconclusive. For those under defined contribution schemes, although APPs could increase the prices of both bonds and equities held in the pension funds, a fall in yields will reduce the annuity rate. For those under defined benefit schemes, while APPs could increase the value of their assets, they could also raise the value of their liabilities due to a fall in yields (BoE, 2012).

36 One study finding a slightly positive overall effect is by Lenza and Slacalek (2018). Based on a sample of four European countries, they estimated that a sudden increase in asset purchases could lower the unemployment rate by 0.7 percentage points. This would mainly benefit the incomes of the bottom 20 per cent of households and slightly reduce the Gini coefficient.

Spillover effects on developing countries

Developed countries' APPs have created significant spillovers

The large-scale APPs introduced by developed country central banks have had significant spillover effects on developing countries through several well-established channels. First, by boosting aggregate demand in the originating country, APPs may generate positive spillovers for developing countries through stronger demand for their goods and services.[37] Second, since APPs reduce long-term bond yields in developed countries, investors turn to assets in developing countries for higher risk-adjusted returns. Consequently, yields in developing countries are expected to fall as asset prices rise.[38] Third, in a world of well-integrated financial markets, APPs are expected to boost global liquidity.[39] Fourth, APPs can impact developing countries' exchange rates, especially where currencies are fully convertible (Fic, 2013).

Countercyclical capital inflows could benefit developing countries...

The additional liquidity generated by central bank asset purchases can benefit developing countries if their business and financial cycles are synchronized with those of developed countries. In this case, stronger capital inflows into developing countries should ease their financing constraints. During both the global financial and COVID-19 crises, developing countries initially experienced sharp reversals of capital flows as capital flew to safety and liquidity dried up (figure II.11). Aggressive monetary easing measures in developed countries, including the introduction of APPs, helped alleviate financial conditions, supporting a revival of portfolio capital flows to developing countries (Batini, 2020).

...while procyclical capital inflows raise overheating and financial stability risks

APPs can increase the procyclicality of capital flows when the origin and destination countries are in different phases of the business cycle. In this case, APP-induced capital flows to developing countries raise the risk of overheating, sudden stops and reversals, increased inflationary pressure and excessive credit growth. This may require domestic policy tightening, which, at least temporarily, may attract even more capital inflows. In the aftermath of the global financial crisis, many developing economies saw growth rebound whereas the major developed countries experienced a slow and fragile recovery. Developed country central banks responded with even larger APPs, triggering major capital flows to developing and emerging economies. The Brazilian economy, for example, experienced a sharp rise in equity prices, credit growth and currency appreciation pressures during the post-APP period (Barroso, da Silva and Sales, 2016). China also observed rising equity prices and inflationary pressure and responded with monetary tightening (Chen and others, 2015).

---

37 Empirical analysis finds that net exports of developing countries do not respond significantly to APPs in developed countries, however, because APP-induced currency appreciation in developing countries offsets increasing demand for their exports (Bhattarai, Chatterjee and Park, 2021).

38 Fic (2013) studied APPs launched by the Federal Reserve, Bank of England, Bank of Japan and ECB during 2018 and 2012, estimating that the programmes could have decreased long-term yields by about 175 basis points in Brazil, and about 25 basis points in China, India and the Russian Federation. Moore and others (2013) estimate that a 10-basis-point decline in long-term United States Treasury yields results in a reduction of approximately 1.7 basis points in emerging market economies' government bond yields.

39 For a sample of 60 developing countries, Lim, Mohapatra and Stocker (2014) estimated that APPs in the United States accounted for more than 20 per cent of the total increase in cross-border capital flows during 2009 and 2013.

Figure II.11

Capital flows to G20 developing countries

Billions of United States dollars, by quarter

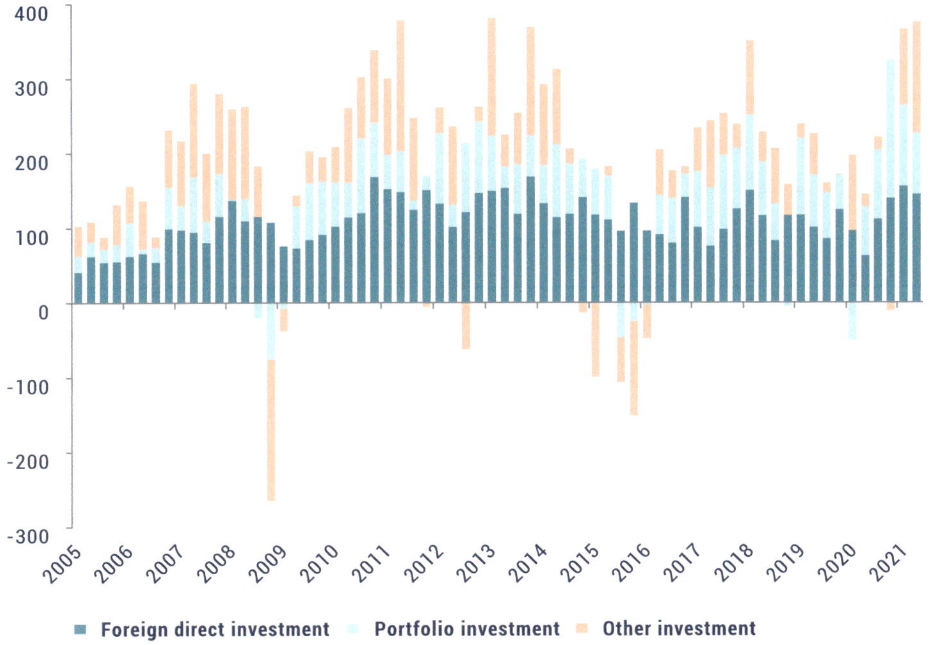

Sources: UN DESA, based on IMF International Financial Statistics (accessed on 22 November 2021).
Note: Values above zero are capital inflows and values below zero are capital outflows.

APPs have supported a borrowing binge in developing countries

APPs in developed economies were among the major triggers of a borrowing binge in a number of developing economies. Public and publicly guaranteed debt in low and lower-middle-income countries owed to private creditors rose by 264 per cent during 2010-2019. In comparison, the public external debt of these countries declined by 7 per cent from 1998 to 2007.[40] The search for higher yields has encouraged private creditors from developed countries to find new debtors in the developing world. In the wake of the global financial crisis, governments and public sector entities in developing countries joined the bandwagon of borrowing from the international capital market, hoping to take advantage of ultralow interest rates.

Sovereign bonds – debt owed to private creditors – now account for 40 per cent of all public and publicly guaranteed debt in low and lower-middle-income countries, up from 23 per cent in 2010. The expectation of lower borrowing costs, however, has often remained elusive for developing countries that have borrowed from the international capital market. As private creditors search for higher yields, the cost of borrowing for developing countries has remained high despite very low interest rates. The coupon rate on developing country sovereign bonds issued during the post-crisis period averaged more than 7 per cent, indicating that these countries continued to pay a very high risk premium.

40 The decline in total external debt during this period is in part due to debt relief provided under the Heavily Indebted Poor Countries Initiative.

Excessive external borrowing, especially from private creditors, along with high borrowing costs have clearly exacerbated debt sustainability concerns for many developing countries. The pandemic further aggravated the situation, with APPs in the developed economies doing little to reduce borrowing costs for developing countries. The latter have faced fewer constraints in borrowing from the international capital market but that has not necessarily reduced their borrowing rates. In March 2021, Ghana, for example, raised $3 billion with Eurobonds as the country continued to grapple with the pandemic, agreeing to pay 7.75-8.875 per cent interest on the debt. Kenya, facing a high risk of debt distress, raised $1 billion with a Eurobond issue in June 2021, with a coupon rate of 6.3 per cent. These high borrowing costs will significantly increase debt-servicing costs and may undermine debt sustainability.

The size of spillover effects depends on economic fundamentals

Developing countries with a more open capital account and greater financial linkages with the United States and euro area economies are more susceptible to APPs pursued by the Federal Reserve and ECB (Apostolou and Beirne, 2017). Countries' economic fundamentals also affect the scale and duration of APP impacts. Developing countries with economic and financial imbalances, especially those with high levels of external debt denominated in foreign currencies prior to the crisis, are facing significant debt distress and default risks.

The bumpy road ahead: looking beyond asset purchase programmes

Unwinding APPs will support future efficacy of this policy tool

Large-scale asset purchases are an effective policy tool to ease financial stress and propel economic recovery following a crisis. But they cannot be a magic wand for boosting investment, employment and economic growth in the long term. Over time, the costs of sustained APPs are likely to outweigh their benefits, as the programmes exacerbate macroeconomic and financial risks, while adversely impacting wealth distribution and debt sustainability. To maintain their efficacy as a monetary policy tool, central banks need to unwind APPs when financial and economic stability objectives are realized.

Challenges in unwinding unconventional monetary policies

As the world economy recovers from the pandemic, higher consumer price inflation and record inflation in asset prices are pressuring major developed country central banks to scale back, if not unwind, their APPs. This time, tapering asset purchases could happen at a much faster pace than after the global financial crisis.[41] The Federal Reserve has already begun to slow monthly asset purchases. The Bank of England has also started reducing the scope of its APP. While tapering is underway, it is unlikely that major central banks will completely exit APPs any time soon. The assets on their balance sheets will likely remain as it will be too costly to push these back to the financial markets.

41 This would follow the breakneck pace of asset purchases undertaken at the outset of the pandemic.

Central banks face difficult trade-offs in unwinding policy support

Unwinding and eventually exiting APPs will not be easy. The developed country central banks, especially the Federal Reserve and the ECB, face the challenge of scaling back bond purchase programmes without creating financial market turmoil and destabilizing global financial flows. The risk of policy mistakes, either by withdrawing stimulus too fast or by waiting too long with tightening, is substantial. Beyond this immediate challenge, the more fundamental question is if – and if so, how quickly – central banks will reverse asset purchases and reduce the size of their balance sheets.[42]

Rising interest rates could create a maturity mismatch on balance sheets

Reducing and eventually stopping new purchases and gradually selling off assets involves risks for monetary and fiscal authorities as well as financial markets. When central banks taper asset purchases and eventually shrink their balance sheets, markets could face upward pressure on the yield curve. Rising interest rates could pose a financial risk for central banks' massive balance sheets as these will increase debt-servicing risks and the roll-over risks of debt (especially public debt). Central banks will need to manage risks from the maturity mismatch of assets and liabilities on their balance sheets. As interest rates rise, the costs of central bank liabilities (in the form of commercial bank reserves bearing floating interest rates) may increase quickly, whereas the interest income from central bank assets (in the form of long-term bonds) could grow more slowly (Allen, Chadha and Turner, 2021). At the same time, central banks face the risk that reducing large holdings of long-term government bonds will disrupt bond markets.

Debt service costs are sensitive to interest rate increases

For fiscal authorities, debt service costs in several developed countries have become more sensitive to short-term interest rates, in part due to APPs. If interest rates were to rise more sharply and rapidly than expected, public finances could come under pressure, especially in countries with high debt burdens, such as Canada, Italy, the United Kingdom and the United States. In the United States, interest expenses accounted for about 10 per cent of total government revenues in 2020. This ratio is forecast to increase to about 14 per cent by 2030 in the baseline scenario but may soar to 22 per cent in 2030 under a higher interest rate scenario, which could force the United States Government to cut back on essential spending.[43] The United Kingdom's Office for Budget Responsibility (OBR, 2021) estimates that if short- and long-term interest rates were both 1 percentage point higher than in the baseline scenario, interest expenditure on debt would increase by 0.8 per cent of GDP in 2025-2026. This "would make the task of keeping debt on a sustainable path more difficult".

The fiscal implications of a sudden unwinding of APPs could be equally consequential for developing countries, especially those with open capital accounts and high levels of external public debt. Higher interest rates, following the end of APPs, will likely trigger capital outflows and further aggravate debt sustainability for many developing countries with high levels of hard currency-denominated external debt.

42 Tapering slows the pace of asset purchases and leads to an outright reduction of the balance sheet. After purchases have ended, central banks are expected to gradually reduce the size of their balance sheets by letting maturing securities roll off (Milstein, Powell and Wessel, 2021).

43 Under the higher interest rate scenario, the interest on 10-year Treasury notes would rise to about 4 per cent in 2025.

Abrupt unwinding of APPs could delay economic recovery

An abrupt unwinding of APPs, in essence, would have the same adverse effect as premature austerity in both developed and developing countries. It would likely lead to cuts in fiscal spending that would not only delay recovery but could also push many economies into recession. It will remain critical for the major central banks to calibrate and coordinate their decisions to taper APPs and reduce their balance sheets, keeping in mind that there will be significant macroeconomic externalities not only in their own economies but also in economies in the rest of the world. Externalities from a sudden unwinding of APPs will be large especially for countries exposed to the international capital market.

The "taper tantrum" of May 2013 serves as a reminder of these risks. At that time, equity and government bond prices dropped immediately. The sell-off of Treasury bonds spilled into corporate bond markets and in less than two months drove a 5 per cent decline in the price of the S&P 500 Investment Grade Corporate Bond Index. The abrupt tightening of financial conditions created major negative spillovers for many developing countries. The sudden stop and reversal of capital flows affected exchange rates and asset prices, resulting in a deterioration of broader balance of payment and economic conditions.

The need for complementary policies

When central banks taper asset purchases and eventually exit from unconventional policies, they will need to ensure that they manage market expectations and minimize both short- and long-term risks. One important lesson from the 2013 "taper tantrum" is that careful communication about balance sheet policies is imperative to avoid market overreaction.

Macroprudential policies can help mitigate the adverse impacts of APPs

Macroprudential policies can play an important role in strengthening the resilience of the financial system, thus helping to limit the adverse effects of APPs and facilitating the unwinding process. Macroprudential measures can slow asset price growth and restrain excessive risk-taking, especially in sectors that pose greater risks to the financial system. For instance, to tackle rising property prices, a few countries (such as Canada, the Netherlands and New Zealand) have tightened loan-to-value limits and applied higher floors on interest rates for banks to evaluate mortgage affordability (BIS, 2021a). Some form of lender-targeted measures can reduce the sensitivity of domestic credit cycles to cross-border capital flows. In the aftermath of the global financial crisis, for example, the Republic of Korea applied a withholding tax on foreign purchases of Treasury and Monetary Stabilization Bonds and imposed a levy on banks' non-deposit foreign exchange liabilities (Ryoo, Kwon and Lee, 2013).

Central banks should green APPs to foster low-carbon activities

APPs offer central banks an opportunity to contribute to mitigating climate risks (Martinez-Diaz and Christianson, 2020). When unwinding their asset purchases, central banks may choose to hold on to assets of sectors and firms with lower carbon footprints. In the process, they would reward climate action and sustainable investments, such as those related to energy efficiency or renewable energy, by private sector firms. At the same time, they could develop new principles and guidelines to acquire low-carbon assets for future APPs.

Fiscal policies are needed to address rising inequalities

Reforms of fiscal and taxation policies are needed to address the adverse distributional effects of APPs. On the revenue side, more progressive income taxation, combined with targeted measures to reduce wealth disparities, can help to reduce inequalities. A levy on capital gains, for example, could partly offset rising wealth inequalities that result from the rapid growth of asset prices. Similarly, taxing corporate stock buy-backs may improve both macroeconomic and distributional outcomes.[44] On the expenditure side, social programmes and targeted government transfers, such as unemployment benefits, along with increased access to and improved quality of education and health care can protect the most vulnerable during crises and enhance their resilience to future shocks.

APPs have allowed central banks to inject liquidity and ease financial stress in times of crisis, especially when policy rates reached their effective lower bound. While the programmes have expanded the monetary policy toolkit, they are no silver bullet. Continuation of APPs cannot replace structural policies to boost investment in the real economy or sustain long-term economic growth. Integrated policy frameworks, including macroprudential and fiscal policy measures, are needed to help countries address APP-related inequalities and climate risks, ensuring fair and sustainable recovery.

44 In the United States, a new legislative proposal includes a 1 per cent excise tax on the amount a publicly traded firm spends on buying back its own stock.

Developed economies

GDP growth

Percentage

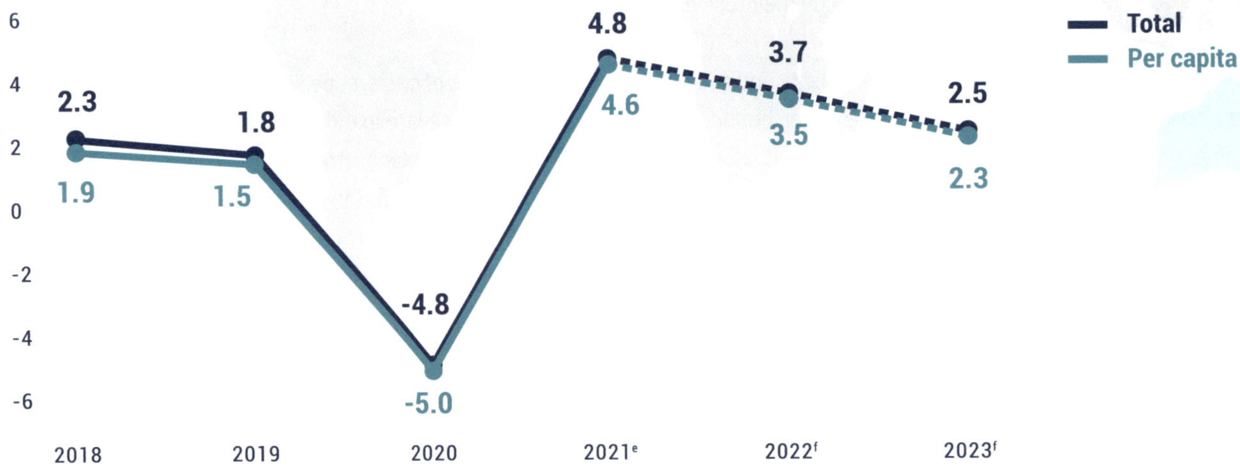

COVID-19 cases & deaths

as of 20 December 2021

Per 100,000 people

Vaccination

as of 20 December 2021

Percentage of population

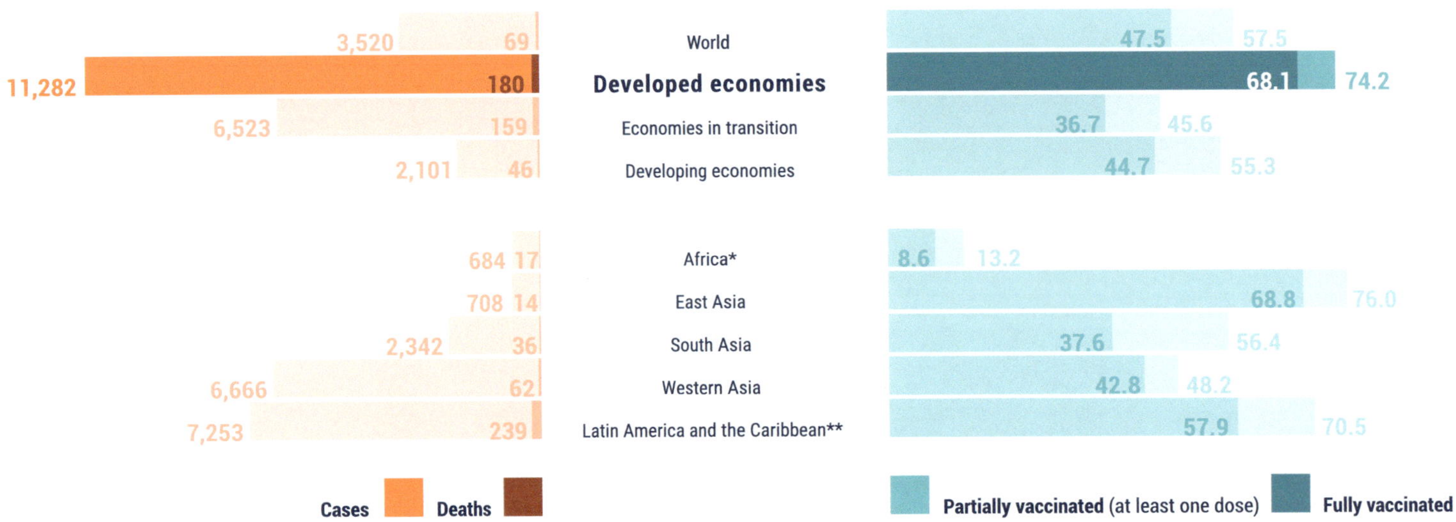

Note: The boundaries and names shown and the designations used on this map do not imply official endorsement or acceptance by the United Nations. The map represents countries and/or territories or parts thereof for which data is available and/or analysed in World Economic Situation and Prospects 2022. The shaded areas therefore do not necessarily overlap entirely with the delimitation of their frontiers or boundaries. Aggregate data for Africa, excluding Libya.

* Excluding Libya; **Excluding Bolivarian Republic of Venezuela. **e:** 2021 estimates. **f:** 2022-2023 forecasts.

Source for COVID-19 data: UN DESA calculations, based on data from Johns Hopkins University.

CHAPTER III

Regional developments and outlooks

Developed economies

- Economic sentiment has improved as vaccination progresses in major developed economies.
- Employment challenges continue with certain sectors experiencing acute labour shortages.
- Inflationary pressures persist amid prolonged supply-chain disruptions; this may further intensify inflationary expectations in some developed countries.

United States: a robust recovery facing supply-side constraints

The economy in the United States grew by an estimated 5.5 per cent in 2021 after a contraction of 3.4 per cent in 2020. A rapid vaccine roll-out and the relaxation of pandemic control measures substantially improved overall economic sentiment and resulted in a quick recovery of output. The current recovery is imbalanced, however, with consumption of goods driving GDP growth (figure III.1).

Figure III.1

The contribution of demand components to GDP growth in the United States

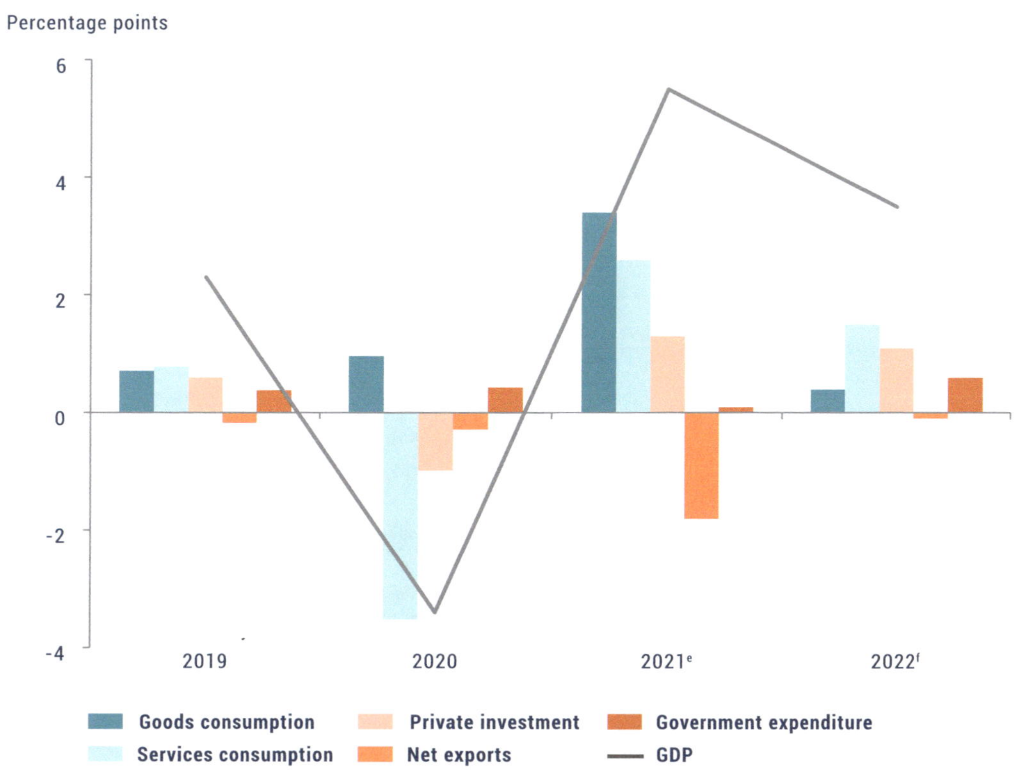

Sources: United States, Bureau of Economic Analysis, Department of Commerce, and UN DESA estimates and forecasts.
Note: e = estimates, f = forecasts.

An imbalanced recovery is overly dependent on goods consumption

A recovery in services consumption accelerated towards the end of 2021 while recovery in investment expenditure was robust. Expenditure on equipment and intellectual property products such as software and research and development registered a rapid climb. In contrast, expenditure on non-residential structures remained extremely weak. The contribution of external demand to economic recovery was anaemic. Growth in gross exports of goods and services is projected to be only slightly positive in 2021; a jump in demand for imports resulted in a significant drag on net exports.

The economy faces increasing supply-side constraints

The economy in the United States has faced increasing supply-side constraints that initially emerged from global supply-chain disruptions triggered by the pandemic. Rapid domestic demand recovery exacerbated logistics backlogs in incoming freight and domestic transport networks. A shortage of industrial parts, mostly notably semiconductors, has worsened due to continuing supply-chain bottlenecks, production disruptions in East Asian countries and the quick drawdown of inventories. Parts shortages have hit the automotive industry particularly hard.

Figure III.2
Labour market indicators in the United States

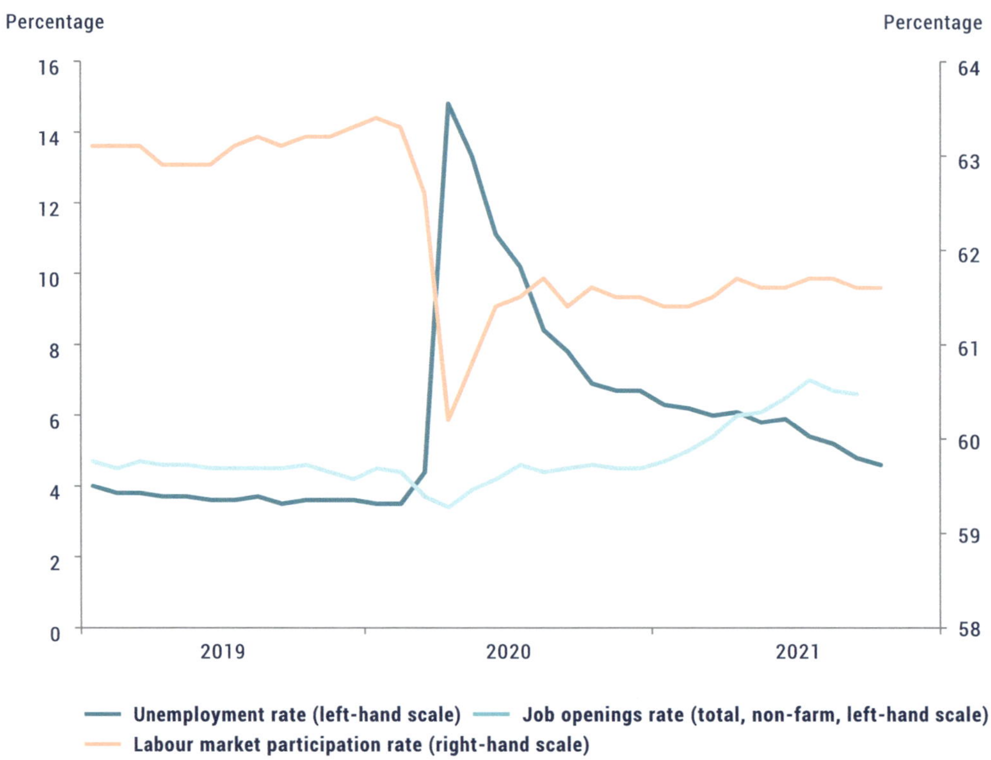

Source: United States, Bureau of Labor Statistics.

Another element of supply-side constraints has been a growing labour shortage. The pace of growth in job openings has consistently been higher than the rate of decline in the unemployment rate; the labour market participation rate has remained lower than the pre-pandemic level (figure III.2). The total non-farm job openings rate hit a historic high of 7 per cent in July and is forecast to remain high. The unemployment rate came down to 4.6 per cent in October, still above the pre-pandemic rate of 3.5 per cent in February 2020. While firms have accelerated hiring, the number of workers who quit their jobs reached a historic high in September 2021. The labour market situation suggests a substantial mismatch between job seekers and firms looking to hire in terms of skills, wages, locations and other working conditions (Lubik, 2021).

Inflationary pressures have been mounting

Along with rising energy prices, domestic supply-side constraints have pushed up prices. The producer price index for final demand increased 8.6 per cent in October 2021 from a year earlier, reflecting higher energy prices and the costs of transportation and warehousing. Nominal wages, in terms of average hourly earnings, registered a 4.8 per cent annual increase in October 2021, well above the pre-pandemic average of 2.4 per cent over the last decade. Although the nominal wage increase is still barely over the core inflation rate of 4.6 per cent in the same month, the wage adjustment to inflation has been noticeably quick. Consumer price inflation is estimated to be 4.3 per cent in 2021.

Policies remain expansionary

Highly accommodative fiscal and monetary policies supported quick recovery as stimulus measures wound down during the second half of 2021. With the expiration of enhanced unemployment benefits in September, the focus of fiscal measures shifted to investment promotion under the Build Back Better Framework.[1] The $1 trillion Infrastructure Investment and Jobs Act was passed by the legislature in November 2021, while the Build Back Better Act, intended to pump $1.7 trillion into the social safety net and climate action, is under legislative review. On the monetary side, the Federal Reserve began to taper its asset purchase programme in November.[2] Policy debate continues regarding the timing of the first policy interest rates hike given inflation prospects.

Growth with a rebalanced demand structure is forecast in 2022

The United States economy is forecast to grow by 3.5 per cent in 2022 amid a rebalancing of demand (figure III.1). Consumption growth is expected to slow; exports are predicted to recover. The consumer inflation rate is forecast at 3.2 per cent with substantial supply-side constraints in the first half of the year. The main downside risks stem from uncertainties regarding the pandemic, inflation prospects and associated monetary policy decisions.

Japan: slow recovery in domestic demand while supply-chain disruptions hit exports

The Japanese economy grew an estimated 2.2 per cent in 2021 after a contraction of 4.6 per cent in 2020. COVID-19 outbreaks and measures to control the pandemic weakened household and economic sentiment, which slowed the recovery of domestic demand during the first three quarters of 2021. Unlike other developed economies, which have witnessed a rapid recovery in residential investment

1 See Zandi and Yanos (2021) for detailed discussions on the macroeconomic impact of the Build Back Better Framework.

2 See Chapter 2 for details on the asset purchase programmes of central banks during the pandemic.

since mid-2020, residential investment in Japan continued its downward trend since peaking in the third quarter of 2019. In the fourth quarter in 2021, however, a decline in COVID-19 cases and progress on vaccination substantially improved economic sentiment.

Supply-chain disruptions hit the automotive sector

Export growth, the main factor contributing to recovery since the second half of 2020, has lost its momentum. Supply-chain disruptions, particularly semiconductor shortages, compelled the automotive sector to operate under full capacity. Exports of automotive products sharply declined in the second half of 2021. Supply-chain disruptions added inflationary pressure on the prices of goods but this barely offset a persistent deflationary trend, particularly in service prices (figure III.3). Consumer price inflation was an estimated 0 per cent for 2021.

Figure III.3
Inflation trends in Japan

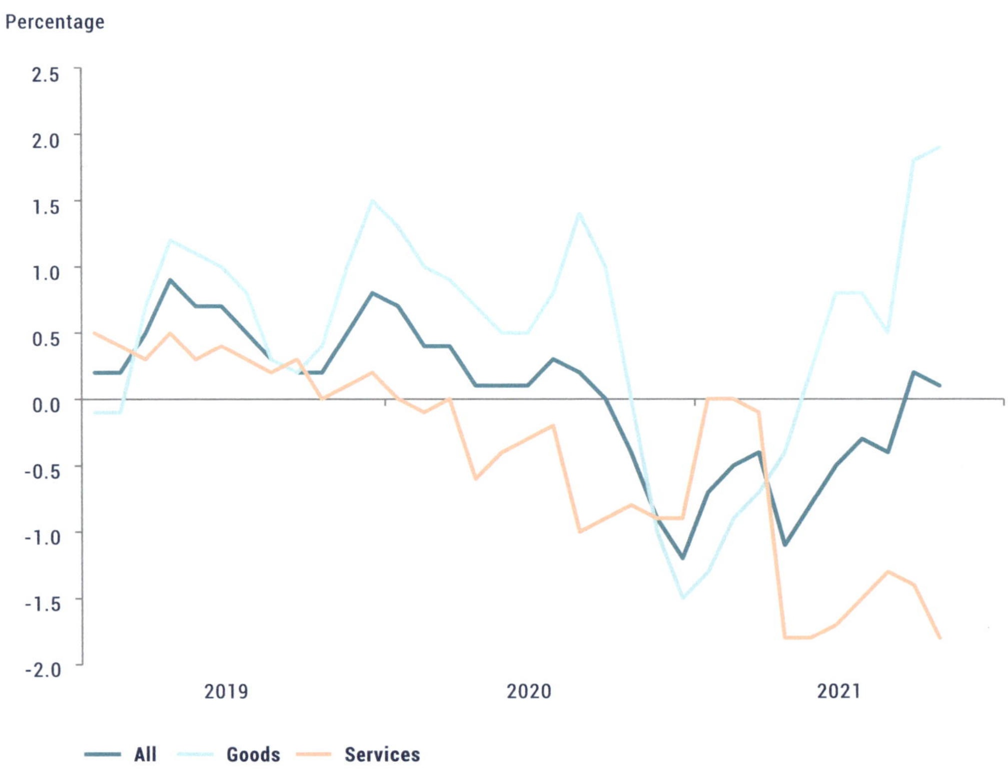

Source: Japan, Ministry of Internal Affairs and Communications.

Expansionary policies contained rising unemployment and bankruptcies

The Government of Japan implemented sizeable fiscal stimulus measures to minimize the impact of the pandemic. The additional stimulus package for the 2021-2022 fiscal year was 40 trillion yen, about 7.5 per cent of GDP. Another package for the 2022-2023 fiscal year amounts to 55.7 trillion yen. Monetary policy continues to be highly expansionary. The Bank of Japan has accelerated its asset purchases along with its existing policy framework for quantitative and qualitative monetary easing with yield curve control. These measures have succeeded in containing rising unemployment and bankruptcies. The unemployment rate peaked at 3 per cent in May 2021 and started declining towards the pre-pandemic rate of 2.4 per cent. Bankruptcy cases have fallen since a peak in July 2020. Policy measures did not induce robust private spending growth in 2021, however.

Robust domestic demand growth is expected in 2022 but downside risks remain

GDP growth is forecast at 3.3 per cent in 2022. Robust domestic demand growth is expected due to increased private consumption reflecting pent-up demand for goods and services. Private investment is also projected to recover along with improving economic sentiment. Both monetary and fiscal policies will likely remain expansionary to support domestic demand recovery. Downside risks stem from uncertainties surrounding the pandemic and supply-chain disruptions. Although the latter have extensively impacted the automotive sector, it is uncertain if they will escalate to broader supply-side constraints.

Australia: strong recovery continues despite a temporary contraction due to Delta variant outbreaks

A strong recovery has resulted in rapid restoration of employment

The Australian economy grew an estimated 3.1 per cent in 2021 after a 2.5 per cent contraction in 2020. A strong recovery in domestic demand promptly led to rapid job recovery in the first half of 2021. The unemployment rate declined to 4.9 per cent in June, below the pre-pandemic level of 5 per cent. During the third quarter, the recovery faced a setback due to outbreaks of the Delta variant of COVID-19, however. The economy shrank on a quarterly basis following stringent lockdown measures in major cities. By the fourth quarter, relaxation of these measures and rapid progress in vaccination restarted economic activities and recovery. Export recovery has gained steam with rising commodity prices.

Robust domestic demand is forecast to continue in 2022

For 2022, the economy is forecast to grow by 4.2 per cent, with robust domestic demand growth. Export growth is projected to accelerate further with a recovery in services trade. Both monetary and fiscal policies are expected to remain expansionary. The Reserve Bank of Australia will probably scale down its bond-buying programme but is not likely to hike its policy rates in 2022 unless rapid wage growth appears. Downside risks stem from uncertainties over the COVID-19 pandemic and global supply-chain disruptions. Compared to other developed countries, however, the impact of the latter is likely to be milder given Australia's service-based domestic demand and commodity-based exports.

Europe: a return to growth but the crisis is not over yet

A strong rebound in the first half of the year, powerful headwinds in the second

The economies of Europe returned to growth in 2021, with the gradual easing of COVID-19 containment measures, continued accommodative macroeconomic policies and a sharp rebound in leading export destinations. Most European economies registered a double-digit year-on-year increase in output in the second quarter; the overall performance of the region in the first half of the year exceeded earlier expectations. Following more than a year of suppression, consumer sentiment improved and private consumption surged as households started to spend savings accumulated due to pandemic-related precautions or limited scope to spend. Amid the reopening of the services sector and lifting of intra-European Union mobility restrictions, economies in countries relatively dependent on tourism, such as Greece, Italy and Spain, saw a sharp increase in tourist arrivals.

In the second half of 2021, however, the region faced serious headwinds. The manufacturing sector, which had recovered to its pre-pandemic level of activity, was severely impacted by supply-chain disruptions in part caused by shortages of shipping containers and lower capacity in Asian ports. Certain industries, in particular the automotive industry – which is of crucial importance for many economies in Europe, including the largest, Germany – have been forced to scale back production because of the global semiconductor shortage. Further, many industries and services have confronted a large-scale lack of workers, especially truck drivers. Supply disruptions and rising costs of input materials brought the construction sector in Europe to a standstill in late 2021. Soaring energy prices, especially for natural gas and LNG,[3] caused a spike in electricity costs and became another hurdle to economic recovery, disrupting output in energy-intensive firms. The Economic Sentiment Indicator for both the euro area and the European Union stabilized at a high level in July after rapidly improving since January 2021 (figure III.4).

The German economy has not regained its pre-crisis size and is expected to expand by only 2.5 per cent in 2021. Growth sharply slowed in the third quarter due to sluggish industrial activity and interruptions in automotive sector output. Disruptions in the supply of intermediate goods were accompanied by rising electricity prices, and in September, producer prices increased by over 14 per cent year on year. Growth should accelerate to 4 per cent in 2022 given an improved outlook for exports and domestic investment, the insourcing of the production of semiconductors and other key inputs, and the gradual shift towards European production chains. An expected increase in the minimum wage should support private consumption. The economy, however, faces medium-term risks associated with slow progress in shifting towards the production of electric vehicles as well as demographic pressures.

Most European countries have accomplished relatively high vaccination rates against COVID-19. Yet, another surge in cases began in the fall of 2021, making the region an epicentre of the pandemic once again. This led to the reintroduction of containment measures in Austria, Denmark, Latvia, the Netherlands and Slovakia. These measures may again disrupt service sectors such as leisure, hospitality and travel. A return to the prolonged full-scale lockdown adopted in 2020 remains unlikely, however.

---

3 The natural gas price increase in Europe in the second half of 2021 was caused by insufficient domestic storage, declining imports from the Russian Federation, a sharp increase in LNG demand from Asia and the shift from long-term gas purchase contracts to spot markets.

Figure III.4

Economic sentiment indicator for the European Union and the euro area

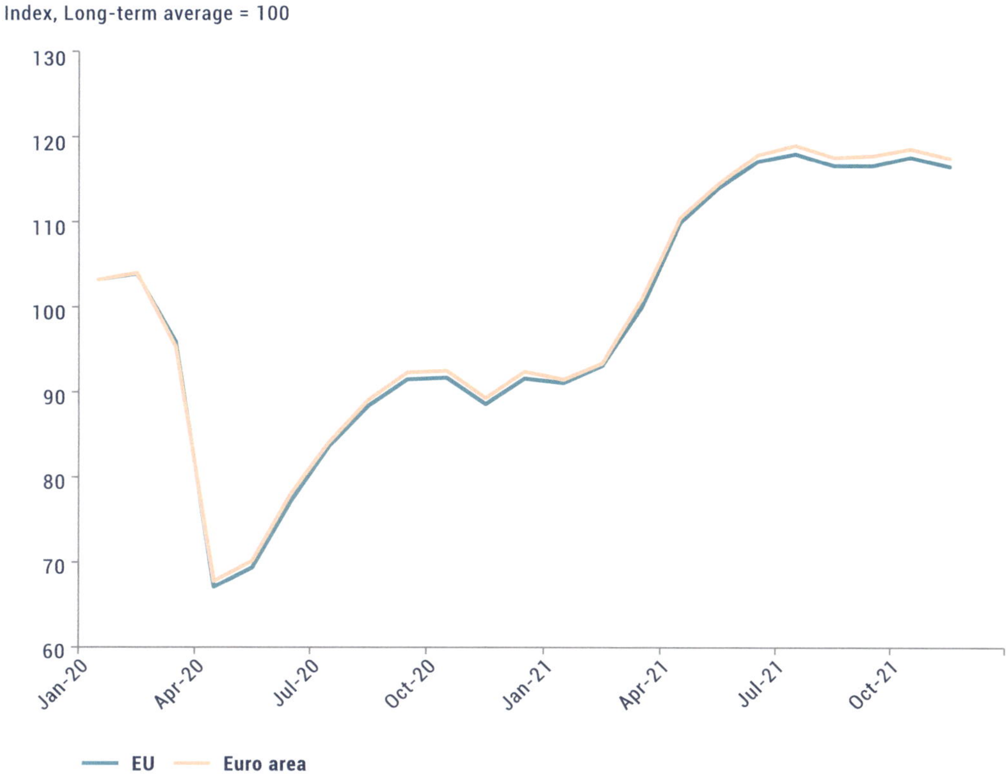

Source: European Commission, 2021.

The consequences of Brexit weighed on production activities in the United Kingdom, despite the Trade and Cooperation Agreement reached with the European Union in 2020. Numerous non-tariff barriers emerged in trade between the two, while significant uncertainty remains around trade in services. After a double-digit year-on-year expansion in the second quarter of 2021, economic growth in the United Kingdom noticeably slowed amid supply-side and fuel shortages. Difficulties in bringing in migrant workers to meet labour demand, a problem that to a certain extent resulted from Brexit,[4] contributed to persistent supply-side bottlenecks.

A massive recovery plan to improve long-term growth prospects

The outlook for European economies for 2022 is mixed, as the weaknesses of late 2021 will carry on to at least the first quarter. Headline growth may taper somewhat due to the weaker base effect and the start of the gradual unwinding of anti-crisis stimulus measures. On the positive side, the European Union will begin benefiting from the largest stimulus package implemented in decades – the combination of the European Community's long-term multi-annual budget running from 2021 to 2027 and the massive Recovery and Resilience Facility, the NextGenerationEU. The latter, worth over 800

4 Although over 6 million foreign workers applied for residency in the United Kingdom after Brexit, many have left the country. In 2020, the net migration of European Union nationals to the United Kingdom was negative. See ONS, 2021.

billion euros, is financed by joint debt issuance. Implementation of the recovery plan, with spending focused on sectors with high growth multipliers, should facilitate the modernization and digitization of infrastructure, bolster research and innovation, expedite the shift towards a sustainable economy, address social problems such as youth unemployment and improve the efficiency of governance. Actual impacts will of course depend on the ability of national governments to use allocated funds.

The aggregate GDP of the EU-27, after shrinking by 6 per cent in 2020, bounced back by an expected 4.7 per cent in 2021. It may be followed by a further 3.9 per cent expansion in 2022, assuming that prolonged lockdowns are not resumed. European Union member States from Eastern Europe are projected to maintain a positive growth differential with their West European peers. Among European countries not in the European Union, the economy of the United Kingdom expanded by an estimated 6.2 per cent in 2021 and is expected to see further growth of 4.5 per cent in 2022. Despite difficulties in late 2021, the outlook for the economy in the United Kingdom is positive. Most of the corporate sector is in a strong financial position, and a two-year tax deduction incentive should encourage investment.

From battling deflation to dealing with inflation worries

Consumer price inflation turned negative in many European countries in 2020. It remained subdued in early 2021 but accelerated markedly in the second half of the year (see Figure III.5). Even in countries with a long record of price stability, annual inflation exceeded 4 per cent in the final quarter of the year, much above the European Central Bank's (ECB) 2 per cent target. Apart from the base year effect, including from a temporary reduction in the value added tax in Germany, the surge in inflation is explained by various factors. These include higher producer prices caused by skyrocketing costs of raw materials and energy, a sharp rise in food prices and persistent supply-chain disruptions. In Eastern European countries with flexible currencies, depreciation added to inflationary pressure. To mitigate the impact of higher gas and electricity prices on households and businesses, several European countries, including France, Italy and Spain, adopted various measures to curb them. In July 2021, the ECB announced that it will tolerate overshooting the inflation target. Most inflationary factors are believed to be transitory; however, a longer-than-anticipated period of above-target inflation may lead to a second-round effect on labour markets and a wage-price spiral.

Employment is recovering; many countries are facing worker shortages

Labour market conditions notably improved in 2021, with a robust increase in working hours in most countries. In the Czech Republic and Germany, unemployment fell to low single-digit levels, while it remains elevated in Greece and Spain. Phasing out furlough schemes implemented in several countries since the beginning of the pandemic may lead to a modest rise in unemployment, but in general, the European economy should add jobs over the next couple of years. Labour demand is expected to strengthen. Several European countries confront labour shortages causing significant logistical bottlenecks and reflecting persistent mismatches between labour supply and demand and different speeds of recovery across sectors (see Chapter 1). Although immigration remains a politically contentious issue, a long-term, comprehensive immigration strategy for bringing in skilled workers may mitigate labour supply pressures. Removing obstacles to internal mobility that emerged from the pandemic may also address labour shortfalls in some countries. Given that virtually all European Union countries are facing demographic shifts, however, alleviating labour shortages in one country via intra-European Union migration would most likely exacerbate shortages in others.

Figure III.5

Annual change in the Harmonized Index of Consumer Prices for select European countries

Source: Eurostat.

A gradual shift to fiscal consolidation

Macroeconomic policies in Europe largely maintained their accommodative stance in 2021, with continuing liquidity and wage support schemes. As an outcome of massive stimulus spending, public debt levels soared in some countries, far exceeding limits set by the Stability and Growth Pact (see figure III.6). Ceilings on the size of budget deficits and public debt were earlier put on hold by the European Commission when it activated the pact's escape clause. Most European countries will nevertheless start putting their public finances in order beginning in 2022. The pace of fiscal consolidation will likely be gradual and decided at a national level. Stronger growth rates will have a modestly positive effect on debt ratios while financing costs should remain low. For the United Kingdom, exiting the European Union allowed greater fiscal flexibility, and the proposed budgetary framework up to 2025 remains accommodative. The ability to borrow in British pounds and the accommodative stance of the Bank of England are expected to provide sufficient fiscal space to support growth.

Figure III.6

Gross public debt-to-GDP ratio for select European countries

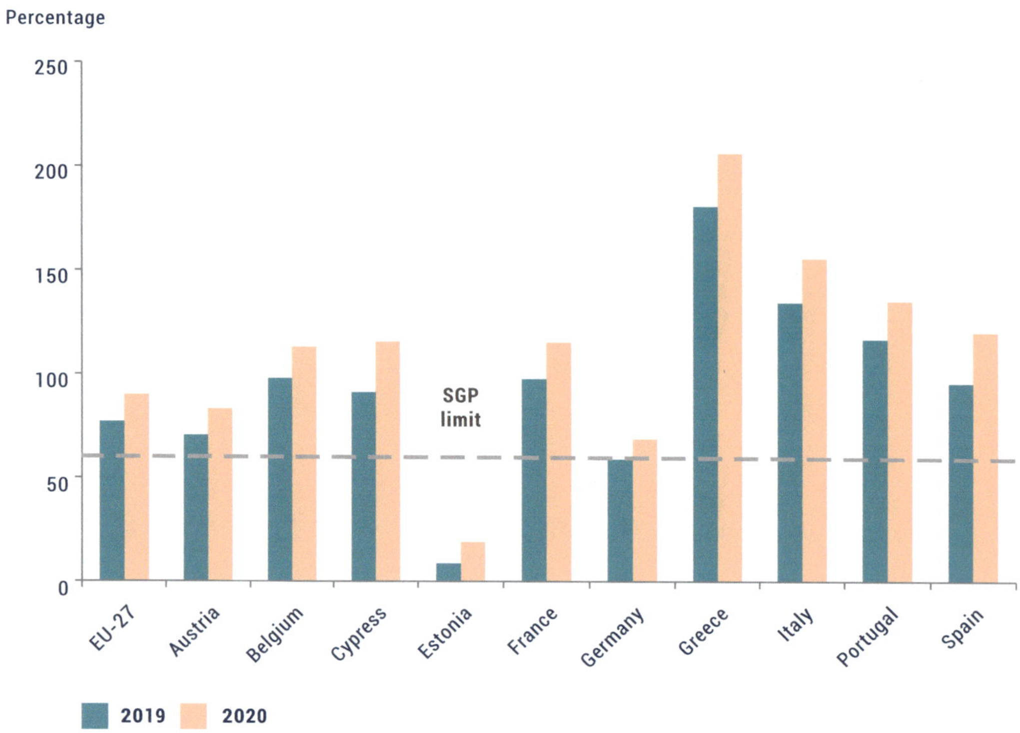

Source: Eurostat.
Note: SGP refers to the Stability and Growth Pact.

The ECB's asset purchases are to be scaled down; Eastern Europe tightens policy

Following the enactment of massive anti-crisis liquidity support schemes, central banks in Europe are expected to start gradual monetary policy normalization. The key policy rates of the ECB, the interest rate on the main refinancing operations and the deposit rate, are likely to be maintained at 0 per cent and minus 0.5 per cent, respectively, at least until early 2023. By contrast, the main policy tool of the ECB since 2020,[5] asset purchases, is expected to be scaled down starting in 2022.[6] The reduction in monthly asset purchases will take place gradually to avoid raising long-term interest rates and prevent disruptions in financial markets. The ECB's balance sheet will likely retain its size in the medium term, with reinvestment of payments from maturing securities.

Outside the euro area, in Sweden, the Riksbank completed its asset purchases by December 2021. In Denmark, where the Government entered the crisis with a large liquidity buffer, the Central Bank, after a series of currency interventions, has reduced the already negative key interest rate further to curb appreciation pressures, defending the peg to the euro. In Eastern Europe, inflation rates not seen for over a decade and concerns about rising inflationary expectations prompted sharp interest rate hikes in the Czech Republic, Hungary, Poland and Romania. In European countries outside the

5 The ECB is running two asset purchase programmes: the Pandemic Emergency Purchase Programme to be phased out in March 2022 and the smaller Asset Purchase Programme.

6 The volume of newly issued sovereign bonds is also expected to shrink along with planned reductions in budget deficits.

European Union, the Bank of England has announced that it plans to begin slowing its asset purchases once interest rates reach 0.5 per cent. Continued favourable monetary conditions in Europe will give a respite to the corporate sector, given elevated business indebtedness. On the other hand, monetary authorities should acknowledge the risks from credit misallocation and elevated asset prices, which could produce unanticipated and sharp price corrections.

Economies in transition

GDP growth

Percentage

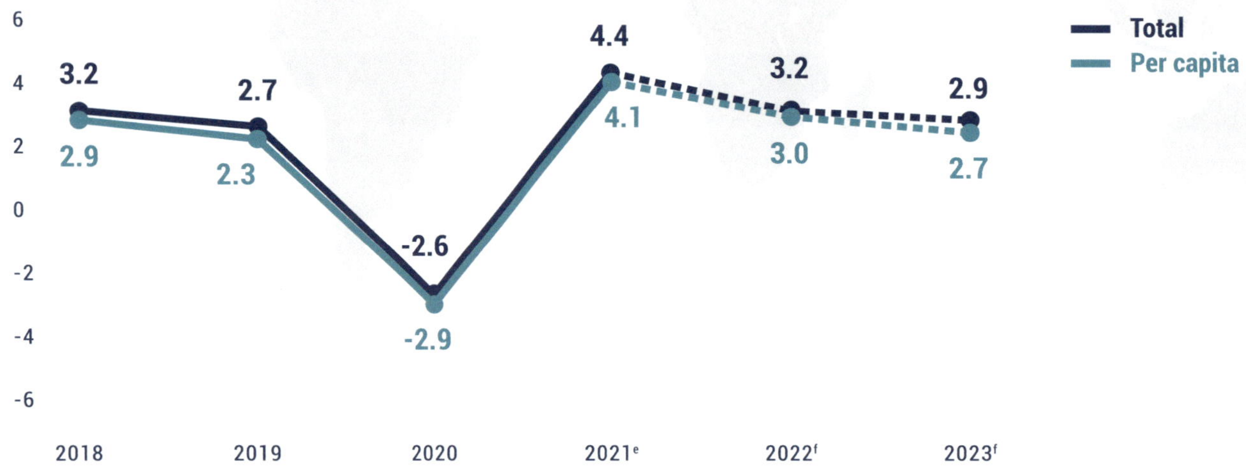

COVID-19 cases & deaths

as of 20 December 2021

Per 100,000 people

Vaccination

as of 20 December 2021

Percentage of population

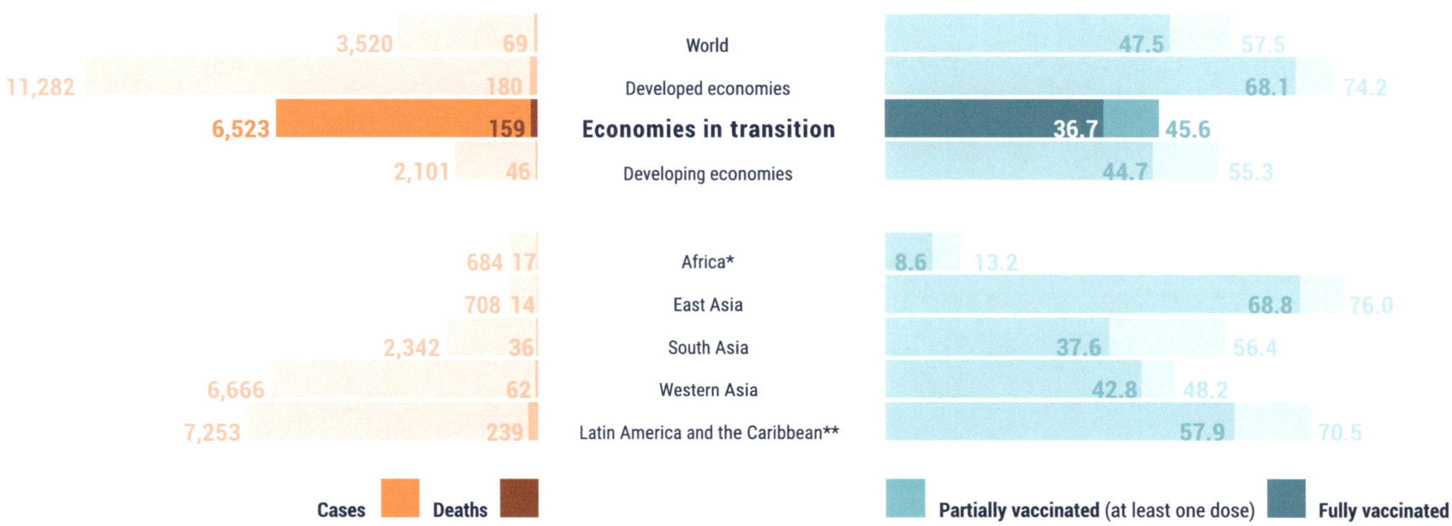

Note: The boundaries and names shown and the designations used on this map do not imply official endorsement or acceptance by the United Nations. The map represents countries and/or territories or parts thereof for which data is available and/or analysed in World Economic Situation and Prospects 2022. The shaded areas therefore do not necessarily overlap entirely with the delimitation of their frontiers or boundaries. Aggregate data for Africa, excluding Libya.

* Excluding Libya; **Excluding Bolivarian Republic of Venezuela. **e:** 2021 estimates. **f:** 2022-2023 forecasts.

Source for COVID-19 data: UN DESA calculations, based on data from Johns Hopkins University.

Economies in transition

- The Commonwealth of Independent States (CIS) and South-Eastern Europe returned to growth amid the lifting of pandemic containment measures, higher commodity prices and an improved external environment.
- Surging inflation is hurting living standards, prompting monetary tightening in the CIS.
- Official development assistance remains important for parts of the region.

The Commonwealth of Independent States and Georgia: the lifting of restrictions and higher commodity prices underpin an economic rebound

Economic growth in the CIS area, including Georgia, resumed in 2021 following contraction in 2020. The turnaround picked up as mobility and activity restrictions were eased or removed. A more favourable external environment, including sharp rises in commodity prices, boosted export volumes and revenues. Services also bounced back while construction activities benefited from support programmes in the Russian Federation and higher remittances sent to Central Asian countries. Better terms of trade for energy-exporting countries improved their current account positions, despite the recovery of imports. In energy-importing countries, remittance flows and tourism revenues along with rebounding domestic demand mitigated current account pressures from import growth.

Private consumption remains the major driver of growth

Growth in the CIS area in 2021 was largely driven by consumer demand, amid raising employment levels, increased retail lending and higher remittances to smaller CIS countries. Investment generally trailed behind amid high uncertainty and subdued foreign direct investment inflows. The relaxation of oil output restrictions under the OPEC Declaration of Cooperation,[7] along with elevated prices for oil and natural gas in late 2021, accelerated recovery in energy-exporting countries.

In the Russian Federation, the main impetus for growth came from the rebound in household spending, boosted by one-off social payments and wage growth due to tight labour market conditions. Investment activity also picked up. The Government launched multiple stimulus packages in 2020-2021, including tax deferrals and guarantees, equivalent to about 6 per cent of 2020 GDP. Despite higher export revenues, protection of reserve buffers against possible external shocks remains a priority. International reserves rocketed to historically high levels in 2021, virtually eliminating debt service risks.[8] That same year, the United States and the European Union introduced additional economic sanctions against the Russian

7 The Declaration of Cooperation is a coordination mechanism for crude oil production by both OPEC member countries and 11 non-OPEC member countries. It is referred to as "the OPEC Plus agreement". See OPEC (2021) for details.

8 In late 2021, international reserves of the Russian Federation exceeded total external debt by around one third.

Federation, in particular forbidding banks based in the United States to purchase Russian sovereign debt on the primary bond market. The decline in the share of non-residents in the Russian domestic bond market was rather limited in 2021, however. The Government in any case was able to issue debt denominated in the local currency and borrow from domestic banks. Economic growth is likely to moderate from the estimated 4.2 per cent in 2021 to 2.7 per cent in 2022 as the Government moves towards fiscal consolidation. The ambitious $360 billion National Development Projects Plan, comprising large investments in infrastructure and the social sphere, was postponed.

In Ukraine, a good harvest, higher steel prices and a surge in construction boosted output in 2021. Economic potential is constrained by the conflict in the East, however, as well as a challenging business environment and large-scale emigration. IMF lending will be important for meeting external debt service obligations in 2022. In Belarus, despite the absence of generalized lockdown measures, domestic demand remained weak amid political tensions. Exports performed well, supported by higher prices for refined oil products and fertilizers, despite sanctions imposed on the country in 2021 by several parties, including the European Union.

In Central Asia, the rebound in remittances in 2021 spurred private consumption; most countries registered high growth rates. Poor performance of the gold sector dampened recovery in the Kyrgyz Republic, however. Pandemic-related restrictions introduced by China in 2020 damaged cross-border trade with Kazakhstan, Kyrgyzstan and Tajikistan, affecting many small businesses.

Following the rebound in 2021, output growth in the CIS area is expected to decelerate in 2022, given weaker base effects, the moderation of consumer demand, more restrictive macroeconomic policies and persistent structural constraints. Without more ambitious reforms, growth will settle around moderate pre-pandemic expansion levels. The aggregate GDP of the CIS and Georgia, after a 2.6 per cent contraction in 2020, increased by an estimated 4.3 per cent in 2021 and is forecast to rise by 3.2 per cent in 2022. Integration processes within the framework of the Eurasian Economic Union[9] are expected to continue, including for financial systems.

Vaccination against COVID-19 is progressing slowly

Vaccination rates in the region remain relatively low, rendering it vulnerable to further waves of infection. In late 2021, the situation in the Russian Federation sharply deteriorated, prompting a one-week lockdown. COVID-19 cases also spiked in Georgia and Ukraine.

Labour markets have improved

Unemployment in the CIS area declined through 2021, approaching pre-pandemic levels in the best-performing countries. They include the Russian Federation, where limited inflows of migrants added to the tightness of labour markets, and numerous sectors such as construction saw shortages of workers. The unemployment rate declined to a record low of 4.3 per cent in September. Authorities relaxed some restrictions imposed earlier, such as by lifting entry bans on Tajik and Uzbek citizens who had committed minor violations.

9 Eurasian Economic Union members are Armenia, Belarus, Kazakhstan, Kyrgyzstan and the Russian Federation. Cuba, Moldova and Uzbekistan are observers.

An upsurge in inflation is eroding living standards

Most of the CIS area experienced a strong upsurge in inflation in 2021, which reached double-digit levels in many countries. The upswing resulted from a combination of supply disruptions, higher food and energy prices, strengthened demand and, in some cases, past exchange rate depreciation. It also came from elevated inflationary expectations and accelerated purchases. Governments responded in various ways. Kazakhstan introduced price controls and export quotas to contain food price pressures. In the Russian Federation, export duties, price controls and agreements with producers were deployed to limit price hikes. In most of the region, inflation is expected to moderate in 2022, except for Moldova, where increases in natural gas tariffs in late 2021 will lead to a double-digit annual consumer price increase.

Monetary policy is significantly tightening

Monetary authorities reacted to the inflationary spike by tightening policies. Interest rate increases in 2021 were substantial, with a series of successive hikes in virtually all countries (see figure III.7). Despite tighter monetary policy, retail lending, in particular mortgage lending, grew rapidly, supporting the recovery of demand. In the Russian Federation, the Central Bank announced plans to curb lending growth in late 2021; a tight monetary policy is expected to continue in 2022 amid concerns about high inflationary expectations.

Figure III.7

Changes in benchmark monetary policy rates in the CIS and Georgia since January 2021

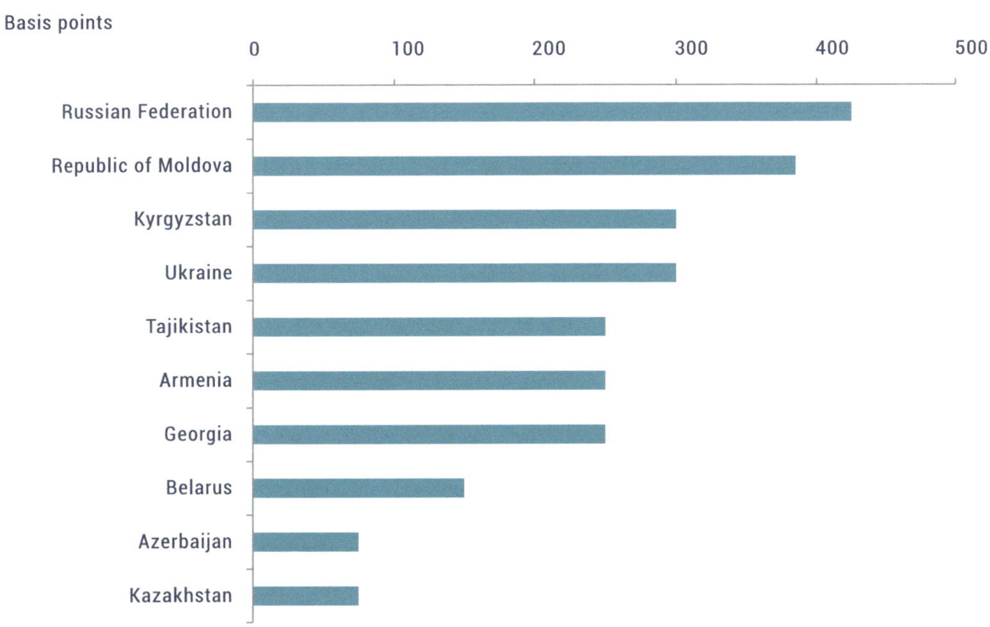

Sources: National central banks data as of 20 December 2021.

The crisis leaves a legacy of public debt

Fiscal policies, although less expansionary than in 2020, have continued to support recovery. Public revenues increased as growth resumed, often exceeding earlier expectations. In the Russian Federation, the deficit fell sharply in 2021 on the back of growing revenues and the return to fiscal consolidation, implying a less supportive fiscal impulse. A tighter fiscal stance is anticipated in 2022, when the fiscal rule is expected to be reinstated. Although public debt in the Russian Federation remains low, at around 20 per cent of GDP, for many other CIS economies, especially energy importers, the crisis has left higher public indebtedness. In Kyrgyzstan, for example, the public debt-to-GDP ratio increased from 54.1 per cent of GDP in 2019 to 68.1 per cent in 2020. The composition of the debt, with a significant share of official financing, represents a mitigating risk factor in the most vulnerable countries. Official financing, critical at the height of the crisis in 2020, remains important, as the recovery of private flows has been limited. Countries from the region have retained good access to international capital markets, however, with a spate of well-received Eurobond issues. The new allocation of the IMF's Special Drawing Rights has alleviated financing needs for many countries, including Ukraine, and helped rebuild reserves.

Looking forward, the region faces multiple downside risks. Volatile commodity prices, especially of oil and natural gas, will remain a major determinant of economic performance. Slow progress in vaccination may lead to a rise in new COVID-19 cases. Mounting geopolitical tensions, internal political strife and the potential for refugee flows from Afghanistan into Central Asia could heighten instability, undermining business and consumer confidence. The banking sector has fared relatively well during the COVID-19 crisis but may come under stress in some countries as temporary forbearance measures are withdrawn and the share of non-performing loans rises, particularly in Ukraine. Persistent price pressures may unleash expectations of rising inflation, leading to quicker policy tightening and domestic tensions.

Box III.1

Sustainable finance in the Commonwealth of Independent States and Georgia

New financial products worldwide are supporting the shift towards sustainable development. This wave of innovation has been accompanied by reflection on the role of financial regulators in both actively contributing to climate change mitigation and adaptation and addressing related risks to the financial system. Sustainable finance is highly relevant for CIS countries, given the importance of hydrocarbons for their economies, including for non-energy-exporting economies through remittances, trade and investment channels, and the related costs of the green energy transition.

Green bonds, where proceeds are used for environmental goals, account for most new offerings. After a slow start compared with other emerging markets, the pace of issuance has picked up. Several financial institutions in Armenia and Kazakhstan and non-financial corporations based in Georgia debuted new products in 2020. Overall issuance in the first nine months of 2021 reached record levels (figure III.1.a). Corporations have pioneered these new financial products and, in line with other emerging markets, financial institutions have been major players. In July 2021, Uzbekistan broke new ground with a sovereign Sustainable Development Goals bond, where proceedings will be allocated to education, water management, health and green transportation, among other ends. The city of Moscow in the Russian Federation issued the first subnational green bond to finance infrastructure projects that reduce air pollution from transport.

New sustainable financial instruments have been accompanied by increased product diversification. For example, some Russian companies in extractive sectors have issued loans linked to sustainability, where interest paid is linked to meeting specified environmental targets. This approach gives issuers more flexibility, as the use of proceeds is not tied to particular projects. Perpetual bonds have been issued by Russian Railways to finance green projects, first in 2020 in the domestic market and then in 2021 in the Eurobond market. While few projects are fully green, the potential pipeline of investable initiatives that could reduce environmental footprints is large. So-called transition bonds, which provide finance for emissions-intensive sectors to meet specific performance criteria, could be of particular interest to the region.

Given the frequent absence of clear comparators, it is difficult to make strong statements on a "greenium" or cost-of-financing advantage. Recent issues have attracted strong investor interest, which has translated into high levels of oversubscription. This has lowered prices and opened access to a broader investor base, which tends to reduce volatility.

From the point of view of issuers, launching a green or sustainable bond has a significance beyond raising revenues at an expected lower financial cost. It allows them to engage with investors and, in the case of corporations, consumers, and to signal their efforts to adopt more sustainable practices and business models. Wide acceptance of these bonds requires alignment with well-established criteria around how proceeds can be used and the existence of suitable monitoring mechanisms, however. According to common practice, issuers have put in place frameworks that detail revenue use and are verified by external parties, but this is a source of additional costs that may deter issuance.

Different forms of financial support have encouraged the development of green finance. For example, under certain conditions, the costs of assessing green bond alignment with globally accepted standards are reimbursed by the Astana International Financial Centre, which aims to become a regional leader in green finance. In the Russian Federation, subsidies to cover part of the cost of the coupon are provided by the national ecology programme. International organizations and multilateral development banks have played roles as anchor investors (European Bank for Reconstruction and Development), helped to identify suitable projects to finance (United Nations Development Programme) or even issued green bonds in domestic markets to raise funding in local currency (Asian Development Bank).

For most countries in the CIS, issuance in external markets is the rule as the investor base for domestic launches remains limited. This relates to the lack of awareness of green instruments among domestic investors but also to shallow domestic capital markets. Judging by developments in other countries and ongoing regulatory initiatives to support demand, green and similar bonds are expected to account for an increased share of total issuance in the future. They still add to the debt burden of issuers,

Author: José Palacin, United Nations Economic Commission for Europe

however, and, in most cases, to their foreign currency exposure. These risks need to be understood and managed, including through regulatory actions to ensure transparency and promote demand. More general initiatives are required to foster domestic capital markets. While sustainable finance carries transformative potential, critical constraints could relate to the appropriate pricing of externalities and regulatory reforms in relevant sectors.

Figure III.1.a
Green bond issuance in the CIS and Georgia

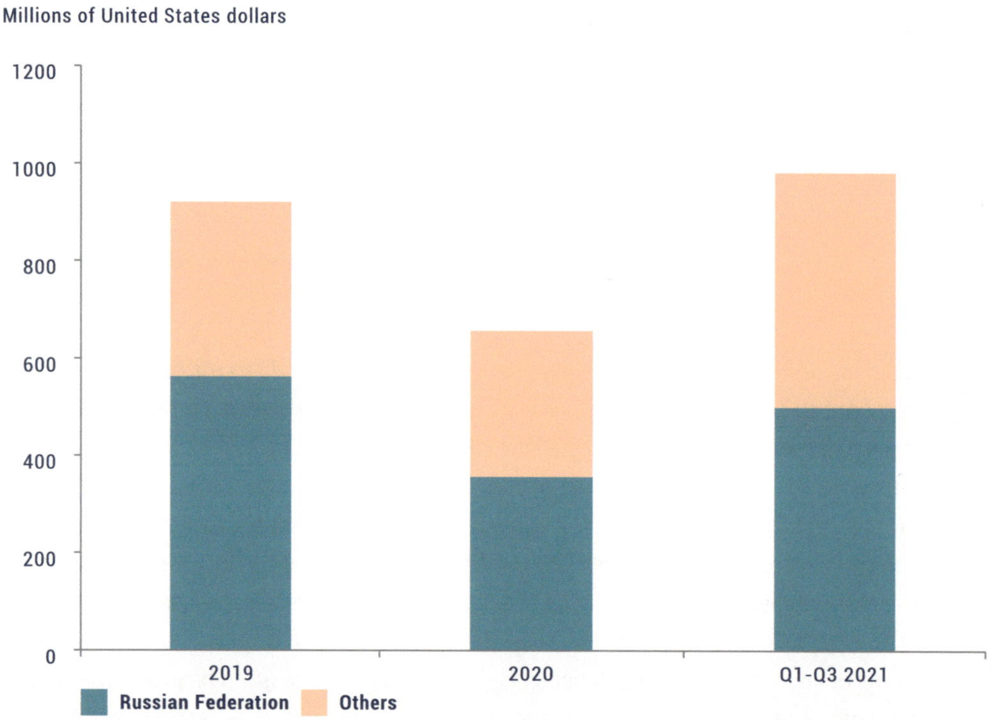

Sources: International Finance Corporation, Amundi, Bloomberg, Climate Bonds Initiative and Environmental Finance.

South-Eastern Europe: growth returns to the region

Economic growth returned to South-Eastern Europe in 2021 after a COVID-19-induced recession in 2020. An improved external environment was a major driver of recovery in these open economies with strong links to the European Union through trade and remittances, and, in the case of Albania and Montenegro, large dependence on the tourism sector. In Serbia, the largest economy in the region, the economy expanded by more than an estimated 6 per cent in 2021 amid soaring private investment and exports. Consumer confidence in South-Eastern Europe has markedly improved; macroeconomic policies have been generally supportive. Investment remained comparatively weak, although in Albania, post-earthquake reconstruction will continue to contribute to recovery. In late 2021, some countries experienced an energy supply crisis induced by the increasing cost of natural gas, leading to more use of coal along with higher prices for it. The pace of economic expansion may slow somewhat in 2022, as fiscal support unwinds to stabilize debt ratios. Aggregate GDP in South-Eastern Europe, after contracting by 3.1 per cent in 2020, is projected to increase by 6.2 per cent in 2021 and a further 4 per cent in 2022.

After years of low inflation, consumer prices have increased

After years of moderate price increases, inflation pressures have returned to the region, driven by the sharp acceleration in food and energy prices and, to a lesser extent, stronger consumer demand. Higher inflation has offset most nominal wage growth and worsened social conditions, with food accounting for up to 30 per cent of consumption spending. Price increases have been steeper in Serbia, while in Bosnia and Herzegovina and Montenegro, a deflationary trend ended. Formal or informal currency pegs constrain monetary policy in the region. While labour markets showed some positive trends in 2021, unemployment remains precariously high in Bosnia and Herzegovina and the Republic of North Macedonia.

Fiscal balances in the region have improved

Fiscal balances in the region improved as revenues increased and spending growth moderated. The fiscal impulse remained positive in 2021 but consolidation is likely in 2022. Countries have retained favourable access to capital markets, despite some deterioration for Montenegro. Several countries issued Eurobonds, including Serbia, which offered its first sovereign green bond. Current account deficits in the region remain high, especially in Albania and Montenegro, and despite a moderate reduction in the latter. Increases in exports and tourism revenues have been offset by stronger domestic demand and higher energy prices.

Structural barriers to growth remain

The outlook for the region is subject to certain risks. Vaccination rates are still relatively low, particularly in Albania and Bosnia and Herzegovina, which could lead to further waves of infection that derail recovery. Structural impediments to growth in South-Eastern Europe remain significant; the pandemic exacerbated already low productivity levels and labour market participation rates. Demographic pressures and outward migration create additional challenges. Geopolitical tensions, while contained, could resurface. Infrastructure deficits, skills shortages and weak governance continue to undermine private investment.

An additional regional cooperation framework was launched

In 2021, Albania, North Macedonia and Serbia agreed to lay the foundation for a single market, including the free movement of labour. This is within the framework of the initial "mini-Schengen" initiative, later renamed "Open Balkans", which is aimed at removing internal borders by 2023. To some extent, the move reflects frustration with slow progress in accession to the European Union, which should nevertheless continue to provide an anchor for domestic policies and remain a source of financing.

Africa

GDP growth

Percentage

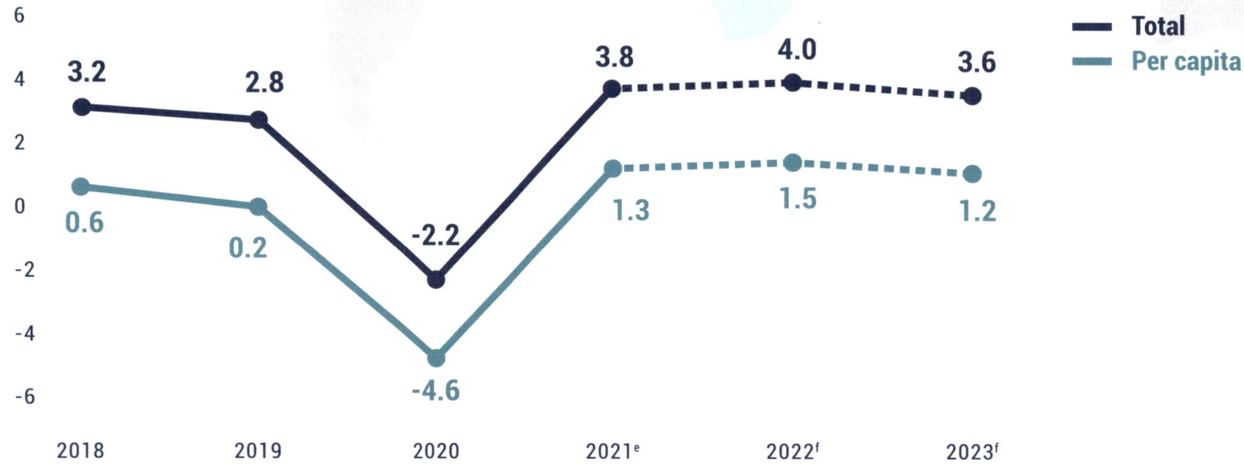

COVID-19 cases & deaths

as of 20 December 2021

Per 100,000 people

Vaccination

as of 20 December 2021

Percentage of population

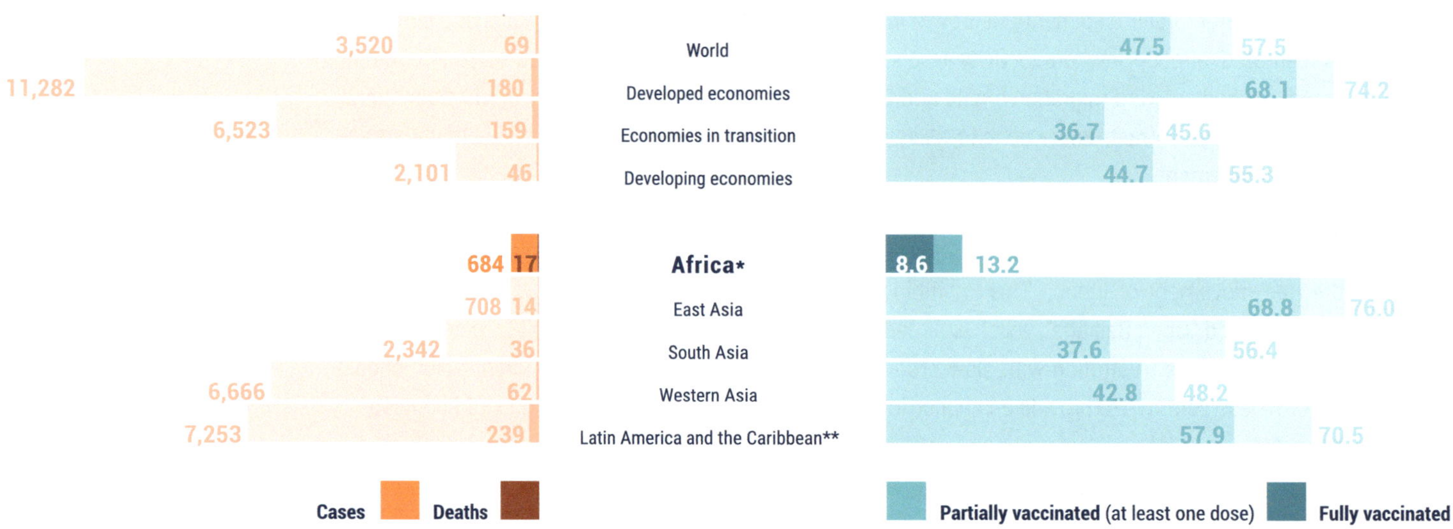

Note: The boundaries and names shown and the designations used on this map do not imply official endorsement or acceptance by the United Nations. The map represents countries and/or territories or parts thereof for which data is available and/or analysed in World Economic Situation and Prospects 2022. The shaded areas therefore do not necessarily overlap entirely with the delimitation of their frontiers or boundaries. Aggregate data for Africa, excluding Libya.

* Excluding Libya; **Excluding Bolivarian Republic of Venezuela. **e:** 2021 estimates. **f:** 2022-2023 forecasts.

Source for COVID-19 data: UN DESA calculations, based on data from Johns Hopkins University.

Developing economies

Africa: rebound in economic growth amid great downside risks

- Economic output in Africa is projected to rise, but it is subject to risks from recurrent waves of COVID-19 and increased instability.
- A boom in commodity prices is providing much needed fiscal space for commodity exporters but tourism-dependent countries may take longer to bounce back.
- Multilateral support to the region will remain critical for full recovery, including to expedite vaccine distribution and facilitate debt relief.

Returning to normal economic activity has been challenging in Africa

Economic activity in Africa continues recovering from the unprecedented events of 2020 but at a fragile pace. A projected expansion is marked by high uncertainty and exposure to repeated waves of COVID-19 infection, as seen recently with the emergence of the Omicron variant. Mitigation measures, such as lockdowns and travel bans, have been the main tool for stopping the spread of the virus due to low vaccination rates. Resulting disruptions in economic activities make a return to pre-pandemic conditions difficult. Although most African economies are witnessing rising output levels, supported by a more favourable global context, economic recovery has been weaker than in other regions.

Economic growth rates are insufficient for a return to pre-pandemic trends

Aggregate output in Africa is projected to recover gradually against a backdrop of subdued investment and high uncertainty. Economic growth is estimated to firm up in 2022, to 4 per cent from 3.8 per cent in 2021 (figure III.8). This should be driven by the gradual rollback of virus containment measures and rising vaccination rates as well as higher commodity prices and incremental improvements in investment rates. Africa observed one of the slowest recoveries in the world in 2021, lagging average growth rates for the developing countries and the globe, which are estimated at 6.4 per cent and 5.5 per cent, respectively. Projections point to a permanent loss of output in the forecast horizon (figure III.9). To return to its pre-pandemic trajectory of output growth, Africa would need to grow by approximately 6 per cent in 2022-2023, which is as fast as South Asia. In per capita terms, real GDP levels are expected to remain below pre-pandemic levels through 2023, especially in southern Africa, representing a significant setback to development gains achieved before the pandemic.

Figure III.8
Real GDP growth in Africa by subregion

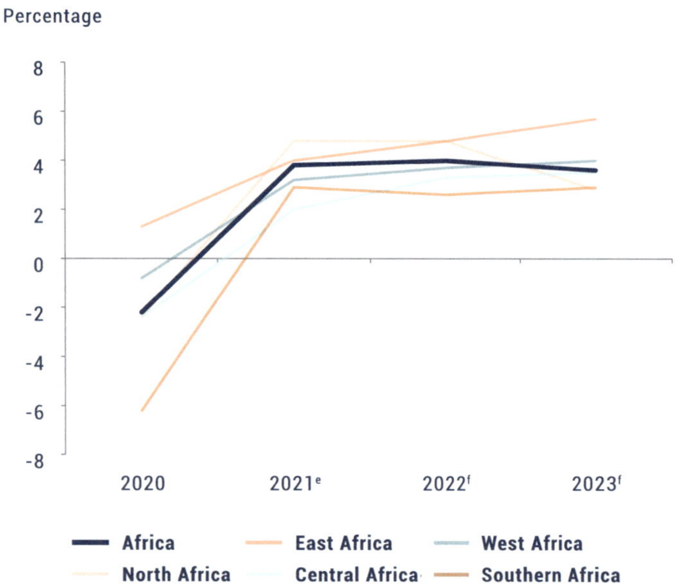

Figure III.9
Real GDP in Africa

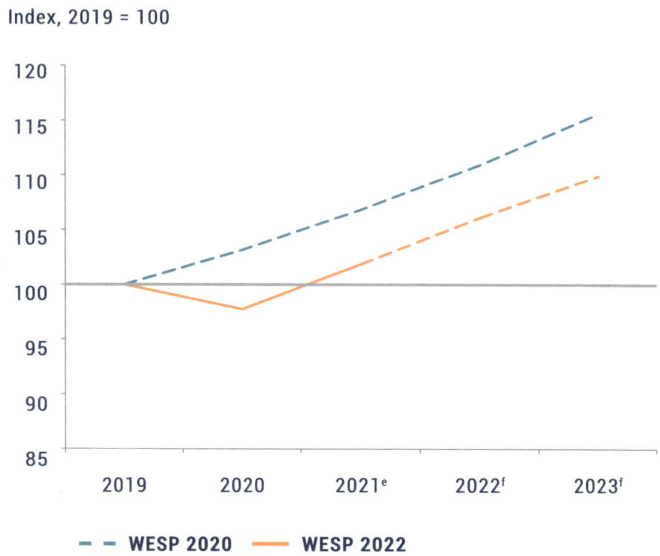

Sources: Source: UN DESA, based on projections produced with the World Economic Forecasting Model.
Note: e = partial estimate, f = forecast. Excludes Libya. The dashed line in Figure III.9 indicates pre-crisis projections.

Low vaccination levels are exposing African countries to repeated COVID-19 waves...

Most African economies remain in the grip of the pandemic. While the third wave of the coronavirus has tapered off, at least 12 countries – Algeria, Benin, Burkina Faso, Egypt, Eritrea, Kenya, Mali, Mauritania, Mauritius, Somalia, South Africa and Tunisia – are battling or have battled their fourth wave. In late November 2021, a new variant, Omicron, was detected in Botswana and put the world on edge after South Africa announced a surge in cases. Though the impact of each wave is unknown, the death toll from future waves in Africa would likely be high, given case fatality rates that rank among the highest in the globe (such as in Egypt, Somalia and Sudan). The continent remains the most undervaccinated in the world, with just over 10 per cent of its 1.3 billion people vaccinated with at least one dose (figure III.10). Most countries have vaccinated less than 5 per cent of their populations, failing to meet the World Health Organization (WHO) vaccination goals of 10 per cent coverage by September 2021 and 40 per cent by the end of 2021. Only five African countries have accomplished the latter (Cabo Verde, Mauritius, Morocco, Seychelles and Tunisia). The vaccine roll-out has been hampered by affordability, hesitancy,[10] logistics, global production constraints and vaccine hoarding abroad. Global solidarity around vaccines has proved widely inadequate, with pledges and deliveries to the WHO's COVAX Facility falling short of requirements. Production facilities in Algeria, Egypt, Nigeria, Senegal and South Africa may help boost vaccination in those countries later this year. The vast majority of countries,

10 A survey by the Africa Centres for Disease Control and Prevention on perceptions of COVID-19 vaccination found that misinformation in Africa is rife. Young, male and unemployed people and urban residents are more likely to be sceptical (Africa CDC, 2021).

however, may not reach 60-70 per cent coverage before 2023 and, in some cases, not at all barring significant changes in vaccine production and distribution.

Figure III.10
COVID-19 vaccination rates by world region (as of 20 December 2021)

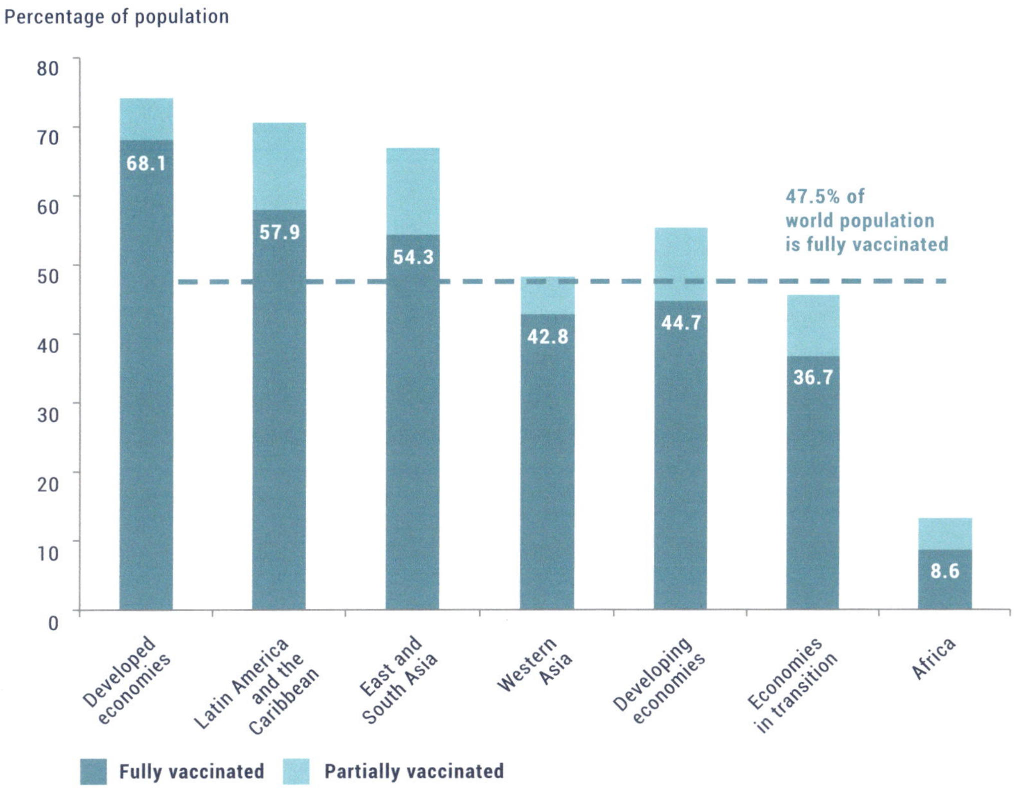

Sources: UN DESA, based on data from Our World in Data (accessed on 20 December 2021).

...and political instability is undermining the economic recovery

Even promising economies face the challenges of conflict and instability. Four military coups occurred last year, in Chad, Guinea, Mali and Sudan, and attempts were foiled in the Central African Republic, Madagascar and Niger. UN Secretary-General António Guterres has referred to "an epidemic of coup d'états". In Ethiopia, Africa's second-most populous nation, civil war in the northern Tigray region since November 2020 is a major source of tension domestically and for countries across the Horn of Africa. A prolonged unsettled dispute will have escalating humanitarian consequences while further destabilizing the region and depressing investment. Tensions are also intensifying among Ethiopia, Egypt and Sudan over the filling of the Grand Ethiopian Renaissance Dam. In the Sahel region, humanitarian and security crises continue to deteriorate, with interethnic violence on the rise in Burkina Faso, Chad, Mali, Mauritania and Niger. Other ongoing conflicts include civil wars in Libya and Somalia, an Islamist insurgency in Mozambique, the "Anglophone crisis" in Cameroon and natural resource-driven conflict in the Democratic Republic of Congo. These crises interact with and aggravate other challenges – such as poverty, unemployment, crime, food insecurity and internal displacement – and undermine the economic potential of the continent.

The main downside risks of the pandemic are elevated food prices and tightening financing conditions

Risks to regional growth skew down due to domestic and external factors. On the domestic front, there is a significant concern that countries will experience recurrent COVID-19 waves with possibly more dangerous variants. Border closures could wreak havoc in African economies, disrupting the flow of medical supplies and tourism. The risks would be aggravated by further delays to vaccination programmes. Vaccine hoarding by developed nations, including for third-dose booster shots, and affordability constraints present serious concerns and may extend the pandemic in the continent. Even as supplies increase, deficient infrastructure, limited access to crucial commodities such as syringes and vaccine hesitancy may continue to slow the roll-out of vaccines. Should COVID-19 become an endemic disease in the region, medium-term prospects would be hampered by lower consumer and investor confidence.

Domestic risks from upsets in crop and livestock production also cloud the outlook. Extreme weather- and conflict-related events may cause these disruptions and increase already elevated food prices, pushing up headline inflation (as in Angola, Egypt, Ethiopia, Guinea and Sierra Leone). Droughts and floods are becoming more frequent as temperatures and sea levels continue to increase faster in Africa than the world average (IPCC, 2021b). Conflict and unrest may escalate given greater instability, poverty and insecurity.

On the external front, rising inflation expectations in advanced economies and other regions threaten financing for the region. A tightening of monetary policy in the United States and global financial conditions would dampen global economic activity and increase risk premiums, especially for more exposed economies in Africa already grappling with elevated debt levels. This situation would decrease access to funds for investment, with dire consequences for social and economic development.

Within the region, prospects remain subdued for the largest economies. Nigerian economic growth is projected to accelerate to 2.8 per cent in 2022 from 2.5 per cent in 2021, as the impact of the health crisis declines and the new oil bill and public infrastructure development boost investment. Nevertheless, there are downside risks from an uncertain evolution of the pandemic given low vaccination rates, high inflation and security threats. South Africa's recovery has faced headwinds due to a sluggish vaccine roll-out and damaging civil unrest during the summer of 2021. Its economy grew by an estimated 3.8 per cent in 2021, not enough to compensate for the 7 per cent drop in 2020. With the outbreak of the Omicron variant spelling dire economic troubles for the country, especially for tourism, prospects are gloomy. Growth is forecast at only 2.3 per cent in 2022. Frequent power outages, high unemployment, inequality and corruption will continue to weigh on productivity growth. In Egypt, after near stagnant economic growth in 2020, a robust recovery is underway with real GDP growth at an estimated 6.1 per cent in 2021 and forecast at 5.7 per cent in 2022. The recovery has been led by solid growth in private consumption, exports and private investment amid easing balance-of-payments constraints due to more favourable external conditions. Both public and external debt are growing at alarming rates, however, posing risks.

Higher commodity prices support some exporters while other countries await the return of tourism

Among commodity exporters, strong global demand and high prices provide a promising outlook. The upturn in global commodity prices is giving some breathing room to energy, metals and agricultural producers after two commodity price crashes in five years. The financial windfall is providing crucial improvements in national income and government spending and investment. The rise in commodity prices will likely be transitory, however, and insufficient to generate robust, sustainable growth. The need for economic reform and diversification will remain high on the development agenda.

Tourism-dependent economies face improving prospects, though from a low base. These are driven by the loosening of travel restrictions and economic recovery in origin markets in Europe and Asia, as well as higher traveller confidence associated with successful containment measures and relatively high vaccination rates (as in Cabo Verde, Comoros, Mauritius, Morocco, Sao Tome and Principe, and Tunisia). Yet global tourist arrivals are not expected to return to 2019 levels before 2023 and quite possibly 2024 (UNWTO, 2021b). Economic recovery in these countries will likely be difficult and vulnerable to renewed shocks to global travel, including from new variants. Tourist-dependent industries, such as wildlife conservation and environmental protection, and informal workers in the sector are expected to face another difficult year, with aggravating long-term effects.

Stagnant working hours and productivity growth contribute to poverty and inequality

Labour markets and social conditions lag economic growth in Africa. Growth in working hours stalled in 2021, remaining 5.3 per cent below levels at the end of 2019 (ILO, 2021d). Labour productivity declined in 2021 with average output per hour worked 1.4 per cent lower than in 2020, except in North Africa. This contrasts with positive productivity growth in developed economies. It follows a medium-term decline in African labour productivity since 2016. With 85.8 per cent of the labour force and 89.7 of the female labour force in informal employment (ILO, 2018), the ability of governments to provide targeted assistance to those in need, especially during the pandemic, proved very limited. The global economic crisis in 2020 increased extreme poverty in Africa by 38.4 million people, and in 2021, another 8.6 million fell below the extreme poverty threshold. Given predicted GDP per capita growth of less than 2 per cent in 2022-2023, the poverty headcount rate in Africa will remain elevated (see box III.2). Women have been disproportionally affected by job losses in hard-hit sectors, increased domestic care, exposure to domestic violence and reduced access to sexual and reproductive care (UN Women, 2020). Young African women are now 60 per cent more likely than men not to be in employment, education or training (ILO, 2020). High unemployment, poverty and inequality afflicting young, increasingly tech-proficient and urbanized populations will present substantial political and policy challenges ahead.

Box III.2

The quantity and quality of economic growth fosters poverty reduction in Africa

Extreme poverty in Africa has dropped from over 50 per cent of the population in 2002 to 41 per cent in 2018 (figure III.2.a). From 2002-2014, the poverty rate fell by 1.2 percentage points per year, mainly due to robust economic growth, with average GDP per capita increasing by 2.6 per cent over this period. Even so, the region added about 13 million poor people due to population growth. Since 2014, reflecting in part the 2014-2015 decline in global commodity prices, annual per capita GDP growth has been negative. Africa's poverty headcount rate decreased by less than 0.5 percentage points per year from 2014-2018.

COVID-19 increased the number of newly poor people in Africa by up to 55 million in one year, more than the combined total since 1999. Achieving the first Sustainable Development Goal, to end extreme poverty by 2030, was unlikely for most African countries even before the pandemic. It is now even further out of reach. Although income growth appears to be the main driver of poverty reduction, its decomposition reveals striking differences across countries in terms of inequality (ECA, 2021).

Figure III.2.a

Poverty headcount rate and annual GDP growth

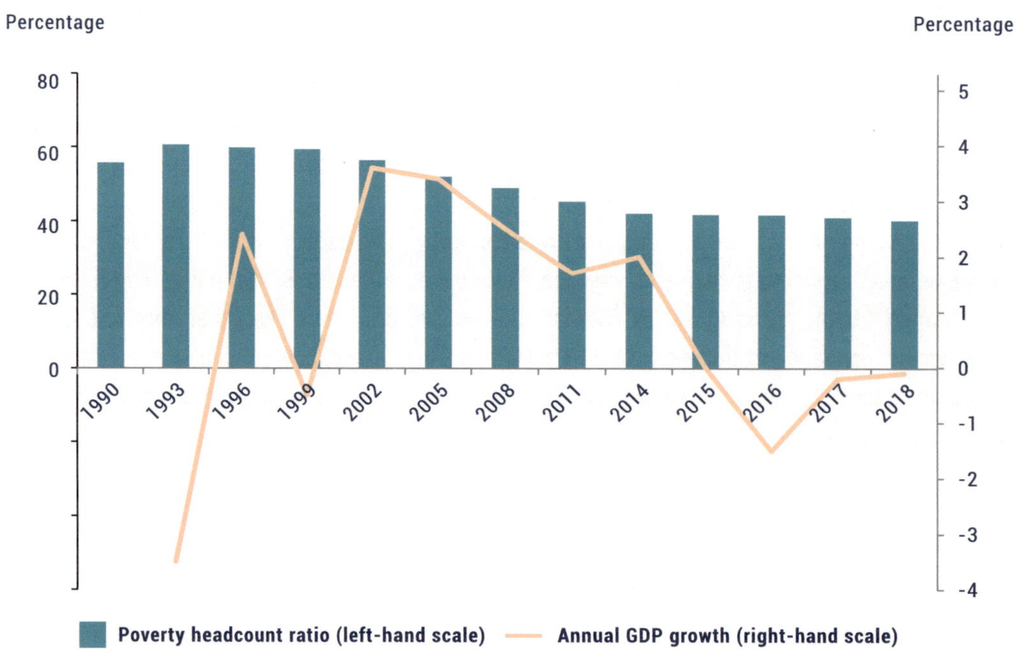

Source: ECA calculations based on data from the World Bank PovcalNet database (accessed in September 2021).

Deep poverty and vulnerability exacerbate poverty reduction challenges

A key challenge to poverty reduction in Africa is how deep poverty remains in many countries. On average, the depth is 13.1 per cent, implying that the average poor person is 13.1 per cent below the poverty threshold (figure III.2.b). There is wide variation, with the poor less than 1 per cent below the poverty line in North Africa, but 13-18 per cent below in the other four subregions. In low-income countries, the average poor person is nearly 20 per cent below the poverty line. The six most-affected countries (Burundi, Democratic Republic of Congo, Central African Republic, Guinea-Bissau, Madagascar and Zambia) have a depth of poverty between 30-39 per cent. The 10 countries in the world with the deepest poverty are all in Africa.

Figure III.2.b

Depth of poverty in Africa

Source: ECA calculations based on data from the World Bank PovcalNet database (accessed in September 2021).
Note: Figures in parantheses are the number of countries in each category.

Another key challenge to ending poverty in Africa is the high proportion of people who live just above the poverty line. About 175 million people have consumption levels about 10-33 per cent above the extreme poverty line. They are not considered poor but remain vulnerable to falling into poverty. About 58 million people are extremely vulnerable as their mean consumption is only 10 per cent above the poverty line. A very small drop in consumption can be enough to push them under the line. This group likely explains the sharp increase in poverty headcount numbers due to COVID-19. West and East Africa have the largest shares of people vulnerable to falling into poverty, with Ethiopia and Nigeria the biggest contributors. East Africa and Southern Africa have the largest proportions of people most vulnerable to staying in poverty (or the chronic poor) at 34.6 and 33.3 per cent, respectively. Unsurprisingly, low-income countries have the largest proportion of people (36.2 per cent) most vulnerable to remaining in poverty after a shock.[a]

Economic performance is key in reducing poverty. The transformation of growth to poverty reduction is mediated by relative contributions of changes in income and inequality. Currently, a return to declining rates of poverty is uncertain given a weak economic recovery with considerable downside risks, such as low vaccine availability and slow roll-outs, the emergence of possible variants, constrained fiscal space and high debt repayment obligations. Those far below the poverty line will require robust targeted income support and other social protection measures.

To revert to the pace of poverty reduction in 2002-2014 and accelerate implementation of the 2030 Agenda and Africa's Agenda 2063, countries need higher growth rates of at least 7 per cent annually. Since high inequality reduces the likelihood that economic growth will translate into poverty reduction, policies must also narrow inequalities in opportunities and set growth on an inclusive path. This could be done through continental initiatives, such as the African Continental Free Trade Area, to stimulate value added intra-Africa trade, structural transformation and job creation. It could build on poverty reduction strategies that hedge against extreme income volatility due to present and future shocks.

With COVID-19 exacerbating economic vulnerabilities, African countries should also emphasize measures including effective debt management, increased expenditure efficiency and greater domestic revenue allocations in sync with the Sustainable Development Goals. They should harness the benefits of international debt relief options, such as the Debt Service Suspension Initiative, the Heavily Indebted Poor Countries Initiative and the Common Framework for Debt Treatment. This would strengthen recovery and eventually diminish the depth of poverty and vulnerability.

a ECA calculations based on data from the World Bank PovcalNet database (accessed in September 2021).

Authors: Adrian Gauci and Hopestone Kayiska Chavula, United Nations Economic Commission for Africa

Fiscal consolidation began during the pandemic

Though African governments initially responded to the crisis by increasing fiscal outlays, fiscal sustainability concerns preceding the pandemic meant a relatively quick return to fiscal consolidation. Governments already had little room to accommodate revenue shortfalls caused by the pandemic and the budgetary costs of response packages. Financing needs were mostly covered by international emergency support, including IMF, World Bank and bilateral assistance, and debt service relief from the G20 Debt Service Suspension Initiative and the IMF Catastrophe Containment and Relief Trust. In 2021, while still fighting second and third waves of COVID-19, governments began fiscal consolidation to maintain sufficient external reserves, protect currency pegs for some and ensure debt servicing capacity, despite weak and fragile economic recoveries. In developed countries, by contrast, greater policy buffers have allowed robust support and a quadrupling of government borrowing since the outbreak of the pandemic (figure III.11). Fiscal balances are expected to continue shrinking across the continent. In August 2021, the $650 billion Special Drawing Rights allocation boosted reserves somewhat and could be amplified by voluntary channelling of allocations elsewhere. China, for instance, announced it would shift $10 billion in its Special Drawing Rights to African nations.

Despite fiscal tightening, debt levels are projected to remain high and rising. Government interest expenditure continues to absorb a rising share of revenues and is already above a third in certain countries in the West African Economic and Monetary Union (IMF, 2021c). This reflects a build-up in debt, persistently weak revenue mobilization and for some countries the end of the Debt Service Suspension Initiative. Rising interest expenditure reduces fiscal space to support economic recovery and the 2030 Agenda for Sustainable Development. Already, several countries spend more on debt servicing than on health care. To this end, a new repo market launched by the United Nations Economic Commission for Africa in November 2021 should trim billions of dollars from government borrowing costs starting in 2022. Still, debt relief as well as emergency assistance may be necessary for countries in higher debt distress.

Figure III.11

Government borrowing as a share of GDP

Index, 2019 = 100

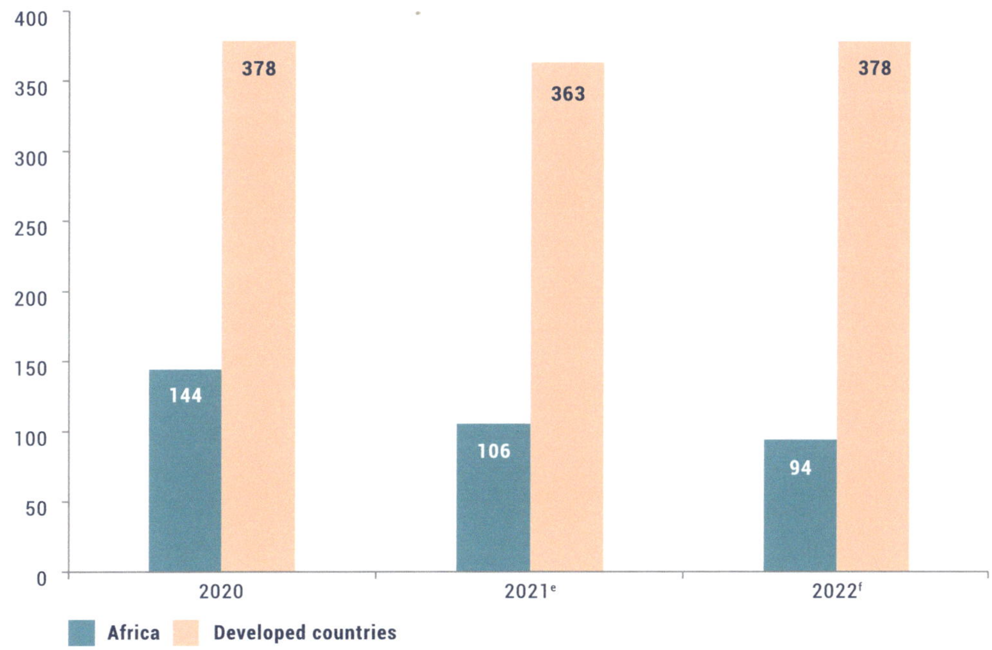

Source: UN DESA, based on projections produced with the World Economic Forecasting Model. Excludes Libya.
Note: e = partial estimate, f = forecast.

Monetary policy stances remain accommodative but global and domestic conditions add pressure

African central banks are mostly maintaining accommodative monetary policy stances but this might change in the short term. In 2021, only a small number of countries changed policy interest rates, either through cuts (as in Ghana, Liberia, the Republic of Congo, Seychelles and Uganda) or hikes (Angola, Ghana, Lesotho, Mozambique, South Africa, Zambia and Zimbabwe). Leniency in developed countries towards rising inflation has allowed crucial policy space for African central banks to prioritize economic growth and narrow output gaps, even if that meant tolerating rising inflationary pressures

(Democratic Republic of the Congo, Nigeria and Sierra Leone). Upside risks to inflation from currency depreciation and planned consumer tax hikes as well as reduced subsidies due to fiscal consolidation may require central bankers to raise interest rates sooner rather than later. Fading monetary stimulus along with fiscal consolidation would complicate already challenging recoveries.

Countries are tasked with fighting the pandemic while boosting growth and development

Moving forward, saving lives from COVID-19 must continue to take precedence. Keeping a close watch on the emergence of more transmissible and lethal variants, at home and abroad, and responding with swift action must be a priority. Faster and more fair distribution of global vaccine supplies, expansion of local vaccine manufacturing, improvements in the distribution infrastructure and measures to combat vaccine hesitancy are necessary to control the pandemic in Africa and avoid stop-and-go economic processes.

For the medium term, the single most viable route to inclusive and sustainable development in Africa is through advancing the structural transformation of economies and building productive capacities. A key focus for many countries will be services and manufacturing-driven industrialization with formal and decent employment. The industrialization of agriculture and minerals processing could be avenues for progress, as recognized in several national development plans. Another key area is to speed the digital revolution. This entails deploying new technologies in areas such as revenue collection and anti-corruption efforts, improving 3G and 4G network coverage, and advancing 5G networks, including beyond major cities. Firms stand to profit from new market opportunities, enhanced supply-chain efficiency and resilience as well as productivity increases. Consumers should see more product choices and learning opportunities through digital transformation.

East Asia

GDP growth

Percentage

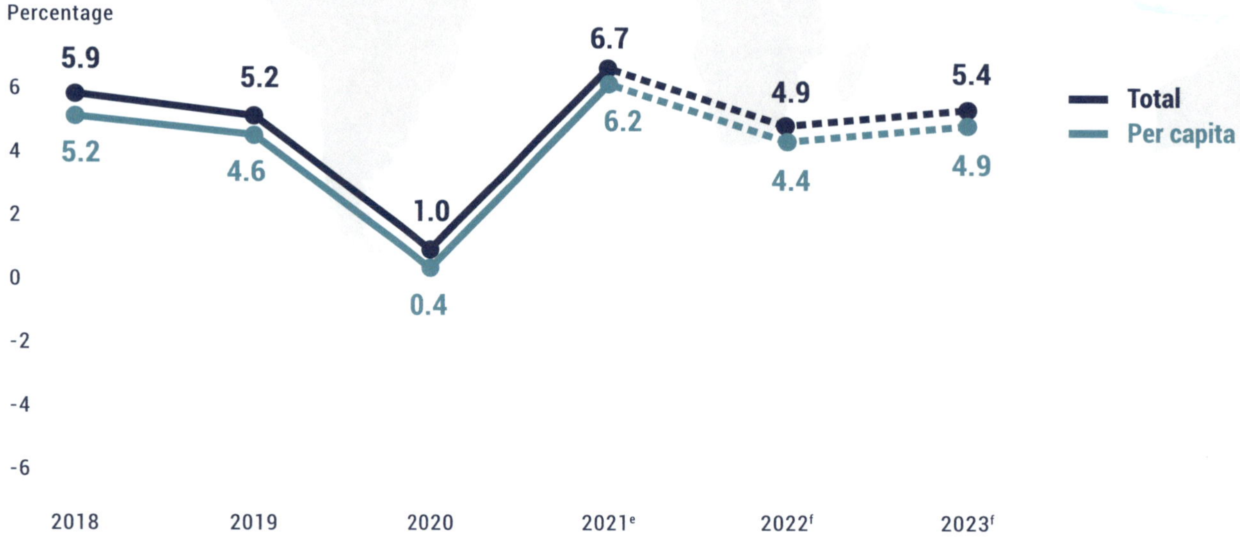

COVID-19 cases & deaths

as of 20 December 2021

Per 100,000 people

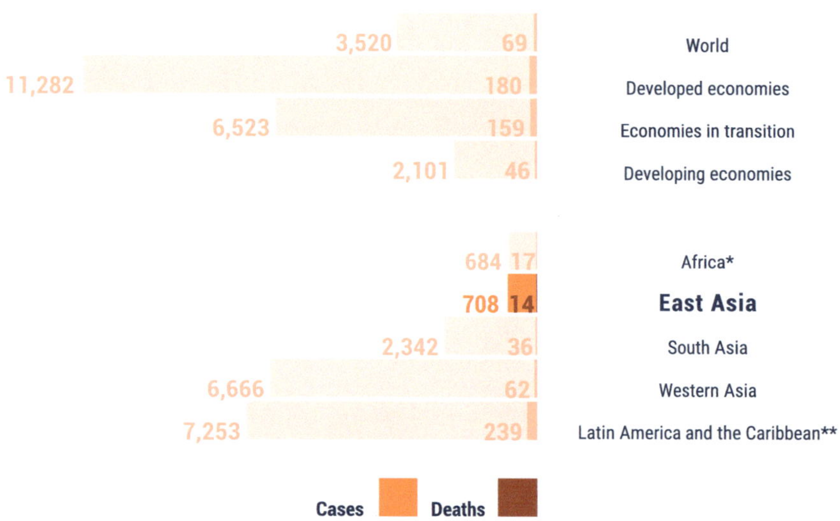

Vaccination

as of 20 December 2021

Percentage of population

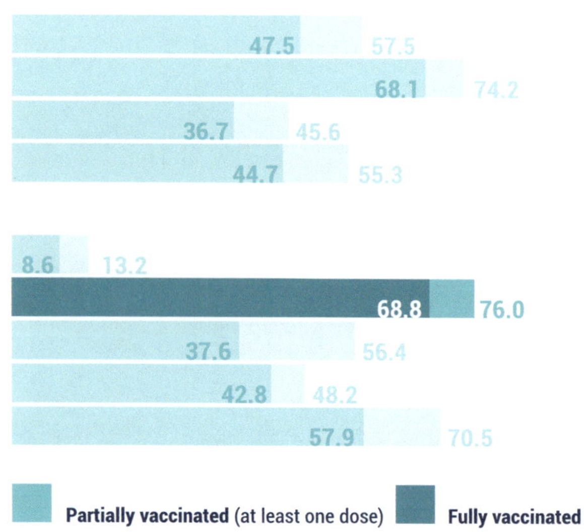

Note: The boundaries and names shown and the designations used on this map do not imply official endorsement or acceptance by the United Nations. The map represents countries and/or territories or parts thereof for which data is available and/or analysed in World Economic Situation and Prospects 2022. The shaded areas therefore do not necessarily overlap entirely with the delimitation of their frontiers or boundaries. Aggregate data for Africa, excluding Libya.
* Excluding Libya; **Excluding Bolivarian Republic of Venezuela. **e:** 2021 estimates. **f:** 2022-2023 forecasts.
Source for COVID-19 data: UN DESA calculations, based on data from Johns Hopkins University.

East Asia: a nascent economic recovery with rising downside risks

- Increasing downside risks and uncertainties cast a shadow on East Asia's nascent economic recovery.
- The lingering pandemic continues to weigh on progress in achieving the 2030 Agenda for Sustainable Development.
- Macroeconomic policies should remain accommodative and targeted to fostering inclusive and sustainable recovery.

East Asia's economies have rebounded from the worst but remain fragile...

East Asia's economic performance largely rebounded in 2021. Headline GDP growth was an estimated 6.7 per cent following the sharp deceleration in 2020. The recovery is nascent, however. A resurgence of COVID-19 has disrupted economic performance supported by strong policy stimulus and a recovery in external demand. Economic growth is forecast to moderate to 4.9 per cent in 2022 as base effects disappear. While countries' reopening could shore up economic activities, the uneven distribution of vaccines, a still low pace of vaccination and unknown vaccine efficacy against new variants of the virus mean that the pandemic will linger and could derail a fragile economic recovery. Additional headwinds come from a possible decline in export demand, prolonged supply-side challenges, rising concerns around financial instability and the possibility of a larger-than-expected slowdown in China's economy amid lingering trade tensions with the United States. Since pandemic control will continue as a policy priority in the near term, macroeconomic policies should remain accommodative and targeted to fostering an inclusive and sustainable recovery.

... and with divergence in economic performance

The uptick in East Asia's headline GDP growth masks large divergence in economic performance across countries. Overall, relatively stronger recovery was seen in China, the Republic of Korea and Singapore, due to early COVID-19 containment measures, quick vaccine roll-outs and strong external demand. In contrast, the Delta variant outbreak slowed recovery in many countries in the Association of Southeast Asian Nations (ASEAN), including Indonesia, Malaysia, the Philippines, Thailand and Viet Nam. Tourism-dependent countries, especially the small island developing States in the Pacific, were hit doubly by new waves of COVID-19 and a plunge in tourist arrivals. Ongoing political turmoil has severely weighed on Myanmar's economy.

Trade, the major growth driver during the pandemic, is losing momentum...

Strong global demand for Asian manufacturing and exports has underpinned the region's headline economic growth. A quick rebound in household spending in the developed countries buoyed demand for electronics, electrical and information technology equipment, and automobiles, which particularly benefited China, the Republic of Korea, Singapore and Taiwan, Province of China (figure III.12).[11] Investment was channelled into machinery and equipment, supporting export manufacturing.

11 Improving external demand also benefited several ASEAN economies (such as Indonesia, Malaysia and Thailand) and commodity exporters (Brunei Darussalam and Mongolia). New waves of COVID-19 cases offset economic gains, however.

Figure III.12

Demand-side contributions to growth in select East Asian countries

Percentage points

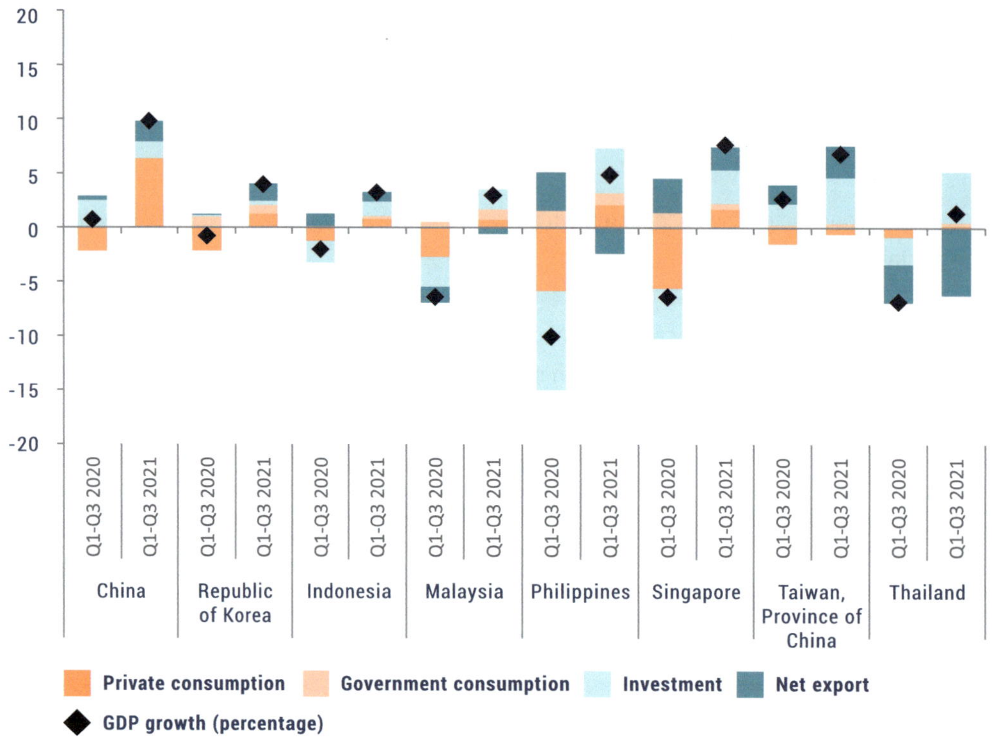

Source: UN DESA, based on data from CEIC (accessed on 29 November 2021).
Note: For China, the consumption bar covers both the private and government sectors.

Shipment backlogs, surging freight costs and temporary quarantine restrictions in key manufacturing and shipping areas have slowed the region's export growth. Semiconductor shortages due to adverse weather events, COVID-19-induced production disruptions and shipping congestion have significantly extended delivery times.[12] Ongoing technology and trade tensions between China and the United States have further hampered production and exports of semiconductors. Rising energy prices and electricity shortages are also weakening exports. Power rationing in China, for instance, has impeded production at numerous factories, including those that supply components to large manufacturers of consumer electronics and automobiles. Going forward, demand for manufactured goods from Asia is expected to gradually decline as economies elsewhere heal from the pandemic and restore their local supplies.

...while strong domestic demand recovery is subject to the progress and efficacy of vaccine programmes

As export growth begins to moderate in the region, domestic demand should, in principle, play a bigger role in driving economic growth. Many East Asian countries have observed stronger domestic demand (figure III.12) through continued policy stimulus and reopening. Ongoing domestic demand as a driver

12 Average delivery times for semiconductors increased from 12 weeks in early 2020 to more than 20 weeks in July 2021 (King, 2021).

of growth is contingent on containing the virus, however. New waves of COVID-19 have triggered containment measures over 2021, which heavily weighed on private consumption and investment.

Vaccinations offer some hope, yet despite gathering pace in the second half of 2021, vaccination progress remains highly uneven. By mid-December 2021, Brunei Darussalam, Cambodia, China, Malaysia, the Republic of Korea and Singapore had over 70 per cent of their populations fully vaccinated. In contrast, some least developed countries and small island developing States lagged behind. Vaccination rates in Myanmar, Papua New Guinea, the Solomon Islands and Vanuatu were still less than 30 per cent (figure III.13). Limited access to vaccines and inadequate capacity for vaccine roll-outs further increase the vulnerability of these countries.

Figure III.13
Vaccination progress in East Asia (as of 20 December 2021)

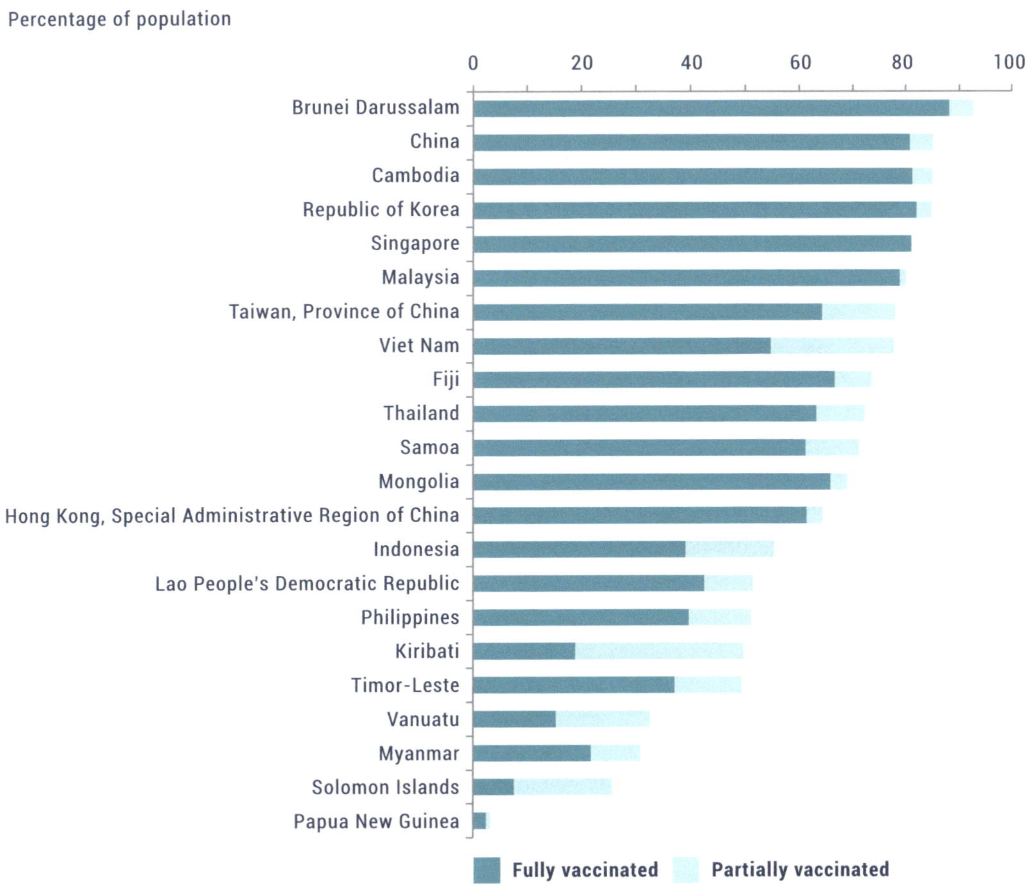

Source: UN DESA, based on data from Our World in Data (accessed on 20 December 2021).

As the pandemic lingers, East Asian countries have started considering long-term strategies to deal with the virus. For instance, while China is sticking with its "zero COVID-19" policy, Indonesia, Malaysia, the Republic of Korea, Singapore and Thailand are pursuing approaches to "coexist" with the virus. No matter which path countries choose, policymakers remain cautious about fully reopening economies; the Delta outbreaks showed the high risks of new and more transmissible variants. While vaccines are assumed to generally reduce the severity and duration of COVID-19 symptoms, their efficacy against new variants is still unknown. This means that some restrictive measures will likely remain in place during the forecast period, with targeted lockdowns and mobility restrictions introduced if infection rates surge again. Border openings are likely to be gradual and come with entry requirements. All such measures will likely further increase social and economic costs and delay full recovery.

China's economic slowdown adds additional headwinds to the region's near-term outlook

China's "zero COVID-19" policy constrains the economy's full recovery. Renewed restrictions in response to a surge in infections in the second half of 2021[13] weighed on consumer spending and weakened the pace of initially strong recovery. At the same time, China's policy efforts to stabilize the property market have slowed investment.[14] This will likely sustain China's long-term resilience for several reasons. First, slower growth in property prices could curb rising inequality and support China's pursuit of "common prosperity".[15] Second, reducing household indebtedness from mortgages, which account for 76 per cent of household debt (People's Bank of China, 2020), could advance China's economic restructuring strategy, which prioritizes domestic consumption. Third, limiting the exposure of highly indebted private property developers will likely reduce financial risks. Given that the property sector potentially contributes about a third of China's GDP (Rogoff and Yang, 2020), a sharp price correction would not only adversely affect investment but also impair household consumption and potentially trigger broader financial instability.

In 2021, China's economy grew an estimated 7.8 per cent with an expectation of moderating to 5.2 per cent in 2022. The slowdown could have regional and global spillovers. For instance, sharp declines in new construction could reduce demand for raw materials from the rest of the world. At the same time, reining in the property market could lead to defaults by several large private property developers. A default would have wide repercussions on banks and other financial institutions as well as investors who hold these companies' offshore bonds. While China is cautiously managing the situation, concerns about a spillover are mounting.

A shift in global liquidity conditions raises financial stability worries

Quicker-than-expected tapering of quantitative easing in the United States raises financial stability concerns for East Asia. As the recovery in the region is in the early stages, a sudden change in global financial conditions could trigger capital outflows and increase exchange rate volatility. Over 2021, while foreign direct investment inflows were steady, a few ASEAN economies (including the Philippines and Thailand) experienced capital outflows through portfolio channels amid the Delta wave. Almost all

13 As of early November 2021, at least 19 of 31 provinces in China have reported infections with the Delta variant. Different provinces re-introduced temporary restrictive measures based on local needs, including mobility restrictions, school closures and quarantines.

14 Investment in construction in China contracted by 1.8 per cent in the third quarter of 2021, compared with an average quarterly growth of 6 per cent during 2015-2019.

15 The concept of "common prosperity" was first put forward by Mao Zedong, Chairperson of the Central Committee of the Communist Party of China, in 1953. China is giving a new push to it in 2021.

currencies in the region depreciated against the United States dollar to some extent, except for China's renminbi. With domestic economic conditions still weak, countries will be highly sensitive to changes in the interest rates of major developed countries. Countries with high debt levels, especially external debts, will be particularly vulnerable, such as Indonesia, Malaysia and Thailand, where external debt was around or above 150 per cent of GDP in the first two to three quarters of 2021.[16]

A lingering pandemic shadows progress on the 2030 Agenda for Sustainable Development

The pandemic is threatening to undermine some development progress in East Asia. The adverse impacts are expected to continue and deepen scarring effects. In particular, temporary restrictive measures have disrupted labour market recovery. The ASEAN region may see working-hour losses of an estimated 7.4 per cent in 2021, which implies only limited improvement compared with 2020 (ILO, 2021a). Working-hour and job losses have caused millions of people to lose at least part of their labour income. In the first half of 2021, labour income in the ASEAN region contracted by 5.7 per cent (ILO, 2021a). Job losses are exacerbating already high inequality as women, young workers and informal workers have been affected disproportionately. Around 8.6 million people in East Asia were pushed into extreme poverty in 2019-2021.

The pandemic's contribution to reducing pollution and emissions due to mobility restriction has proven short-lived. Air pollution (measured by PM2.5 emissions) has exceeded pre-pandemic levels. The recent energy crunch risks derailing the transition to low-carbon energy. Some firms may turn to "dirtier" energy such as diesel. This comes as rising climate risks already threaten the region's recovery. For instance, Fiji and Papua New Guinea experienced cyclones and floods in early 2021, adding economic costs to recovery. Taiwan, Province of China experienced its worst drought in 56 years in April 2021, which affected semiconductor production. East Asian countries are taking actions to address climate risks, with China and the Republic of Korea announcing they intend to reach carbon neutrality by 2060 and 2050, respectively. The Philippines and Viet Nam have committed to moving away from coal.

Inflationary pressure is still low

Inflation is expected to remain largely in check in East Asia. In 2021, headline inflation was an estimated 1.5 per cent. Most countries had inflation below or within central bank targets (figure III.14) although it trended upward due to rising food and fuel prices and supply-chain disruptions. Some countries observed above-target inflation related to particular factors, such as the Republic of Korea (higher costs of petroleum, housing rentals and services) and the Philippines (a spike in food inflation caused by adverse weather conditions). Going forward, headline inflation is projected at 2 per cent in 2022. While rebounding commodity prices and supply bottlenecks could increase prices, broader inflationary pressure is unlikely as the reopening of economies will be very cautious. Most economies are expected to operate below pre-crisis levels (figure III.15) with low consumer purchasing power likely keeping a surge in producer prices from passing through to consumer prices. Ongoing supply shortages and network disruptions are anticipated to recede over time as more countries reopen and demand shifts away from goods to services.

16 UN DESA estimate, based on data from CEIC (accessed on 29 November 2021).

Figure III.14
Inflation and inflation targets in East Asia

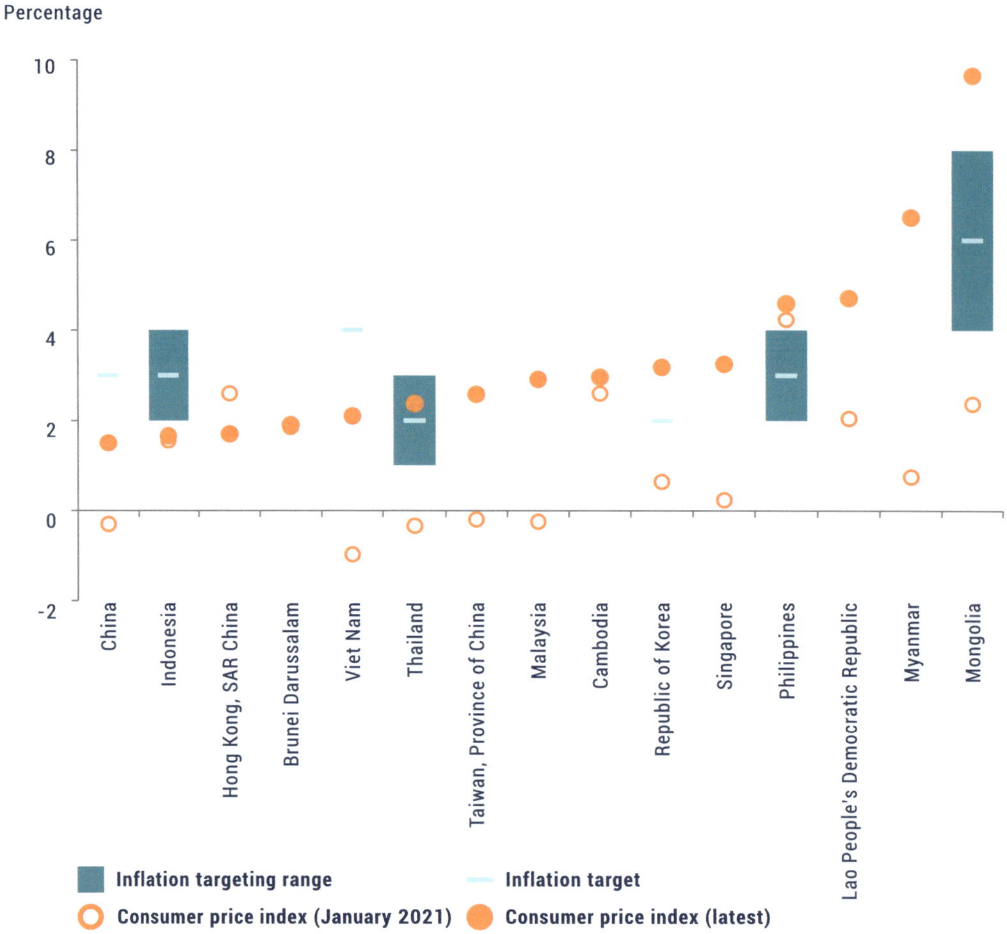

Source: UN DESA, based on data from CEIC and Central Bank News (both accessed on 29 November 2021).

Fiscal policies could be more targeted to support an inclusive and green recovery

Supportive fiscal policies are critical to shore up the region's domestic demand, especially during new waves of COVID-19 and new rounds of restrictive policies. From January to October 2021, total COVID-19 policy responses cost an estimated $266 billion, equivalent to 1.4 per cent of the region's GDP.[17] Countries have extended fiscal stimuli introduced in 2020 (such as Indonesia[18]), implemented new programmes to contain the pandemic and fund social security programmes (Lao People's Democratic Republic and Malaysia[19]) and introduced new tax relief to support small firms (China, Malaysia and the Philippines).

17 In 2020, policy responses totalled about $970 billion in East Asia. The amount of fiscal stimulus is estimated based on the IMF's Policy Responses to COVID-19 and the Asian Development Bank's COVID-19 Policy Database (both accessed on 13 November 2021).

18 Indonesia increased the budgeted amount of a national economic recovery programme from IDR579.8 trillion in 2020 to IDR699.4 trillion in 2021.

19 Lao People's Democratic Republic allocated LAK100 billion in 2021 for prevention, control and treatment of COVID-19 cases; Malaysia accelerated social security payments and provided additional funds for vaccine procurement.

Figure III.15

Growth of real GDP from 2019 to 2022, based on projections made in 2022 and 2020

Source: UN DESA.

Increasing public spending and decreasing tax revenue (due to economic output that is below the pre-pandemic level along with tax cuts) have widened fiscal deficits and increased public debt-to-GDP ratios. The region's median fiscal deficit as a share of GDP increased from 1.7 per cent in 2019 to an estimated 5.8 per cent in 2021. The gross government debt-to-GDP ratio grew from 40.5 to an estimated 47.8 per cent over the same period.[20] While premature fiscal consolidation should be avoided to prevent reversal of recovery gains, shrinking fiscal space requires more targeted public spending that is better aligned with the 2030 Agenda.[21] At the same time, countries could turn to various policy options to better mobilize domestic and international financial resources (box III.3).

20 Calculated based on October 2021 data from the IMF's World Economic Outlook Database (accessed on 14 November 2021).

21 The United Nations Economic and Social Commission for Asia and the Pacific (2021) points out that only a small share of the stimulus in Asia and the Pacific supported gender equality. A large part of the spending encouraged more production and consumption of fossil fuels without green commitments.

Box III.3

Fiscal policy and financing options to build forward better

The scars of past economic and non-economic shocks could last for a long time in East and South Asia (ESCAP, 2021). The region has high-quality public infrastructure and strong human capital, and even during the pandemic maintained ample fiscal space to help withstand the crisis. Sizeable fiscal stimulus buoyed domestic demand and supported households and companies in need. While accommodative fiscal policies are still required for recovery, however, fiscal space constraints will tighten in some countries. For example, while gross financing needs (the sum of the primary fiscal deficit and maturing debt obligations) in selected East and South Asian economies are expected to fall during 2021-2023 from the level in 2020, projected levels are far higher than in 2019 (figure III.3.a). Public debt sustainability is tenuous in some countries, more so given prospects for tightening global financing conditions and higher borrowing costs.

Figure III.3.a

Gross financing needs in selected East and South Asian countries

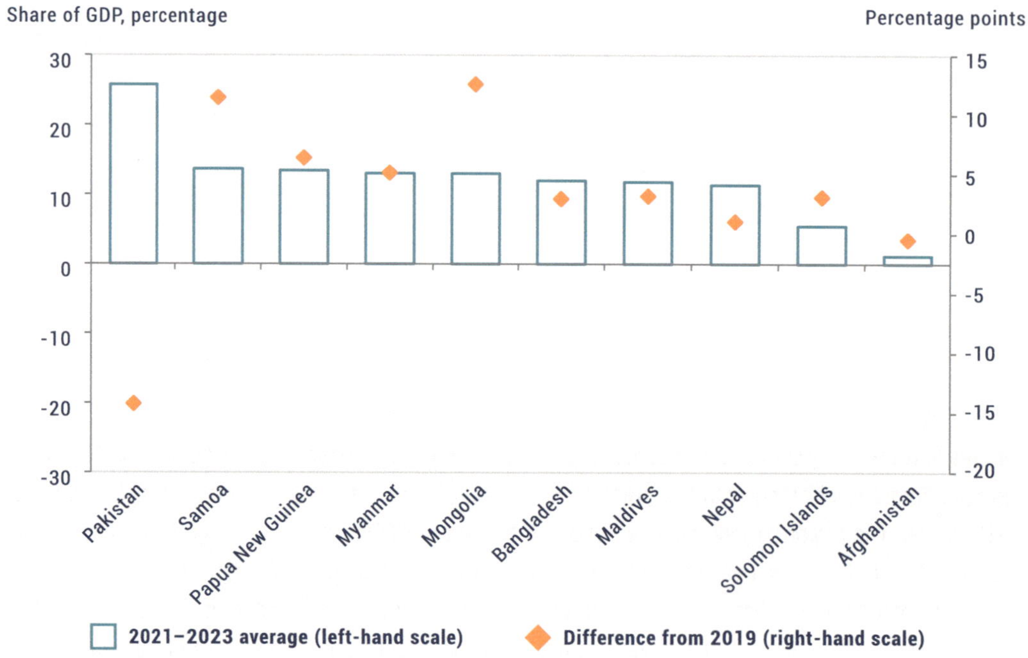

Source: ESCAP, based on Munevar, 2020.

Governments are exploring options to mobilize fiscal resources beyond traditional sources of borrowing and to improve public debt management. Tighter fiscal space also means that countries need to consider risk sharing to cope with coming shocks and rely less on fiscal resources. There are several different fiscal and financing policy options in the region.

Offshore sovereign and diaspora bonds: During 2013-2020, the Government of Lao People's Democratic Republic and other public entities issued 43 Thai baht-denominated bonds in Thailand, with an outstanding value of $2.1 billion at the end of 2020. These issuances benefitted from Thailand's relaxation of investment rules and close economic ties with Lao People's Democratic Republic. In a similar vein, smaller countries in Asia and the Pacific could tap domestic savings in neighbouring emerging economies with close economic connections. Examples include China for Mongolia, and India for Bhutan and Nepal. Multilateral development partners could support these initiatives by developing common market practices for cross-border bond issuances. In addition to offshore bonds, governments could also consider diaspora bonds, especially in countries with large remittance flows as a share of GDP, such as Nepal and Tonga. To benefit from this type of bond, issuing countries could conduct demand analysis to gauge the willingness and ability of diaspora communities to invest in bonds, offer diversity in bond structures and launch marketing campaigns.

Debt swaps for development: Bangladesh, Indonesia, Pakistan and the Philippines engaged in debt swaps during the 1980s and early 2000s. While these agreements were broadly consistent with national development policies, strong frontloading of counterpart payments reduced fiscal space in Indonesia in the first few years. The overall impact on public debt reduction was small given the modest scale of debt relief. Learning from past lessons, countries should conduct independent feasibility studies to identify the amount and profile of swappable public debt, beneficiary projects, co-financing sources and the debt discount rate. Relevant stakeholders could seek to reduce the transaction costs of debt swaps, since elements such as a time-consuming negotiation process, feasibility studies and financial and legal fees can add up to 5 per cent of the debt value. Other efforts can be made to scale up debt swaps and minimize fund fungibility.

Emergency financing mechanisms: Many countries in East and South Asia have dedicated reserve funds for natural disasters. But catastrophic risk insurance schemes, based on a risk-transfer modality and especially important during low-frequency, high-impact events, remain uncommon. Some examples of existing schemes include agricultural insurance in Bangladesh, India and Mongolia, earthquake insurance in China and public asset insurance in Indonesia and Viet Nam. Covered losses are mostly small, however. At a subregional level, a catastrophe risk insurance pool for the Pacific islands was set up in 2016 and has so far made three payouts worth $6.7 million to Tonga and Vanuatu. To enhance emergency financing mechanisms, countries need to incorporate sovereign catastrophic risks into government financial planning and explore risk-transfer financial instruments for emergencies. Development partners can help by establishing more regional catastrophic risk-sharing initiatives and coordinating regional emergency funds.

Sustainable investing by public institutional investors: Financial assets under management by pension funds and sovereign wealth funds in Asia and the Pacific stood at about $8.5 trillion at the end of 2020. Relative to GDP, these assets are particularly large in Brunei Darussalam, Solomon Islands, Timor-Leste and Tuvalu. Yet the extent of sustainable investing by public institutional investors appears limited. Moving forward, one policy option is to relax investment rules in line with a careful review of the impact on portfolio risk. For example, certain pension funds in India, Pakistan and the Republic of

Author: Vatcharin Sirimaneetham, United Nations Economic and Social Commission for Asia and the Pacific

Korea are not allowed to invest in domestic equities or allowed but with maximum limits. Similarly, there are often maximum portfolio limits on investments in sovereign bonds and requirements to invest only in corporate bonds with certain ratings. Pension funds in India and Indonesia are prohibited from investing in foreign equities and bonds.

Still low inflation leaves room to maintain accommodative monetary policies

Low and relatively stable inflation offers some flexibility for central banks. Most kept accommodative monetary policy stances in 2021, maintaining policy rates at historically low levels after massive rate cuts in 2020. Central banks have also used other tools, including lowering reserve requirement ratios, extending lending operations and purchasing assets. Rising inflationary pressure in some countries has prompted central banks to change policy direction. The Bank of Korea raised its policy rate in August 2021, aiming to cool the real estate sector. The Monetary Authority of Singapore unexpectedly tightened policy in October 2021 to counter imported cost pressures. In 2022, overall monetary stances still need to be accommodative to sustain a fledgling recovery, however. While changing monetary policy stances in major developed countries, especially the tapering of quantitative easing in the United States, may pressure East Asian central banks to begin tightening, a cautious approach is warranted if changes in interest rates are not driven by better economic conditions.

South Asia

GDP growth

Percentage

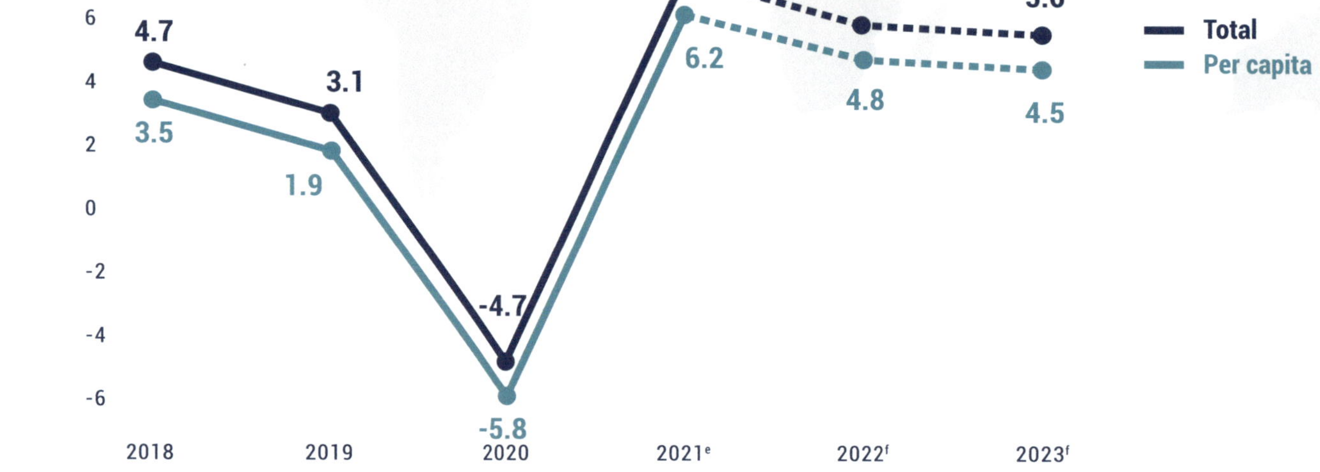

COVID-19 cases & deaths

as of 20 December 2021

Per 100,000 people

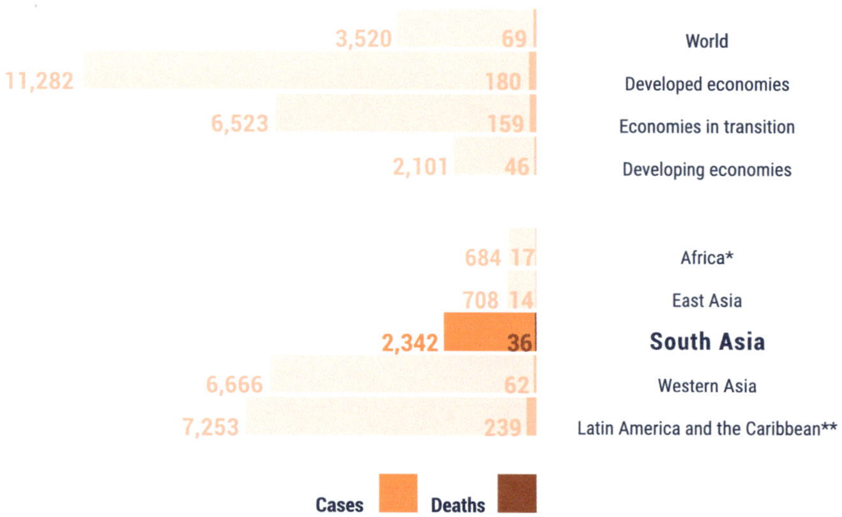

Vaccination

as of 20 December 2021

Percentage of population

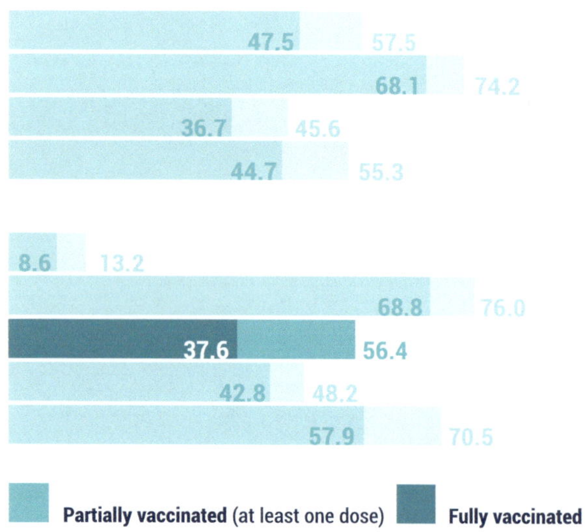

Note: The boundaries and names shown and the designations used on this map do not imply official endorsement or acceptance by the United Nations. The map represents countries and/or territories or parts thereof for which data is available and/or analysed in World Economic Situation and Prospects 2022. The shaded areas therefore do not necessarily overlap entirely with the delimitation of their frontiers or boundaries. Aggregate data for Africa, excluding Libya.

* Excluding Libya; **Excluding Bolivarian Republic of Venezuela. **e:** 2021 estimates. **f:** 2022-2023 forecasts.

Source for COVID-19 data: UN DESA calculations, based on data from Johns Hopkins University.

South Asia: moderate economic prospects amid large uncertainties and more constrained policy space

- South Asia's recovery is gathering steam but remains fragile and subject to downside risks.
- Revitalizing employment growth is crucial to tackle worsening poverty and inequality.
- Amid higher public debt and prospects for tightening financial conditions, fiscal policy faces increasing constraints.

South Asia confronts challenges to achieving robust and inclusive growth

The economic recovery continues to gain momentum in South Asia amid contained COVID-19 infections and higher mobility, robust remittance inflows and broadly supportive macroeconomic policy stances. After an estimated expansion of 7.4 per cent in 2021, regional GDP is projected to expand at a more moderate pace of 5.9 per cent in 2022 as base effects gradually disappear.[22] The recovery, however, is still fragile, uneven and subject to pandemic-related uncertainties and downside risks. A lagging labour market recovery illustrates the severe socioeconomic difficulties for large segments of the population. Achieving robust, sustained and inclusive growth will be critical in tackling the region's recent rise in poverty and inequality, with the pandemic erasing years of progress on poverty reduction and an estimated 30 million more people in extreme poverty in 2020. A sustained recovery may prove challenging as global financial conditions tighten, however, and monetary and fiscal policy space become more constrained. Policymakers need to maintain essential support for the recovery and job creation, such as by prioritizing public infrastructure and green investments that crowd-in private finance.

The outlook is highly uncertain and subject to downside risks

South Asia faces major downside risks that can strengthen headwinds in achieving the 2030 Agenda. Relatively slow vaccination progress leaves the region vulnerable to new variants and recurrent outbreaks. Financial constraints and an inadequate global vaccine supply continue to drag down full recovery in some countries. As of early December 2021, Bangladesh, Nepal and Pakistan had less than 26 per cent of their populations fully vaccinated (figure III.16). By contrast, the fully vaccinated population is above 64 per cent in Bhutan, Maldives and Sri Lanka. In India, a deadly wave of infection with the Delta variant stole 240,000 lives between April and June and disrupted economic recovery. Similar episodes could take place in the near term.

Accelerated global monetary tightening could increase volatility, trigger capital outflows and disrupt credit growth, especially in countries with elevated debt, large financing needs and high levels of foreign-currency-denominated debt. Significant financial distress could emerge as highly leveraged firms face greater refinancing costs, particularly in sectors hit harder by lockdowns, even more so if the removal of forbearance measures uncovers a large deterioration in balance sheets. In Bangladesh and Bhutan, non-performing loans were elevated even before the pandemic. While still vulnerable, India is in a better position to navigate financial turbulence compared to its situation during the "taper tantrum"

22 All growth figures for South Asia are on a calendar year basis. For fiscal year growth figures, please refer to the Statistical Annex.

episode after the 2008-2009 global financial crisis. This is due to a stronger external position and measures to minimize risks to bank balance sheets. In the medium-term, scarring effects from higher public and private debt or permanent impacts on labour markets could reduce potential growth and prospects for poverty reduction.

Figure III.16
South Asia's vaccination progress (as of 20 December 2021)

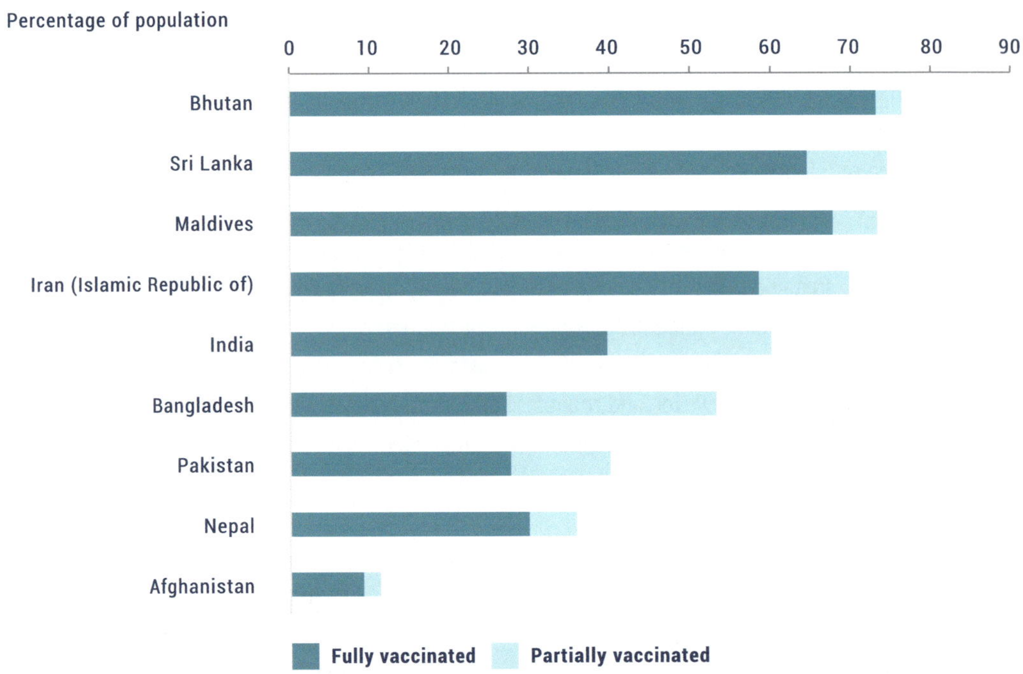

Source: UN DESA, based on data from Our World in Data (accessed on 20 December 2021).

Economic activity has gathered pace in Bangladesh and India

India's economic recovery is on a solid path, amid rapid vaccination progress, less stringent social restrictions and still supportive fiscal and monetary stances. GDP is projected to expand by 6.7 per cent in 2022 (figure III.17) after a 9 per cent expansion in 2021, as base effects wane. Robust export growth and public investments underpin economic activity, but high oil prices and coal shortages could put the brakes on economic activity in the near term. It will remain crucial to encourage private investment to support inclusive growth beyond the recovery. India has taken an important step by committing to 50 per cent of its energy mix coming from renewable sources by 2030 and to reaching net-zero emissions by 2070. Amid sound macroeconomic policies, Bangladesh has navigated the COVID-19 pandemic relatively well. GDP is projected to expand by 6 per cent in 2022. Economic activity rides on export growth and the rising demand for apparel, robust remittance inflows, and accommodative fiscal and monetary policies. The economy of Pakistan also remains on a relatively robust recovery path. After an economic expansion of 4.5 per cent in 2021, GDP growth is projected at 3.9 per cent in 2022, driven by private consumption, record-high remittances and fiscal support. The outlook for the Islamic Republic of Iran continues to improve after severe difficulties in recent years, supported by rising gas and oil exports. GDP is projected to expand by 3.1 per cent in 2022, following an expansion of 2.9 per cent in 2021.

Figure III.17

GDP growth in select South Asian countries

Source: UN DESA.
Note: e = estimates, f = forecasts.

Sri Lanka faces major challenges; Afghanistan is on the brink of economic meltdown

The outlook is more challenging for other countries in South Asia, including those more dependent on tourism. In the Maldives, economic activity is gradually improving partly due to a solid rebound in international tourism. But renewed COVID-19 outbreaks, locally and abroad, could easily derail recovery. GDP may remain well below pre-pandemic levels; the risk of debt distress could be high. In Sri Lanka, GDP growth is projected at 2.6 per cent in 2022. Its major challenges include food shortages, dwindling foreign reserves and sovereign debt risks. Afghanistan's severe downturn has come amid drastic political changes, a decline in international aid and a lack of access to offshore assets. The worsening situation is leading to extreme poverty and food insecurity with the risk of the entire country becoming a humanitarian catastrophe.[23]

More constrained fiscal policy space

In South Asia, fiscal responses to the crisis were relatively restrained compared to other regions, largely due to sovereign credit ratings and debt-to-GDP ratios. Fiscal policies remain moderately supportive as the recovery gathers pace. In India and Pakistan, fiscal deficits are projected to decline gradually. At the same time, policy priorities have shifted towards capital expenditure. Pressures for fiscal consolidation will likely increase from higher public debt and rising borrowing costs (figure III.18). Amid elevated social needs, a still fragile recovery and lagging employment, it is imperative to avoid premature consolidation, however. The weak debt situation emphasizes the need for revenue mobilization (box III.3) as well as further multilateral support, especially for countries with elevated sovereign risks. Yet the G20 Debt Service Suspension Initiative did not provide substantial relief to eligible countries, namely, Afghanistan, Maldives, Nepal and Pakistan. Relief stood at less than 20 per cent of debt service obligations or about 1.6 per cent of GDP, on average.

Figure III.18

Public debt over GDP in select South Asian countries

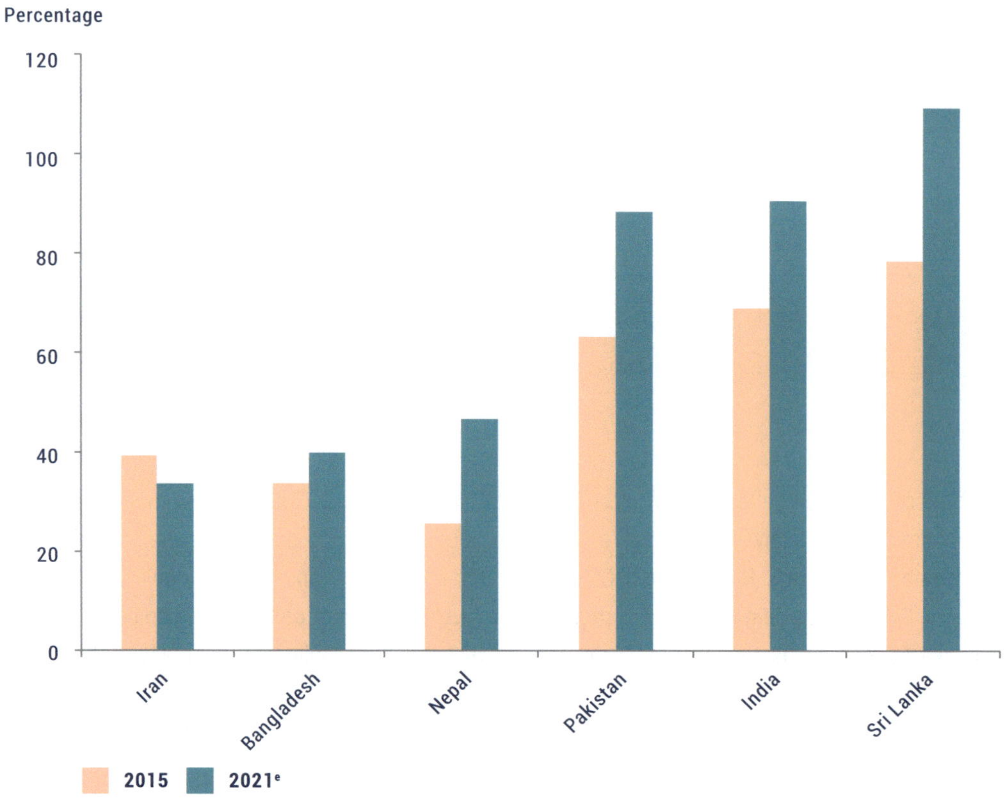

Source: UN DESA based on IMF, 2021a.
Note: e = estimates.

23 The United Nations estimated that about 23 million people would be at risk of acute hunger, with 3.2 million children expected to suffer from malnutrition (IPC, 2021).

Inflation prospects remain largely stable

Inflation is projected to remain largely stable in most economies in South Asia, which offers flexibility to central banks before they move to more restrictive monetary stances. After inflationary pressures gained momentum in early 2021 due to supply constraints and rising energy prices, consumer price inflation has tended to subside. At the aggregate level, it is projected at 8.4 per cent in 2022. In India, inflation is expected to decelerate throughout 2022, continuing a trend observed since the second half of 2021 when relatively restrained food prices compensated for higher oil prices. A sudden and renewed rise in food inflation, however, due to unpredictable weather, broader supply disruptions and higher agricultural prices, could undermine food security, reduce real incomes and increase hunger across the region. In the Islamic Republic of Iran, inflation remains elevated due to depreciation of the domestic currency and the monetization of fiscal deficits.

The monetary cycle is gradually shifting towards a less accommodative stance

Monetary policies remain accommodative with interest rates close to record lows and liquidity measures still in place in most economies. Yet the monetary cycle is gradually shifting as global financial conditions tighten and the recovery gains steam. The Reserve Bank of India has begun to taper liquidity by increasing the volume of reverse repo operations and the cash reserve ratio; it is expected to raise interest rates throughout 2022. The central banks of Pakistan and Sri Lanka increased interest rates in the second half of 2021 amid rising inflation and widening current account deficits. Central banks need to assess the magnitude and timing of policy changes to support an inclusive recovery and maintain financial and price stability.

Western Asia

GDP growth

Percentage

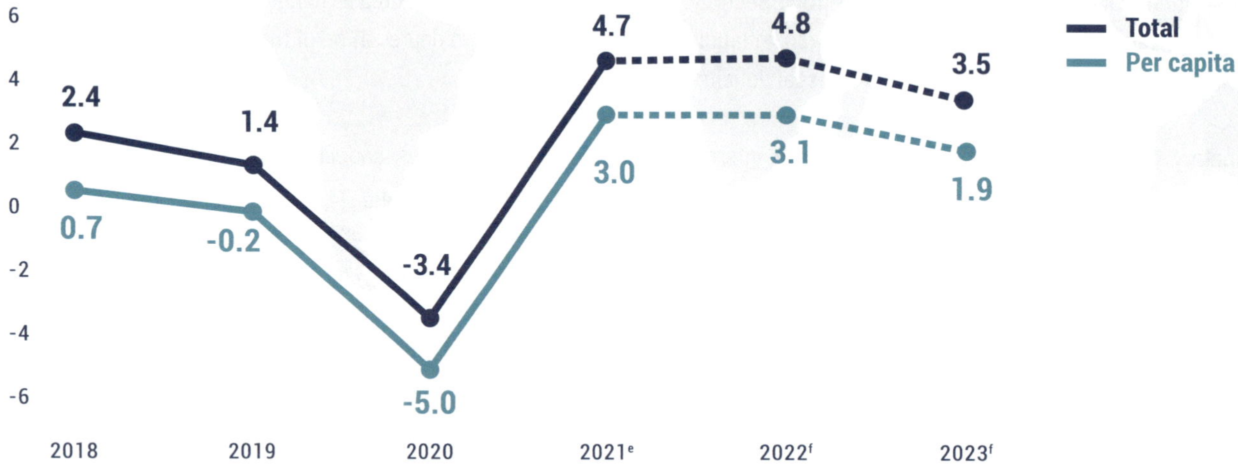

COVID-19 cases & deaths

as of 20 December 2021

Per 100,000 people

Vaccination

as of 20 December 2021

Percentage of population

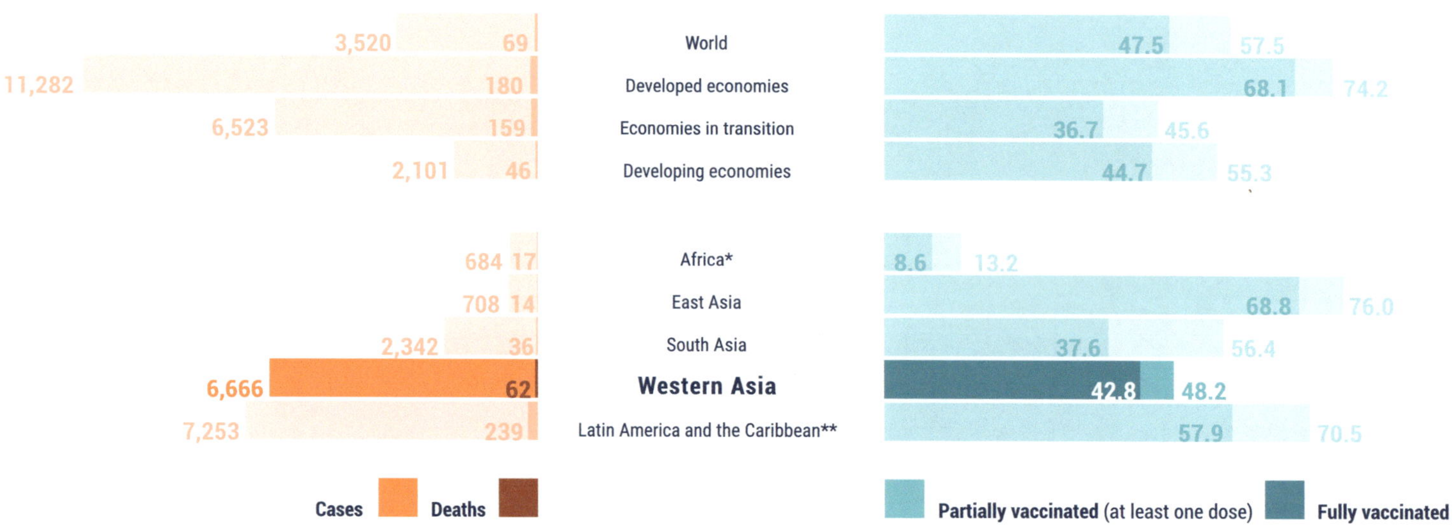

Note: The boundaries and names shown and the designations used on this map do not imply official endorsement or acceptance by the United Nations. The map represents countries and/or territories or parts thereof for which data is available and/or analysed in World Economic Situation and Prospects 2022. The shaded areas therefore do not necessarily overlap entirely with the delimitation of their frontiers or boundaries. Aggregate data for Africa, excluding Libya.

* Excluding Libya; **Excluding Bolivarian Republic of Venezuela. **e:** 2021 estimates. **f:** 2022-2023 forecasts.

Source for COVID-19 data: UN DESA calculations, based on data from Johns Hopkins University.

Western Asia: recovery to continue in 2022

- The slow recovery of crude oil production countered the rapid recovery of domestic demand.
- Economic sentiment improved in the second half of 2021 with progress on vaccination.
- A robust recovery is forecast to continue in 2022 with an expected increase in crude oil production.

The Western Asian economies grew an estimated 4.7 per cent in 2021. With the relaxation of pandemic control measures and the progress of vaccination, economic activities recovered rapidly particularly in the second half of the year. Strong domestic demand was seen after the substantial plunge in the previous year, leading recovery in Israel and Turkey. While the unemployment rate declined towards pre-pandemic trends in Israel, Saudi Arabia and Turkey, the speed of employment recovery has been slower in other countries. The employment situation is dire in Iraq, Lebanon, the State of Palestine, the Syrian Arab Republic and Yemen.

Figure III.19
Recovery forecast for Western Asia

Source: UN DESA, based on projections produced with the World Economic Forecasting Model.
Note: e = estimates, f = forecasts.

GDP growth is modest in Gulf Cooperation Council countries due to little expansion in crude oil production

Estimated GDP growth in 2021 was modest in major crude oil producers, namely the member countries of the Gulf Cooperation Council (GCC): Bahrain, Kuwait, Oman, Qatar, Saudi Arabia and the United Arab Emirates. Strongly recovering energy prices contributed to overall improved economic sentiment but production coordination under OPEC[24] meant that crude oil production in the GCC countries likely increased only slightly from 2020. In real terms, the oil sector's contribution to GDP growth is estimated as extremely modest relative to the contribution from the rapidly recovering non-oil sector. Iraq is following a similar recovery path although the recovery of its non-oil sector has been more modest.

Recovery has stagnated in other countries in the region

Despite resilience in 2020, Jordan has seen a slow recovery due to the stagnation of service exports, namely tourism. The economic situation in Lebanon further deteriorated against a deepening financial crisis (see box III.4). Ongoing armed conflict has hampered economic recovery in the Syrian Arab Republic and Yemen.

Box III.4

The anatomy of the Lebanese financial crisis

Lebanon faces an unprecedented economic and financial crisis, with GDP growth contracting by 7.2 per cent in 2019 and 37.1 per cent in 2020. While COVID-19, the subsequent loss of tourism revenues and the devastating Beirut port explosion were major drivers of the downturn, an unravelling financial crisis is also a significant factor. In March 2020, Prime Minister Hassan Diab announced that Lebanon would not be able to pay a Eurobond of $1.2 billion. As of November 2021, a new Government, formed after a year-long political vacuum, is about to restart difficult negotiations with the IMF on debt restructuring and default.

For almost two decades, Lebanon received huge foreign currency inflows. These primarily comprised remittances from the very large Lebanese diaspora, which may total 15.4 million people, greatly outstripping an internal population of 6 million (Pukas, 2018). Lebanon also benefited from its reputation as a safe haven for savings from war-torn Syria. Inflows were directed to domestic banks, which bought Eurobonds issued by the Government. In 2019, as the supply of foreign currency significantly decreased, the Government faced difficulties in financing the debt and maintaining the official exchange rate. It announced measures to improve liquidity, including taxes on gasoline, tobacco and VoIP applications. These plans triggered massive social protests dubbed the 17 October Revolution. The unrest combined with a worsening economic situation to propel a bank run with depositors rushing to withdraw foreign currency deposits from Lebanese banks. Facing shortages of cash, banks froze foreign currency deposits on 17 October 2019 and began limiting withdrawals to $1,000 per month. Withdrawals were halted completely a few months later without any official capital control measure.

24 See OPEC (2021) for details.

Figure III.4.a

The structure of Lebanese public debt

Percentage of GDP

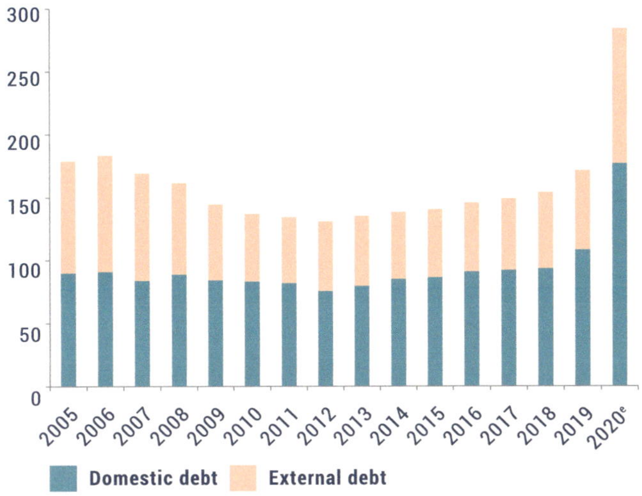

Source: Lebanon, Ministry of Finance and Central Administration of Statistics.
Note: e = estimation.

Figure III.4.b

The composition of Lebanese GDP

Billions of Lebanese pounds, current prices

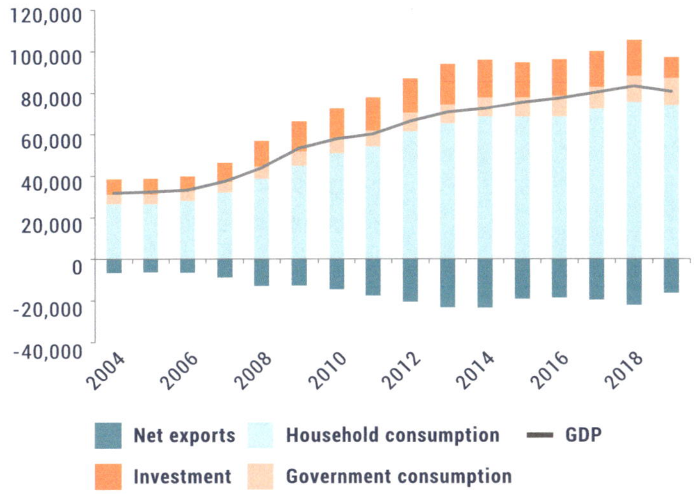

Source: Lebanon, Central Administration of Statistics.

The freeze on foreign currency deposits led to the immediate birth of a black market for cash dollars. Initially, the Central Bank provided importers with currency to finance the huge Lebanese current account deficit. This meant the black market rate hovered around LBP2,000-2,500 per dollar, with the official peg maintained at LBP1,507 per dollar. With dwindling foreign reserves, however, the portfolio of products financed at the official rate began shrinking. By the beginning of 2021, only medicines, essential food products, medical equipment and fuel imports were financed at the official rate in ever smaller amounts, leading to huge shortages in Lebanese pharmacies and petrol stations. As of September 2021, the Central Bank announced that it will no longer finance these imports, which caused massive price increases. At the same time, the black market exchange rate had risen to almost LBP21,000 per dollar, meaning the Lebanese pound had lost 93 per cent of its value even as the official peg was maintained.[a] These developments spurred inflation to enormous levels of 85 per cent in 2020 and an estimated 128 per cent in 2021.

This situation has several consequences for negotiations on debt restructuring. First, pound-denominated debt has become less of a concern because a default has effectively taken place through inflation, even though the debt is still officially being repaid. Second, a significant share of Lebanese market-issued Eurobonds, which constitute 94 per cent of total foreign debt, is held by local banks and the Central Bank ($11 billion and $5 billion out of $31.3 billion in outstanding debt, respectively). This means that a significant haircut in dollar-denominated deposits is inevitable. A question hangs over whether such a solution will be accepted by depositors, even though these deposits have been effectively frozen for more than two years despite some measures to allow small withdrawals in pounds at unfavourable rates (Banque du Liban, 2021).

a As of November 2021, the official exchange rate stood at LBP1,507 per dollar. Three other officially designated exchange rates were in place serving different purposes, including LBP3,900 per dollar and LBP12,000 per dollar for bank withdrawals under different conditions. The Central Bank's Sayrafa platform supplied dollars for importers at a rate that reached LBP19,000 per dollar.

Another element is that two decades of massive foreign inflows financed huge current account deficits (figure III.4.2), leading to the overvaluation of the pound and dampening export competitiveness. Amid minimal investment in public infrastructure and productive sectors and the lack of a 24-hour electricity supply, restoring the current account balance will be painful, requiring a major wage adjustment. This problem is especially acute given that the main Lebanese export sectors – tourism and knowledge-intensive services – were severely damaged by the pandemic, on top of the brain drain triggered by the economic situation.

Due to the toxic combination of the financial crisis, the COVID-19 pandemic and the Beirut blast, Lebanon's poverty rate has shot up from 42 per cent in 2019 to 82 per cent in 2021. Among the poor, 40 per cent suffer extreme multidimensional poverty (ESCWA, 2021b). Safeguarding them against further deterioration in dignity and well-being is of primary importance and needs to be taken seriously in further negotiations with international donors.

Authors: Ahmed Moummi and Jan Gaska, United Nations Economic and Social Commission for Western Asia

In Western Asia, COVID-19 outbreaks were generally contained by the end of 2021, after multiple surges in cases. Israel and Turkey went through Delta variant outbreaks in the second half of 2021. Further outbreaks in all countries remain a possibility.

Figure III.20

Vaccination progress in Western Asia (as of 20 December 2021)

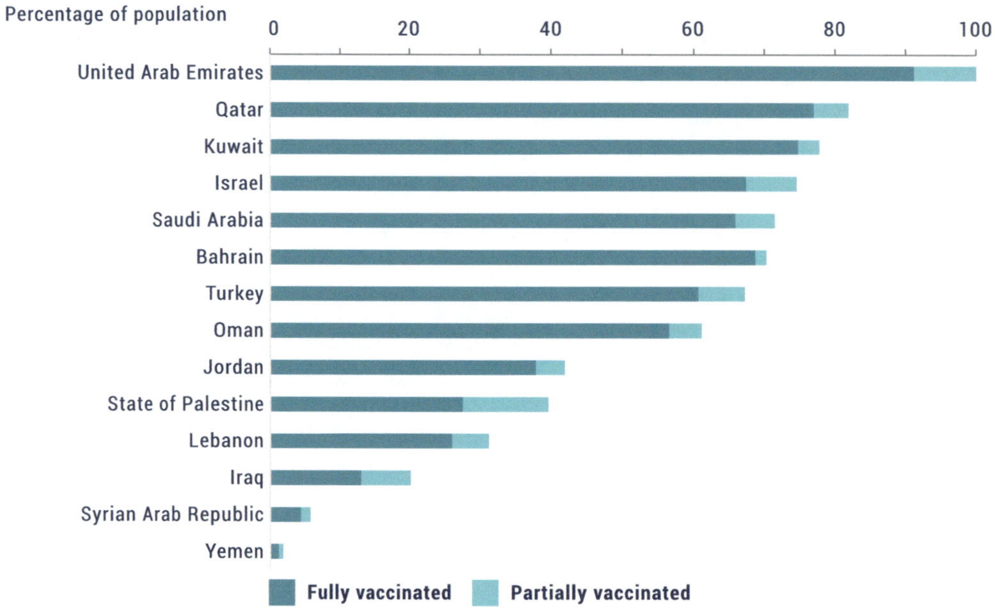

Source: UN DESA, based on data from Our World in Data (accessed on 20 December 2021).

Vaccination programmes progressed quickly in the GCC countries, Israel and Turkey, with more than half of the population having received two shots by October 2021 (figure III.20). In Israel, Turkey and the United Arab Emirates, additional booster shots were administered in the second half of the year. Other countries struggled to raise the vaccination rate amid supply constraints and vaccine hesitancy. Despite these difficulties, vaccination has steadily progressed in Iraq, Jordan, Lebanon and the State of Palestine. The vaccination rate is likely extremely low for Syria and Yemen.

Pandemic control measures eased in the second half of 2021

In the first half of 2021, COVID-19 outbreaks compelled governments to introduce lockdowns, curfews, social distancing and mask requirements. Stringent lockdowns of various duration were implemented in most countries. These measures were eased in the second half of the year, replaced by vaccination promotion, including booster shots, and with softer social distancing measures. Border entry restrictions have also gradually lifted, replaced by COVID-19 test and vaccination requirements, although Israel temporarily closed its borders due to the emergence of the Omicron variant.

Fiscal balances improved with recovering energy export prices and tax revenues

In 2021, recovering energy export prices and tax revenues improved fiscal balances after a sharp deterioration in the previous fiscal year. Fiscal expenditure growth in 2021 was estimated as moderate, however, focusing on public health and other essential areas. Governments were obliged to step up fiscal consolidation in the face of rapidly growing public debt (ESCWA, 2021a). Fiscal expenditure in real terms significantly declined in Lebanon and Syria amid high inflation rates.

Efforts to diversify fiscal revenue sources in the GCC countries continued. Oman introduced a value added tax with a 5 per cent rate in April 2021, with Kuwait and Qatar expected to follow in the near future. Bahrain, Saudi Arabia and the United Arab Emirates had already introduced a 5 per cent value added tax in 2016, in accordance with the GCC Common Value Added Tax Agreement. Saudi Arabia raised the rate to 15 per cent in 2020, and Bahrain is scheduled to raise it to 10 per cent in 2022.

Monetary policy has remained expansionary for most countries

Monetary policy has remained expansionary in the GCC countries, Iraq, Israel, Jordan and Turkey. For Lebanon and Syria, the monetary stance has resulted in extremely tight financial conditions through a substantial devaluation of the national currency.

Despite global supply-chain disruptions, inflation pressures generally remain weak

Inflationary pressures have remained weak except in Lebanon, Syria, Turkey and Yemen. The main factor contributing to high inflation in these countries has been a tight balance-of-payments condition that resulted in a substantial devaluation of the national currency. Inflation in Lebanon reached an estimated 128 per cent in 2021 due to an exchange rate pass through. Inflationary pressure from global supply-chain disruptions remained weak in Western Asia in 2021 although supply-chain disruptions remain a risk into 2022.

A robust recovery is forecast to continue in 2022 amid downside risks

The region's economy is projected to grow by 4.8 per cent in 2022. The expected expiration of the OPEC+ crude production coordination in 2022 will allow oil-exporting countries to increase crude oil production towards pre-pandemic levels. The resumption of international tourism will support further recovery. Significant downside risks remain from geopolitical tensions and high unemployment, however. Prolonged conflict in the State of Palestine, Syria and Yemen largely explains uneven recovery in the region, especially where the economic situation was dire even before the pandemic. High unemployment rates remain among the region's most important socioeconomic concerns and need to be resolved.

Latin America and the Caribbean

GDP growth

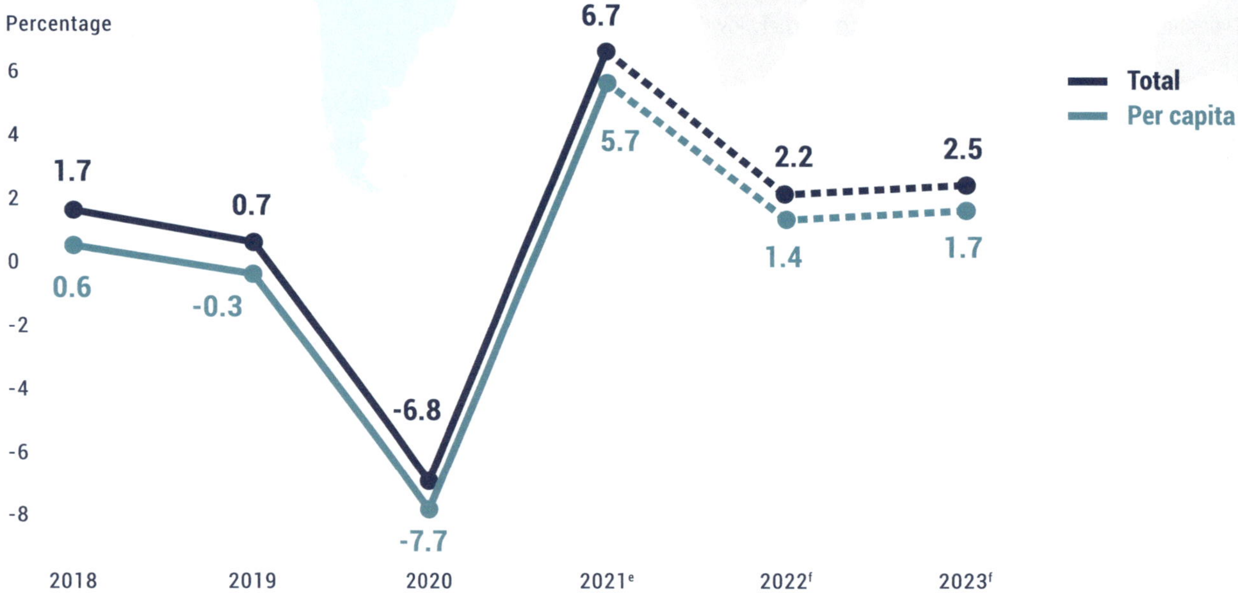

COVID-19 cases & deaths

as of 20 December 2021

Per 100,000 people

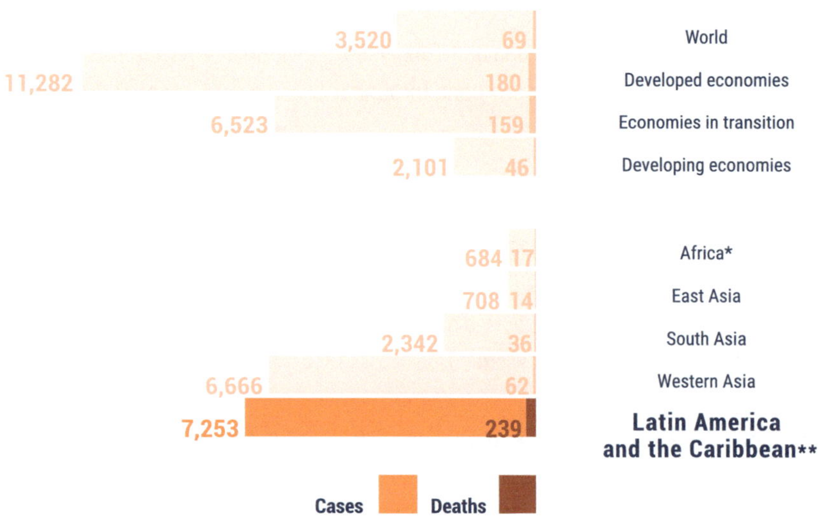

Vaccination

as of 20 December 2021

Percentage of population

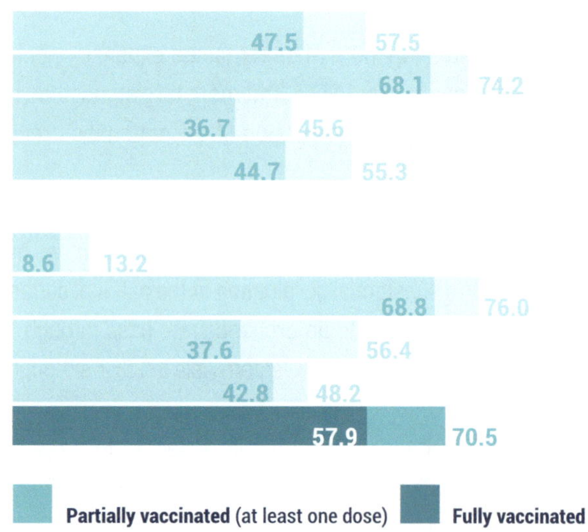

Note: The boundaries and names shown and the designations used on this map do not imply official endorsement or acceptance by the United Nations. The map represents countries and/or territories or parts thereof for which data is available and/or analysed in World Economic Situation and Prospects 2022. The shaded areas therefore do not necessarily overlap entirely with the delimitation of their frontiers or boundaries. Aggregate data for Africa, excluding Libya.
* Excluding Libya; **Excluding Bolivarian Republic of Venezuela. **e:** 2021 estimates. **f:** 2022-2023 forecasts.
Source for COVID-19 data: UN DESA calculations, based on data from Johns Hopkins University.

Latin America and the Caribbean: recovery to lose steam amid fading external tailwinds and policy tightening

- Despite a faster-than-expected rebound in economic activity, the region faces lasting damage from the pandemic.
- Governments and central banks are expected to withdraw policy support to address fiscal pressures and combat rapidly rising inflation.
- The spread of new COVID-19 variants, a sharp tightening of global financial conditions, and social and political instability pose significant downside risks.

After a strong recovery from COVID-19, a slowdown is looming

Economies in Latin America and the Caribbean have largely rebounded from the COVID-19-induced recession, amid favourable external conditions, successful vaccine roll-outs and strong domestic policy support. But recovery has been insufficient to reverse damage from the pandemic, which has pushed millions out of work and into poverty. As global tailwinds recede and structural weaknesses exacerbated by the pandemic resurface, the region faces the prospect of a sharp economic slowdown, with growth returning to its weak pre-crisis trend. Real GDP expanded by an estimated 6.5 per cent in 2021 following the 7.4 per cent contraction in 2020, the region's deepest pull back in 120 years (Maddison Project Database, 2020). Growth is projected to average only 2.2 per cent in 2022 and 2.5 per cent in 2023. Uncertainties surrounding these forecasts remain exceptionally large as the region confronts significant downside risks, including the spread of more contagious or deadly COVID-19 variants, a sharp tightening of global financial conditions, and mounting social and political instability.

The region has experienced faster-than-expected but uneven recovery in economic activity over the past year. The growth rebound in 2021 was partly due to strong base effects, stemming from the output collapse at the beginning of the pandemic, but also reflected improved domestic conditions and supportive external factors. Many countries in Central America and South America recorded high growth rates, with annual GDP expanding at double-digit rates in Chile, Panama and Peru. The Caribbean small island developing States recovered more slowly as fiscal policy was less supportive, due to high levels of debt, and because they depend on international travel, which resumed only gradually.

The pandemic has loosened its grip on the region's economy

The pandemic has loosened its grip as governments, businesses and households have adapted to restrictions, which are having much less of an impact on output than in the early stages of the crisis (Oliveros-Rosen, 2021). The release of pent-up demand has driven higher private consumption and investment. With the numbers of daily COVID-19 cases and deaths declining sharply since mid-2021 amid significant progress on vaccination, governments have also more assertively eased restrictions and reopened economies.[25] In about half of the countries, more than 50 per cent of people were fully

25 Latin America and the Caribbean's share of the death toll from COVID-19 is the highest in the world. In mid-November 2021, the region accounted for 30.1 per cent of global deaths from the pandemic while having only 8.4 per cent of the world's population.

vaccinated by the end of November 2021 (figure III.21). Disparities in vaccination rates remain large, however. In Bermuda, Chile, Cuba and Uruguay, more than 75 per cent of people are fully vaccinated compared to less than 20 per cent in Jamaica and under 1 per cent in Haiti.

Figure III.21

Vaccination progress in Latin America and the Caribbean (as of 20 December 2021)

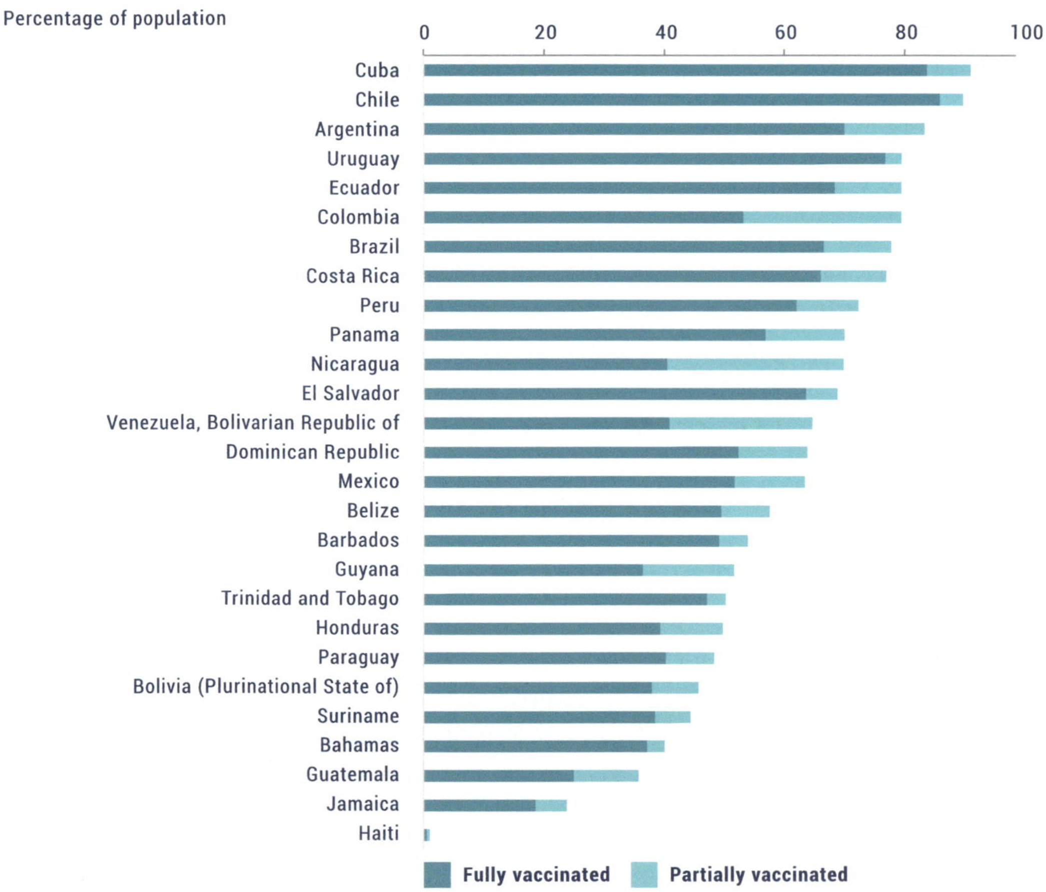

Source: UN DESA, based on data from Our World in Data (accessed on 20 December 2021).

Favourable external conditions supported economic recovery

The region has benefited from supportive external conditions. Strong demand from its main trading partners, notably China, the European Union and the United States, has boosted export growth. The global recovery has also led to sharp increases in the prices of oil, metals and agricultural goods, with South America's commodity exporters recording significant improvements in their terms of trade (ECLAC, 2021a).[26] At the same time, rapid growth in remittance inflows, driven by a recovering economy in the United States, has supported private demand in Mexico, Central America and parts of

26 By contrast, Mexico, Central America and the Caribbean experienced a slight worsening in the terms of trade in 2021.

the Caribbean.[27] Total remittance flows to the region reached an estimated record high of $126 billion in 2021, up 21.6 per cent over 2020 (World Bank, 2021c). Exceptionally accommodative global financial conditions have allowed governments and businesses across the region to access international financing on favourable terms.

Fading external tailwinds and policy tightening weigh on growth

While South America's commodity exporters have led the region's pandemic recovery, their growth prospects for 2022 and 2023 are subdued. Tailwinds from higher commodity prices, buoyant demand from China and the United States and favourable global financial conditions will gradually fade. At the same time, central banks are expected to tighten monetary policy to combat rapidly rising inflationary pressures. Governments will increasingly move away from fiscal stimulus and towards the consolidation of public finances. Altogether, these factors are expected to lower GDP growth in South America to only 1.6 per cent in 2022. Short-term growth prospects are more favourable for Central America and especially the Caribbean, where the continued resumption of tourism will stimulate economic activities.

Labour market recovery has been slow and uneven

The region's labour markets have seen only a partial and uneven recovery after suffering an unprecedented shock during the early stages of the COVID-19 crisis. While economic activity rebounded, job creation has been insufficient in terms of quantity and quality. In most countries, unemployment rates have remained significantly higher and participation rates lower than before the pandemic (figure III.22). In addition, informal employment has accounted for a large portion of the jobs created during the recovery (ILO, 2021b). ECLAC (2021a) warns that unemployment rates may increase even further in the coming years as people re-enter the labour market. Risks of long-term unemployment are greatest for groups hit particularly hard by the pandemic, including young people, women and less educated workers. Box III.5 examines the pandemic's disproportionate impact on the employment of vulnerable groups, underscoring the need to adopt comprehensive macroeconomic and labour market policy packages.

27 In El Salvador, Guatemala, Honduras and Jamaica, the value of remittances exceeded 18 per cent of GDP in 2021.

Figure III.22

Unemployment rates in select Latin American countries

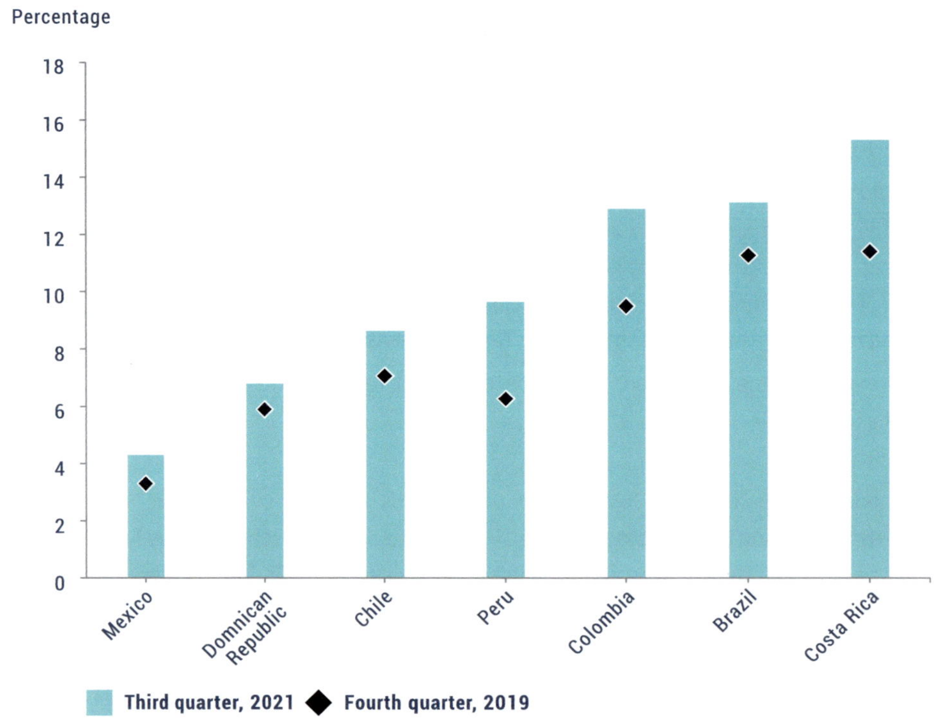

Source: CEIC, national data.

Box III.5

Healing from the pandemic: the impact of COVID-19 on labour markets in Latin America and the Caribbean and policies to promote a transformative recovery

The pandemic triggered an unprecedented crisis in labour markets across Latin American and the Caribbean. Although the entire global economy was affected in 2020, countries in this region saw the largest contraction in employment. It declined 3.5 per cent on average around the world but 9 per cent in Latin America and the Caribbean. Before the crisis, the region's pace of employment growth was already slowing, with 2010-2019 producing the most sluggish growth in the number of employed people since 1950.

For various reasons, the crisis weighed most heavily on employed women and the most vulnerable social groups, such as young people, migrants and less-educated workers. Between 2019 and 2020, the number of people in employment fell by almost 25 million, including about 13 million women. This resulted in a female unemployment rate of 11.9 per cent, up from 9.3 per cent in 2019. The unemployment rate for men in 2020 was 9.3 per cent compared with 6.9 per cent in 2019. These unemployment levels would have been higher (15.3 per cent for men and 22.2 per cent for women) if many workers had not withdrawn from the labour market altogether.

Figure III.5.a

Latin America and the Caribbean's labour force participation rate by gender

Percentage

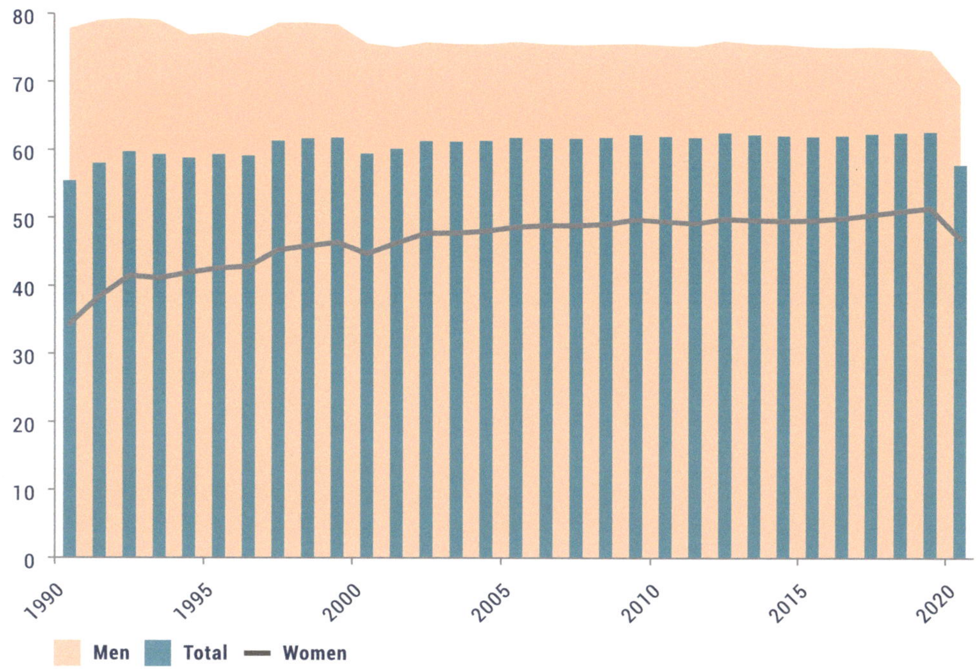

Source: ECLAC, based on official national data.

The crisis prompted a marked decline in labour force participation, especially among women, bringing an end to more than 30 years of continuous growth. By the close of 2020, women's participation rate was similar to that of 2001 (see figure III.5.a). This noticeable impact stems from women's strong presence in activities that were highly restricted during the pandemic, such as commerce and tourism, but also from the greater burden of unpaid work linked to household care for children, older persons and the sick that typically falls on women and in many cases grew worse during pandemic-related lockdowns.

Informal employment was heavily affected by the COVID-19 crisis, even as it provided work for nearly half of the people employed in Latin America and the Caribbean. In contrast to previous crises, informal employment did not act as a buffer in the labour market but actually fluctuated more than formal employment, as shown in figure III.5.b.

Figure III.5.b

People in formal and informal employment and total employed, first quarter of 2019 to fourth quarter of 2020

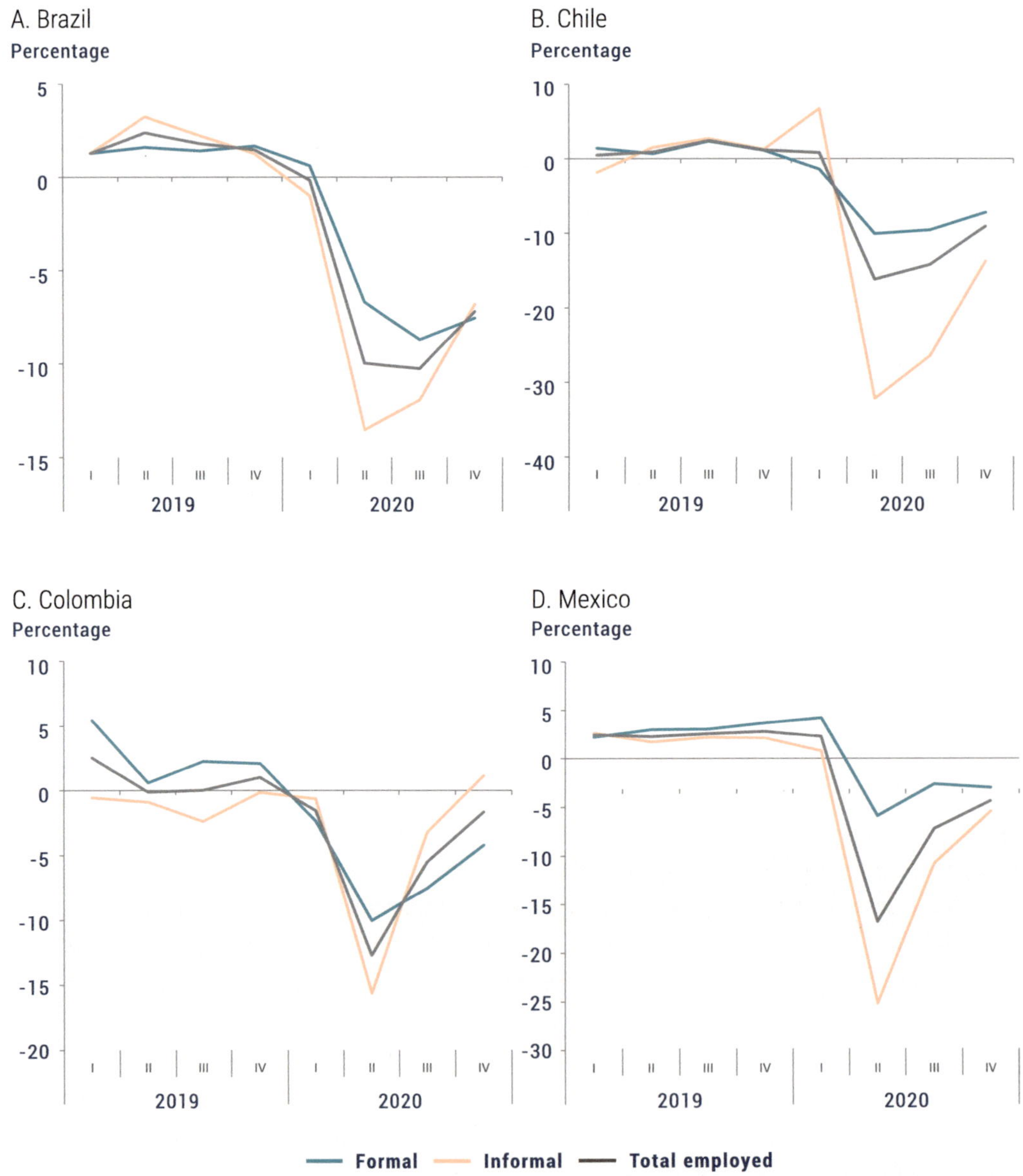

Source: ECLAC, based on official national data.
Note: Percentage change from the same quarter of the previous year.

The 2021 economic recovery boosted employment in the region but for most countries, neither economic activity nor employment returned to pre-crisis levels. In fact, in 2020, the number of employed persons fell by 25.3 million, of whom 17.3 million (68 per cent) returned to the labour force in 2021. This means the number of employed persons in the region was 2.8 per cent lower in 2021 than in 2019.

The total unemployment rate rose to 11 per cent, a rate worse for women at 12.7 per cent, 3 percentage points higher than the rate for men at 9.7 per cent.

Beyond the rebound in 2021, economic growth is likely to remain sluggish, which will not support rapid recovery in employment or improvements in the quality of jobs. Policies to drive the creation of high-quality jobs will be essential. These should focus on strengthening employment among groups most affected during the crisis, including women, young people and migrants. It is also necessary to support productive sectors with the greatest potential for job creation and labour market formalization, and to advance care systems that modify the traditional gender-based division of labour. Such systems should enshrine the right to care and the right to be cared for under conditions of quality and equality. All these steps should be taken in the medium term as the challenges will only grow if the region fails to break the pattern of weak growth seen before the COVID-19 crisis.

Fiscal stimulus packages to respond to COVID-19, particularly job support measures, have played a crucial role in protecting households and businesses and boosting aggregate demand. This support must be maintained in coming years to halt rising inequalities in the region. Furthermore, comprehensive short-term policies should support jobs and productivity and protect the incomes of the most disadvantaged groups, aiming for productive transformation capable of creating and maintaining high-quality jobs.

This comprehensive vision requires training, public employment programmes, employment subsidies, self-employment and microentrepreneurship programmes, employment services and infrastructure for labour intermediation, among other core measures.[a]

a See United Nations Economic Commission for Latin America and the Caribbean (2021a) for the strategies followed by Latin American economies to mitigate the impacts of the crisis and promote job creation during the recovery. UN Women and United Nations Economic Commission for Latin America and the Caribbean (2021) show the importance of comprehensive national care systems to foster growth and gender equality in the region.

Author: United Nations Economic Commission for Latin America and the Caribbean

Soaring food and energy prices have pushed inflation higher

The strong rebound in economic growth in Latin America and the Caribbean has been accompanied by rapidly rising inflationary pressures. Excluding the Bolivarian Republic of Venezuela, average consumer price inflation accelerated to an estimated 11.3 per cent in 2021, the fastest annual pace in more than two decades. In October, year-on-year inflation exceeded the central bank target range in all large economies (Argentina, Brazil, Chile, Colombia, Mexico and Peru). In contrast, upward pressures on prices have been more limited in most Central American countries. The recent surge in inflation reflects several factors, which vary in importance by country: the release of pent-up demand as pandemic-related restrictions have eased; supply shortages, for example, in the electronics, automotive and agricultural industries; higher prices of imported goods and services due to exchange rate depreciation; and, most importantly, soaring food and energy prices, which make up a larger share of consumer price indices in Latin America and the Caribbean than in developed countries. The spike in food prices has particularly affected low-income households, many of which are still reeling from the pandemic.

Inflation expectations have so far remained well anchored

Medium-term inflation expectations have so far remained well anchored, reflecting improved monetary policy frameworks and greater central bank credibility in much of the region, even though the growth outlook for major economies remains weak. In August 2021, three-year-ahead inflation expectations were below 4 per cent in Brazil, Chile, Colombia, Mexico and Peru (IMF, 2021b). Although core inflation, which excludes volatile food and energy prices, has accelerated, most factors pushing prices up are likely temporary. Food and energy prices are expected to plateau in 2022, while demand pressures and supply-chain bottlenecks will likely ease gradually in the coming year. A baseline forecast projects average consumer price inflation in the region to moderate to 9.6 per cent in 2022 and 7.2 per cent in 2023. But large uncertainties surrounding the inflation outlook and concerns over deteriorating growth prospects present monetary policymakers with a challenging environment to navigate.

Several central banks have tightened monetary policy

After providing unprecedented monetary policy support in response to the pandemic, central banks started to withdraw monetary stimulus in 2021. Many have raised their policy rates, aiming to rein in inflationary pressures and prevent de-anchoring of inflation expectations (figure III.23). The Central Bank of Brazil has embarked on the most aggressive tightening cycle in the region, lifting its main policy rate from 2 per cent at the start of the year to 7.75 per cent in late October and projecting the rate will reach 9.75 per cent in 2022. Several other central banks, for example, in Chile, Colombia and Peru, accelerated tightening in late 2021. While the monetary tightening cycle is set to continue in 2022, the question is how aggressively central banks will raise borrowing costs. Since current upward pressure is partly due to global and supply-side factors, sharp tightening of monetary policy may not be effective in reducing inflation and could undermine a fragile and incomplete recovery. If it leads to increased capital inflows and exchange rate appreciations, it could hurt exports.

Figure III.23

Central bank policy rates in select Latin American countries

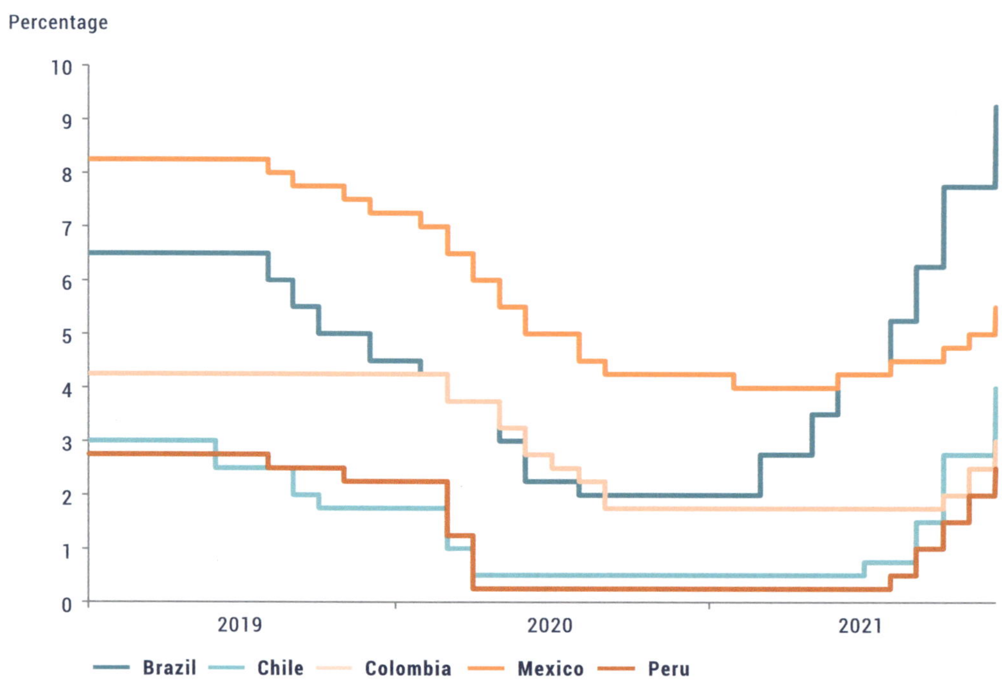

Source: Bank for International Settlements.

Pressures to consolidate public finances are likely to rise

Large-scale fiscal stimulus measures were vital in cushioning social fallout from the pandemic and supporting economic recovery in the region. Most governments, with major exceptions being Chile and Peru, started scaling back their extraordinary policy support in 2021 but spending levels remained significantly higher than before the crisis. At the same time, public revenues recovered through higher economic growth and rising commodity prices. This temporary cyclical improvement, however, should not obscure a still challenging fiscal outlook. With global financial conditions expected to tighten, pressures to consolidate public finances are likely to increase, especially for countries with large dollar-denominated debt (for example, Argentina and the Dominican Republic). In many countries, fiscal space will further shrink as the debt-servicing burden continues to rise. Given large and increasing demands for greater spending, including to strengthen health and education systems, expand social protection coverage, facilitate energy transition and carry forward policies to support industry and technology, additional resource mobilization will remain critical. Above all, this requires increasing contributions from direct taxes. More progressive taxation, coupled with increased efforts to close loopholes and combat tax evasion, can put public finances on a more solid footing while reducing income inequalities (Hanni and others, 2015; Martorano, 2018).

Statistical Annex

Data sources, country classifications and aggregation methodology

The statistical annex contains a set of data that the *World Economic Situation and Prospects (WESP)* employs to delineate trends in various dimensions of the world economy.

Data sources

The annex was prepared by the Economic Analysis and Policy Division (EAPD) of the Department of Economic and Social Affairs of the United Nations Secretariat (UN DESA). It is based on information obtained from the Statistics Division and the Population Division of UN DESA, as well as from the five United Nations regional commissions, the United Nations Conference on Trade and Development (UNCTAD), the International Monetary Fund (IMF), the World Bank, the Organization for Economic Cooperation and Development (OECD), Eurostat and national sources. Estimates for 2021 and forecasts for 2022 and 2023 were made by EAPD in consultation with the regional commissions and UNCTAD, partly guided by the World Economic Forecasting Model (WEFM) of EAPD.[1] Longer-term projections are based on a technical model-based extension of the WEFM. Data presented in the WESP may differ from those published by other organizations for several reasons, including differences in timing, sample composition and aggregation methods. Historical data may differ from those in previous editions of the WESP because of updating and changes in the availability of data for individual countries.

Country classifications

For analytical purposes, the WESP classifies all countries of the world into one of three broad categories: developed economies, economies in transition and developing economies.[2] The composition of these analytical groupings, specified in tables A, B and C, is intended to reflect basic economic country conditions, and are not strictly aligned with the regional classifications defined by the Statistics Division of UN DESA known as M49.[3] Table A.4 reports estimates for regional GDP growth according to the M49 definitions for comparison. Several countries (in particular the economies in transition) have characteristics that could place them in more than one category; however, for purposes of analysis, the groupings have been made mutually exclusive. Within each broad category, some subgroups are defined based either on geographical location or on ad hoc criteria, such as the subgroup of "major developed economies", which is based on the membership of the Group of Seven.

In parts of the analysis, a distinction is made between fuel exporters and fuel importers. An economy is classified as a fuel exporter if the share of fuel exports in its total merchandise exports is greater

1 See Altshuler et al. (2016).
2 These analytical groupings are not strictly aligned with geographic groupings of Developed Regions and Developing Regions designated by the Statistics Division of UN DESA.
3 Full details of the M49 standard can be found on the **Statistics Division website**.

than 20 per cent and the level of fuel exports is at least 20 per cent higher than that of the country's fuel imports (table D). This criterion is drawn from the share of fuel exports in the total value of world merchandise trade. Fuels include coal, oil and natural gas.

For other parts of the analysis, countries have been classified by their level of development as measured by per capita gross national income (GNI). Accordingly, countries have been grouped as high-income, upper-middle-income, lower-middle-income and low-income (table E). To maintain compatibility with similar classifications used elsewhere, the threshold levels of GNI per capita are those established by the World Bank. Countries with less than $1,046 GNI per capita are classified as low-income countries, those with between $1,046 and $4095 as lower-middle-income countries, those with between $4096 and $12,695 as upper-middle-income countries, and those with incomes of more than $12,695 as high-income countries. GNI per capita in dollar terms is estimated using the World Bank Atlas method,[4] and the classification in table E is based on data for 2020.

The list of the least developed countries (LDCs) is determined by the United Nations Economic and Social Council and, ultimately, by the General Assembly, on the basis of recommendations made by the Committee for Development Policy. The basic criteria for inclusion require that certain thresholds be met with regard to per capita GNI, a human assets index and an economic and environmental vulnerability index.[5] As of February 2021, there were 46 LDCs (table F).

The WESP also makes reference to the group of heavily indebted poor countries (HIPCs), which are considered by the World Bank and IMF as part of their debt-relief initiative (the Enhanced HIPC Initiative).[6] In March 2020, there were 39 HIPCs (table G).

Aggregation methodology

Aggregate data are either sums or weighted averages of individual country data. Unless otherwise indicated, multi-year averages of growth rates are expressed as compound annual percentage rates of change. The convention followed is to omit the base year in a multi-year growth rate. For example, the 10-year average growth rate for the decade of the 2000s would be identified as the average annual growth rate for the period from 2001 to 2010.

The WESP utilizes market exchange rate conversions of national data in order to aggregate output of individual countries into regional and global totals. The growth of output in each group of countries is calculated from the sum of gross domestic product (GDP) of individual countries measured at 2015 prices and exchange rates. This method supplies a reasonable set of aggregate growth rates for a period of about 15 years, centered on 2015.

---

4 See http://data.worldbank.org/about/country-classifications.

5 Handbook on the Least Developed Country Category: Inclusion, Graduation and Special Support Measures, 4th ed. (United Nations publication, Sales No. E.22.II.A.1).

6 International Monetary Fund, Debt Relief Under the Heavily Indebted Poor Countries (HIPC) Initiative.

The exchange rate-based aggregation method differs from the one mainly applied by the IMF for their estimates of world and regional economic growth, which is based on purchasing power parity (PPP) weights. Over the past two decades, the growth of world gross product (WGP) on the basis of the exchange rate-based approach has been below that based on PPP weights. This is because developing countries, in the aggregate, have seen significantly higher economic growth than the rest of the world in the 1990s and 2000s and the share in WGP of these countries is larger under PPP measurements than under market exchange rates. Table I.1 in Chapter I reports world output growth with PPP weights as a comparator.

Table A
Developed economies

Northern America	Europe		Major developed economies (G7)
	European Union	Other Europe	
Canada	*EU-15*	Iceland	Canada
United States	Austria[a]	Norway	France
	Belgium[a]	Switzerland	Germany
	Denmark[a]	United Kingdom[c]	Italy
	Finland[a]		Japan
	France[a]		United Kingdom
	Germany[a]		United States
	Greece[a]		
	Ireland[a]		
	Italy[a]		
	Luxembourg[a]		
	Netherlands[a]		
	Portugal[a]		
	Spain[a]		
	Sweden		
Developed Asia and Pacific	*EU-13*[b]		
Australia	Bulgaria		
Japan	Croatia		
New Zealand	Cyprus[a]		
	Czechia		
	Estonia[a]		
	Hungary		
	Latvia[a]		
	Lithuania[a]		
	Malta[a]		
	Poland		
	Romania		
	Slovakia[a]		
	Slovenia[a]		

a Member of euro area.
b Used in reference to the 13 countries that joined the EU since 2004.
c The United Kingdom withdrew from the EU on 31 January 2020 and is therefore excluded from all EU aggregations.

Table B
Economies in transition

South-Eastern Europe	Commonwealth of Independent States and Georgia[a]	
Albania	Armenia	Republic of Moldova
Bosnia and Herzegovina	Azerbaijan	Russian Federation
Montenegro	Belarus	Tajikistan
North Macedonia	Georgia[a]	Turkmenistan
Serbia	Kazakhstan	Ukraine[b]
	Kyrgyzstan	Uzbekistan

a Georgia officially left the Commonwealth of Independent States on 18 August 2009. However, its performance is discussed in the context of this group of countries for reasons of geographic proximity and similarities in economic structure.

b Starting in 2010, data for the Ukraine excludes the temporarily occupied territory of the Autonomous Republic of Crimea and Sevastopol.

Table C
Developing economies by region[a]

Africa		Asia	Latin America and the Caribbean
North Africa	**Southern Africa**	**East Asia[b]**	**Caribbean**
Algeria	Angola	Brunei Darussalam	Bahamas
Egypt	Botswana	Cambodia	Barbados
Libya	Eswatini	China	Belize
Mauritania	Lesotho	Democratic People's Republic of Korea	Guyana
Morocco	Malawi	Fiji	Jamaica
Sudan	Mauritius	Hong Kong SAR[c]	Suriname
Tunisia	Mozambique	Indonesia	Trinidad and Tobago
Central Africa	Namibia	Kiribati	**Mexico and Central America**
Cameroon	South Africa	Lao People's Democratic Republic	Costa Rica
Central African Republic	Zambia	Malaysia	Cuba
Chad	Zimbabwe	Mongolia	Dominican Republic
Congo	**West Africa**	Myanmar	El Salvador
Equatorial Guinea	Benin	Papua New Guinea	Guatemala
Gabon	Burkina Faso	Philippines	Haiti
Sao Tome and Prinicipe	Cabo Verde	Republic of Korea	Honduras
East Africa	Côte d'Ivoire	Samoa	Mexico
Burundi	Gambia	Singapore	Nicaragua
Comoros	Ghana	Solomon Islands	Panama
Democratic Republic of the Congo	Guinea	Taiwan Province of China	**South America**
Djibouti	Guinea-Bissau	Thailand	Argentina
Eritrea	Liberia	Timor-Leste	Bolivia (Plurinational State of)
Ethiopia	Mali	Vanuatu	Brazil
Kenya	Niger	Viet Nam	Chile
Madagascar	Nigeria	**South Asia**	Colombia
Rwanda	Senegal	Afghanistan	Ecuador
Somalia	Sierra Leone	Bangladesh	Paraguay
South Sudan	Togo	Bhutan	Peru
Uganda		India	Uruguay
United Republic of Tanzania		Iran (Islamic Republic of)	Venezuela (Bolivarian Republic of)
		Maldives	
		Nepal	
		Pakistan	
		Sri Lanka	
		Western Asia	
		Bahrain	
		Iraq	
		Israel	
		Jordan	
		Kuwait	
		Lebanon	
		Oman	
		Qatar	
		Saudi Arabia	
		State of Palestine	
		Syrian Arab Republic	
		Turkey	
		United Arab Emirates	
		Yemen	

a Economies systematically monitored for the World Economic Situation and Prospects report. These analytical groupings differ from the geographical aggregations defined according to M49.
b Throughout the report the term 'East Asia' is used in reference to this set of developing countries, and excludes Japan.
c Special Administrative Region of China.

Table D
Fuel-exporting countries

Developed countries	Economies in transition	Developing countries: Latin America and the Caribbean	Developing countries: Africa	Developing countries: East Asia	Developing countries: Western Asia
Norway	Azerbaijan	Bolivia (Plurinational State of)	Algeria	Brunei Darussalam	Bahrain
	Kazakhstan	Colombia	Angola	Indonesia	Iraq
	Russian Federation	Ecuador	Cameroon	Mongolia	Kuwait
	Turkmenistan	Trinidad and Tobago	Chad	Papua New Guinea	Oman
		Venezuela (Bolivarian Republic of)	Congo		Qatar
			Equatorial Guinea	**South Asia**	Saudi Arabia
			Gabon	Iran (Islamic Republic of)	United Arab Emirates
			Ghana		Yemen
			Libya		
			Mozambique		
			Nigeria		

Source: UN DESA, based on data from UNCTAD.

Table E
Economies by per capita GNI as of 1 July 2021[a]

High-income	
Australia	Latvia
Austria	Lithuania
Bahamas	Luxembourg
Bahrain	Malta
Barbados	Netherlands
Belgium	New Zealand
Brunei Darussalam	Norway
Canada	Oman
Chile	Poland
Croatia	Portugal
Cyprus	Qatar
Czechia	Republic of Korea
Denmark	Saudi Arabia
Estonia	Singapore
Finland	Slovakia
France	Slovenia
Germany	Spain
Greece	Sweden
Hong Kong SAR[d]	Switzerland
Hungary	Taiwan Province of China
Iceland	Trinidad and Tobago
Ireland	United Arab Emirates
Israel	United Kingdom
Italy	United States
Japan	Uruguay
Kuwait	

Upper-middle-income	
Albania	Jordan
Argentina	Kazakhstan
Armenia	Lebanon
Azerbaijan	Libya
Belarus	Malaysia
Bosnia and Herzegovina	Maldives
Botswana	Mauritius[b]
Brazil	Mexico
Bulgaria	Montenegro
China	Namibia
Colombia	North Macedonia
Costa Rica	Panama[b]
Cuba	Paraguay
Dominican Republic	Peru
Ecuador	Republic of Moldova
Equatorial Guinea	Romania[b]
Fiji	Russian Federation
Gabon	Serbia
Georgia	South Africa
Guatemala	Suriname
Guyana	Thailand
Iraq	Turkey
Jamaica	Turkmenistan

Lower-middle-income	
Algeria	Lesotho
Angola	Mauritania
Bangladesh	Mongolia
Belize[b]	Morocco
Benin	Myanmar
Bhutan	Nepal
Bolivia (Plurinational State of)	Nicaragua
Cabo Verde	Nigeria
Cambodia	Pakistan
Cameroon	Papua New Guinea
Comoros	Philippines
Congo	Samoa[b]
Côte d'Ivoire	Sao Tome and Principe
Djibouti	Senegal
Egypt	Solomon Islands
El Salvador	Sri Lanka
Eswatini	State of Palestine
Ghana	Tajikistan[c]
Haiti[c]	Timor-Leste
Honduras	Tunisia
India	Ukraine
Indonesia[b]	United Republic of Tanzania
Iran (Islamic Republic of)[b]	Uzbekistan
Kenya	Vanuatu
Kiribati	Viet Nam
Kyrgyzstan	Zambia
Lao People's Democratic Republic	Zimbabwe

Low-income			
Afghanistan	Democratic Republic of the Congo	Madagascar	Sudan
Burkina Faso	Eritrea	Malawi	Syrian Arab Republic
Burundi	Ethiopia	Mali	Togo
Central African Republic	Gambia	Mozambique	Uganda
Chad	Guinea	Niger	Yemen
Democratic People's Republic of Korea	Guinea-Bissau	Rwanda	
	Liberia	Sierra Leone	
		Somalia	
		South Sudan	

Source: World Bank, Country classification by income (https://datahelpdesk.worldbank.org/knowledgebase/articles/906519).
Note: Venezuela (Bolivarian Republic of) has been temporarily unclassified in July 2021 pending release of revised national accounts statistics.

a Economies systematically monitored for the World Economic Situation and Prospects report, based on World Bank country classifications by income.
b Indicates the country has been shifted downward by one category from previous year's classification.
c Indicates the country has been shifted upward by one category from previous year's classification.
d Special Administrative Region of China.

Table F
Least developed countries (*24 November 2021*)

Africa		East Asia	South Asia	Western Asia	Latin America and the Caribbean
Angola	Malawi	Cambodia	Afghanistan	Yemen	Haiti
Benin	Mali	Kiribati	Bangladesh		
Burkina Faso	Mauritania	Lao People's Democratic Republic	Bhutan		
Burundi	Mozambique	Myanmar	Nepal		
Central African Republic	Niger	Solomon Islands			
Chad	Rwanda	Timor Leste			
Comoros	Sao Tome and Principe	Tuvalu[a]			
Democratic Republic of the Congo	Senegal				
Djibouti	Sierra Leone				
Eritrea	Somalia				
Ethiopia	South Sudan				
Gambia	Sudan				
Guinea	Togo				
Guinea-Bissau	Uganda				
Lesotho	United Republic of Tanzania				
Liberia	Zambia				
Madagascar					

Source: UN DESA (https://www.un.org/development/desa/dpad/wp-content/uploads/sites/45/publication/ldc_list.pdf).
a Economies not systematically monitored for the World Economic Situation and Prospects report.

Table G
Heavily indebted poor countries (*as of March 2020*)

Post-completion point HIPCs[a]		Pre-decision point HIPCs[b]
Afghanistan	Haiti	Eritrea
Benin	Honduras	Sudan
Bolivia	Liberia	
Burkina Faso	Madagascar	
Burundi	Malawi	
Cameroon	Mali	
Central African Republic	Mauritania	
Chad	Mozambique	
Comoros	Nicaragua	
Congo	Niger	
Côte D'Ivoire	Rwanda	
Democratic Republic of the Congo	Sao Tome and Principe	
Ethiopia	Senegal	
Gambia	Sierra Leone	
Ghana	Somalia	
Guinea	Togo	
Guinea-Bissau	Uganda	
Guyana	United Republic of Tanzania	
	Zambia	

Source: The World Bank and the International Monetary Fund (https://www.worldbank.org/en/topic/debt/brief/hipc).
a Countries that have qualified for irrevocable debt relief under the HIPC Initiative.
b Countries that are potentially eligible and may wish to avail themselves of the HIPC Initiative or the Multilateral Debt Relief Initiative (MDRI).

Table H
Small island developing States

United Nations members		Non-UN members/Associate members of the Regional Commissions[a]
Antigua and Barbuda[a]	Marshall Islands[a]	American Samoa
Bahamas	Mauritius	Anguilla
Bahrain	Nauru[a]	Aruba
Barbados	Palau[a]	Bermuda
Belize	Papua New Guinea	British Virgin Islands
Cabo Verde	Saint Kitts and Nevis[a]	Cayman Islands
Comoros	Saint Lucia[a]	Commonwealth of Northern Marianas
Cuba	Saint Vincent and the Grenadines[a]	Cook Islands
Dominica[a]	Samoa	Curaçao
Dominican Republic	Sao Tome and Príncipe	French Polynesia
Federated States of Micronesia[a]	Seychelles[a]	Guadeloupe
Fiji	Singapore	Guam
Grenada[a]	Solomon Islands	Martinique
Guinea-Bissau	Suriname	Montserrat
Guyana	Timor-Leste	New Caledonia
Haiti	Tonga[a]	Niue
Jamaica	Trinidad and Tobago	Puerto Rico
Kiribati	Tuvalu[a]	Sint Maarten
Maldives	Vanuatu	Turks and Caicos Islands
		U.S. Virgin Islands

Source: UN DESA (https://sustainabledevelopment.un.org/topics/sids/list).
a Economies not systematically monitored for the World Economic Situation and Prospects report.

Table I
Landlocked developing countries

Landlocked developing countries		
Afghanistan	Ethiopia	North Macedonia
Armenia	Kazakhstan	Paraguay
Azerbaijan	Kyrgystan	Republic of Moldova
Bhutan	Lao People's Democratic Republic	Rwanda
Bolivia (Plurinational State of)	Lesotho	South Sudan
Botswana	Malawi	Tajikistan
Burkina Faso	Mali	Turkmenistan
Burundi	Mongolia	Uganda
Central African Republic	Nepal	Uzbekistan
Chad	Niger	Zambia
Eswatini		Zimbabwe

Source: UN-OHRLLS (http://unohrlls.org/about-lldcs/country-profiles/).

Table J
International Organization for Standardization of Country Codes

ISO Code	Country
AFG	Afghanistan
AGO	Angola
AIA	Anguilla
ALB	Albania
AND	Andorra
ARE	United Arab Emirates
ARG	Argentina
ARM	Armenia
ATG	Antigua and Barbuda
AUS	Australia
AUT	Austria
AZE	Azerbaijan
BDI	Burundi
BEL	Belgium
BEN	Benin
BFA	Burkina Faso
BGD	Bangladesh
BGR	Bulgaria
BHR	Bahrain
BHS	Bahamas
BIH	Bosnia and Herzegovina
BLR	Belarus
BLZ	Belize
BOL	Bolivia (Plurinational State of)
BRA	Brazil
BRB	Barbados
BRN	Brunei Darussalam
BTN	Bhutan
BWA	Botswana
CAF	Central African Republic
CAN	Canada
CHE	Switzerland
CHL	Chile
CHN	China
CIV	Côte D'Ivoire
CMR	Cameroon
COD	Democratic Republic of the Congo
COG	Congo
COL	Colombia
COM	Comoros
CPV	Cabo Verde
CRI	Costa Rica
CUB	Cuba
CYP	Cyprus
CZE	Czechia
DEU	Germany
DJI	Djibouti
DMA	Dominica
DNK	Denmark
DOM	Dominican Republic
DZA	Algeria
ECU	Ecuador
EGY	Egypt
ERI	Eritrea
ESP	Spain
EST	Estonia
ETH	Ethiopia
FIN	Finland
FJI	Fiji
FRA	France
FSM	Micronesia (Federated States of)
GAB	Gabon
GBR	United Kingdom of Great Britain and Northern Ireland
GEO	Georgia
GHA	Ghana
GIN	Guinea
GMB	Gambia
GNB	Guinea-Bissau
GNQ	Equatorial Guinea
GRC	Greece
GRD	Grenada
GTM	Guatemala
GUY	Guyana
HND	Honduras
HRV	Croatia
HTI	Haiti
HUN	Hungary
IDN	Indonesia
IND	India
IRL	Ireland
IRN	Iran (Islamic Republic of)
IRQ	Iraq
ISL	Iceland
ISR	Israel
ITA	Italy
JAM	Jamaica
JOR	Jordan
JPN	Japan
KAZ	Kazakhstan
KEN	Kenya
KGZ	Kyrgyzstan
KHM	Cambodia
KIR	Kiribati
KNA	Saint Kitts and Nevis
KOR	Republic of Korea
KWT	Kuwait
LAO	Lao People's Democratic Republic
LBN	Lebanon
LBR	Liberia
LBY	Libya
LCA	Saint Lucia
LIE	Liechtenstein
LKA	Sri Lanka
LSO	Lesotho
LTU	Lithuania
LUX	Luxembourg
LVA	Latvia
MAR	Morocco
MCO	Monaco
MDA	Republic of Moldova
MDG	Madagascar
MDV	Maldives
MEX	Mexico
MHL	Marshall Islands
MKD	North Macedonia
MLI	Mali
MLT	Malta
MMR	Myanmar
MNE	Montenegro
MNG	Mongolia
MOZ	Mozambique
MRT	Mauritania
MSR	Montserrat
MUS	Mauritius
MWI	Malawi
MYS	Malaysia
NAM	Namibia
NER	Niger
NGA	Nigeria
NIC	Nicaragua
NLD	Netherlands
NOR	Norway
NPL	Nepal
NRU	Nauru
NZL	New Zealand
OMN	Oman
PAK	Pakistan
PAN	Panama
PER	Peru
PHL	Philippines
PLW	Palau
PNG	Papua New Guinea
POL	Poland
PRK	Democratic People's Republic of Korea
PRT	Portugal
PRY	Paraguay
PSE	State of Palestine
QAT	Qatar
ROU	Romania
RUS	Russian Federation
RWA	Rwanda
SAU	Saudi Arabia
SDN	Sudan
SEN	Senegal
SGP	Singapore
SLB	Solomon Islands
SLE	Sierra Leone
SLV	El Salvador
SMR	San Marino
SOM	Somalia
SRB	Serbia
SSD	South Sudan
STP	Sao Tome and Principe
SUR	Suriname
SVK	Slovakia
SVN	Slovenia
SWE	Sweden
SWZ	Eswatini
SYC	Seychelles
SYR	Syrian Arab Republic
TCD	Chad
TGO	Togo
THA	Thailand
TJK	Tajikistan
TKM	Turkmenistan
TLS	Timor-Leste
TON	Tonga
TTO	Trinidad and Tobago
TUN	Tunisia
TUR	Turkey
TUV	Tuvalu
TZA	United Republic of Tanzania
UGA	Uganda
UKR	Ukraine
URY	Uruguay
USA	United States of America
UZB	Uzbekistan
VCT	Saint Vincent and the Grenadines
VEN	Venezuela (Bolivarian Republic of)
VNM	Viet Nam
VUT	Vanuatu
WSM	Samoa
YEM	Yemen
ZAF	South Africa
ZMB	Zambia
ZWE	Zimbabwe

Annex tables

Table A.1

Developed economies: rates of growth of real GDP

Annual percentage change

	1999–2013[a]	2014	2015	2016	2017	2018	2019	2020	2021[b]	2022[c]	2023[c]
Developed economies	**1.8**	**1.9**	**2.3**	**1.7**	**2.4**	**2.3**	**1.8**	**-4.8**	**4.8**	**3.7**	**2.5**
United States	2.1	2.3	2.7	1.7	2.3	2.9	2.3	-3.4	5.5	3.5	2.4
Canada	2.4	2.9	0.7	1.0	3.0	2.4	1.9	-5.3	5.1	3.9	2.7
Japan	0.8	0.3	1.6	0.8	1.7	0.6	0.0	-4.6	2.2	3.3	2.7
Australia	3.1	2.5	2.3	2.7	2.4	2.9	1.9	-2.5	3.1	4.2	3.0
New Zealand	2.8	3.3	4.2	4.2	4.0	4.3	3.0	-1.2	4.3	3.3	3.3
European Union	**1.4**	**1.6**	**2.3**	**2.0**	**2.8**	**2.1**	**1.8**	**-6.0**	**4.7**	**3.9**	**2.6**
Austria	1.7	0.7	1.0	2.0	2.4	2.6	1.4	-6.3	4.5	4.0	2.0
Belgium	1.8	1.6	2.0	1.3	1.6	1.8	1.8	-6.3	5.2	3.2	1.8
Bulgaria	2.9	1.9	4.0	3.8	3.5	3.1	3.7	-4.2	4.3	4.0	3.5
Croatia	1.6	-0.3	2.4	3.5	3.4	2.8	2.9	-8.0	7.8	4.3	3.3
Cyprus	2.3	-1.8	3.2	6.4	5.2	5.2	3.1	-5.1	3.1	3.5	3.5
Czechia	2.5	2.3	5.4	2.5	5.2	3.2	3.0	-5.8	3.6	3.5	2.9
Denmark	1.1	1.6	2.3	3.2	2.8	2.0	2.1	-2.1	3.5	3.3	2.9
Estonia	3.7	3.0	1.9	3.2	5.8	4.1	4.1	-3.0	6.8	3.5	3.5
Finland	1.9	-0.4	0.5	2.8	3.2	1.1	1.3	-2.9	3.2	2.5	2.5
France	1.5	1.0	1.1	1.1	2.3	1.9	1.8	-7.9	6.0	3.6	2.5
Germany	1.2	2.2	1.5	2.2	2.7	1.1	1.1	-4.9	2.5	3.9	2.1
Greece	0.2	0.7	-0.4	-0.5	1.3	1.6	1.9	-8.2	8.0	5.0	3.9
Hungary	2.1	4.2	3.8	2.1	4.3	5.4	4.6	-5.0	6.8	4.3	4.2
Ireland	3.3	8.7	25.2	2.0	8.9	9.0	4.9	5.9	12.0	5.2	4.0
Italy	0.3	0.0	0.8	1.3	1.7	0.9	0.3	-8.9	6.0	4.2	2.6
Latvia	3.9	1.1	4.0	2.4	3.3	4.0	2.0	-3.6	4.3	4.4	4.5
Lithuania	4.0	3.5	2.0	2.5	4.3	3.9	4.3	-0.9	4.2	3.5	3.8
Luxembourg	3.3	4.3	4.3	4.6	1.8	3.1	2.3	-1.3	5.0	2.9	2.0
Malta	2.8	7.6	9.6	3.8	11.0	6.1	5.7	-7.8	5.2	5.2	3.0
Netherlands	1.5	1.4	2.0	2.2	2.9	2.4	2.0	-3.8	3.9	3.0	2.0
Poland	3.7	3.4	4.2	3.1	4.8	5.4	4.7	-2.7	5.0	4.0	4.5
Portugal	0.5	0.8	1.8	2.0	3.5	2.8	2.5	-7.6	4.2	4.8	3.1
Romania	3.5	3.6	3.0	4.7	7.3	4.5	4.1	-3.9	7.1	4.2	3.9
Slovakia	3.7	2.6	4.8	2.1	3.0	3.7	2.5	-4.8	4.5	3.5	3.8
Slovenia	2.2	2.8	2.2	3.2	4.8	4.4	3.3	-4.2	5.6	4.0	3.9
Spain	1.7	1.4	3.8	3.0	3.0	2.4	2.0	-10.8	4.5	5.2	3.0
Sweden	2.3	2.7	4.5	2.1	2.6	2.0	2.0	-2.8	4.2	3.0	2.0
Other Europe	**1.9**	**2.7**	**2.2**	**1.7**	**1.8**	**1.5**	**1.3**	**-7.7**	**5.4**	**4.0**	**2.1**
Iceland	2.9	1.7	4.4	6.3	4.2	4.9	2.4	-6.5	3.5	4.5	3.6
Norway	1.7	2.0	2.0	1.1	2.3	1.1	0.9	-0.8	3.0	3.0	2.6
Switzerland	2.0	2.4	1.7	2.0	1.6	2.9	1.2	-2.4	3.6	2.7	2.3
United Kingdom[d]	1.8	2.9	2.4	1.7	1.7	1.3	1.4	-9.8	6.2	4.5	2.0
Memorandum items:											
Northern America	2.1	2.3	2.5	1.6	2.3	2.9	2.3	-3.6	5.5	3.5	2.4
Developed Asia and the Pacific	1.3	0.9	1.8	1.3	1.9	1.2	0.5	-4.0	2.5	3.5	2.8
Europe	1.5	1.6	2.3	2.0	2.8	2.1	1.7	-5.7	4.6	3.8	2.6
Major developed economies	1.7	1.9	2.1	1.5	2.2	2.1	1.7	-4.9	4.9	3.7	2.4
Euro area	1.3	1.4	2.1	1.9	2.6	1.9	1.5	-6.5	4.7	4.0	2.5

Source: UN DESA, based on data of the United Nations Statistics Division and individual national sources.

Note: Regional aggregates calculated at 2015 prices and exchange rates.

a Average percentage change.

b Partly estimated.

c Baseline scenario forecasts, based on UN DESA World Economic Forecasting Model.

d The United Kingdom withdrew from the EU on 31 January 2020 and is therefore excluded from all EU aggregations.

Table A.2

Economies in transition: rates of growth of real GDP

Annual percentage change

	1999–2013[a]	2014	2015	2016	2017	2018	2019	2020	2021[b]	2022[c]	2023[c]
Economies in transition	**5.2**	**1.2**	**-1.2**	**0.8**	**2.4**	**3.2**	**2.7**	**-2.6**	**4.4**	**3.2**	**2.9**
South-Eastern Europe	**3.4**	**0.2**	**2.4**	**3.2**	**2.6**	**4.1**	**3.5**	**-3.1**	**6.2**	**4.0**	**3.6**
Albania	5.3	1.8	2.2	3.3	3.8	4.1	2.2	-3.3	6.8	5.0	3.8
Bosnia and Herzegovina	3.5	1.2	3.1	3.1	3.2	3.7	2.8	-4.3	5.6	3.3	3.7
Montenegro	2.8	1.8	3.4	2.9	4.7	5.1	4.1	-15.3	10.3	5.2	3.8
North Macedonia	2.9	3.6	3.9	2.8	1.1	2.9	3.2	-4.5	4.4	3.9	3.5
Serbia	3.1	-1.6	1.8	3.3	2.1	4.5	4.2	-1.0	6.4	4.0	3.5
Commonwealth of Independent States and Georgia[d]	**5.3**	**1.2**	**-1.4**	**0.7**	**2.4**	**3.2**	**2.6**	**-2.6**	**4.3**	**3.2**	**2.8**
Commonwealth of Independent States and Georgia – net fuel exporters	**5.3**	**1.4**	**-1.3**	**0.3**	**2.2**	**3.0**	**2.4**	**-2.7**	**4.2**	**3.0**	**2.7**
Azerbaijan	11.4	2.8	1.0	-3.1	0.2	1.5	2.2	-4.3	4.9	4.0	4.1
Kazakhstan	7.5	4.2	1.2	1.1	4.1	4.1	4.5	-2.6	3.6	4.0	4.0
Russian Federation	4.9	0.7	-2.0	0.2	1.8	2.8	2.0	-3.0	4.2	2.7	2.3
Turkmenistan	9.0	10.3	6.5	6.2	6.5	6.2	3.0	5.9	6.1	5.7	6.0
Commonwealth of Independent States and Georgia – net fuel importers	**5.0**	**0.4**	**-1.8**	**2.7**	**3.8**	**4.3**	**4.0**	**-1.8**	**4.7**	**4.2**	**3.6**
Armenia	7.0	3.6	3.2	0.2	7.5	5.2	7.6	-7.6	5.2	4.4	4.0
Belarus	6.1	1.7	-3.8	-2.5	2.5	3.2	1.2	-0.9	2.9	1.8	2.1
Georgia[d]	5.6	4.4	3.0	2.9	4.8	4.8	5.1	-6.2	9.5	4.4	4.0
Kyrgyzstan	4.4	4.0	3.9	4.3	4.7	3.8	4.5	-8.6	1.5	3.5	4.0
Republic of Moldova	4.3	5.0	-0.3	4.4	4.7	4.3	3.5	-7.0	6.5	4.0	3.5
Tajikistan	7.3	6.7	6.0	6.9	12.7	7.1	7.5	4.5	6.0	4.0	3.4
Ukraine[e]	3.4	-6.6	-9.8	2.4	2.5	3.4	3.2	-4.0	3.2	4.0	3.8
Uzbekistan	6.7	7.2	7.4	6.1	4.5	5.4	5.6	1.6	6.2	5.6	4.0

Source: UN DESA, based on data of the United Nations Statistics Division and individual national sources.

Note: Regional aggregates calculated at 2015 prices and exchange rates.

a Average percentage change.

b Partly estimated.

c Baseline scenario forecasts, based in part on the UN DESA World Economic Forecasting Model.

d Georgia officially left the Commonwealth of Independent States on 18 August 2009. However, its performance is discussed in the context of this group of countries for reasons of geographic proximity and similarities in economic structure.

e Data for the Ukraine excludes the temporarily occupied territory of the Autonomous Republic of Crimea and Sevastopol.

Table A.3

Developing economies: rates of growth of real GDP

Annual percentage change

	1999–2013[a]	2014	2015	2016	2017	2018	2019	2020	2021[b]	2022[c]	2023[c]
Developing countries[d]	**5.7**	**4.7**	**4.4**	**4.2**	**4.7**	**4.4**	**3.5**	**-1.6**	**6.4**	**4.5**	**4.7**
Africa	**4.6**	**3.3**	**2.8**	**1.7**	**3.3**	**3.4**	**2.8**	**-3.0**	**4.7**	**4.0**	**3.7**
North Africa	**3.5**	**-0.9**	**2.0**	**2.9**	**4.8**	**4.2**	**2.9**	**-4.6**	**7.6**	**4.9**	**3.1**
Algeria	3.6	3.8	3.7	3.2	1.3	1.2	0.8	-5.1	3.8	4.7	3.3
Egypt[e]	4.5	2.9	4.4	4.3	4.2	5.3	5.1	2.5	3.3	5.9	3.9
Libya	-2.0	-50.1	-45.5	-16.1	64.0	17.9	9.9	-62.1	198.0	8.8	9.2
Mauritania	3.4	4.3	5.4	1.3	3.5	2.1	5.9	-2.9	3.1	3.8	5.2
Morocco	4.7	2.7	4.5	1.1	4.2	3.1	2.6	-6.3	6.1	3.5	3.1
Sudan[e]	6.2	7.0	4.0	3.6	4.7	2.8	-2.2	-1.1	0.7	2.5	3.8
Tunisia	3.8	2.9	1.2	1.2	1.9	2.7	1.0	-8.8	3.8	6.2	3.2
East Africa	**5.5**	**7.8**	**6.5**	**5.5**	**5.7**	**6.6**	**6.6**	**1.3**	**4.0**	**4.8**	**5.7**
Burundi	2.9	4.2	-0.4	3.2	3.8	5.3	4.5	-0.3	2.9	3.5	3.2
Comoros	2.4	3.9	2.0	2.8	5.6	3.8	2.0	0.2	2.0	3.5	3.6
Democratic Republic of the Congo	3.8	9.5	6.9	2.4	3.7	5.8	4.4	0.8	3.5	4.5	5.9
Djibouti	7.1	7.1	7.7	6.7	5.4	8.4	6.6	1.2	5.1	5.9	6.5
Eritrea	0.9	30.9	-20.6	7.4	-10.0	13.0	3.8	-1.8	1.5	2.5	2.1
Ethiopia	8.8	10.3	9.0	8.5	8.2	7.6	8.9	3.5	3.5	4.9	7.0
Kenya	4.2	5.4	5.7	5.9	4.8	6.3	5.4	-0.3	4.7	5.0	4.8
Madagascar	2.8	3.3	3.1	4.0	3.9	3.2	4.4	-4.2	3.4	4.4	4.6
Rwanda	8.2	6.2	8.9	6.0	4.0	8.6	9.4	-3.4	4.5	6.2	6.5
Somalia	2.9	3.7	2.7	2.9	1.4	2.8	2.9	-0.7	1.1	2.0	3.6
South Sudan	1.8	30.3	7.9	-7.0	-3.7	3.8	0.9	-7.2	2.0	2.2	8.9
Uganda	6.9	4.5	5.7	2.6	7.1	5.7	7.7	-0.8	3.9	4.7	4.6
United Republic of Tanzania	6.3	6.7	6.2	6.9	6.8	7.0	7.0	4.8	4.5	4.8	5.4
Central Africa	**4.7**	**4.2**	**1.3**	**-1.0**	**-0.2**	**0.6**	**1.9**	**-2.4**	**2.0**	**3.3**	**3.5**
Cameroon	4.1	5.9	5.7	4.6	3.5	4.1	3.9	-1.5	3.4	4.1	4.6
Central African Republic	-0.8	0.1	4.3	4.8	4.5	3.8	3.0	1.0	0.0	4.1	4.7
Chad	8.1	3.8	4.6	-2.7	-2.4	2.3	3.0	-0.9	1.5	3.6	3.8
Congo	4.6	6.0	-3.2	-10.2	-4.6	-6.2	-0.9	-7.5	-1.6	3.3	3.0
Equatorial Guinea	13.0	0.4	-9.1	-8.8	-5.7	-6.4	-5.6	-4.9	1.9	-0.6	-0.7
Gabon	1.1	4.3	3.9	2.1	0.5	1.2	3.6	-1.7	1.5	3.7	3.5
Sao Tome and Principe	4.5	6.5	3.9	4.2	3.8	2.9	1.3	2.9	2.5	3.6	3.8
West Africa	**6.2**	**6.5**	**3.7**	**0.4**	**2.6**	**3.3**	**3.4**	**-0.8**	**3.2**	**3.7**	**4.0**
Benin	5.5	13.1	13.0	3.3	5.7	6.7	6.9	3.8	3.9	5.1	5.5
Burkina Faso	5.7	4.3	3.9	6.0	6.2	6.7	5.7	1.9	5.0	5.5	5.3
Cabo Verde	5.1	0.6	1.0	4.7	3.7	4.5	5.7	-14.8	3.8	5.0	5.1
Côte D'Ivoire	3.2	14.8	14.9	7.2	7.4	6.9	6.2	2.0	6.2	6.7	6.6
Gambia	3.2	-1.4	4.1	1.9	4.8	7.7	6.1	-0.2	4.8	5.3	5.8
Ghana	6.4	2.9	2.2	3.4	8.1	6.3	6.5	0.4	4.2	4.8	4.3
Guinea	3.5	3.7	3.8	10.8	10.3	6.2	5.6	7.1	5.2	6.4	6.0
Guinea-Bissau	3.1	1.0	6.1	6.3	5.9	3.4	4.5	-1.4	2.6	3.6	4.4
Liberia	7.8	5.2	9.3	-0.5	2.5	1.2	-2.3	-3.0	2.9	4.1	4.5
Mali	9.0	7.8	7.5	8.9	6.7	6.8	6.6	-1.6	3.0	4.3	4.2
Niger	4.4	7.5	4.3	5.7	5.0	7.0	5.8	3.6	4.6	7.1	9.9
Nigeria	6.7	6.3	2.7	-1.6	0.8	1.9	2.2	-1.8	2.5	2.8	3.0
Senegal	4.0	4.1	6.4	6.4	7.4	6.4	5.2	1.5	4.8	6.0	9.6

Table A.3

Developing economies: rates of growth of real GDP (continued)

Annual percentage change

	1999–2013[a]	2014	2015	2016	2017	2018	2019	2020	2021[b]	2022[c]	2023[c]
Sierra Leone	8.3	4.6	-20.5	6.3	3.8	3.4	5.5	-2.2	2.9	4.4	4.1
Togo	3.9	11.3	11.1	10.9	4.3	4.9	5.3	1.8	4.3	5.0	5.4
Southern Africa	**4.3**	**3.0**	**1.5**	**0.2**	**1.4**	**0.8**	**-0.2**	**-6.2**	**2.9**	**2.6**	**2.9**
Angola	7.3	4.8	0.9	-2.6	-0.1	-2.0	-1.5	-4.0	0.0	2.4	3.3
Botswana	4.9	4.1	-1.7	4.3	2.9	4.5	3.0	-7.9	5.7	4.5	4.8
Eswatini	3.2	0.9	2.3	1.3	2.0	2.4	2.2	-2.3	1.4	2.7	5.0
Lesotho	4.1	1.7	3.1	3.6	-3.2	-1.2	-0.4	-9.5	3.6	4.6	6.8
Malawi	4.1	6.2	3.3	2.7	5.2	3.9	5.2	0.8	2.5	4.0	4.3
Mauritius	4.1	3.7	3.6	3.8	3.8	3.8	3.0	-14.9	3.8	6.7	5.1
Mozambique	7.6	7.4	6.7	3.8	3.7	3.4	2.3	-1.3	2.1	3.8	5.1
Namibia	4.6	6.1	4.3	0.0	-1.0	1.1	-0.6	-8.0	2.1	2.9	3.7
South Africa	3.3	1.8	1.2	0.4	1.4	0.8	0.2	-7.0	3.8	2.3	2.1
Zambia	6.7	4.7	2.9	3.8	3.5	4.0	1.4	-3.0	1.5	0.9	4.5
Zimbabwe	3.3	2.4	1.8	0.8	4.7	4.8	-8.1	-8.0	6.3	4.1	4.2
Africa - net fuel exporters	**4.9**	**1.4**	**0.9**	**-0.8**	**2.1**	**1.9**	**2.0**	**-4.5**	**5.0**	**3.5**	**3.5**
Africa - net fuel importers	**4.4**	**4.6**	**4.2**	**3.4**	**4.1**	**4.3**	**3.4**	**-2.1**	**4.5**	**4.4**	**3.8**
East and South Asia	**7.4**	**6.3**	**6.0**	**6.2**	**6.2**	**5.7**	**4.9**	**0.0**	**6.8**	**5.0**	**5.4**
East Asia	**7.8**	**6.3**	**6.0**	**5.9**	**6.1**	**5.9**	**5.2**	**1.0**	**6.7**	**4.9**	**5.4**
Brunei Darussalam	1.5	-2.5	-0.4	-2.5	1.3	0.1	3.9	1.1	0.0	3.5	5.0
Cambodia	8.2	7.1	7.0	6.9	7.0	7.5	7.1	-3.1	1.9	5.5	6.2
China	9.8	7.4	7.0	6.8	6.9	6.7	6.0	2.3	7.8	5.2	5.5
Democratic People's Republic of Korea	1.4	1.0	-1.1	3.9	-3.5	-4.1	0.4	-5.5	2.8	1.5	1.4
Fiji	2.1	27.5	4.7	2.5	5.4	3.5	0.5	-15.7	-4.1	6.2	5.0
Hong Kong SAR[f]	4.0	2.8	2.4	2.2	3.8	2.8	-1.7	-6.1	6.7	3.0	3.4
Indonesia	5.0	5.0	4.9	5.0	5.1	5.2	5.0	-2.1	3.4	4.9	6.0
Kiribati	1.4	-0.6	10.3	1.1	4.9	2.3	2.3	0.6	0.3	2.3	3.0
Lao People's Democratic Republic	7.3	7.6	7.3	7.0	6.9	6.2	5.5	3.3	2.1	4.2	7.2
Malaysia	5.1	6.0	5.1	4.4	5.8	4.8	4.4	-5.6	3.5	5.6	5.7
Mongolia	7.3	7.9	2.4	2.0	5.4	7.0	4.9	-5.4	4.6	6.0	6.8
Myanmar[e]	11.0	7.5	6.4	5.8	6.4	6.8	2.9	-3.3	-18.1	-0.8	7.3
Papua New Guinea	3.1	13.5	6.6	5.5	3.5	-0.3	5.9	-3.8	1.0	5.7	4.3
Philippines	4.8	6.1	6.1	6.9	6.7	6.2	6.1	-9.6	4.9	5.5	7.7
Republic of Korea	5.1	3.2	3.1	3.0	2.9	2.8	2.2	-0.9	4.3	3.0	4.5
Samoa	2.5	2.6	6.7	3.7	-0.6	0.7	2.3	-2.7	-7.8	3.0	2.6
Singapore	5.9	3.9	3.0	3.2	4.3	3.4	1.3	-5.4	6.9	3.8	4.0
Solomon Islands	3.1	1.0	1.4	5.9	5.3	3.9	1.2	-4.5	1.0	4.1	5.4
Taiwan, Province of China	4.2	4.7	1.5	2.2	3.3	2.8	3.0	3.1	6.0	3.1	5.1
Thailand	4.4	1.0	3.1	3.4	4.0	4.2	2.3	-6.1	1.1	4.0	3.5
Timor-Leste	1.6	4.5	2.9	3.4	-4.1	-1.1	18.7	-8.5	2.2	4.0	-0.2
Vanuatu	2.9	2.3	0.2	3.5	4.4	2.9	2.8	-2.3	4.0	4.5	2.9
Viet Nam	6.4	6.0	6.7	6.2	6.8	7.1	7.0	2.9	2.5	6.8	5.4
South Asia	**5.6**	**6.3**	**6.3**	**8.0**	**6.6**	**4.7**	**3.1**	**-4.7**	**7.4**	**5.9**	**5.6**
Afghanistan[e]	7.8	3.1	-1.4	1.7	2.7	1.6	2.0	-8.9	-5.8	4.8	5.6
Bangladesh[e]	5.8	6.1	6.6	7.1	7.3	7.9	8.2	3.5	5.5	5.8	6.4
Bhutan	7.9	4.0	6.6	8.1	4.7	3.0	3.8	-0.8	-2.3	4.5	4.8
India[e]	6.5	7.4	8.0	8.3	6.8	6.5	4.0	-10.6	8.4	6.5	5.9

Table A.3

Developing economies: rates of growth of real GDP (continued)

Annual percentage change

	1999–2013[a]	2014	2015	2016	2017	2018	2019	2020	2021[b]	2022[c]	2023[c]
Iran (Islamic Republic of)[e]	3.1	4.6	-1.3	13.4	3.8	-5.4	-6.5	-5.7	2.9	3.1	2.6
Maldives	5.1	7.3	2.9	6.3	7.2	8.1	7.0	-31.5	17.9	16.5	9.5
Nepal[e]	4.2	6.0	3.3	0.6	8.2	6.7	7.0	-8.5	-1.7	5.5	3.9
Pakistan[e]	4.1	4.7	5.5	5.6	5.8	1.1	-0.9	4.7	0.8	4.2	3.8
Sri Lanka	5.5	5.0	5.0	4.5	3.6	3.3	2.3	-3.6	3.4	2.6	3.5
East and South Asia – net fuel exporters	**4.3**	**4.6**	**3.3**	**6.5**	**5.2**	**2.3**	**1.7**	**-0.6**	**3.2**	**4.4**	**5.2**
East and South Asia – net fuel importers	**7.7**	**6.5**	**6.2**	**6.2**	**6.2**	**6.0**	**5.1**	**0.1**	**7.1**	**5.1**	**5.5**
Western Asia	**4.4**	**3.4**	**3.8**	**3.3**	**2.5**	**2.4**	**1.4**	**-3.4**	**4.7**	**4.8**	**3.5**
Western Asia – net fuel exporters	**4.5**	**2.7**	**3.2**	**3.3**	**-0.4**	**1.7**	**1.4**	**-5.7**	**2.5**	**5.6**	**3.8**
Bahrain	5.2	4.4	2.9	3.6	3.9	1.8	1.8	-5.5	2.6	3.4	3.2
Iraq	4.8	0.2	4.7	13.8	-3.8	0.9	4.4	-11.2	2.4	6.2	4.2
Kuwait	4.4	0.5	0.6	2.9	-4.7	2.4	-0.6	-8.9	2.0	5.8	3.9
Oman	3.6	1.5	4.6	5.1	0.3	0.9	-0.8	-3.2	2.2	4.5	3.5
Qatar	10.9	4.0	3.7	2.1	1.6	1.5	-0.2	-3.9	2.3	4.2	3.3
Saudi Arabia	3.5	3.7	4.1	1.7	-0.7	2.4	0.3	-4.1	2.4	6.0	3.5
United Arab Emirates	4.8	4.3	5.1	3.1	2.4	1.2	3.4	-6.1	3.0	5.9	4.2
Yemen	3.1	-10.6	-30.5	-14.6	-10.0	-1.3	2.1	-5.2	1.1	2.5	3.2
Western Asia – net fuel importers	**4.2**	**4.3**	**4.6**	**3.4**	**6.2**	**3.1**	**1.5**	**-0.9**	**7.0**	**3.9**	**3.3**
Israel	3.8	4.4	2.1	4.5	4.4	4.1	3.7	-2.1	6.8	4.3	4.0
Jordan	5.2	3.4	2.5	2.0	2.1	1.9	2.0	-1.6	2.1	2.8	2.8
Lebanon	4.3	2.5	0.6	1.6	0.8	-1.7	-7.2	-37.1	-16.2	10.1	6.7
State of Palestine	4.3	-0.2	3.7	8.9	1.4	1.2	1.4	-12.3	7.1	2.4	2.0
Syrian Arab Republic	-0.7	-10.3	-3.2	-5.6	-0.7	1.5	3.7	-11.7	2.1	2.2	5.0
Turkey	4.5	4.9	6.1	3.3	7.5	3.0	0.9	1.8	8.1	3.7	3.0
Latin America and the Caribbean[g]	**3.0**	**1.0**	**0.1**	**-1.2**	**1.0**	**0.7**	**-0.6**	**-7.4**	**6.5**	**2.2**	**2.5**
South America	**3.2**	**0.2**	**-1.3**	**-3.0**	**0.3**	**-0.1**	**-1.1**	**-7.0**	**6.7**	**1.6**	**2.4**
Argentina	2.5	-2.5	2.7	-2.1	2.7	-2.5	-2.2	-9.9	9.8	2.2	2.6
Bolivia (Plurinational State of)	3.9	5.5	4.9	4.3	4.2	4.2	2.2	-8.0	5.2	3.2	3.0
Brazil	3.3	0.5	-3.5	-3.3	1.3	1.8	1.4	-4.1	4.7	0.5	1.9
Chile	4.0	1.8	2.3	1.7	1.2	3.9	0.9	-5.8	11.8	1.9	2.6
Colombia	3.6	4.5	3.0	2.1	1.4	2.5	3.3	-6.8	9.5	3.7	3.3
Ecuador	3.7	3.8	0.1	-1.2	2.4	1.3	0.1	-7.8	3.1	2.6	2.0
Paraguay	4.1	4.9	3.1	4.3	5.0	3.4	0.2	-0.6	4.6	3.8	3.7
Peru	5.2	2.4	3.3	4.0	2.5	4.0	2.2	-11.0	13.5	3.0	2.9
Uruguay	2.6	3.2	0.4	1.7	2.6	1.6	0.2	-5.9	3.9	3.1	2.3
Venezuela (Bolivarian Republic of)	2.6	-3.9	-6.2	-17.0	-15.7	-19.6	-35.0	-30.0	-3.0	3.0	6.5
Mexico and Central America	**2.5**	**3.0**	**3.6**	**3.1**	**2.5**	**2.5**	**0.5**	**-8.2**	**6.1**	**3.4**	**2.7**
Costa Rica	4.1	3.5	3.6	4.2	3.9	2.7	2.1	-4.1	5.5	3.7	3.3
Cuba	4.8	1.0	4.4	0.5	1.8	2.2	2.0	-10.8	0.5	3.5	4.5
Dominican Republic	4.8	7.1	6.9	6.7	4.7	7.0	5.1	-6.8	10.4	5.5	5.2
El Salvador	2.0	1.4	2.4	2.5	2.2	2.4	2.4	-7.9	10.0	3.8	2.6
Guatemala	3.5	4.4	4.1	2.7	3.0	3.2	3.8	-1.5	5.4	4.3	3.6
Haiti[e]	1.1	2.8	1.2	1.5	1.2	1.5	-1.7	-3.3	-1.4	2.0	1.6
Honduras	3.7	3.1	3.8	3.9	4.8	3.7	2.7	-9.0	9.0	4.5	3.4

Table A.3

Developing economies: rates of growth of real GDP (continued)

Annual percentage change

	1999–2013[a]	2014	2015	2016	2017	2018	2019	2020	2021[b]	2022[c]	2023[c]
Mexico	2.1	2.8	3.3	2.9	2.1	2.1	-0.3	-8.3	5.8	2.9	2.2
Nicaragua	3.9	4.8	4.8	4.6	4.6	-4.0	-3.9	-2.0	7.4	3.0	2.5
Panama	6.2	5.1	5.7	5.0	5.6	3.6	3.0	-17.9	12.4	7.3	4.5
Caribbean	**2.8**	**0.2**	**0.8**	**-1.5**	**0.2**	**1.5**	**0.4**	**-7.2**	**3.2**	**11.5**	**3.7**
Bahamas	1.3	1.1	0.2	1.4	3.1	3.0	1.2	-14.5	2.3	8.5	4.0
Barbados	0.6	-0.1	2.4	2.5	0.5	-0.6	-0.1	-18.0	1.5	7.5	3.3
Belize	4.3	3.6	2.8	0.1	1.9	2.1	0.3	-14.0	2.7	6.2	2.8
Guyana	6.1	1.7	0.7	3.8	3.7	4.4	5.4	43.0	18.5	46.0	8.7
Jamaica	0.6	0.7	0.9	1.4	1.0	1.9	0.9	-10.2	4.0	5.7	2.7
Suriname	4.0	0.3	-3.4	-5.6	1.8	2.6	0.3	-15.9	-1.0	1.5	1.7
Trinidad and Tobago	5.2	-0.9	1.5	-5.6	-3.0	0.1	-1.2	-7.8	-1.0	5.7	1.9
Latin America and the Caribbean – net fuel exporters	**3.2**	**0.2**	**-1.6**	**-7.0**	**-5.3**	**-5.5**	**-8.9**	**-12.1**	**5.6**	**3.4**	**3.5**
Latin America and the Caribbean – net fuel importers	**3.0**	**1.1**	**0.4**	**-0.2**	**2.0**	**1.7**	**0.6**	**-6.7**	**6.6**	**2.1**	**2.4**
Memorandum items:											
Least developed countries	6.0	5.7	3.7	4.0	4.9	5.2	4.5	0.8	1.4	4.0	5.7
Africa (excluding Libya)	5.0	4.9	3.5	1.9	3.0	3.2	2.8	-2.2	3.8	4.0	3.6
North Africa (excluding Libya)	4.3	3.9	4.2	3.3	3.7	3.8	2.7	-2.4	4.8	4.8	2.8
East Asia (excluding China)	4.9	4.1	3.7	3.8	4.2	4.0	3.2	-2.4	3.8	4.0	5.0
South Asia (excluding India)	4.2	4.7	3.3	7.5	5.3	0.8	-0.2	0.8	3.9	4.1	4.4
Western Asia (excluding Israel and Turkey)	4.4	2.5	3.0	3.2	-0.3	1.7	1.3	-6.6	2.2	5.6	3.8
Arab States[h]	4.1	1.5	2.7	3.1	1.2	2.5	1.8	-6.0	4.0	5.4	3.5
Landlocked developing economies	6.6	5.6	3.8	3.3	4.7	4.9	4.4	-1.6	4.1	4.4	4.8
Small island developing States	4.9	3.9	3.5	2.9	3.5	3.3	2.1	-6.8	5.5	4.9	4.2

Source: UN DESA, based on data of the United Nations Statistics Division and individual national sources.

Note: Regional aggregates calculated at 2015 prices and exchange rates.

a Average percentage change.

b Partly estimated.

c Baseline scenario forecasts, based in part on the UN DESA World Economic Forecasting Model.

d Covering countries that account for 98 per cent of the population of all developing countries.

e Fiscal year basis.

f Special Administrative Region of China.

g Figures for Latin America and the Caribbean for 2021–2022 were provided by UN ECLAC.

h Currently includes data for Algeria, Bahrain, Comoros, Djibouti, Egypt, Iraq, Jordan, Kuwait, Lebanon, Libya, Mauritania, Morocco, Oman, Qatar, Saudi Arabia, Somalia, Sudan, Syrian Arab Republic, Tunisia, United Arab Emirates, and Yemen.

Table A.4

Growth of world output and gross domestic product by SDG regions

Annual percentage change

	2019	2020	2021[a]	2022[b]	2023[b]
World	**2.5**	**-3.4**	**5.5**	**4.0**	**3.5**
Africa	**2.8**	**-3.0**	**4.7**	**4.0**	**3.7**
North Africa	2.9	-4.6	7.7	4.9	3.0
East Africa	5.4	0.1	3.9	4.6	5.4
Middle Africa	0.8	-2.5	1.4	3.1	3.9
Southern Africa	0.3	-7.0	3.8	2.5	2.4
West Africa	3.4	-0.8	3.2	3.7	4.0
Americas	**1.7**	**-4.3**	**5.7**	**3.3**	**2.4**
Northern America	2.3	-3.6	5.5	3.5	2.4
Latin America and the Caribbean	-0.6	-7.4	6.5	2.2	2.5
Caribbean	2.5	-9.1	4.4	4.8	4.3
Central America	0.2	-8.2	6.1	3.2	2.4
South America	-1.1	-6.9	6.7	1.7	2.5
Asia	**3.8**	**-1.1**	**6.0**	**4.8**	**4.9**
Central Asia	4.7	-0.4	4.7	4.7	4.2
East Asia	4.2	0.4	6.4	4.6	4.9
South Asia	3.1	-4.7	7.4	5.9	5.6
South-east Asia	4.4	-3.9	2.8	4.8	5.5
Western Asia	1.5	-3.5	4.7	4.8	3.6
Europe	**1.7**	**-6.1**	**4.8**	**3.9**	**2.5**
Eastern Europe	3.0	-3.4	4.6	3.3	3.1
Northern Europe	1.8	-6.2	5.8	4.1	2.4
Southern Europe	1.2	-9.2	5.5	4.6	2.9
Western Europe	1.5	-5.6	4.0	3.6	2.2
Oceania	**2.1**	**-2.4**	**3.2**	**4.1**	**3.0**

Source: UN DESA, based on data of the United Nations Statistics Division and UN DESA forecasts.

Notes: Regional aggregates in this table follow geographic regions defined under the Standard Country or Area Codes for Statistical Use (known as M49) and are not strictly comparable to those in the WESP. Full details on the M49 standard can be found at the United Nations Statistics Division. Calculated at 2015 prices and exchange rates. Figures are based on the countries actively monitored for the World Economic Situation and Prospects report.

a Partly estimated.

b Baseline scenario forecasts, based in part on UN DESA World Economic Forecasting Model.

Table A.5

Developed economies: consumer price inflation

Annual percentage change[a]

	2013	2014	2015	2016	2017	2018	2019	2020	2021[b]	2022[c]	2023[c]
Developed economies	**1.4**	**1.4**	**0.3**	**0.8**	**1.8**	**2.0**	**1.5**	**0.8**	**3.2**	**2.6**	**2.0**
United States	1.5	1.6	0.1	1.3	2.1	2.4	1.8	1.2	4.6	3.6	2.5
Canada	0.9	1.9	1.1	1.4	1.6	2.3	1.9	0.7	3.5	3.1	2.5
Japan	0.3	2.8	0.8	-0.1	0.5	1.0	0.5	0.0	0.0	1.0	1.1
Australia	2.5	2.5	1.5	1.3	1.9	1.9	1.6	0.8	3.2	2.7	2.2
New Zealand	1.1	1.2	0.3	0.6	1.9	1.6	1.6	1.7	3.9	2.8	2.5
European Union	**1.4**	**0.4**	**0.2**	**0.2**	**1.5**	**1.8**	**1.4**	**0.5**	**2.5**	**2.0**	**1.5**
Austria	2.1	1.5	0.8	1.0	2.2	2.1	1.5	1.4	2.7	2.3	2.0
Belgium	1.2	0.5	0.6	1.8	2.2	2.3	1.2	0.4	2.4	1.6	1.5
Bulgaria	0.4	-1.6	-1.1	-1.3	1.2	2.6	2.4	1.2	3.0	1.9	1.9
Croatia	2.3	0.2	-0.3	-0.6	1.3	1.5	0.8	0.0	2.5	2.0	1.5
Cyprus	0.4	-0.3	-1.5	-1.2	0.7	0.8	0.5	-1.1	1.5	1.5	1.5
Czechia	1.3	0.5	0.2	0.7	2.4	1.9	2.6	3.3	3.8	2.5	2.5
Denmark	0.5	0.4	0.2	0.0	1.1	0.7	0.7	0.4	1.4	1.0	1.3
Estonia	3.2	0.5	0.1	0.8	3.7	3.4	2.3	-0.6	3.1	2.5	2.1
Finland	2.2	1.2	-0.2	0.4	0.8	1.2	1.1	0.4	2.0	1.7	1.7
France	1.0	0.6	0.1	0.3	1.2	2.1	1.3	0.5	1.9	2.0	1.5
Germany	1.6	0.7	0.7	0.4	1.7	1.9	1.4	0.4	2.9	1.9	1.5
Greece	-0.9	-1.4	-1.1	0.0	1.1	0.8	0.5	-1.3	1.2	1.6	1.5
Hungary	1.7	0.0	0.1	0.4	2.4	2.9	3.4	3.4	4.8	3.8	3.0
Ireland	0.5	0.3	0.0	-0.2	0.3	0.7	0.9	-0.5	2.7	2.0	1.5
Italy	1.3	0.2	0.1	-0.1	1.4	1.2	0.7	-0.2	1.9	1.9	1.2
Latvia	0.0	0.7	0.2	0.1	2.9	2.6	2.7	0.1	2.9	1.5	2.0
Lithuania	1.2	0.2	-0.7	0.7	3.7	2.5	2.2	1.1	3.5	2.5	2.3
Luxembourg	1.7	0.7	0.1	0.0	2.1	2.0	1.7	0.0	3.1	1.6	1.2
Malta	1.0	0.8	1.2	0.9	1.3	1.7	1.5	0.8	1.0	1.5	1.5
Netherlands	2.6	0.3	0.2	0.1	1.3	1.6	2.7	1.1	2.3	2.1	1.7
Poland	0.8	0.1	-0.7	-0.2	1.6	1.2	2.1	3.6	5.1	3.4	3.0
Portugal	0.4	-0.2	0.5	0.6	1.6	1.2	0.3	-0.1	1.0	1.0	1.0
Romania	3.2	1.4	-0.4	-1.1	1.1	4.1	3.9	2.3	4.4	3.5	2.1
Slovakia	1.5	-0.1	-0.3	-0.5	1.4	2.5	2.8	2.0	3.0	2.5	2.3
Slovenia	1.9	0.4	-0.8	-0.1	1.6	1.9	1.7	-0.3	2.5	2.0	2.0
Spain	1.5	-0.2	-0.6	-0.3	2.0	1.7	0.8	-0.3	2.7	1.9	1.3
Sweden	0.4	0.2	0.7	1.1	1.9	2.0	1.7	0.7	1.9	1.5	1.3
Other European countries	**2.0**	**1.3**	**0.1**	**0.8**	**2.2**	**2.2**	**1.6**	**0.7**	**2.4**	**2.1**	**2.2**
Iceland	4.1	1.0	0.3	0.8	-1.6	0.7	2.0	2.9	4.5	2.7	2.3
Norway	2.0	1.9	2.0	3.9	1.8	3.0	2.3	1.2	3.5	2.5	0.1
Switzerland	0.1	0.0	-0.8	-0.5	0.6	0.9	0.4	-0.8	0.5	1.1	1.2
United Kingdom[d]	2.5	1.5	0.0	0.7	2.7	2.4	1.8	1.0	2.7	2.2	2.7
Memorandum items:											
Northern America	1.4	1.6	0.2	1.3	2.1	2.4	1.8	1.2	4.5	3.5	2.5
Developed Asia and the Pacific	0.8	2.7	0.9	0.2	0.8	1.2	0.7	0.2	0.8	1.4	1.4
Europe	1.3	0.4	0.2	0.3	1.5	1.7	1.4	0.5	2.4	2.0	1.5
Major developed economies	1.4	1.5	0.3	0.8	1.8	2.1	1.5	0.8	3.3	2.7	2.1
Euro area	1.4	0.4	0.2	0.3	1.5	1.7	1.3	0.3	2.4	1.9	1.5

Source: UN DESA, based on OECD Main Economic Indicators, Eurostat and individual national sources.

a Data for country groups are weighted averages, where weights for each year are based on 2015 GDP in United States dollars.

b Partly estimated.

c Baseline scenario forecasts, based on UN DESA World Economic Forecasting Model.

d The United Kingdom withdrew from the EU on 31 January 2020 and is therefore excluded from all EU aggregations.

Table A.6

Economies in transition: consumer price inflation

Annual percentage change[a]

	2013	2014	2015	2016	2017	2018	2019	2020	2021[b]	2022[c]	2023[c]
Economies in transition	**6.6**	**7.7**	**14.6**	**8.0**	**5.4**	**4.4**	**5.0**	**4.1**	**6.7**	**4.0**	**3.5**
South-Eastern Europe	**4.5**	**1.1**	**1.1**	**0.3**	**2.5**	**2.0**	**1.3**	**1.0**	**3.0**	**2.5**	**2.4**
Albania	1.9	1.6	3.5	-0.4	2.1	2.0	1.4	1.6	3.3	3.2	2.0
Bosnia and Herzegovina	-0.1	-0.9	-1.0	-1.6	0.8	1.4	0.6	-1.1	1.7	1.5	1.9
Montenegro	2.2	-0.7	1.5	-0.3	2.4	2.6	0.4	-0.3	2.8	1.7	0.9
North Macedonia	2.7	0.0	0.1	0.2	2.1	2.3	0.7	1.2	3.0	2.0	1.6
Serbia	7.7	2.3	1.5	1.3	3.4	2.0	1.9	1.7	3.4	2.9	3.0
Commonwealth of Independent States and Georgia[d]	**6.7**	**8.0**	**15.2**	**8.3**	**5.5**	**4.5**	**5.1**	**4.3**	**6.9**	**4.0**	**3.5**
Commonwealth of Independent States and Georgia – net fuel exporters	**6.5**	**7.4**	**13.9**	**8.0**	**4.5**	**3.5**	**4.5**	**3.9**	**6.4**	**3.5**	**3.4**
Azerbaijan	2.4	1.4	4.0	12.4	12.9	2.3	2.6	2.8	4.5	3.8	3.1
Kazakhstan	5.8	6.7	6.7	14.5	7.4	6.0	5.2	6.7	6.4	5.0	4.5
Russian Federation	6.8	7.8	15.5	7.0	3.7	2.9	4.5	3.4	6.4	3.2	3.2
Turkmenistan	6.8	6.0	7.4	3.6	8.0	13.3	5.1	7.6	10.5	6.1	4.8
Commonwealth of Independent States and Georgia – net fuel importers	**7.7**	**11.1**	**22.2**	**10.0**	**10.9**	**10.2**	**8.7**	**6.7**	**9.4**	**7.1**	**4.5**
Armenia	5.8	3.0	3.7	-1.4	1.0	2.5	1.4	1.2	7.6	4.1	3.8
Belarus	18.3	18.1	13.5	11.8	6.0	4.9	5.6	5.5	8.4	5.3	4.8
Georgia[d]	-0.5	3.1	4.0	2.1	6.0	2.6	4.9	5.2	8.9	4.6	2.6
Kyrgyzstan	6.6	7.5	6.5	0.4	3.2	1.5	1.1	6.3	10.7	6.1	5.4
Republic of Moldova	4.6	5.1	9.7	6.4	6.6	3.0	4.8	3.8	4.4	12.0	5.0
Tajikistan	5.0	6.1	5.7	6.0	7.3	3.8	7.8	8.6	10.0	8.8	8.0
Ukraine[e]	-0.2	12.1	48.7	13.9	14.4	11.0	7.9	2.7	9.0	6.8	5.6
Uzbekistan	11.7	9.1	8.5	8.8	13.9	17.5	14.5	12.9	11.1	9.0	3.0

Source: UN DESA, based on data of the United Nations Statistics Division and individual national sources.
Note: Regional aggregates calculated at 2015 prices and exchange rates.
a Average percentage change.
b Partly estimated.
c Baseline scenario forecasts, based in part on the UN DESA World Economic Forecasting Model.
d Georgia officially left the Commonwealth of Independent States on 18 August 2009. However, its performance is discussed in the context of this group of countries for reasons of geographic proximity and similarities in economic structure.
e Starting in 2010, data for the Ukraine excludes the temporarily occupied territory of the Autonomous Republic of Crimea and Sevastopol.

Table A.7

Developing economies: consumer price inflation

Annual percentage change[a]

	2013	2014	2015	2016	2017	2018	2019	2020	2021[b]	2022[c]	2023[c]
Developing countries by region[d]	**4.8**	**4.2**	**3.8**	**4.7**	**4.2**	**3.6**	**5.2**	**5.5**	**8.1**	**5.5**	**4.6**
Africa	**7.5**	**7.3**	**7.3**	**11.8**	**14.4**	**10.9**	**10.8**	**17.2**	**22.0**	**12.4**	**9.2**
North Africa	**9.5**	**9.5**	**8.2**	**10.6**	**18.9**	**15.1**	**10.3**	**19.2**	**43.2**	**18.5**	**10.9**
Algeria	3.3	2.9	4.8	6.4	5.6	4.3	2.0	2.4	5.1	5.0	3.4
Egypt	9.5	10.1	10.4	13.8	29.5	14.4	9.2	5.0	5.6	7.4	8.1
Libya	2.6	2.4	9.9	25.9	25.8	13.6	-2.1	1.5	3.1	3.5	4.0
Mauritania	4.1	3.5	3.2	1.5	2.3	3.0	2.3	2.4	3.5	4.2	4.8
Morocco	1.9	0.4	1.6	1.6	0.8	1.8	0.3	0.7	1.0	1.5	2.0
Sudan	36.5	36.9	16.9	17.8	32.4	63.3	51.0	150.3	368.1	126.6	54.2
Tunisia	5.3	4.6	4.4	3.6	5.3	7.3	6.7	5.6	5.5	5.8	6.5
East Africa	**5.6**	**5.2**	**7.3**	**14.3**	**15.8**	**11.5**	**8.9**	**9.9**	**8.5**	**6.9**	**6.9**
Burundi	7.9	4.4	5.5	5.6	16.1	-2.0	-0.8	7.3	5.0	5.1	5.1
Comoros	-4.3	0.0	0.9	0.8	0.1	1.7	3.7	0.9	1.7	2.3	2.4
Democratic Republic of the Congo	0.8	1.2	0.7	2.9	35.8	29.3	4.7	11.3	9.4	6.4	6.6
Djibouti	2.7	1.3	-0.8	2.7	0.6	0.1	3.3	1.8	3.4	3.4	3.3
Eritrea	5.9	10.0	28.5	-5.6	-13.3	-14.4	-16.4	4.9	2.9	4.4	4.4
Ethiopia	7.5	6.9	9.6	6.6	10.7	13.8	15.8	20.4	14.9	11.9	11.4
Kenya	5.7	6.9	6.6	6.3	8.0	4.7	5.2	5.4	6.5	4.5	4.6
Madagascar	5.8	6.1	7.4	6.0	8.6	8.6	5.6	4.2	5.6	5.8	6.1
Rwanda	5.9	2.4	2.5	7.2	8.3	-0.3	3.3	9.9	6.9	5.1	4.4
Somalia	-3.2	-5.6	-5.6	0.5	3.9	1.6	1.5	0.7	1.7	1.4	1.4
South Sudan	-0.1	1.7	52.8	380.0	187.9	83.5	87.2	29.7	33.0	29.1	25.2
Uganda	4.9	3.1	5.4	5.4	5.6	2.6	2.9	2.8	3.5	3.8	4.2
United Republic of Tanzania	7.9	6.1	5.6	5.2	5.3	3.5	3.5	3.3	2.7	2.9	3.7
Central Africa	**2.2**	**2.8**	**2.3**	**1.4**	**0.8**	**2.2**	**1.8**	**2.7**	**2.0**	**2.5**	**2.5**
Cameroon	2.1	1.8	2.7	0.9	0.6	1.1	2.5	2.4	2.3	2.1	2.0
Central African Republic	7.0	14.9	1.4	4.9	4.2	1.6	2.7	2.3	3.7	2.6	2.5
Chad	0.2	1.7	4.4	-0.8	-1.5	4.3	-1.0	3.5	2.2	2.8	3.0
Congo	4.6	0.9	3.2	3.2	0.5	1.2	2.2	1.8	2.0	2.8	3.0
Equatorial Guinea	2.9	4.3	1.7	1.4	0.7	1.3	1.2	4.8	0.5	3.1	3.1
Gabon	0.5	4.7	-0.3	2.1	2.7	4.7	2.5	1.2	2.0	2.0	2.0
Sao Tome and Principe	8.1	7.0	5.3	5.4	5.7	7.9	7.7	9.8	8.3	7.8	5.8
West Africa	**7.5**	**7.2**	**8.2**	**13.0**	**13.4**	**9.3**	**9.0**	**11.1**	**13.8**	**11.0**	**9.8**
Benin	0.4	-0.5	0.2	-0.8	1.8	0.6	-0.7	3.0	3.0	2.0	2.0
Burkina Faso	0.5	-0.3	0.7	0.4	1.5	2.0	-3.2	1.9	3.0	2.6	2.5
Cabo Verde	1.5	-0.2	0.1	-1.4	0.8	1.3	1.1	0.6	1.5	1.6	1.7
Côte D'Ivoire	2.6	0.4	1.3	0.7	0.7	0.4	-1.1	2.4	3.0	2.5	2.2
Gambia	5.7	5.9	6.8	7.2	8.0	6.5	7.1	5.9	7.0	6.3	6.1
Ghana	11.7	15.5	17.1	17.5	11.7	0.4	7.2	10.0	9.3	8.8	8.0
Guinea	11.9	7.1	10.8	8.2	8.9	9.8	9.5	10.6	11.6	9.9	8.0
Guinea-Bissau	1.2	-1.5	1.5	1.5	1.7	0.4	0.2	1.5	1.9	2.0	2.0
Liberia	7.6	9.9	7.7	8.8	12.4	23.6	27.0	17.0	5.9	11.8	9.6
Mali	-0.6	0.9	1.5	-1.8	1.8	0.3	-1.7	0.4	3.0	2.0	2.0
Niger	2.3	-0.9	-0.6	1.7	2.8	3.0	-2.5	2.8	2.9	2.5	2.0
Nigeria	8.5	8.1	9.0	15.7	16.5	12.1	11.4	13.2	17.0	13.3	11.8
Senegal	0.7	-1.1	0.1	0.8	1.3	0.5	1.8	2.5	2.4	2.0	1.5
Sierra Leone	5.5	4.6	6.7	10.9	18.2	16.0	14.8	13.4	11.3	13.3	11.4

Table A.7

Developing economies: consumer price inflation *(continued)*

Annual percentage change[a]

	2013	2014	2015	2016	2017	2018	2019	2020	2021[b]	2022[c]	2023[c]
Togo	1.8	0.2	2.6	1.3	-1.0	0.9	0.7	1.8	2.7	2.5	2.2
Southern Africa	**6.5**	**6.2**	**5.5**	**12.2**	**10.7**	**8.1**	**16.3**	**28.3**	**13.2**	**10.0**	**8.5**
Angola	8.8	7.3	9.2	30.7	29.8	19.6	17.1	22.3	25.9	22.3	17.3
Botswana	5.9	4.4	3.1	2.8	3.3	3.2	2.8	1.9	6.8	2.6	3.8
Lesotho	5.6	5.7	5.0	7.8	6.2	4.8	2.6	3.9	4.7	5.0	5.5
Malawi	4.9	5.4	3.2	6.6	4.4	4.8	5.2	5.0	5.1	5.3	5.3
Mauritius	27.3	23.8	21.9	21.7	11.5	12.4	9.4	8.6	7.9	6.0	4.9
Mozambique	3.5	3.2	1.3	1.0	3.7	3.2	0.4	2.5	2.9	3.5	3.6
Namibia	4.3	2.6	3.6	17.4	15.1	3.9	2.8	3.1	8.4	8.3	7.6
South Africa	5.6	5.4	3.4	6.7	6.1	4.3	3.7	2.2	2.8	3.4	4.2
Eswatini	5.8	6.1	4.5	6.6	5.2	4.5	4.1	3.2	5.1	5.3	5.6
Zambia	7.0	7.8	10.1	17.9	6.6	7.5	9.2	15.7	19.9	8.3	6.3
Zimbabwe	1.6	-0.2	-2.4	-1.5	0.9	10.6	255.3	557.2	84.9	29.9	17.9
Africa – net fuel exporters	**7.0**	**6.8**	**8.0**	**15.0**	**14.8**	**10.1**	**9.0**	**11.0**	**13.9**	**11.5**	**9.8**
Africa – net fuel importers	**7.8**	**7.6**	**6.7**	**9.6**	**14.1**	**11.5**	**12.1**	**21.5**	**27.6**	**12.9**	**8.9**
East and South Asia	**4.4**	**3.0**	**2.3**	**2.5**	**2.2**	**2.8**	**4.0**	**3.2**	**3.0**	**3.0**	**3.4**
East Asia	**2.6**	**2.1**	**1.5**	**1.9**	**2.0**	**2.1**	**2.5**	**1.9**	**1.5**	**2.0**	**2.6**
Brunei Darussalam	0.4	-0.2	-0.5	-0.3	-1.3	1.0	-0.4	1.9	1.5	0.7	2.5
Cambodia	2.9	3.9	1.2	3.0	2.9	2.5	2.0	2.9	2.9	2.5	1.6
Democratic People's Republic of Korea	2.6	1.9	1.4	2.0	1.6	2.1	2.9	2.4	1.3	1.9	2.6
China	1.6	3.7	3.1	-0.6	7.2	2.3	-4.6	-2.1	2.5	3.4	3.6
Fiji	2.9	0.5	1.4	3.9	3.3	4.1	1.8	-2.6	1.0	3.0	0.5
Hong Kong SAR[e]	-0.3	0.8	2.0	2.0	4.3	0.6	2.3	0.3	1.5	2.1	3.3
Indonesia	6.4	6.4	6.4	3.5	3.8	3.2	3.0	1.9	1.6	2.8	2.6
Kiribati	-1.5	2.1	0.6	1.9	0.4	0.6	-1.9	2.5	1.1	1.5	2.2
Lao People's Democratic Republic	6.4	4.1	1.3	1.6	0.8	2.0	3.3	5.1	3.7	4.0	3.5
Malaysia	2.1	3.1	2.1	2.1	3.9	0.9	0.7	-1.1	2.5	2.3	1.4
Mongolia	10.5	12.3	5.7	0.7	4.3	6.8	7.3	3.7	7.0	8.5	9.2
Myanmar	5.6	5.0	9.5	6.9	4.6	6.9	8.8	5.7	6.2	4.0	4.3
Papua New Guinea	5.0	5.2	6.0	6.7	5.4	4.4	2.7	5.1	4.5	4.0	3.5
Philippines	2.6	3.6	0.7	1.3	2.9	5.2	2.5	2.6	4.8	3.9	3.4
Republic of Korea	1.3	1.3	0.7	1.0	1.9	1.5	0.4	0.5	2.1	1.5	2.4
Samoa	0.6	-0.4	0.7	1.3	1.7	4.2	1.0	-1.6	-3.0	2.7	2.7
Singapore	1.7	0.4	1.0	2.1	6.6	0.6	2.8	-0.2	1.7	1.5	2.5
Solomon Islands	5.4	5.2	-0.6	0.5	0.5	3.5	1.6	3.0	2.5	3.5	2.1
Taiwan, Province of China	0.8	1.2	-0.3	1.4	0.6	1.4	0.6	-0.2	1.7	1.0	2.3
Thailand	2.2	1.9	-0.9	0.2	0.7	1.1	0.7	-0.8	1.1	1.0	1.6
Timor-Leste	11.0	0.8	0.6	-1.5	0.5	2.3	1.0	0.5	1.6	2.2	2.4
Vanuatu	1.5	0.8	2.5	0.8	3.1	2.3	2.8	2.9	4.1	3.6	2.5
Viet Nam	6.6	4.1	0.6	2.7	3.5	3.5	2.8	3.2	2.0	2.5	4.0
South Asia	**13.5**	**7.7**	**6.4**	**5.2**	**3.7**	**6.5**	**11.7**	**9.9**	**10.4**	**8.4**	**7.5**
Afghanistan	7.4	4.7	-0.7	4.4	5.0	0.6	2.3	5.6	5.9	4.7	3.9
Bangladesh	7.5	7.0	6.2	5.5	5.7	5.5	5.6	5.7	5.5	5.4	5.3
Bhutan	7.0	8.3	4.5	3.2	5.0	2.7	2.7	5.6	6.8	6.5	5.2
India	10.9	6.4	5.9	4.9	2.5	4.9	7.7	5.6	5.9	5.6	5.3
Iran (Islamic Republic of)	36.6	16.6	12.5	7.2	8.0	18.0	39.9	36.5	40.0	26.2	21.7

Table A.7

Developing economies: consumer price inflation *(continued)*

Annual percentage change[a]

	2013	2014	2015	2016	2017	2018	2019	2020	2021[b]	2022[c]	2023[c]
Maldives	3.8	2.1	1.0	0.5	2.8	-0.1	0.2	-1.4	1.4	2.3	2.2
Nepal	9.0	8.4	7.9	8.8	3.6	4.1	5.6	5.1	4.5	5.5	5.4
Pakistan	7.7	7.2	2.5	3.8	4.1	5.1	10.6	9.7	8.6	8.3	6.1
Sri Lanka	6.9	3.2	3.8	4.0	7.7	2.1	3.5	6.2	5.5	5.9	5.2
East and South Asia – net fuel exporters	**15.5**	**9.5**	**8.1**	**4.6**	**5.1**	**7.7**	**14.2**	**12.5**	**13.3**	**9.9**	**8.5**
East and South Asia – net fuel importers	**3.6**	**2.6**	**1.9**	**2.3**	**2.0**	**2.4**	**3.2**	**2.5**	**2.2**	**2.5**	**3.0**
Western Asia	**4.3**	**4.3**	**3.8**	**3.8**	**4.1**	**6.5**	**4.2**	**6.4**	**9.7**	**6.5**	**3.9**
Net fuel exporters	**2.7**	**2.5**	**2.4**	**2.2**	**0.9**	**2.4**	**-1.1**	**1.3**	**2.7**	**2.3**	**1.8**
Bahrain	3.3	2.6	1.8	2.8	1.4	2.1	1.0	-2.3	-0.4	1.0	2.1
Iraq	1.9	2.2	1.4	0.6	0.2	0.4	-0.2	0.6	5.8	3.6	3.0
Kuwait	2.7	2.9	3.3	3.2	2.2	0.5	1.1	2.1	3.1	2.7	2.5
Oman	1.0	1.0	0.1	1.1	1.6	0.9	0.1	-0.9	1.6	2.4	2.8
Qatar	3.2	3.3	1.8	2.7	0.4	0.3	-0.7	-2.5	1.9	2.2	2.6
Saudi Arabia	3.5	2.2	1.2	2.1	-0.8	2.5	-2.1	3.4	3.2	2.1	0.7
United Arab Emirates	1.1	2.3	4.1	1.6	2.0	3.1	-1.9	-2.1	0.3	1.0	1.7
Yemen	11.0	8.1	22.0	21.3	30.4	27.6	10.0	26.2	12.0	15.4	15.0
Net fuel importers	**6.2**	**6.6**	**5.5**	**5.7**	**8.1**	**11.5**	**10.8**	**12.8**	**18.3**	**11.7**	**6.4**
Israel	1.6	0.5	-0.6	-0.5	0.2	0.8	0.8	-0.6	1.7	1.8	1.8
Jordan	4.8	2.9	-0.9	-0.8	3.3	4.5	0.8	0.3	1.5	1.9	2.2
Lebanon	4.8	1.9	-3.7	-0.8	4.3	6.1	3.0	84.9	128.0	64.9	8.5
State of Palestine	1.7	1.7	1.4	-0.2	0.2	-0.2	1.6	-0.7	1.4	1.9	2.1
Syrian Arab Republic	27.8	20.1	38.2	47.7	19.4	0.9	13.4	84.7	33.7	19.6	15.7
Turkey	7.5	8.9	7.7	7.7	11.1	16.3	15.2	12.3	18.4	12.4	7.8
Latin America and the Caribbean[d]	**5.3**	**7.0**	**7.6**	**10.1**	**6.8**	**7.5**	**8.4**	**8.1**	**11.5**	**10.5**	**7.4**
South America[d]	**6.1**	**8.5**	**10.1**	**13.7**	**7.6**	**9.1**	**10.9**	**10.5**	**14.6**	**13.6**	**9.2**
Argentina	10.6	21.4	21.5	40.5	25.7	34.2	41.0	42.6	48.2	46.5	33.0
Bolivia (Plurinational State of)	5.8	5.8	4.1	3.6	2.8	2.3	1.9	1.0	0.5	1.7	1.9
Brazil	6.2	6.3	9.0	8.7	3.4	3.7	4.4	3.2	8.4	6.9	3.8
Chile	1.9	4.7	4.3	3.8	2.2	2.4	2.3	3.0	4.5	4.6	2.8
Colombia	2.0	2.9	5.0	7.5	4.3	3.2	3.5	2.5	3.4	4.1	3.7
Ecuador	2.7	3.6	4.0	1.7	0.4	-0.2	0.0	-0.3	0.1	1.2	1.0
Paraguay	2.7	5.0	3.1	4.1	3.6	4.0	3.2	1.8	4.3	4.1	3.2
Peru	2.8	3.2	3.6	3.6	2.8	1.3	2.1	1.8	4.1	4.2	2.9
Uruguay	8.6	8.9	8.7	9.6	6.2	7.6	7.6	9.8	7.7	7.0	6.7
Venezuela (Bolivarian Republic of)	40.6	62.2	121.7	254.9	438.1	...	...	...	...	...	...
Mexico and Central America	**3.8**	**3.8**	**2.6**	**2.5**	**5.0**	**4.4**	**3.5**	**3.5**	**9.0**	**5.6**	**4.0**
Costa Rica	5.2	4.5	0.9	0.0	1.6	2.2	2.0	0.7	1.6	2.4	2.1
Cuba	0.6	1.1	4.9	-0.5	-1.1	1.9	5.6	9.9	71.0	29.8	7.0
Dominican Republic	4.8	3.0	0.8	1.6	3.3	3.6	1.8	3.8	7.7	4.6	4.4
El Salvador	0.8	1.1	-0.7	0.6	1.0	1.1	1.7	-0.4	3.4	2.5	2.2
Guatemala	4.3	3.4	2.4	4.4	4.4	3.8	4.3	3.2	4.5	4.0	4.1
Haiti	5.9	4.6	9.0	13.8	14.7	14.0	16.9	20.3	23.8	24.8	23.6
Honduras	5.2	6.1	3.2	2.7	3.9	4.3	4.2	3.5	4.6	4.2	4.1

Table A.7

Developing economies: consumer price inflation *(continued)*

Annual percentage change[a]

	2013	2014	2015	2016	2017	2018	2019	2020	2021[b]	2022[c]	2023[c]
Mexico	3.8	4.0	2.8	2.8	6.0	4.9	3.6	3.4	5.5	4.2	3.8
Nicaragua	7.1	6.0	3.9	3.4	4.0	4.8	4.4	3.7	4.6	4.3	4.0
Panama	4.0	2.6	0.1	0.7	0.9	0.8	0.4	-1.5	1.6	1.8	1.4
Caribbean	**4.4**	**4.5**	**3.2**	**5.6**	**4.0**	**2.4**	**2.4**	**4.3**	**6.6**	**6.2**	**4.5**
Bahamas	0.3	1.2	1.9	-0.3	1.5	2.3	2.5	0.0	1.7	2.4	1.9
Barbados	1.8	1.9	-1.1	1.1	4.7	3.7	4.1	2.9	2.5	3.0	2.2
Belize	0.5	1.0	-0.7	0.7	1.1	0.3	0.2	0.1	2.2	2.5	2.2
Guyana	2.1	0.6	-1.0	0.8	1.9	1.2	2.4	3.2	3.3	5.9	3.1
Jamaica	9.4	8.3	3.7	2.3	4.4	3.7	4.2	5.2	5.3	4.7	4.6
Suriname	1.9	3.4	6.9	53.0	21.5	6.9	4.4	34.9	58.0	47.9	27.0
Trinidad and Tobago	5.2	5.7	4.6	3.1	1.9	1.0	0.8	0.6	1.5	1.7	2.1
Latin America and the Caribbean – net fuel exporters	**2.6**	**3.4**	**4.7**	**5.7**	**3.2**	**2.3**	**2.5**	**1.7**	**2.4**	**3.2**	**2.9**
Latin America and the Caribbean – net fuel importers	**5.6**	**7.3**	**8.0**	**10.6**	**7.1**	**1.4**	**8.3**	**8.9**	**21.9**	**11.8**	**7.9**
Memorandum items:											
Least developed countries	9.0	8.2	7.9	12.8	14.1	14.3	11.7	21.7	39.6	18.3	11.5
East Asia (excluding China)	2.6	2.6	1.8	1.8	2.8	2.0	1.6	0.8	2.1	2.0	2.5
South Asia (excluding India)	19.0	10.5	7.4	5.6	6.3	9.9	20.2	18.9	19.9	14.4	12.0
Western Asia (excluding Israel and Turkey)	3.1	2.7	2.6	2.6	1.3	2.5	-0.8	4.7	6.7	4.3	2.2
Arab States[f]	5.1	4.7	4.3	5.0	6.7	6.3	2.6	9.1	17.8	8.6	4.9
Landlocked developing economies	6.1	5.7	6.2	11.3	8.8	7.7	13.3	21.9	9.6	6.7	5.2
Small island developing States	2.5	1.7	2.1	2.4	4.5	1.8	3.1	2.6	72.8	6.8	3.9

Source: UN DESA, based on data of the United Nations Statistics Division, individual national sources and UN DESA forecasts.
a Data for country groups are weighted averages, where weights for each year are based on 2015 GDP in United States dollars.
b Partly estimated.
c Baseline scenario forecasts, based in part on UN DESA World Economic Forecasting Model.
d Regional aggregates exclude Venezuela (Bolivarian Republic of).
e Special Administrative Region of China.
f Includes data for Algeria, Bahrain, Comoros, Djibouti, Egypt, Iraq, Jordan, Kuwait, Lebanon, Libya, Mauritania, Morocco, Oman, Qatar, Saudi Arabia, Somalia, Sudan, Syrian Arab Republic, Tunisia, United Arab Emirates, and Yemen.

Table A.8

Selected economies: real effective exchange rates, broad measurement[a, b]

	2012	2013	2014	2015	2016	2017	2018	2019	2020	2021[c]
Developed economies										
Australia	100.0	94.9	90.2	81.0	81.6	84.0	80.9	77.0	75.6	80.1
Austria	100.0	101.7	103.2	101.1	102.5	103.3	104.3	103.4	105.0	105.4
Belgium	100.0	101.2	101.3	97.5	100.0	101.2	102.9	101.4	102.2	102.6
Bulgaria	100.0	99.9	99.6	96.9	96.8	96.5	100.2	100.0	102.6	104.0
Canada	100.0	96.5	90.3	81.3	79.3	80.4	79.8	79.0	77.9	82.1
Croatia	100.0	100.7	100.4	98.6	99.6	99.6	101.3	100.0	98.5	99.0
Czechia	100.0	97.4	92.3	91.4	93.8	96.8	100.8	101.0	101.5	105.2
Denmark	100.0	100.7	101.6	97.3	98.2	98.3	99.3	97.5	98.7	97.3
Finland	100.0	102.3	104.9	101.9	103.1	102.0	104.1	102.7	104.1	103.6
France	100.0	101.2	101.3	96.3	97.4	97.6	99.2	97.7	98.7	98.7
Germany	100.0	102.0	102.7	98.3	99.7	100.3	102.2	100.6	101.6	102.2
Greece	100.0	99.3	98.0	92.0	93.0	92.5	90.6	88.2	87.5	86.9
Hungary	100.0	98.4	95.1	92.6	93.2	94.3	93.6	92.6	88.8	92.0
Ireland	100.0	101.5	100.5	92.7	93.9	94.0	94.9	92.2	92.1	92.8
Italy	100.0	101.6	101.8	97.0	97.9	98.1	98.8	96.5	96.8	96.9
Japan	100.0	80.3	75.5	70.1	78.7	74.6	74.3	76.1	76.7	70.8
Netherlands	100.0	102.9	102.9	98.4	99.5	99.4	100.6	100.5	102.4	102.7
New Zealand	100.0	103.7	108.4	102.1	104.6	107.6	101.8	100.9	102.2	108.5
Norway	100.0	97.9	92.7	84.9	86.1	86.7	87.4	85.4	79.6	83.8
Poland	100.0	100.0	101.1	98.4	94.8	96.7	97.3	96.2	96.9	97.5
Portugal	100.0	100.0	99.3	96.9	98.3	97.4	96.1	95.1	96.6	95.8
Romania	100.0	103.7	105.1	102.5	101.3	99.0	101.1	100.6	101.5	101.1
Slovakia	100.0	101.1	101.9	99.8	100.0	99.0	100.4	101.0	103.5	103.5
Spain	100.0	101.7	101.0	95.8	96.3	97.0	96.2	94.7	95.2	96.0
Sweden	100.0	101.3	96.3	91.1	91.7	90.6	86.3	83.2	85.2	88.3
Switzerland	100.0	98.6	99.4	104.9	102.8	100.5	97.5	98.2	101.9	98.4
United Kingdom	100.0	98.8	105.6	110.3	98.4	93.3	94.9	94.4	94.6	98.8
United States	100.0	100.2	102.1	112.9	116.5	114.3	109.2	113.3	115.7	113.1
Economies in transition										
Azerbaijan	100.0	99.8	103.5	95.5	70.1	71.0	72.6	75.4	77.8	77.0
Belarus	100.0	107.8	119.6	110.1	101.4	98.9	97.1	99.3	93.0	89.7
Kazakhstan	100.0	100.6	93.3	93.2	70.9	76.7	75.8	72.4	71.8	70.6
Russian Federation	100.0	100.2	90.0	74.4	74.3	86.1	78.7	79.9	73.2	71.5
Ukraine[d]	100.0	96.4	73.9	69.9	70.2	73.5	78.0	89.3	88.1	89.1
Developing economies										
Algeria	100.0	98.0	99.9	95.3	94.5	95.3	91.9	93.7	90.3	84.3
Argentina	100.0	90.9	74.4	87.5	75.8	78.9	52.7	38.4	38.8	37.1
Bangladesh	100.0	110.9	118.8	135.5	143.0	143.7	141.3	148.8	154.9	154.1
Brazil	100.0	94.6	92.5	75.5	78.8	84.9	67.7	61.1	45.0	42.2
Chile	100.0	99.0	89.7	87.1	87.9	90.5	88.9	81.4	73.2	75.0
China	100.0	104.5	107.8	115.7	109.9	105.5	105.4	104.1	106.1	109.9
Colombia	100.0	96.3	91.5	74.0	70.4	71.2	58.2	45.5	37.1	32.3
Dominican Republic	100.0	96.8	94.8	96.2	95.1	90.9	80.0	72.4	64.5	59.3

Table A.8

Selected economies: real effective exchange rates, broad measurement[a, b] *(continued)*

	2012	2013	2014	2015	2016	2017	2018	2019	2020	2021[c]
Egypt	100.0	94.3	101.2	112.1	98.5	69.5	78.3	91.9	101.6	95.6
Ethiopia	100.0	99.9	99.8	108.3	109.8	106.9	108.8	121.0	118.5	117.8
Guatemala	100.0	102.0	106.5	114.5	121.1	127.1	122.5	119.8	120.4	114.8
Hong Kong SAR[e]	100.0	97.5	97.0	102.5	106.7	109.1	105.4	108.8	108.3	103.0
India	100.0	99.6	101.5	107.8	108.4	111.3	105.9	108.4	106.1	105.7
Indonesia	100.0	95.3	89.4	89.9	93.7	94.2	88.7	92.1	90.5	89.1
Iran (Islamic Republic of)	100.0	88.6	72.7	76.6	78.1	77.2	72.5	99.4	135.7	166.3
Israel	100.0	106.5	107.7	106.3	108.2	112.7	111.2	113.6	116.1	120.0
Korea, Republic of	100.0	103.5	109.0	107.8	106.4	109.0	110.2	104.6	102.6	103.3
Kuwait	100.0	100.7	102.0	104.8	108.0	107.8	105.8	106.6	105.6	104.2
Malaysia	100.0	99.6	99.1	89.9	86.2	83.7	87.4	85.5	82.8	82.3
Mexico	100.0	105.6	104.4	92.4	79.9	81.2	59.5	57.9	52.3	55.2
Morocco	100.0	101.6	102.1	101.9	104.0	102.7	103.2	103.8	105.4	105.8
Nigeria	100.0	106.8	114.0	110.4	98.0	91.5	99.5	111.1	107.2	107.5
Pakistan	100.0	97.3	103.8	109.6	112.9	114.3	100.9	91.2	91.7	93.3
Peru	100.0	98.8	96.8	95.1	93.7	96.2	91.7	90.6	86.7	74.6
Philippines	100.0	102.3	101.4	105.4	101.9	96.4	94.3	98.4	104.3	105.1
Qatar	100.0	103.7	106.4	115.6	118.3	116.4	113.1	113.1	108.6	104.8
Saudi Arabia	100.0	103.0	104.5	112.2	114.6	111.2	111.1	109.5	111.8	108.9
Singapore	100.0	101.3	100.4	99.7	101.3	105.6	104.8	107.1	104.6	104.2
South Africa	100.0	88.9	83.8	81.1	76.6	85.6	86.8	81.1	69.3	74.9
Sri Lanka	100.0	104.5	105.8	110.5	107.6	107.1	98.9	91.3	91.8	85.2
Taiwan, Province of China	100.0	100.5	99.4	99.6	99.4	103.9	103.3	101.4	105.0	106.4
Thailand	100.0	104.0	100.4	100.3	97.1	99.5	103.0	108.2	105.4	100.2
Turkey	100.0	98.9	94.6	92.4	91.1	80.9	68.6	67.5	60.0	58.1
United Arab Erirates	100.0	101.1	103.7	113.4	115.3	115.1	117.0	113.0	106.9	100.8
Uruguay	100.0	106.9	103.4	104.5	103.6	106.5	88.5	72.0	61.9	54.6
Viet Nam	100.0	105.1	107.8	112.2	114.6	113.3	112.8	114.7	116.8	112.5

Sources: UN DESA, Bank for International Settlements, IMF International Financial Statistics.
a 2012=100.
b CPI-based indices. The real effective exchange rate gauges the effect on international price competitiveness of currency changes and inflation differentials. A rise in the index implies a fall in competitiveness and vice versa.
c Average for the first ten months.
d Data for Ukraine excludes the temporarily occupied territory of the Autonomous Republic of Crimea and Sevastopol.
e Special Administrative Region of China.

Table A.9

Free market commodity price indices

Index: Year 2015 = 100

	Non-fuel commodities							
	Food	Tropical beverages	Vegetable oilseeds and oils	Agricultural raw materials	Minerals and metals	All groups	All groups excluding fuels	Fuels
2012	127	112	152	143	153	177	145	197
2013	120	90	136	131	138	170	131	194
2014	118	111	123	115	121	157	119	180
2015	100	100	100	100	100	100	100	100
2016	104	97	107	100	105	91	104	83
2017	103	94	106	105	116	106	110	104
2018	96	86	100	103	118	123	109	133
2019	98	81	93	99	125	114	112	116
2020	102	85	106	97	145	96	124	79
2018								
I	100	90	107	105	124	120	114	124
II	100	90	106	105	121	126	112	135
III	92	80	95	102	113	126	104	140
IV	94	82	92	100	114	121	105	131
2019								
I	96	79	94	101	120	115	109	119
II	97	79	89	101	123	117	110	121
III	98	80	92	97	130	112	114	110
IV	102	87	98	97	127	113	114	112
2020								
I	103	87	99	97	129	101	116	91
II	99	83	92	91	134	82	116	61
III	100	86	104	96	155	98	130	78
IV	104	85	127	105	160	105	137	85
2021								
I	113	91	150	110	170	128	147	115
II	122	99	163	110	184	140	158	128
III	123	111	159	110	180	149	157	145

Sources: UNCTAD, *Monthly Commodity Price Bulletin*; UN DESA.

Table A.10

World oil supply and demand

	2013	2014	2015	2016	2017	2018	2019	2020	2021[a]
World oil supply[b,c] (millions of barrels per day)	**89.3**	**91.7**	**94.3**	**94.7**	**95.5**	**98.2**	**97.1**	**94.1**	**92.5**
Developed economies	18.1	20.1	21.4	21.0	22.0	24.7	26.5	25.6	25.8
Economies in transition	13.9	14.0	14.1	14.3	14.4	14.7	15.0	13.5	13.8
Developing economies	55.1	55.3	56.6	57.1	56.8	56.5	53.3	52.6	50.6
OPEC	37.7	37.7	39.1	39.6	39.5	39.5	36.7	32.6	30.9
Non-OPEC	17.4	17.6	17.6	17.5	17.2	16.9	16.5	20.1	19.7
Processing gains[d]	2.2	2.2	2.2	2.3	2.3	2.3	2.4	2.4	2.4
Global biofuels[e]	2.0	2.2	2.3	2.4	2.4	2.6	2.8	2.8	2.8
World total demand[f]	**92.0**	**93.2**	**95.0**	**96.1**	**97.9**	**99.2**	**100.5**	**92.1**	**97.4**
Oil prices (dollars per barrel)									
OPEC basket[g]	105.9	96.3	49.5	40.8	52.4	69.8	64.1	41.5	69.4
Brent oil	108.9	98.9	52.3	43.7	54.2	71.2	64.3	41.7	71.6

Sources: UN DESA, International Energy Agency; U.S. Energy Information Administration; and OPEC.
a Partly estimated.
b Including global biofuels, crude oil, condensates, natural gas liquids (NGLs), oil from non-conventional sources and other sources of supply.
c Totals may not add up because of rounding.
d Net volumetric gains and losses in the refining process and marine transportation losses.
e Global biofuels comprise all world biofuel production including fuel ethanol from Brazil and the United States.
f Measured as deliveries from refineries and primary stocks, comprises inland deliveries, international marine bunkers, refinery fuel, crude for direct burning, oil from non-conventional sources and other sources of supply. Includes Biofuels.
g As of 6 March 2020: The basket price excludes the Ecuadorean crude "Oriente".

Table A.11

World trade[a]: Changes in value and volume of exports and imports, by major country group

Annual percentage change

	2013	2014	2015	2016	2017	2018	2019	2020	2021[b]	2022[c]	2023[c]
Dollar value of exports											
World	**2.6**	**1.5**	**-11.1**	**-1.7**	**10.7**	**9.0**	**-1.6**	**-11.4**	**22.2**	**7.4**	**4.7**
Developed economies	**3.1**	**3.1**	**-9.6**	**0.4**	**8.8**	**8.9**	**-1.4**	**-10.6**	**18.9**	**8.2**	**4.4**
Northern America	2.7	3.6	-6.3	-1.8	7.0	6.5	-0.5	-15.5	16.1	9.7	5.0
Europe	5.0	3.0	-10.8	1.5	9.6	9.9	-1.9	-8.0	19.8	7.7	4.2
Developed Asia and the Pacific	-6.6	1.8	-11.7	3.4	10.5	7.3	-1.2	-12.2	21.1	6.2	5.0
Economies in transition	**-0.5**	**-5.7**	**-28.7**	**-11.7**	**21.2**	**21.0**	**-2.0**	**-18.5**	**35.1**	**8.2**	**3.1**
South-Eastern Europe	15.5	4.1	-10.0	9.3	15.1	16.4	1.2	-9.5	27.7	6.8	3.2
Commonwealth of Independent States and Georgia[d]	-1.1	-6.1	-29.5	-12.8	21.6	21.3	-2.2	-19.1	35.7	8.3	3.1
Developing economies	**2.3**	**0.2**	**-11.3**	**-3.7**	**12.5**	**8.2**	**-1.8**	**-11.9**	**25.7**	**6.3**	**5.2**
Latin America and the Caribbean	-0.2	-4.0	-12.7	-0.8	20.0	-3.8	1.0	-14.6	21.2	5.2	5.1
Africa	-10.3	-3.5	-27.9	-7.6	17.0	14.6	-3.3	-19.7	33.9	5.3	6.8
East Asia	5.1	3.0	-5.9	-3.9	10.4	8.9	-1.6	-9.2	27.1	6.9	4.9
South Asia	3.2	-4.3	-9.1	2.3	13.4	6.9	-4.9	-6.6	20.0	6.4	5.3
Western Asia	0.8	-2.9	-24.1	-6.8	13.2	15.1	-2.7	-20.8	23.1	4.4	5.7
Dollar value of imports											
World	**2.7**	**2.0**	**-9.8**	**-2.2**	**14.2**	**10.1**	**412.3**	**-35.5**	**6.7**	**10.1**	**5.6**
Developed economies	**1.6**	**3.0**	**-9.9**	**-0.4**	**8.7**	**9.5**	**-0.8**	**-10.4**	**23.4**	**5.9**	**3.4**
Northern America	-0.1	3.6	-4.2	-2.2	6.8	6.9	-0.5	-11.2	21.4	3.9	4.0
Europe	3.6	2.7	-11.5	1.6	10.2	10.7	-0.8	-8.7	24.0	6.8	3.3
Asia and Oceaia	-5.4	1.7	-16.8	-4.1	9.4	10.2	-2.4	-13.3	26.1	2.8	2.1
Economies in transition	**3.3**	**-9.1**	**-28.3**	**-4.8**	**19.0**	**9.4**	**4.4**	**-13.2**	**27.0**	**7.0**	**2.9**
South-Eastern Europe	4.8	4.0	-13.8	5.4	14.6	16.6	2.4	-8.7	23.9	6.1	3.5
Commonwealth of Independent States and Georgia[d]	3.2	-9.9	-29.3	-5.7	19.4	8.7	4.6	-13.7	27.3	7.1	2.8
Developing economies	**4.2**	**1.7**	**-8.2**	**-4.3**	**21.5**	**10.9**	**934.7**	**-38.6**	**3.7**	**11.0**	**6.1**
Latin America and the Caribbean	4.8	-0.1	3.5	-9.7	73.7	12.6	4105.1	-40.9	0.2	11.6	6.1
Africa	5.2	2.1	-16.0	-7.6	4.7	11.2	0.4	-10.6	27.3	4.9	7.7
East Asia	4.9	2.5	-10.2	-2.5	12.6	12.5	-3.1	-7.4	33.8	6.5	4.5
South Asia	-3.6	-3.9	-7.7	1.0	17.8	7.5	-5.0	-12.2	39.4	10.4	14.2
Western Asia	5.7	4.0	-8.2	-6.6	8.0	2.1	-2.7	-9.7	26.0	6.9	7.3
Volume of exports											
World	**2.5**	**3.8**	**3.0**	**2.3**	**5.6**	**4.3**	**1.2**	**-8.7**	**11.0**	**6.0**	**4.0**
Developed economies	**2.6**	**4.3**	**4.6**	**2.8**	**5.0**	**3.5**	**1.8**	**-10.1**	**9.2**	**7.0**	**3.6**
Northern America	2.9	4.3	0.8	0.6	3.6	3.0	0.2	-12.9	8.1	8.1	4.0
Europe	2.8	4.2	6.5	3.6	5.3	3.7	2.6	-8.3	9.7	6.4	3.3
Developed Asia and the Pacific	1.9	8.5	4.1	2.9	6.0	3.4	0.1	-11.3	11.6	5.9	4.5
Economies in transition	**2.5**	**-0.8**	**1.8**	**3.2**	**5.4**	**5.5**	**2.3**	**-6.2**	**10.6**	**5.6**	**3.1**
South-Eastern Europe	11.5	5.3	8.2	10.8	9.0	7.8	5.8	-10.6	12.9	6.3	2.6
Commonwealth of Independent States and Georgia[d]	2.1	-1.1	1.5	2.8	5.2	5.4	2.1	-5.9	10.4	5.6	3.1
Developing economies	**2.3**	**3.6**	**1.0**	**1.5**	**6.3**	**5.3**	**0.2**	**-7.0**	**13.4**	**4.9**	**4.5**
Latin America and the Caribbean	1.1	1.3	4.7	1.8	3.7	3.6	0.3	-9.0	8.5	2.3	3.5

Table A.11

World trade[a]: Changes in value and volume of exports and imports by major country group *(continued)*

Annual percentage change

	2013	2014	2015	2016	2017	2018	2019	2020	2021[b]	2022[c]	2023[c]
Africa	-26.3	-6.6	-2.9	2.7	13.0	4.4	1.9	-15.5	15.3	2.8	5.2
East Asia	6.8	5.8	1.0	0.8	7.2	4.8	0.7	-5.4	15.9	6.0	4.5
South Asia	4.2	3.0	-1.5	6.6	5.8	6.4	-4.1	-4.2	9.8	4.3	4.2
Western Asia	2.1	0.9	0.6	1.6	1.9	8.7	-0.3	-10.4	6.2	2.2	5.4
Volume of imports											
World	**3.0**	**3.1**	**2.0**	**1.5**	**5.8**	**4.7**	**1.1**	**-7.9**	**10.9**	**5.3**	**4.1**
Developed economies	**2.0**	**4.6**	**5.7**	**3.0**	**4.7**	**3.9**	**2.8**	**-9.3**	**7.8**	**4.9**	**2.9**
Northern America	1.4	4.7	4.4	1.2	4.5	4.0	1.0	-9.3	6.2	3.0	3.5
Europe	2.2	4.6	7.3	4.5	5.1	3.9	4.1	-8.2	8.4	5.8	2.8
Developed Asia and the Pacific	1.9	5.7	0.9	-0.6	4.6	4.3	0.5	-9.5	8.3	2.2	2.0
Economies in transition	**2.8**	**-6.3**	**-16.7**	**-0.3**	**12.9**	**5.1**	**5.5**	**-10.9**	**10.3**	**5.2**	**2.4**
South-Eastern Europe	3.0	6.5	3.5	8.1	9.0	8.4	7.2	-8.7	9.0	4.8	2.9
Commonwealth of Independent States and Georgia[d]	2.8	-7.1	-18.2	-1.0	13.3	4.8	5.3	-11.1	10.5	5.3	2.3
Developing economies	**4.2**	**1.9**	**-1.2**	**-0.5**	**6.7**	**5.8**	**-1.5**	**-5.8**	**15.1**	**5.8**	**5.6**
Latin America and the Caribbean	-0.6	-4.9	-6.6	-11.2	1.4	4.0	-3.1	-13.7	12.7	4.7	3.7
Africa	6.5	-1.4	-3.4	-0.7	5.8	6.4	2.0	-7.0	7.6	2.8	6.6
East Asia	7.2	4.9	1.3	3.1	7.8	6.5	-1.5	-3.2	17.4	5.9	4.3
South Asia	-6.0	-1.3	-3.9	2.5	13.5	7.0	-1.0	-8.3	15.9	9.9	14.3
Western Asia	5.7	3.9	-0.9	-3.2	4.4	2.9	-1.6	-7.3	10.5	5.6	6.9

Source: UN DESA.

a Includes goods and services.

b Partly estimated.

c Baseline scenario forecasts, based in part on UN DESA World Economic Forecasting Model.

d Georgia officially left the Commonwealth of Independent States on 18 August 2009. However, its performance is discussed in the context of this group of countries for reasons of geographic proximity and similarities in economic structure.

Table A.12

Balance of payments on current accounts, by country or country group, summary table

Billions of dollars

	2012	2013	2014	2015	2016	2017	2018	2019	2020	2021[a]
Developed economies	**-141.1**	**24.4**	**-9.4**	**10.8**	**113.5**	**228.4**	**147.4**	**97.4**	**-86.6**	**-57.1**
Japan	59.7	46.0	36.8	136.4	197.8	203.5	177.8	176.5	164.4	176.9
United States	-418.1	-339.5	-370.0	-408.9	-397.6	-361.7	-438.2	-472.1	-616.1	-796.1
Europe	356.3	433.2	416.7	399.6	405.9	474.3	486.2	425.0	360.5	502.5
Europe excluding the United Kingdom	450.9	569.4	566.4	547.0	552.8	574.7	591.5	512.6	461.1	607.1
Other Europe[b]	44.2	0.0	-35.2	-43.3	-66.2	-26.8	-20.6	-25.5	-64.8	-13.9
Economies in transition	**59.4**	**11.5**	**51.1**	**47.7**	**-4.4**	**13.4**	**105.8**	**43.3**	**22.9**	**82.5**
South-Eastern Europe	-8.4	-5.6	-6.1	-3.8	-3.9	-5.1	-5.1	-6.5	-5.9	-6.2
Commonwealth of Independent States and Georgia[c]	69.6	18.1	58.9	53.3	1.4	19.8	112.0	50.8	30.8	90.5
Developing economies	**507.7**	**370.3**	**384.3**	**178.2**	**179.6**	**277.9**	**165.2**	**216.9**	**427.1**	**585.2**
Net fuel exporters	420.8	348.2	198.2	-167.0	-108.7	15.6	132.9	27.6	-82.1	86.4
Net fuel importers	86.9	22.1	186.1	345.3	288.3	262.3	32.4	189.4	509.3	498.8
Latin America and the Caribbean	**-148.8**	**-172.5**	**-185.9**	**-172.1**	**-100.6**	**-94.1**	**-140.0**	**-102.3**	**2.0**	**-27.4**
Net fuel exporters	-3.4	-2.3	-11.3	-37.5	-18.2	-2.7	-6.6	-10.0	-9.1	-9.3
Net fuel importers	-145.5	-170.2	-174.6	-134.6	-82.4	-91.4	-133.4	-92.3	11.1	-18.2
Africa	**-47.1**	**-64.1**	**-91.9**	**-143.6**	**-112.0**	**-84.1**	**-80.2**	**-100.0**	**-89.3**	**-80.9**
Net fuel exporters	34.5	15.8	-25.5	-72.9	-42.0	-19.9	-13.1	-34.9	-45.2	-32.0
Net fuel importers	-81.7	-79.8	-66.4	-70.7	-70.0	-64.2	-67.1	-65.1	-44.1	-48.9
Western Asia	**336.8**	**284.5**	**200.9**	**-72.0**	**-83.2**	**-14.3**	**122.0**	**100.0**	**-47.7**	**109.1**
Net fuel exporters	399.8	348.4	243.6	-47.0	-51.4	32.2	151.8	95.3	-25.7	111.6
Net fuel importers	-63.0	-63.9	-42.7	-25.0	-31.8	-46.4	-29.8	4.7	-22.0	-2.4
East and South Asia	**272.4**	**287.8**	**432.4**	**543.6**	**459.9**	**405.5**	**172.6**	**272.1**	**576.4**	**543.9**
Net fuel exporters	-10.2	-13.7	-8.6	-9.6	2.9	6.0	0.7	-22.8	-2.2	16.2
Net fuel importers	282.6	301.4	441.0	553.3	457.0	399.4	171.8	294.9	578.6	527.8
World residual[d]	**426.0**	**406.2**	**426.0**	**236.6**	**288.7**	**519.7**	**418.4**	**357.6**	**363.5**	**610.7**

Sources: International Monetary Fund (IMF), World Economic Outlook database, October 2022

a Partially estimated

b Other Europe consists of Iceland, Norway, Switzerland and the United Kingdom (Table A).

c Georgia officially left the Commonwealth of Independent States on 18 August 2009. However, its performance is discussed in the context of this group of countries for reasons of geographic proximity and similarities in economic structure.

d Statistical discrepancy.

Other Notes: Africa includes South Sudan; Western Asia excludes the State of Palestine; and East Asia excludes Democratic People's Republic of Korea.

Table A.13

Net ODA from major sources, by type

Donor group or country	Growth rate of ODA (2018 prices and exchange rates)					ODA as a percentage of GNI	Total ODA (millions of dollars)	Percentage distribution of ODA by type, 2020			
								Bilateral	Multilateral		
	1999–2008	2009–2017	2018	2019	2020	2020	2020	Total	Total (United Nations & other)	United Nations	Other
Total DAC countries	**4.9**	**5.3**	**-2.3**	**-0.5**	**7.1**	**0.32**	**161027**	**70.0**	**30.0**	**5.1**	**24.9**
Total EU	**4.8**	**5.4**	**-0.5**	**-1.5**	**7.6**	**0.54**	**93974**	**63.3**	**36.7**	**4.8**	**31.9**
Austria	4.7	4.6	-12.4	9.0	4.6	0.31	1316	42.7	57.3	3.2	54.2
Belgium	6.3	9.1	0.5	-2.5	3.5	0.48	2341	43.5	56.5	12.7	43.9
Denmark	0.2	0.2	0.1	3.4	0.6	0.73	2638	64.1	35.9	10.2	25.7
Finland	7.4	7.4	-14.9	21.0	6.4	0.47	1275	50.6	49.4	13.5	36.0
France[a]	3.5	3.9	7.2	-2.8	26.6	0.60	15833	66.0	34.0	2.1	31.8
Germany	4.1	5.0	-3.6	-3.1	16.0	0.74	28886	77.7	22.3	2.8	19.5
Greece	6.8	4.9	-11.4	33.2	-36.2	0.13	238	1.9	98.1	1.5	96.6
Ireland	10.6	8.0	6.2	6.9	-4.1	0.31	972	52.4	47.6	11.9	35.7
Italy	-1.0	0.4	-17.7	-12.5	-1.0	0.23	4348	29.4	70.6	4.7	65.9
Luxembourg	7.1	6.5	4.0	1.6	-9.2	1.02	450	67.6	32.4	13.3	19.0
Netherlands	2.5	2.3	5.6	-3.5	-2.8	0.59	5359	66.8	33.2	9.8	23.4
Portugal	1.3	3.1	-4.5	2.0	-8.9	0.16	364	31.6	68.4	3.5	65.0
Spain	9.4	8.8	-4.5	8.8	-2.2	0.22	2722	27.6	72.4	4.0	68.4
Sweden	7.8	6.5	7.1	-8.1	15.5	1.13	6261	55.8	44.2	11.6	32.6
Australia	4.2	5.4	4.0	-4.4	-10.6	0.19	2563	76.3	23.7	7.1	16.6
Canada	3.1	4.5	5.7	-1.8	9.2	0.30	4896	75.4	24.6	5.9	18.7
Japan	-3.0	-2.0	-13.5	14.3	13.1	0.26	13666	75.0	25.0	4.7	20.3
New Zealand	4.2	3.2	25.5	2.4	-5.2	0.27	531	81.6	18.4	9.7	8.7
Norway	3.8	3.5	-4.8	9.7	8.4	1.11	4198	75.2	24.8	9.7	15.1
Switzerland	5.1	3.4	-2.9	1.6	13.9	0.50	3722	76.5	23.5	7.3	16.2
United Kingdom	8.5	10.9	1.5	1.8	-6.6	0.72	19245	63.2	36.8	3.8	33.0
United States	9.1	9.0	-5.0	-4.1	5.3	0.16	35124	82.5	17.5	4.9	12.6

Source: UN DESA, based on OECD/DAC online database.
a Excluding flows from France to the Overseas Departments, namely Guadeloupe, French Guiana, Martinique and Réunion.

Table A.14

Total net ODA flows from OECD Development Assistance Committee countries, by type

	Net disbursements at current prices and exchange rates (billions of dollars)									
	2011	2012	2013	2014	2015	2016	2017	2018	2019	2020
Official Development Assistance	**135.1**	**127.0**	**134.8**	**137.5**	**131.6**	**144.9**	**147.2**	**150.1**	**146.5**	**161.0**
Bilateral official development assistance	**94.8**	**88.5**	**93.5**	**94.8**	**94.2**	**103.1**	**105.6**	**105.2**	**103.3**	**112.7**
in the form of:										
Technical cooperation	18.0	18.2	16.9	17.3	14.9	15.7	16.5	15.8	16.9	...
Humanitarian aid	9.7	8.5	10.5	13.1	13.4	14.4	16.1	16.0	16.5	...
Debt forgiveness	6.3	3.3	6.1	1.4	0.3	2.1	0.4	0.3	0.1	...
Bilateral loans	1.9	2.6	1.4	5.3	6.0	5.8	6.6	6.3	6.3	...
Contributions to multilateral institutions[a]	**40.3**	**38.6**	**41.4**	**42.7**	**37.3**	**41.8**	**41.6**	**44.9**	**43.2**	**48.3**
of which are:										
UN agencies	6.5	6.6	6.9	6.8	6.1	5.9	6.2	6.6	7.6	8.2
EU institutions	13.8	12.0	12.8	13.3	11.9	13.8	13.9	15.2	15.5	16.3
World Bank	10.2	8.6	9.4	9.8	8.6	8.8	8.2	11.3	9.3	8.7
Regional development banks	4.1	3.9	3.9	4.0	3.2	4.6	4.2	4.2	3.9	2.9
Others	4.4	6.4	7.2	7.5	6.7	7.8	8.1	6.3	6.0	...
Memorandum item										
Bilateral ODA to least developed countries	30.7	27.4	29.9	26.4	25.0	24.6	27.4	27.8	28.2	...

Source: UN DESA, based on OECD/DAC online database.

a Grants and capital subscriptions. Does not include concessional lending to multilateral agencies.

Table A.15

Commitments and net flows of financial resources, by selected multilateral institutions

Billions of dollars

	2011	2012	2013	2014	2015	2016	2017	2018	2019	2020
Resource commitments[a]	**163.8**	**189.8**	**130.8**	**185.0**	**119.9**	**245.4**	**256.7**	**224.8**	**225.0**	**247.1**
Financial institutions, excluding International Monetary Fund (IMF)	106.8	96.5	98.8	99.2	99.9	106.9	108.0	114.6	129.3	143.7
Regional development banks[b]	46.9	43.0	45.8	41.1	46.9	49.8	54.0	56.0	59.8	56.5
World Bank Group[c]	59.9	53.5	53.0	58.1	53.0	57.0	54.0	58.6	69.5	87.2
International Bank for Reconstruction and Development (IBRD)	26.7	20.6	15.2	18.6	23.5	29.7	22.6	23.0	28.0	30.5
International Development Association (IDA)	16.3	14.8	16.3	22.2	19.0	16.2	19.5	24.0	30.4	36.0
International Financial Corporation (IFC)[d]	16.9	9.2	11.0	10.0	10.5	11.1	11.9	11.6	11.1	20.7
International Fund for Agricultural Development (IFAD)	1.0	1.0	0.8	0.7	1.3	0.8	1.3	1.3	1.7	0.8
International Monetary Fund (IMF)	45.7	82.5	19.6	72.7	6.2	123.9	132.9	89.9	75.6	73.5
United Nations operational agencies[e]	11.3	10.8	12.4	13.1	13.7	14.7	15.8	20.4	20.1	29.8
Net flows	**78.7**	**35.1**	**8.8**	**-5.1**	**17.7**	**32.2**	**36.3**	**82.6**	**62.8**	**84.4**
Financial institutions, excluding IMF	38.0	26.3	22.2	25.0	35.5	33.8	36.6	46.8	49.4	61.1
Regional development banks[b]	10.5	8.6	5.7	11.2	15.4	14.2	13.1	14.2	15.2	24.0
World Bank Group[c]	27.6	17.7	16.5	13.8	20.1	19.6	23.6	32.7	34.2	37.1
International Bank for Reconstruction and Development (IBRD)	17.2	8.0	7.8	6.4	9.0	10.0	13.2	17.4	17.4	16.9
International Development Association (IDA)	9.1	7.8	7.0	7.4	9.9	8.8	8.8	14.7	15.3	19.6
International Financial Corporation (IFC)	1.2	1.9	1.6	0.1	1.3	0.8	1.6	0.6	1.6	0.6
International Fund for Agricultural Development (IFAD)	0.3	0.3	0.2	0.2	0.2	0.2	0.3	0.3	0.3	0.2
International Monetary Fund (IMF)	40.7	8.9	-13.4	-30.1	-17.9	-1.5	-0.4	35.8	13.4	23.3

Source: Annual reports of the relevant multilateral institutions, various issues.

a Loans, grants, technical assistance and equity participation, as appropriate; all data are on a calendar-year basis.

b African Development Bank (AfDB), Asian Development Bank (ADB), Caribbean Development Bank (CDB), European Bank for Reconstruction and Development (EBRD), and the Inter-American Development Bank (IDB).

c Data is for fiscal year.

d Effective 2012, data does not include short-term finance.

e United Nations Development Program (UNDP), United Nations Population Fund (UNFPA), United Nations Children's Fund (UNICEF), and the World Food Programme (WFP).

Bibliography

A

Acharya, V. V., and others (2019). Whatever It Takes: The Real Effects of Unconventional Monetary Policy. *The Review of Financial Studies* 32(9): 3366–3411.

Adalet McGowan, M., D. Andrews and V. Millot (2017). The Walking Dead: Zombie Firms and Productivity Performance in OECD Countries. OECD Economics Department Working Papers No. 1372. Paris: OECD.

Africa Centres for Disease Control and Prevention (Africa CDC) (2021). COVID 19 Vaccine Perceptions: A 15 Country Study. Addis Ababa: Africa CDC.

Allen, W. A., J. S. Chadha and P. Turner (2021). Quantitative Tightening: Protecting Monetary Policy from Fiscal Encroachment. London: National Institute of Economic and Social Research.

Altshuler, Clive, and others (2016). The World Economic Forecasting Model at the United Nations. New York: United Nations Department of Economic and Social Affairs.

Amaral, P. (2017). Monetary Policy and Inequality. Economic commentary, January. Cleveland, United States: Federal Reserve Bank of Cleveland.

Andrade, P., and others (2016). The ECB's Asset Purchase Programme: An Early Assessment. European Central Bank Working Paper 1956. Frankfurt am Main, Germany: ECB.

Andrews, D., J. Hambur and E. Bahar (2021). The COVID-19 Shock and Productivity-Enhancing Reallocation in Australia: Real-Time Evidence from Single Touch Payroll. OECD Economics Department Working Paper No. 1677. Paris: OECD.

Apostolou, A., and J. Beirne (2017). Volatility Spillovers of Federal Reserve and ECB Balance Sheet Expansions to Emerging Market Economies. ECB Working Paper No. 2044. Frankfurt am Main, Germany: ECB.

Aramonte, S. (2020). Mind the Buybacks, Beware of The Leverage. Bank for International Settlements Quarterly Review, September. Basel, Switzerland: BIS.

Autor, D., and others (2020). An Evaluation of the Paycheck Protection Program Using Administrative Payroll Microdata. Cambridge, United States: Massachusetts Institute of Technology.

B

Baldwin, R., and others (2015). Rebooting the Eurozone: Step 1—Agreeing A Crisis Narrative. Washington, DC: Centre for Economic Policy Research.

Banerjee, R., and B. Hofmann (2018). The Rise of Zombie Firms: Causes and Consequences. Bank for International Settlements Quarterly Review, September. Basel, Switzerland: BIS.

Bank for International Settlements (BIS) (2021a). A Global Database on Central Banks' Monetary Responses to COVID-19. Basel, Switzerland: BIS.

——— (2021b). *Annual Economic Report 2021.* Basel, Switzerland: BIS.

Bank of England (BoE) (2012). The Distributional Effects of Asset Purchases. Quarterly Bulletin, 2012 Q3. London: BoE.

——— (2021). Greening our Corporate Bond Purchase Scheme (CBPS). London: BoE.

Bank of Japan (2021). Statement on Monetary Policy, 18 June 2021. Tokyo: Bank of Japan.

Banque du Liban (2021). Exceptional Measures for the Gradual Withdrawal of Deposits in Foreign Currencies. Basic Circular No. 158 (Arabic). Beirut: Banque du Liban.

Barker, A. (2015). ECB Suspends Purchase of Loans Backed by VW Assets. *Financial Times*, 27 September.

Barroso, J.B.R.B., L.A.P. da Silva and A. S. Sales (2016). Quantitative Easing and Related Capital Flows into Brazil: Measuring Its Effects and Transmission Channels Through a Rigorous Counterfactual Evaluation. *Journal of International Money and Finance* 67: 102–122.

Bartholomew, L., and P. Diggle (2021). The Lasting Impact of the Covid Crisis on Economic Potential. VOXEU, 21 September.

Bartsch, E., and others (2020). It's All in the Mix: How Can Monetary and Fiscal Policies Work or Fail Together? VOXEU, 15 December.

Batini, N. (2020). The COVID-19 Crisis and Capital Flows. Washington, DC: IMF.

Benigno, G., and P. Pesenti (2021). The International Experience of Central Bank Asset Purchases and Inflation. New York: Federal Reserve Bank of New York.

Bernanke, B. (2020). The New Tools of Monetary Policy. American Economic Association Presidential Address, 4 January.

Bernoth, K., P. König, and B. Beckers (2016). ECB Asset Purchases May Affect Wealth Distribution. *DIW Economic Bulletin* 6(7): 75–81.

Bhattarai, S., A. Chatterjee and W. Y. Park (2021). Effects of US Quantitative Easing on Emerging Market Economies. *Journal of Economic Dynamics and Control* 122.

Bishop, J., and I. Day (2020). How Many Jobs Did JobKeeper Keep? Research Discussion Paper. Sydney: Reserve Bank of Australia.

Blofield, M., C. Giambruno and F. Filgueira (2020). Policy Expansion in Compressed Time: Assessing the Speed, Breadth and Sufficiency of Post-COVID-19 Social Protection Measures in 10 Latin American Countries. *Social Policy 235,* Economic Commission for Latin America and the Caribbean (ECLAC).

Bonifacio, V., and others (2021). Distributional Effects of Monetary Policy. IMF Working Paper WP/21/201. Washington, DC: IMF.

Brunnermeier, M., and others (2016). The Sovereign-Bank Diabolic Loop and ESBies. *American Economic Review* 106(5): 508–512.

Bundesbank (2016). The Macroeconomic Impact of Quantitative Easing in the Euro Area. Frankfurt, Germany: Bundesbank.

C

Caballero, R. J., T. Hoshi and A. K. Kashyap (2008). Zombie Lending and Depressed Restructuring in Japan. *American Economic Review* 98(5): 1943–1977.

Cakmakli, C. and others (2021). The Economic Case for Global Vaccinations: An Epidemiological Model with International Production Networks. Working paper. Cambridge, United States: Center for International Development at Harvard University.

Caldentey, E. P. (2017). Quantitative Easing (QE), Changes in Global Liquidity, and Financial Instability. *International Journal of Political Economy* 46(2–3): 91–112.

Cantú, C., and others (2021). A Global Database on Central Banks' Monetary Responses to COVID-19. BIS Working Paper No. 934. Basel, Switzerland: BIS, Monetary and Economic Department.

Casanova, C., B. Hardy and M. Onen (2021). COVID-19 Policy Measures to Support Bank Lending. BIS Quarterly Review, September. Basel, Switzerland: BIS.

Chen, Q., and others (2015). Financial Crisis, US Unconventional Monetary Policy and International Spillovers. IMF Working Paper WP/15/85. Washington, DC: IMF.

Christensen, J. H., and G. D. Rudebusch (2012). The Response of Interest Rates to US and UK Quantitative Easing. *The Economic Journal* 122(564): F385–F414.

Clemens, M., S. Gebauer and M. Rieth (2017). Early Exit from ECB Bond Purchase Program Could Reduce GDP Growth and Inflation. *DIW Economic Bulletin* 7(49): 533–540.

Climate Action Tracker (2021). Warming Projections Global Update. 9 November.

Corradin, S., N. Grimm and B. Schwaab (2021). Euro Area Sovereign Bond Risk Premia During the COVID-19 Pandemic. ECB Working Paper No. 2561. Frankfurt am Main, Germany: ECB.

COVID-19 Vaccines Global Access (COVAX) (2021). COVAX Global Supply Forecast.

D

Dafermos, Y., and others (2020a). Decarbonising Is Easy: Beyond Market Neutrality in the ECB's Corporate QE. London: New Economics Foundation.

——— (2020b). Decarbonising the Bank of England's Pandemic QE: Perfectly Sensible. London: New Economics Foundation.

Delatte, A. L., and A. Guillaume (2020). COVID-19: A New Challenge for the EMU. CEPII Working Paper. Paris: Centre d'Etudes Prospectives et d'Informations Internationales.

Dell' Ariccia, G., P. Rabanal and D. Sandri (2018). Unconventional Monetary Policies in the Euro Area, Japan, and the United Kingdom. *Journal of Economic Perspectives* 32(4): 147–172.

Domanski, D., M. Scatigna and A. Zabai (2016). Wealth Inequality and Monetary Policy. BIS Quarterly Review, March. Basel, Switzerland: BIS.

E

The Economist (2017). The World's Largest Online-Travel Company. 29 July.

Eggertsson, G. B., and M. Woodford (2003). The Zero Bound on Interest Rates and Optimal Monetary Policy. Washington, DC: The Brookings Institution.

Eichengreen, B., and others (2021). In Defense of Public Debt. Oxford, United Kingdom: Oxford University Press.

English, B., K. Forbes and A. Ubide (2021). Monetary Policy and Central Banking in the COVID Era. VOXEU, 3 June.

European Central Bank (ECB) (2021). ECB to Accept Sustainability-Linked Bonds as Collateral. Press release. Frankfurt am Main, Germany: ECB.

European Commission (2021). Latest Business and Consumer Surveys. Brussels: European Commission.

F

Fabrizio, S., and others (2021). COVID-19 She-Cession: The Employment Penalty of Taking Care of Young Children. IMF Working Paper, WP/21/58, March. Washington, DC: IMF.

Fatás, A., and L. Summers (2018). The Permanent Effects of Fiscal Consolidations. *Journal of International Economics* 112 (May): 238–250.

Fatouh, M., S. Markose and S. Giansante (2019). The Impact of Quantitative Easing on UK Bank Lending: Why Banks Do Not Lend to Businesses? *Journal of Economic Behavior & Organization* 183: 928–953.

Federal Reserve (2021). Federal Reserve Issues FOMC statement. Press release, 22 September.

Feldkircher, M., F. Huber and M. Pfarrhofer (2021). Measuring the Effectiveness of US Monetary Policy During the COVID-19 Recession. *Scottish Journal of Political Economy* 68: 287–297.

Ferdinandusse, M., M. Freier and A. Ristiniemi (2020). Quantitative Easing and the Price-Liquidity Trade-off. European Central Bank Working Paper No. 2399. Frankfurt am Main, Germany: ECB.

Fic, T. (2013). The Spillover Effects of Unconventional Monetary Policies in Major Developed Countries on Developing Countries. UN DESA Working Paper No. 131. New York: United Nations Department of Economic and Social Affairs.

Food and Agricultural Organization of the United Nations (FAO) (2021). FAO Food Price Index. Rome: FAO.

Food and Agriculture Organization of the United Nations (FAO) and World Food Programme (WFP) (2021). Hunger Hotspots: FAO-WFP Early Warnings on Acute Food Insecurity, March to July 2021 Outlook. Rome: FAO and WFP.

Fratto, C., and others (2021). Unconventional Monetary Policies in Emerging Markets and Frontier Countries. Washington, DC: IMF.

Furman, J. (2021). What the Federal Reserve Should Do Now: An Elaboration. Paper prepared for delivery at the Peterson Institute for International Economics, 18 November, Washington, DC.

G

Gagnon, J. (2016). Quantitative Easing: An Underappreciated Success. PIIE Policy Brief, 16. Washington, DC: Peterson Institute for International Economics.

Gambetti, L., and A. Musso (2017). The Macroeconomic Impact of the ECB's Expanded Asset Purchase Programme (APP). European Central Bank Working Paper Series. No 2075. Frankfurt am Main, Germany: ECB.

Gentilini, U., and others (2020). Social Protection and Jobs Responses to COVID-19: A Real-Time Review of Country Measures. Washington, DC: World Bank.

Georgieva, K. (2021). Managing Director Kristalina Georgieva's Remarks at the Summit on the Financing of African Economies, 18 May, Paris.

Gern, K-J., and others (2015). Quantitative Easing in the Euro Area: Transmission Channels and Risks. Intereconomics 2015(4).

Gerszon Maler, D., and others (2021). Updated Estimates of the Impact of COVID-19 on Global Poverty: Turning the Corner on the Pandemic in 2021? World Bank blog, 24 June. Washington, DC: World Bank.

Gilchrist, S., D. López-Salido and E. Zakrajšek (2015). Monetary Policy and Real Borrowing Costs at the Zero Lower Bound. *American Economic Journal: Macroeconomics* 7(1): 77–109.

Gourinchas, P. O., and others (2021). Fiscal Policy in the Age of COVID: Does It 'Get in All of the Cracks?' Working paper. Kansas City: Federal Reserve Bank of Kansas City.

Group of 20 (G20) (2021). G20 Rome Leaders' Declaration. Rome: G20 Information Centre.

Guerrieri, V., and others (2021). Monetary Policy in Times of Structural Reallocation. Working paper prepared for the 2021 Jackson Hole Economic Policy Symposium. Cambridge, United States: Harvard University.

H

Hallegatte, S., J. Rentschler and J. Rozenberg (2019). Lifelines: The Resilient Infrastructure Opportunity. Sustainable Infrastructure Series. Washington, DC: World Bank.

Hanni, M., R. Martner and A. Podestá (2015). The Redistributive Potential of Taxation in Latin America. CEPAL Review 116. Santiago: ECLAC.

Heredia, L., and others (2021). The $100 Trillion Machine. Boston, United State: Boston Consulting Group.

Hesse, H., B. Hofmann and J. M. Weber (2018). The Macroeconomic Effects of Asset Purchases Revisited. *Journal of Macroeconomics* 58: 115–138.

Hofman, D., and G. Kamber (2020). Unconventional Monetary Policy in Emerging Market and Developing Economies. International Monetary Fund, Special Series on COVID-19. Washington, DC: IMF.

Horst, M., and U. Neyer (2019). The Impact of Quantitative Easing on Bank Loan Supply and Monetary Policy Implementation in the Euro Area. DICE Discussion Paper, No. 325. Düsseldorf, Germany: Düsseldorf University Press.

I

Ibarrarán, P., and D. Rosas (2009). Evaluating the Impact of Job Training Programs in Latin America: Evidence from IDB Funded Operations. *Journal of Development Effectiveness* 1: 195–216.

Independent Commission for the Reform of International Corporate Taxation (ICRICT) (2021). ICRICT Open Letter to G20 Leaders: A Global Tax Deal for the Rich. 12 October.

Integrated Food Security Phase Classification (IPC) (2021). Afghanistan: Acute Food Insecurity Situation September – October 2021 and Projection for November 2021 – March 2022. Rome: IPC.

Intergovernmental Panel on Climate Change (IPCC) (2018). Special Report on Impacts of 1.5 ºC Global Warming. Geneva: IPCC.

——— (2021a). AR6 Climate Change 2021: The Physical Science Basis. Geneva: IPCC.

——— (2021b). Climate Change 2021: The Physical Science Basis. Geneva: IPCC.

International Labour Organization (ILO) (2018). Women and Men in the Informal Economy: A Statistical Picture. Third edition. Geneva: ILO.

——— (2020). Global Employment Trends for Youth 2020: Africa. Briefing note. Geneva: International Labour Office.

——— (2021a). COVID-19 and the ASEAN Labour Market: Impact and Policy Response. ILO Policy Brief. Geneva: International Labour Office.

——— (2021b). Employment and Informality in Latin America and the Caribbean: An Insufficient and Unequal Recovery. Technical note, September. Geneva: International Labour Office.

——— (2021c). ILO Monitor: COVID-19 and the World of Work. Seventh edition, 25 January. Geneva: ILO.

——— (2021d). ILO Monitor: COVID-19 and the World of Work. Eighth edition, 27 October.

——— (2021e). World Employment and Social Outlook. Trends 2021. Geneva: ILO.

International Monetary Fund (IMF) (2020). *Global Financial Stability Report 2020: Bridge to Recovery*. Washington, DC: IMF.

——— (2021a). Fiscal Monitor, October 2021: Strengthening the Credibility of Public Finances. Washington, DC: IMF.

——— (2021b). Regional Economic Outlook, Western Hemisphere: A Long and Winding Road to Recovery. Washington, DC: IMF.

——— (2021c). West African Economic and Monetary Union: Staff Report on Common Policies for Member Countries. Washington, DC: IMF.

——— (2021d). World Economic Outlook: Recovery During a Pandemic. Washington, DC: IMF.

International Monetary Fund (IMF) and World Bank (2021). Joint IMF-WBG Staff Note: DSSI Fiscal Monitoring Update. IMF Policy Papers, September. Washington, DC: IMF and World Bank.

International Telecommunication Union (ITU) (2019). Small Island Developing States (SIDS) and ICTs: Mid-term Review of the Samoa Pathway. Geneva: ITU.

J

Johnson, M. (2021). Connecting the World Means Connecting Small Islands Too. Geneva: ITU.

K

Kim, K., T. Laubach and M. Wei (2020). Macroeconomic Effects of Large-Scale Asset Purchases: New Evidence. Finance and Economics Discussion Series 2020-047. Washington, DC: Board of Governors of the Federal Reserve System.

King, I. (2021). Chip Delivery Time Surpasses 20 Weeks in No Sign Shortage Easing. Bloomberg, 10 August.

Kluve, J. (2016). A Review of the Effectiveness of Active Labour Market Programmes with a Focus on Latin America and the Caribbean. Working Paper No. 9, March. Geneva: ILO.

Krishnamurthy, A., and A. Vissing-Jorgensen (2011). The Effects of Quantitative Easing on Interest Rates: Channels and Implications for Policy. NBER No. 17555. Cambridge, United States: National Bureau of Economic Research.

L

Lenza, M., and J. Slacalek (2018). How Does Monetary Policy Affect Income and Wealth Inequality? Evidence from Quantitative Easing in the Euro Area. Working Paper Series No. 2190. Frankfurt am Main, Germany: ECB.

Lim, J. J., S. Mohapatra and M. Stocker (2014). Tinker, Taper, QE, Bye? The Effect of Quantitative Easing on Financial Flows to Developing Countries. Policy Research Working Paper 6820. Washington, DC: World Bank.

Lubik, T. A. (2021). Revisiting the Beveridge Curve: Why Has It Shifted So Dramatically? Economic Brief, October, No. 21-36. Richmond, United States: Federal Reserve Bank of Richmond.

M

Macklem, T. (2021). The Benefits of an Inclusive Economy. Remarks delivered to the universities of Atlantic Canada, Halifax, Nova Scotia, Bank of Canada.

Maddison Project Database (2020). Maddison Style Estimates of the Evolution of the World Economy: A New 2020 Update. The Maddison Project.

Martinez-Diaz, L., and G. Christianson (2020). Economic Recovery Efforts Must Consider Climate Change. GreenBiz.

Martorano, B. (2018). Taxation and Inequality in Developing Countries: Lessons from the Recent Experience of Latin America. *Journal of International Development* 30: 256-273.

Mathieu, E., and others (2021) A Global Database of COVID-19 Vaccinations. Our World in Data.

Matikainen, S., E. Campiglio and D. Zenghelis (2017). The Climate Impact of Quantitative Easing. Policy Paper No. 36. London: Centre for Climate Change Economics and Policy and Grantham Research Institute on Climate Change and the Environment.

Mercure, J-F., and others (2021). Reframing Incentives for Climate Policy Action. *Nature Energy* 6: 1133–1143.

Metzger, M., and B. Young (2020). No Gender Please, We're Central Bankers: Distributional Impacts of Quantitative Easing. Working Paper No. 136/2020. Berlin: Institute for International Political Economy.

Milstein, E., T. Powell and D. Wessel (2021). What Does the Federal Reserve Mean When It Talks About Tapering? Washington, DC: The Brookings Institution.

Monioudi, I., and others, (2018). Climate Change Impacts on Critical International Transportation Assets of Caribbean Small Island Developing States (SIDS): The Case of Jamaica and Saint Lucia. *Regional Environmental Change 2018*: 2211–2225.

Moore, J., and others (2013). Estimating the Impacts of U.S. LSAPs on Emerging Market Economies' Local Currency Bond Markets. Staff Report No. 595. New York: Federal Reserve Bank of New York.

Munevar, D. (2020). Arrested Development: International Monetary Fund Lending and Austerity Post COVID-19. European Network on Debt and Development, 6 October.

O

Ocampo, J. A. (2021). Rich Countries' Double Standards on Taxation. Project Syndicate, 16 November.

Occhino, F. (2020). Quantitative Easing and Direct Lending in Response to the COVID-19 Crisis. Working Paper No. 2029. Cleveland, United States: Federal Reserve Bank of Cleveland.

Oliveros-Rosen, E. (2021). Economic Outlook Latin America Q4 2021: Settling into the New Post-Pandemic Normal of Slow Growth. New York: S&P Global.

Organisation for Economic Co-operation and Development (OECD) (2020). COVID-19 And Global Capital Flows. OECD Policy Responses to Coronavirus (COVID-19), 3 July. Paris: OECD.

——— (2021a). Employment Outlook 2021. Paris: OECD.

——— (2021b). International Community Strikes a Ground-breaking Tax Deal for the Digital Age. Press release, 10 October. Paris: OECD.

——— (2021c). Statement on a Two-Pillar Solution to Address the Tax Challenges Arising from the Digitalisation of the Economy. 8 October. Paris: OECD.

Organization of Petroleum Exporting Countries (OPEC) (2021). Declaration of Cooperation. Vienna: OPEC.

Ortmans, A., and F. Tripier (2021). COVID-induced Sovereign Risk in the Euro Area: When Did the ECB Stop the Spread? CEPII Working Paper, No. 20–11. Paris: Centre d'Etudes Prospectives et d'Informations Internationales.

P

Papoutsi, M., M. Piazzesi and M. Schneider (2021). How Unconventional Is Green Monetary Policy? Working paper.

People's Bank of China (2020). Survey on Chinese Urban Households' Assets and Liabilities 2019. Sina Finance.

Pukas, A. (2018). Lebanese Across the Globe: How the Country's International Community Came to Be. *Arab News*, 4 May.

R

Reis, R. (2016). Funding Quantitative Easing to Target Inflation. LSE Research Online Documents on Economics 86222. London: London School of Economics and Political Science.

Rieth, M., and L. Gehrt (2016). ECB Asset Purchase Programs Raise Inflation Expectations in the Euro Area. *DIW Economic Bulletin* 6(38): 463–469.

Riksbank (2020). Programme for the Riksbank's Asset Purchases for Monetary Policy Purposes in 2021. Stockholm: Riksbank.

Rodnyansky, A., and O. Darmouni (2015). The Effects of Quantitative Easing on Bank Lending Behavior. *Review of Financial Studies*, 12 June.

Rogoff, K. S., and Y. Yang (2020). Peak China Housing. NBER Working Paper 27697. Cambridge, United States: National Bureau of Economic Research.

Ryoo, S., T. Kwon and H. Lee (2013). Foreign Exchange Market Developments and Intervention in Korea. In *Market Volatility and Foreign Intervention in EMEs: What has Changed?* BIS Papers No 73. Basel, Switzerland: BIS.

S

Sanchez-Paramo, C., and others (2021). COVID-19 Leaves a Legacy of Rising Poverty and Widening Inequality. World Bank blog, 7 October. Washington, DC: World Bank.

Schnabel, I. (2021). Asset Purchases: From Crisis to Recovery. Speech delivered at the Annual Conference of Latvijas Banka on Sustainable Economy in Times of Change, ECB.

Schrimpf, A., H. S. Shin and V. Sushko (2020). Leverage and Margin Spirals in Fixed Income Markets During the COVID-19 Crisis. BIS Bulletin No.2. Basel, Switzerland: BIS.

Sever, C., and others (2020). Effects of Emerging Market Asset Purchase Program Announcements on Financial Markets During the COVID-19 Pandemic. IMF Working Paper WP/20/292. Washington, DC: IMF.

Shin, H. S. (2021). Bottlenecks, Labour Markets and Inflation in the Wake of the Pandemic. Paper delivered at the Recover Together, Recover Stronger G20 international seminar, 9 December, Bali.

Sims, E. R., and J. C. Wu (2020). Wall Street vs. Main Street QE. NBER Working Paper 27295. Cambridge, United States: National Bureau of Economic Research.

Smart, T. (2021). Who Owns Stocks in America? Mostly, It's the Wealthy and White. *U.S. News*, 15 March.

Standard and Poor's (S&P) (2021). Credit Trends: Global Financing Conditions: Bond Issuance Is Expected to Finish the Year Close to 2020 Levels; Drop 2% Next Year. 25 October. New York: S&P Global Ratings.

T

Tax Justice Network (2021). Losses to OECD Tax Havens Could Vaccinate Global Population Three Times Over, Study Reveals. 16 November.

Torslov, T., L. Wier and G. Zucman (2021). The Missing Profits of Nations. Working paper, 10 August.

U

United Kingdom, House of Lords (2021). Quantitative Easing: A Dangerous Addiction? First report of Session 2021–22, House of Lords, Economic Affairs Committee. London: House of Lords.

United Kingdom, Office for Budget Responsibility (OBR) (2021). Economic and Fiscal Outlook – March 2021. London: OBR.

United Kingdom, Office for National Statistics (ONS) (2021). Long-Term International Migration, Provisional: Year Ending December 2020. 25 November. London: ONS.

United Nations (2020). World Economic Situation and Prospects 2020. New York: United Nations.

——— (2021a). Liquidity and Debt Solutions to Invest in the SDGs: The Time to Act Is Now. Policy brief, March. New York: United Nations.

——— (2021b). World Economic Situation and Prospects: November 2021 Briefing, No. 155. New York: United Nations.

United Nations Children's Fund (UNICEF) (2021). COVID-19 and the Looming Debt Crisis. April. New York: UNICEF.

United Nations Conference on Trade and Development (UNCTAD) (2018). Review of Maritime Transport 2018. Geneva: UNCTAD.

——— (2021a). Investment Trends Monitor. Issue 39, 21 October. Geneva: UNCTAD.

——— (2021b). Review of Maritime Transport 2021: Challenges Faced by Seafarers in View of the COVID-19 Crisis. Geneva: UNCTAD.

——— (2021c). SDG Pulse. Sustainable and Resilient Transport Amidst Rising Uncertainty, Disruptions and Climate Risks. Geneva: UNCTAD.

——— (2021d). Trade and Development Report 2021: From Recovery to Resilience: The Development Dimension. Geneva: UNCTAD.

United Nations Development Program (UNDP) (2021). Impact of Vaccine Inequity on Economic Recovery. New York: UNDP.

United Nations Development Program (UNDP) and Oxford Poverty and Human Development Initiative (OPHI) (2021). Global Multidimensional Poverty Index 2021: Unmasking Disparities by Ethnicity, Caste and Gender. New York and Oxford, United Kingdom: UNDP and OPHI.

United Nations Economic Commission for Africa (ECA) (2021). Economic Report on Africa 2021: Addressing the Challenges of Poverty and Vulnerability in the Time of COVID-19. Addis Ababa: ECA.

United Nations Economic Commission for Latin America and the Caribbean (ECLAC) (2021a). Economic Survey of Latin America and the Caribbean: Labour Dynamics and Employment Policies for Sustainable and Inclusive Recovery Beyond the COVID-19 Crisis. Santiago, ECLAC.

——— (ECLAC) (2021b). Social Panorama of Latin America 2020. March, LC/PUB.2021/2-P/Rev.1. Santiago, ECLAC.

United Nations Economic and Social Commission for Asia and the Pacific (ESCAP) (2021). Economic and Social Survey of Asia and the Pacific 2021: Towards Post-COVID-19 Resilient Economies. Bangkok, ESCAP.

United Nations Economic and Social Commission for Western Asia (ESCWA) (2021a). Liquidity Shortage and Debt: Obstacles to Recovery in the Arab Region. E/ESCWA/CL3.SEP/2021/POLICY BRIEF.3. Beirut: ESCWA.

——— (2021b). Multidimensional Poverty in Lebanon (2019-2021): Painful Reality and Uncertain Prospects. E/ESCWA/CL3.SEP/2021/POLICY BRIEF.2). Beirut: ESCWA.

United Nations Entity for Gender Equality and the Empowerment of Women (UN Women) (2020). From Insights to Action: Gender Equality in the Wake of COVID-19. New York: UN Women.

United Nations Entity for Gender Equality and the Empowerment of Women (UN Women) and United Nations Economic Commission for Latin America and the Caribbean (ECLAC) (2021). Towards the Construction of Comprehensive Care Systems in Latin America and the Caribbean: Elements for Implementation. New York and Santiago: UN Women and ECLAC.

United Nations World Tourism Organization (UNWTO) (2021a). World Tourism Barometer. November. Madrid: UNWTO.

——— (2021b). World Tourism Barometer. September. Madrid: UNWTO.

V

Volz, U. and others (2020). Climate Change and Sovereign Risk. London, Tokyo, Singapore and Berkeley, United States: SOAS University of London, Asian Development Bank Institute, World Wide Fund for Nature Singapore and Four Twenty Seven.

W

Woodford, M. (2012). Methods of Policy Accommodation at the Interest-Rate Lower Bound. New York: Columbia University.

World Bank (2021a). Commodity Market Outlook. Urbanization and Commodity Demand. October. Washington, DC: World Bank.

——— (2021b). COP26: The World Is Watching. 31 October. Washington, DC: World Bank.

——— (2021c). Recovering Growth: Rebuilding Dynamic Post-COVID-19 Economies amid Fiscal Constraints. LAC Semiannual Report, October. Washington, DC: World Bank.

——— (2021d). World Bank: Pandemic Threatens to Drive Unprecedented Number of Children into Learning Poverty. 29 October. Washington, DC: World Bank.

World Bank and United Nations Educational, Scientific and Cultural Organization (UNESCO) (2021). Education Finance Watch 2021. 22 February. Washington, DC and Paris: World Bank and UNESCO.

World Health Organization (WHO) (2021). Strategy to Achieve Global COVID-19 Vaccination by Mid-2022. Geneva: WHO.

World Trade Organization (WTO) (2021). Trade Statistics and Outlook: Global Trade Rebound Beats Expectations but Marked by Regional Divergences. Geneva: WTO.

World Travel and Tourism Council (WTTC) (2017). 5 Ways Tourism Can Support Local Economies. London: WTTC.

Y

Yoshino, N., F. Taghizadeh-Hesary and S. Shimizu (2018). Impact of Quantitative Easing and Tax Policy on Income Inequality: Evidence from Japan. Working Paper Series No. 891. Manila: Asian Development Bank Institute.

Yu, E. (2016). Did Quantitative Easing Work? *Economic Insights* 1(1): 5–13.

Z

Zandi, M., and B. Yanos (2021). Macroeconomic Consequences of the Infrastructure Investment and Jobs Act & Build Back Better Framework. Moody's Analytics.